"No other guide has as muc[...]
a pleasure to read."   Gene[...]

". . . Excellently organized for the casual traveler who is looking for a mix of recreation and cultural insight."
Washington Post

★ ★ ★ ★ ★ (5-star rating) "Crisply written and remarkably personable. Cleverly organized so you can pluck out the minutest fact in a moment. Satisfyingly thorough."
Réalités

"The information they offer is up-to-date, crisply presented but far from exhaustive, the judgments knowledgeable but not opinionated."   *New York Times*

"The individual volumes are compact, the prose succinct, and the coverage up-to-date and knowledgeable . . . The format is portable and the index admirably detailed."
John Barkham Syndicate

". . . An abundance of excellent directions, diversions, and facts, including perspectives and getting-ready-to-go advice — succinct, detailed, and well organized in an easy-to-follow style."   *Los Angeles Times*

"They contain an amount of information that is truly staggering, besides being surprisingly current."
Detroit News

"These guides address themselves to the needs of the modern traveler demanding precise, qualitative information . . . Upbeat, slick, and well put together."
Dallas Morning News

". . . Attractive to look at, refreshingly easy to read, and generously packed with information."   *Miami Herald*

"These guides are as good as any published, and much better than most."   *Louisville* (Kentucky) *Times*

Stephen Birnbaum Travel Guides

Acapulco
Bahamas, Turks & Caicos
Barcelona
Bermuda
Boston
Canada
Cancun, Cozumel, and Isla Mujeres
Caribbean
Chicago
Disneyland
Eastern Europe
Europe
Europe for Business Travelers
Florence
France
Great Britain
Hawaii
Ireland
Italy
Ixtapa & Zihuatanejo
London
Los Angeles
Mexico
Miami
New York
Paris
Portugal
Rome
San Francisco
South America
Spain
United States
USA for Business Travelers
Venice
Walt Disney World
Western Europe

CONTRIBUTING EDITORS

Stephanie Curtis
Joan Gannij
Rochelle Goldstein
Melinda Tang

MAPS   B. Andrew Mudryk
SYMBOLS   Gloria McKeown

A Stephen Birnbaum Travel Guide

Birnbaum's
PARIS
1992

Stephen Birnbaum
Alexandra Mayes Birnbaum
EDITORS

Lois Spritzer
EXECUTIVE EDITOR

Laura L. Brengelman
Managing Editor

Mary Callahan
Ann-Rebecca Laschever
Beth Schlau
Dana Margaret Schwartz
Associate Editors

Gene Gold
Assistant Editor

HarperPerennial
A Division of HarperCollins*Publishers*

FIRST EDITION

ISSN: 0749-2561 (Stephen Birnbaum Travel Guides)
ISSN: 1056-4438 (Paris)
ISBN: 0-06-278029-8 (pbk.)

92 93 94 95 96 CC/OPM 10 9 8 7 6 5 4 3 2 1

Contents

USEFUL WORDS AND PHRASES

THE CITY

Thorough, qualitative guide to Paris. Each section offers a comprehensive report on the city's most compelling attractions and amenities, designed to be used on the spot.

DIVERSIONS

A selective guide to more than a dozen active and/or cerebral vacation themes including the best places to pursue them.

For the Experience

For the Body

For the Mind

DIRECTIONS

Eight of the most delightful walks through Paris.

A Word from the Editor

I really thought of myself as worldly; after all, I'd been going to school in the US while my parents lived in the Caribbean, so I'd been traveling back and forth on school holidays and thought international roamings a bit of a bore. As only an arrogant teenager can convey, I pooh-poohed the idea of my first trip to Europe, explaining that it couldn't be that much different from trips to the capitals of South America, with which I had become more or less familiar. Then I saw Paris.

To say that that first look at l'Etoile made a difference is to understate the impact; finally, I had how much I didn't know driven home, and (best of all) I recognized that it wouldn't be the worst thing if I spent a significant portion of the rest of my life learning what all was out there. Even after dozens of visits to Paris, I never fail to find something I missed last time through.

My own evolution as a traveler (which happily continues) is mirrored by the evolution of our guidebook series. When we began our series of modern travel guides, we logically began with "area" books, attempting to publish guides that would include the widest possible number of attractive destinations. When the public seemed to accept our new way of delivering travel data, we added titles covering only a single country, and when these became popular we began our newest expansion phase, which centers on a group of books that deal with only a single city. Now we not only can highlight our favorite urban destinations, but can really describe how to get the very most out of a visit.

Such treatment of travel information only mirrors an increasingly pervasive trend among travelers — the frequent return to a treasured foreign travel spot. Once upon a time, even the most dedicated travelers would visit distant parts of the world no more than once in a lifetime — usually as part of that fabled Grand Tour. But greater numbers of would-be sojourners are now availing themselves of the opportunity to visit a favored part of the world over and over again.

So where once it was routine to say you'd "seen" a particular country after a very superficial, once-over-lightly encounter, the more perceptive travelers of today recognize that it's entirely possible to have only skimmed the surface of a specific travel destination even after having visited that place more than a dozen times. Similarly, repeated visits to a single site permit true exploration of special interests, whether they be sporting, artistic, or intellectual.

For those of us who spent the several years working out the special system under which we present information in this series, the luxury of being able to devote nearly as much space as we'd like to just a single city is as close to paradise for guide writers and editors as any of us expects to come. But clearly this is not the first guide to the glories of Paris — one suspects that guides of one sort or another have existed at least since the Capetian kings took over the Ile St.-Louis. Guides to Paris have probably existed in one form or another for centuries, so a traveler might logically ask why a new one is suddenly necessary.

Our answer is that the nature of travel to Paris — and even of the travelers who now routinely make the trip — has changed dramatically of late. For the past 2,000 years or so, travel to any foreign address was an extremely elaborate undertaking, one that required extensive advance planning. Even as recently as the 1950s, a person who had actually been to Paris — to say nothing of Lyons, Marseilles, or Nice — could dine out on his or her experiences for years, since such adventures were quite extraordinary and usually the province of the privileged alone.

With the advent of jet air travel in the late 1950s, however, and of increased-capacity, wide-body aircraft during the 1960s, travel to and around once distant destinations became extremely common. In fact, in more than 2 decades of nearly unending inflation, airfares may be the only commodity in the world that has actually gone down in price.

Attitudes as well as costs have also changed significantly in the last couple of decades. Beginning with the so-called flower children of the 1960s, international travel lost much of its aura of mystery. Whereas their parents might have been happy with just a superficial sampling of Paris, these young people simply picked up and settled in various parts of Europe for an indefinite stay. While living as inexpensively as possible, they adapted to the local lifestyle, and generally immersed themselves in things European.

Thus began an explosion of travel. And over the years, the development of inexpensive charter flights and packages fueled and sharpened the new American interest in and appetite for more extensive exploration.

Now, in the 1990s, those same flower children who were in the forefront of the modern travel revolution have undeniably aged. While it may be impolite to point out that they are probably well into their untrustworthy thirties and forties, their original zeal for travel remains undiminished. For them, it's hardly news that the way to get to l'Etoile is to head up the Champs-Elysées. Such experienced and knowledgeable travelers have decided precisely where they want to go and are more often searching for ideas and insights to expand their already sophisticated travel consciousnesses.

Obviously, any new guidebook to Paris must keep pace with and answer the real needs of today's travelers. That's why we've tried to create a guide that's specifically organized, written, and edited for this more demanding modern audience, travelers for whom qualitative information is infinitely more desirable than mere quantities of unappraised data. We think that this book and the other guides in our series represent a new generation of travel guides, one that is especially responsive to modern needs and interests.

For years, dating back as far as Herr Baedeker, travel guides have tended to be encyclopedic, seemingly much more concerned with demonstrating expertise in geography and history than with making a real analysis of the sorts of things that actually concern a typical modern tourist. But today, when it is hardly necessary to tell a traveler where Paris is (in many cases, the traveler has been there nearly as often as the guidebook editors), it becomes the responsibility of those editors to provide new perspectives and to suggest new directions in order to make the guide genuinely valuable.

That's exactly what we've tried to do in this series. I think you'll notice a different, more contemporary tone to the text, as well as an organization and focus that are distinctive and more functional. And even a random reading of what follows will demonstrate a substantial departure from the standard guidebook orientation, for not only have we attempted to provide information of a more compelling sort, but we also have tried to present the data in a format that makes it particularly accessible.

Needless to say, it's difficult to decide precisely what to include in a guidebook of this size — and what to omit. Early on, we realized that giving up the encyclopedic approach precluded our listing every single route and restaurant, a realization that helped define our overall editorial focus. Similarly, when we discussed the possibility of presenting certain information in other than strict geographic order, we found that the new format enabled us to arrange data in a way we feel best answers the questions travelers typically ask.

Large numbers of specific questions have provided the real editorial skeleton for this book. The volume of mail I regularly receive emphasizes that modern travelers want very precise information, so we've tried to organize our material in the most responsive way possible. Readers who want to know the best restaurants or the best places to find inexpensive couturier fashions in Paris will have no trouble extracting that data from this guide.

Travel guides are, understandably, reflections of personal taste, and putting one's name on a title page obviously puts one's preferences on the line. But I think I ought to amplify just what "personal" means. I don't believe in the sort of personal guidebook that's a palpable misrepresentation on its face. It is, for example, hardly possible for any single travel writer to visit thousands of restaurants (and nearly as many hotels) in any given year and provide accurate appraisals of each. And even if it were physically possible for one human being to survive such an itinerary, it would of necessity have to be done at a dead sprint and the perceptions derived therefrom would probably be less valid than those of any other intelligent individual visiting the same establishments. It is, therefore, impossible (especially in a large, annually revised guidebook *series* such as we offer) to have only one person provide all the data on the entire world.

I also happen to think that such individual orientation is of substantially less value to readers. Visiting a single hotel for just one night or eating one hasty meal in a random restaurant hardly equips anyone to provide appraisals that are of more than passing interest. No amount of doggedly alliterative or oppressively onomatopoeic text can camouflage a technique that is essentially specious. We have, therefore, chosen what I like to describe as the "thee and me" approach to restaurant and hotel evaluation and, to a somewhat more limited degree, to the sites and sights we have included in the other sections of our text. What this really reflects is a personal sampling tempered by intelligent counsel from informed local sources, and these additional friends-of-the-editor are almost always residents of the city and/or area about which they are consulted.

Despite the presence of several editors, writers, researchers, and local correspondents, very precise editing and tailoring keep our text fiercely subjective. So what follows is the gospel according to the Birnbaums, and represents as much of our own taste and instincts as we can manage. It is probable, therefore, that if you like your cities stylish and prefer small hotels with personality to huge high-rise anonymities, we're likely to have a long and meaningful relationship. Readers with dissimilar tastes may be less enraptured.

I also should point out something about the person to whom this guidebook is directed. Above all, he or she is a "visitor." This means that such elements as restaurants have been specifically picked to provide the visitor with a representative, enlightening, stimulating, and, above all, pleasant experience. Since so many extraneous considerations can affect the reception and service accorded a regular restaurant patron, our choices can in no way be construed as an exhaustive guide to resident dining. We think we've listed all the best places, in various price ranges, but they were chosen with a visitor's enjoyment in mind.

Other evidence of how we've tried to tailor our text to reflect modern travel habits is most apparent in the section we call DIVERSIONS. Where once it was common for travelers to spend a foreign visit in a determinedly passive state, the emphasis is far more active today. So we've organized every activity we could reasonably evaluate and presented the material in a way that is especially accessible to activists of either athletic or cerebral bent. It is no longer necessary, therefore, to wade through a pound or two of superfluous prose just to find the very best shop or the quaintest country inn within a reasonable distance of the city.

If there is a single thing that best characterizes the revolution in and evolution of current holiday habits, it is that most travelers now consider travel a right rather than a privilege. No longer is a trip to the far corners of the globe necessarily a once-in-a-lifetime thing; nor is the idea of visiting exotic, faraway places in the least worrisome. Travel today translates as the enthusiastic desire to sample all of the world's opportunities, to find that elusive quality of experience that is not only enriching but comfortable. For that reason, we've tried to make what follows not only helpful and enlightening but the sort of welcome companion of which every traveler dreams.

Finally, I also should point out that every good travel guide is a living enterprise; that is, no part of this text is carved in stone. In our annual revisions, we refine, expand, and further hone all our material to serve your travel needs better. To this end, no contribution is of greater value to us than your personal reaction to what we have written, as well as information reflecting your own experiences while using the book. We earnestly and enthusiastically solicit your comments about this guide *and* your opinions and perceptions about places you have recently visited. In this way, we will be able to provide the most current information — including the actual experiences of recent travelers — and to make those experiences more readily available to others. Please write to us at 60 E. 42nd St., New York, NY 10165.

We sincerely hope to hear from you.

STEPHEN BIRNBAUM

How to Use This Guide

A great deal of care has gone into the organization of this guidebook, and we believe it represents a real breakthrough in the presentation of travel material. Our aim is to create a new, more modern generation of travel books and to make this guide the most useful and practical travel tool available today.

Our text is divided into five basic sections in order to present information in the best way on every possible aspect of a Paris vacation. This organization itself should alert you to the vast and varied opportunities available, as well as indicate all the specific data necessary to plan a successful trip. You won't find much of the conventional "swaying palms and shimmering sand" text here; we've chosen instead to deliver more useful and practical information. Prospective itineraries tend to speak for themselves, and with so many diverse travel opportunities, we feel our main job is to highlight what's where and to provide basic information — how, when, where, how much, and what's best — to assist you in making the most intelligent choices possible.

Here is a brief summary of the five basic sections and what you can expect to find in each. We believe that you will find both your travel planning and en route enjoyment enhanced by having this book at your side.

GETTING READY TO GO

This mini-encyclopedia of practical travel facts is a sort of know-it-all companion with all the precise information necessary to create a successful trip to Paris. There are entries on more than 2 dozen separate topics, including how to get where you're going, what preparations to make before leaving, what your trip is likely to cost, and how to avoid prospective problems. The individual entries are specific, realistic, and where appropriate, cost-oriented.

We expect you to use this section most in the course of planning your trip, for its ideas and suggestions are intended to simplify this often confusing period. Entries are intentionally concise, in an effort to get to the meat of the matter with the least extraneous prose. These entries are augmented by extensive lists of specific sources from which to obtain even more specialized data, plus some suggestions for obtaining travel information on your own.

USEFUL WORDS AND PHRASES

Though most hotels and restaurants in Paris have at least one English-speaking staff member, at smaller establishments a little knowledge of French will go a long way. This collection of often-used words and phrases will help you to make a hotel or dinner reservation, order a meal, mail a letter — and even buy toothpaste.

THE CITY

The individual report on Paris has been created with the assistance of researchers, contributors, professional journalists, and experts who live in the city. Although useful at the planning stage, THE CITY is really designed to be taken along and used on the spot. The reports offer a short-stay guide, including an essay introducing the city as a historic entity and as a contemporary place to visit. *At-a-Glance* material is actually a site-by-site survey of the most important, interesting (and sometimes most eclectic) sights to see and things to do. *Sources and Resources* is a concise listing of pertinent information meant to answer a range of potentially pressing questions as they arise — simple things such as the address of the local tourist office, how to get around, which sightseeing tours to take, when special events occur, where to find the best nightspot or hail a taxi, which are the chic places to shop, and where the best museums and theaters are to be found. *Best in Town* is our collection of cost-and-quality choices of the best places to eat and sleep on a variety of budgets.

DIVERSIONS

This section is designed to help travelers find the best places in which to pursue a wide range of physical and cerebral activities, without having to wade through endless pages of unrelated text. This very selective guide lists the broadest possible range of activities, including all the best places to pursue them.

We start with a list of possibilities that offer various places to stay and eat, move to those that require some perspiration — sports preferences and other rigorous pursuits — and go on to report on a number of more cerebral and spiritual vacation opportunities. In every case, our suggestion of a particular location — and often our recommendation of a specific hotel — is intended to guide you to that special place where the quality of experience is likely to be the highest. Whether you seek a romantic hostelry or an inspiring cooking school, each category is the equivalent of a comprehensive checklist of the absolute best in Paris.

DIRECTIONS

Here are eight walks that cover the city, along its main thoroughfares and side streets, past its most spectacular landmarks and magnificent parks. DIRECTIONS is the only section of this book that is organized geographically; itineraries can be "connected" for longer sojourns or used individually for short, intensive explorations.

Although each of the book's sections has a distinct format and a special function, they have all been designed to be used together to provide a complete inventory of travel information. To use this book to full advantage, take a few minutes to read the table of contents and random entries in each section to get a firsthand feel of how it all fits together.

Pick and choose needed information. Assume, for example, that you have always wanted to take that typically Parisian vacation, an eating tour of the city's temples of gastronomy — but you never really knew how to organize it or where to go. Choose specific restaurants from the selections offered in the Paris chapter in THE CITY, in each walking tour in DIRECTIONS, and in the roundup of the best in the city called *Haute Gastronomie* in the DIVER-SIONS section. Then, refer to USEFUL WORDS AND PHRASES to help you with everything from making reservations to deciphering the menu. We've even provided instructions on how to write a letter requesting reservations (an important prelude to visiting many of Paris's great restaurants, which are often booked weeks — or months — in advance), as well as a discussion of special food and wine tours and some of their suppliers.

In other words, the sections of this book are building blocks designed to help you put together the best possible trip. Use them selectively as a tool, a source of ideas, a reference work for accurate facts, and a guidebook to the best buys, the most exciting sights, the most pleasant accommodations, the tastiest food — *the best travel experience* that you can possibly have in Paris.

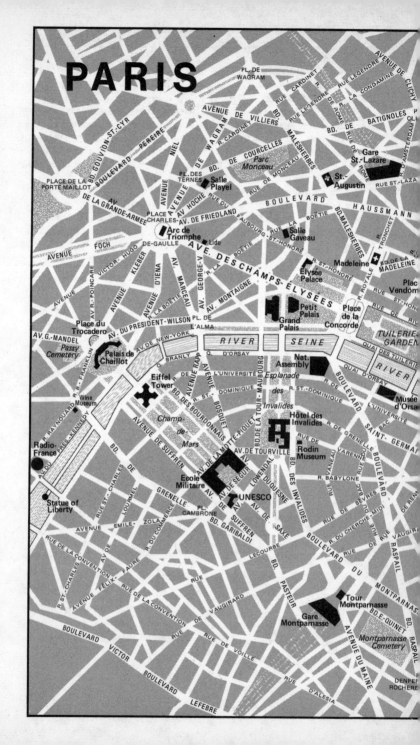

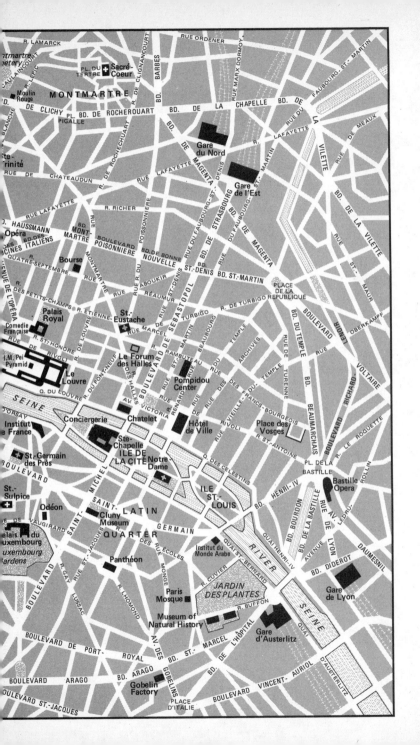

GETTING READY
TO GO

When and How to Go

When to Go

 There really isn't a "best" time to visit Paris. For North Americans, as well as Europeans, the period from April to mid-September has long been — and remains — the peak travel period, traditionally the most popular vacation time.

It is important to emphasize that Paris, like the rest of France, is hardly a single-season destination; more and more vacationers who have a choice are enjoying the substantial advantages of off-season travel. Though some tourist attractions may close during the off-season — roughly November to March — the major ones remain open and tend to be less crowded. During the off-season, people relax and French life proceeds at a more leisurely pace. What's more, travel generally is less expensive.

For some, the most convincing argument in favor of off-season travel is the economic one. Getting there and staying there are less expensive during less popular travel periods, as airfares, hotel rooms, and car rental rates go down and less expensive package tours become available; the independent traveler can go farther on less, too.

A definite bonus to visiting during the off-season is that even the most basic services are performed more efficiently. In theory, off-season service is identical to that offered during high season, but the fact is that the absence of demanding crowds inevitably begets much more thoughtful and personal attention.

Even during the off-season, high-season rates may prevail because of an important local event. Particularly in the larger cities, and Paris is a major commercial city, special events and major trade shows or conferences held at the time of your visit are sure to affect not only the availability of discounts on accommodations, but the basic availability of a place to stay.

It also should be noted that the months immediately before and after the peak summer months — what the travel industry refers to as shoulder seasons — often are sought out because they offer fair weather and somewhat smaller crowds.

In short, like many other popular places, in France and elsewhere, Paris's vacation appeal has become multi-seasonal. But the noted exceptions notwithstanding, most travel destinations are decidedly less heavily trafficked and less expensive during the winter.

CLIMATE: Paris maintains fairly moderate temperatures year-round. For example, the average temperature range is 41–50F (5–10C) in January, 61–64F (16–18C) in April, 57–72F (14–22C) in July, and 50–63F (10–17C) in October. Winter is the wettest season, with an average of 25 days of rain in January.

Travelers can get current readings and 3-day Accu-Weather forecasts through *American Express Travel Related Services*' Worldwide Weather Report number. By dialing 900-WEATHER and punching in the access code for numerous travel destinations worldwide, an up-to-date recording will provide current temperature, sky conditions, wind speed and direction, heat index, relative humidity, local time, highway reports, and beach and boating reports or ski conditions (where appropriate). For the weather in Paris, punch in PAR. This 24-hour service can be accessed from any touch-tone phone in the US or Canada and costs 95¢ per minute. The charge will show up on your phone bill. For a free list of the areas covered, send a self-addressed, stamped envelope to *1-900-WEATHER,* 261 Central Ave., Farmingdale, NY 11735.

SPECIAL EVENTS: For runners and sports enthusiasts, a series of major events are held starting in April with the *Paris Marathon.* The *French Open Tennis Championships* take place in May. The *Tour de France,* the celebrated 3-week cycling race, finishes in Paris in July.

Music lovers eagerly await the *Festival du Marais,* a month-long event of music and dance performances held in historic surroundings in the Marais district in June. In July and August, the *Festival Estival* features classical music in various locations throughout the city. Contemporary music, dance, and theater are the focus of the *Festival d'Automne,* held from September through December.

Bastille Day, the national holiday that commemorates the storming of the Bastille prison in Paris in 1789, which began the French Revolution and led to the declaration of the French Republic, is widely celebrated throughout the country with elaborate fireworks, parades, music, and dancing.

Traveling by Plane

Flying is the most efficient way to get to Paris, and it is the quickest, most convenient means of travel between different parts of France once you are there.

The air space between North America and Europe is the most heavily trafficked in the world. It is served by dozens of airlines, almost all of which sell seats at a variety of prices under a vast spectrum of requirements and restrictions. You probably will spend more for your airfare than for any other single item in your travel budget, so try to take advantage of the lowest fares offered by either scheduled airlines or charter companies. You should know what kinds of flights are available, the rules under which air travel operates, and all the special package options.

GATEWAYS: At present, nonstop flights to Paris leave from Atlanta, Boston, Chicago, Cincinnati, Dallas/Ft. Worth, Detroit, Los Angeles, Miami, Newark, New York, St. Louis, and Washington, DC. Additional connecting flights depart from some of the above cities and a few others as well.

SCHEDULED FLIGHTS: US airlines offering regularly scheduled flights to Paris are *American, Continental, Delta, Northwest, TWA, United,* and *USAir. Delta* flies nonstop to Paris only from Atlanta and Cincinnati; *Northwest,* only from Detroit. In addition, *Air France* operates nonstop flights to Paris from Boston, Chicago, Houston, Los Angeles, Miami, Newark, New York, and Washington, DC. *Air Outre Mer,* a new French airline, recently launched nonstop service between Miami and Paris.

Nonstop or direct, flights to Paris land either at Charles de Gaulle or Orly airports.

A number of other European carriers serve Paris from the US with connecting flights through their main hubs: *British Airways* from numerous US cities via London's Heathrow Airport; *Iberia* from Los Angeles, Miami, and New York via Madrid; *KLM* from Atlanta, Baltimore, Chicago, Houston, Los Angeles, and New York via Amsterdam; *Sabena* from Boston, Chicago, and New York via Brussels; and *TAP Air Portugal* from Boston, Newark, and New York by way of Lisbon.

Tickets – When traveling on one of the many regularly scheduled flights, a full-fare ticket provides maximum travel flexibility (although at considerable expense) because there are no advance booking requirements. A prospective passenger can buy a ticket for a flight right up to the minute of takeoff — if a seat is available. If your ticket is for a round trip, you can make the return reservation whenever you wish — months before you leave or the day before you return. Assuming foreign immigration requirements are met, you can stay at your destination for as long as you like. (Tickets generally are good for a year and can be renewed if not used.) You also can cancel your flight at any time without penalty. However, while it is true that this category of ticket can be purchased at the last minute, it is advisable to reserve well in advance during popular vacation periods and around holiday times.

Fares – Airfares continue to change so rapidly that even experts find it difficult to keep up with them. This ever-changing situation is due to a number of factors, including airline deregulation, volatile labor relations, increasing fuel costs, and vastly increased competition.

Perhaps the most common misconception about fares on scheduled airlines is that the cost of the ticket determines how much service will be provided on the flight. This is true only to a certain extent. A far more realistic rule of thumb is that the less you pay for your ticket, the more restrictions and qualifications are likely to come into play *before* you board the plane (as well as after you get off). These qualifying aspects relate to the months (and the days of the week) during which you must travel, how far in advance you must purchase your ticket, the minimum and maximum amount of time you may or must remain away, your willingness to decide on a return date at the time of booking — and your ability to stick to that decision. It is not uncommon for passengers sitting side by side on the same wide-body jet to have paid fares varying by hundreds of dollars, and all too often the traveler paying more would have been equally willing (and able) to accept the terms of the far less expensive ticket.

In general, the great variety of fares between the US and Paris can be reduced to four basic categories — first class, business class, coach (also called economy or tourist class), and excursion or discount fares. In addition, Advance Purchase Excursion (APEX) fares offer savings under certain conditions.

In a class by itself is the *Concorde,* the supersonic jet developed jointly by France and Great Britain that cruises at speeds of 1,350 miles per hour (almost twice the speed of sound) and makes transatlantic crossings in half the time (3¾ hours from New York to Paris) of conventional, subsonic jets. *Air France* offers *Concorde* service to Paris from New York. Service is "single" class (with champagne and caviar all the way), and the fare is expensive, about 20% more than a first class ticket on a subsonic aircraft. Some discounts have been offered, but time is the real gift of the *Concorde.*

A **first class** ticket admits you to the special section of the aircraft with larger seats, more legroom, better (or more elaborately served) food, free drinks and headsets for movies and music channels, and above all, personal attention. First class fares are about twice those of full-fare (often called "regular") economy.

Behind first class often lies **business class**, usually a separate cabin or cabins. While standards of comfort and service are not as high as in first class, they represent a considerable improvement over conditions in the rear of the plane, with roomier seats, more leg and shoulder space between passengers, and fewer seats abreast. Free liquor and headsets, a choice of meal entrées, and a separate counter for speedier check-in are other inducements. Note that airlines often have their own names for their business class service — such as Le Club on *Air France,* Medallion Class on *Delta,* and Ambassador Class on *TWA.*

The terms of the **coach** or **economy** fare may vary slightly from airline to airline; from time to time airlines may be selling more than one type of economy fare. Coach or economy passengers sit more snugly, as many as 10 in a single row on a wide-body jet, behind the first class and business class sections. Normally, alcoholic drinks are not free, nor are the headsets.

In first, business, and economy class, passengers are entitled to reserve seats and are sold tickets on an open reservation system, with tickets sold up to the last minute if seats are available. The passengers may travel on any scheduled flight they wish, buy a one-way or round-trip ticket, and have the ticket remain valid for a year. There are no requirements for a minimum or maximum stay or for advance booking and no cancellation penalties. The first class and business tickets also allow free stopover privileges; limited free stopovers often are permitted in some economy fares, while with others a surcharge may apply. The cost of economy and business class tickets between the US and Paris does not vary much in the course of the year.

Excursion and other **discount** fares are the airlines' equivalent of a special sale and usually apply to round-trip bookings only. These fares generally differ according to the season and the number of travel days permitted. They are only a bit less flexible than full-fare economy tickets, and are, therefore, often useful for both business and holiday travelers. Most round-trip excursion tickets include strict minimum and maximum stay requirements and can be changed only within prescribed time limits. So don't count on extending a ticket beyond the specified time of return or staying less time than required. Different airlines may have different regulations concerning the number of stopovers permitted, and sometimes excursion fares are less expensive during midweek. The availability of these reduced-rate seats is most limited at busy times such as holidays. Discount or excursion fare ticket holders sit with the coach passengers and, for all intents and purposes, are indistinguishable from them. They receive all the same basic services, even though they may have paid anywhere between 30% and 55% less for the trip. Obviously, it's wise to make plans early enough to qualify for this less expensive transportation if possible.

These discount or excursion fares may masquerade under a variety of names and invariably have strings attached. A common requirement is that the ticket be purchased a certain number of days — usually no fewer than 7 or 14 days — in advance of departure, though it may be booked weeks or months in advance (it has to be "ticketed," or paid for, shortly after booking, however). The return reservation usually has to be made at the time of the original ticketing and cannot be changed later than a certain number of days (again, usually 7 or 14) before the return flight. If events force a passenger to change the return reservation after the date allowed, the difference between the round-trip excursion rate and the round-trip coach rate probably will have to be paid, though most airlines allow passengers to use their discounted fares by standing by for an empty seat, even if the carrier doesn't otherwise have standby fares. Another common condition is the minimum and maximum stay requirement; for example, 1 to 6 days or 6 to 14 days (but including a Saturday night). Last, cancellation penalties of up to 50% of the full price of the ticket have been assessed — check the specific penalty in effect when you purchase your discount/excursion ticket — so careful planning is imperative.

Of even greater risk — and bearing the lowest price of all the current discount fares — is the ticket where no change at all in departure and/or return flights is permitted, and where the ticket price is totally nonrefundable. If you do buy a nonrefundable ticket, you should be aware of a new policy followed by many airlines that may make it easier to change your plans if necessary. For a fee — set by each airline and payable at the airport when checking in — you *may* be able to change the time or date of a return flight on a nonrefundable ticket. However, if the nonrefundable ticket price for the replacement flight is higher than that of the original (as often is the case when trading in a weekday for a weekend flight), you also will have to pay the difference. Any such change must be made a certain number of days in advance — in some cases as little as 2 days — of either the original or the replacement flight, whichever is earlier; restrictions are set by the individual carrier. (Travelers holding a nonrefundable or other restricted ticket who must change their plans due to a family emergency should know that some carriers may make special allowances in such situations; see *Medical and Legal Aid and Consular Services,* in this section.)

One excursion fare available for travel between the US and Paris, but not to the majority of other European destinations, comes unencumbered by advance booking requirements and cancellation penalties, permits one stopover (for a fee) in each direction, and has "open jaws," meaning that you can fly to one city and depart from another, arranging and paying for your own transportation between the two. The ticket costs about a third less than economy — during the off-season. High-season prices may be less attractive. The ticket currently is good for a minimum of 7 days and a maximum of 6 months abroad.

There also is a newer, often less expensive, type of excursion fare, the **APEX**, or **Advanced Purchase Excursion** fare. (In the case of flights to Europe, this type of fare also may be called a "Eurosaver" fare.) As with traditional excursion fares, passengers paying an APEX fare sit with and receive the same basic services as any other coach or economy passengers, even though they may have paid up to 50% less for their seats. In return, they are subject to certain restrictions. In the case of flights to Paris, the ticket usually is good for a minimum of 7 days abroad and a maximum, currently, of 2 months (depending on the airline and the destination); and as its name implies, it must be "ticketed," or paid for in its entirety, a certain period of time before departure — usually 21 days, although in the case of Paris it may be as little as 14 days.

The drawback to an APEX fare is that it penalizes travelers who change their minds — and travel plans. The return reservation must be made at the time of the original ticketing, and if for some reason you change your schedule, you will have to pay a penalty of $100 or 10% of the ticket value, whichever is greater, as long as you travel within the validity period of your ticket. But if you change your return to a date less than the minimum stay or more than the maximum stay, the difference between the round-trip APEX fare and the full round-trip coach rate will have to be paid. There also is a penalty of anywhere from $75 to $125 or more for canceling or changing a reservation *before* travel begins — check the specific penalty in effect when you purchase your ticket. No stopovers are allowed on an APEX ticket, but it is possible to create an open-jaw effect by buying an APEX on a split ticket basis; for example, flying to Paris and returning from Nice. The total price would be half the price of an APEX to Paris plus half the price of an APEX to Nice. APEX tickets to Paris are sold at basic and peak rates (peak season is around May through September) and may include surcharges for weekend flights.

There also is a Winter or Super APEX, which may go under different names for different carriers. Similar to the regular APEX fare, it costs slightly less but is more restrictive. Depending on the airline and destination, it usually is available only for off-peak winter travel and is limited to a stay of between 7 and 21 days. Advance purchase still is required (currently, 30 days prior to travel), and ticketing must be completed within 48 hours of reservation. The fare is nonrefundable, except in cases of hospitalization or death.

At the time of this writing, *Air France* offered Super APEX on transatlantic flights to most destinations in France during the off-season.

Another type of fare that sometimes is available is the youth or student fare. At present, most US airlines and *Air France* offer a special form of APEX fare for travelers through age 26. The maximum stay is extended to a year. Seats can be reserved no more than 3 days before departure, and tickets must be purchased when the reservation is made. The return is booked at time of reservation, or it can be left open. There is no cancellation penalty, but the fare is subject to availability, so it may be difficult to book a return during peak travel periods, and as with the regular APEX fare, it may not even be available for travel to or from Paris during high season, especially if you have a strict traveling schedule.

The major airlines serving Paris from the US also may offer individual excursion fares in conjunction with ground accommodation packages. Previously called ITX, and sometimes referred to as individual tour-basing fares, these fares generally are offered as part of "air/hotel/car/transfer packages," and can reduce the cost of an economy fare by more than a third. The packages are booked for a specific length of time, with return dates specified; rescheduling and cancellation restrictions and penalties vary from carrier to carrier. At the time of this writing, airlines that offer this type of fare to Paris include *Air France, British Airways, KLM,* and most US airlines. Note that their offerings may or may not represent substantial savings over standard economy fares, so check at the time you plan to travel. (For further information on package options, see *Package Tours,* in this section.)

Travelers looking for the least expensive possible airfares should, finally, scan the travel pages of their hometown newspapers (especially the Sunday travel sections) for announcements of special promotional fares. Most airlines traditionally have offered their most attractive special fares to encourage travel during slow seasons, and to inaugurate and publicize new routes. Even if none of these factors apply, prospective passengers can be fairly sure that the number of discount seats per flight at the lowest price is strictly limited, or that the fare offering includes a set expiration date — which means it's absolutely necessary to move fast to enjoy the lowest possible price.

It's always wise to ask about discount or promotional fares and about any conditions that might restrict booking, payment, cancellation, and changes in plans. Check the prices from other neighboring cities. A special rate may be offered in a nearby city but not in yours, and it may be enough of a bargain to warrant your leaving from that city. Ask if there is a difference in price for midweek versus weekend travel, or if there is a further discount for traveling early in the morning or late at night. Also be sure to investigate package deals, which are offered by virtually every airline. These may include a car rental, accommodations, and dining and/or sightseeing features in addition to the basic airfare, and the combined cost of packaged elements usually is considerably less than the cost of the exact same elements when purchased separately.

If in the course of your research you come across a deal that seems too good to be true, keep in mind that logic may not be a component of deeply discounted airfares — there's not always any sane relationship between miles to be flown and the price to get there. More often than not, the level of competition on a given route dictates the degree of discount, and don't be dissuaded from accepting an offer that sounds irresistible just because it also sounds illogical. Better to buy that inexpensive fare while it's being offered and worry about the sense — or absence thereof — while you're flying to your desired destination.

When you're satisfied that you've found the lowest possible price for which you can conveniently qualify, make your booking. You may have to call the airline more than once, because different airline reservations clerks have been known to quote different prices, and different fares will be available at different times for the same flight because of a relatively new computerized airline practice called yield management, which adds or subtracts low-fare seats to a given flight depending on how well it is selling.

To protect yourself against fare increases, purchase and pay for your ticket as soon as possible after you've received a confirmed reservation. Airlines generally will honor their tickets, even if the operative price at the time of your flight is higher than the price you paid; if fares go up between the time you *reserve* a flight and the time you *pay* for it, you likely will be out of luck. Finally, with excursion or discount fares, it is important to remember that when a reservation clerk says that you must purchase a ticket by a specific date, this is an absolute deadline. Miss it and the airline may automatically cancel your reservation without telling you.

Frequent Flyers – The leading carriers serving Paris — including *Air France, American, British Airways, Continental, Delta, Northwest, TWA,* and *United* — offer a bonus system to frequent travelers. After the first 10,000 miles, for example, a passenger might be eligible for a first class seat for the coach fare; after another 10,000 miles, he or she might receive a discount on his or her next ticket purchase. The value of the bonuses continues to increase as more miles are logged.

Bonus miles also may be earned by patronizing affiliated car rental companies or hotel chains, or by using one of the credit cards that now offers this reward. In deciding whether to accept such a credit card from one of the issuing organizations that tempt you with frequent flyer mileage bonuses on a specific airline, first determine whether the interest rate charged on the unpaid balance is the same as (or less than) possible alternate credit cards, and whether the annual "membership" fee also is equal or lower. If these charges are slightly higher than those of competing cards, weigh the difference against the potential value in airfare savings. Also ask about any bonus miles awarded just for signing up — 1,000 is common, 5,000 generally the maximum.

For the most up-to-date information on frequent flyer bonus options, you may want to send for the monthly newsletter *Frequent.* Issued by Frequent Publications, it provides current information about frequent flyer plans in general, as well as specific data about promotions, awards, and combination deals to help you keep track of the profusion — and confusion — of current and upcoming availabilities. For a year's subscription, send $33 to Frequent Publications, 4715-C Town Center Dr., Colorado Springs, CO 80916 (phone: 800-333-5937).

There also is a monthly magazine called *Frequent Flyer,* but unlike the newsletter mentioned above, its focus is primarily on newsy articles of interest to business travelers and other frequent flyers. Published by Official Airline Guides (PO Box 58543, Boulder, CO 80322-8543; phone: 800-323-3537), *Frequent Flyer* is available for $24 for a 1-year subscription.

Low-Fare Airlines – Increasingly, the stimulus for special fares is the appearance of airlines associated with bargain rates. On these airlines, all seats on any given flight generally sell for the same price, which is somewhat below the lowest discount fare offered by the larger, more established airlines. It is important to note that tickets offered by the smaller airlines specializing in low-cost travel frequently are not subject to the same restrictions as the lowest-priced ticket offered by the more established carriers. They may not require advance purchase or minimum and maximum stays, may involve no cancellation penalties, and may be available one way or round trip. A disadvantage to low-fare airlines, however, is that when something goes wrong, such as delayed baggage or a flight cancellation due to equipment breakdown, their smaller fleets and fewer flights mean that passengers may have to wait longer for a solution than they would on one of the equipment-rich major carriers.

At press time, one of the few airlines offering a consistently low fare to Europe was *Virgin Atlantic* (phone: 800-862-8621 or 212-242-1330), which flies daily from New York (Newark) to London's Gatwick Airport. The airline sells tickets in several categories, including business or "upper" class, economy, APEX, and nonrefundable variations on standby. Fares from New York to London include Late Saver fares — which must be purchased not less than 7 days prior to travel — and Late Late Saver fares — which are purchased no later than 1 day prior to travel. Travelers to Paris then have to take a second flight there from London, but still may save money. To determine the potential savings, add the cost of these transatlantic fares and the cost of connecting flights to come up with the total ticket price. Remember, too, that since Paris is such a popular holiday destination with the British, ultra-low-priced package programs are frequently available from British-based tour operators and bucket shops.

In a class by itself is *Icelandair,* which always has been a scheduled airline but long has been known as a good source of low-cost flights to Europe. *Icelandair* flies from Baltimore/Washington, DC, New York, and Orlando to Copenhagen (Denmark), Glasgow and London (Great Britain), Gothenburg and Stockholm (Sweden), Helsinki (Finland), Luxembourg (in the country of the same name), Oslo (Norway), Paris

(France), and Reykjavik (Iceland). In addition, the airline increases the options for its passengers by offering "thru-fares" on connecting flights to other European cities. (The price of the intra-European flights — aboard Luxembourg's *Luxair* — is included in the price *Icelandair* quotes for the transatlantic portion of the travel to these additional destinations.)

Icelandair sells tickets in a variety of categories, from unrestricted economy fares to a sort of standby "3-days-before" fare (which functions just like the youth fares described above but has no age requirement). Travelers should be aware, however, that most *Icelandair* flights stop in Reykjavik, Iceland, for 45 minutes — a minor delay for most, but one that further prolongs the trip for passengers who will wait again to board connecting flights to their ultimate destination of Paris. (At the time of this writing, *Icelandair* did not offer connecting flights to France; however, connecting flight options are available through other carriers.) It may be a better choice for travelers intending to visit *other* destinations on the Continent when taking both this delay and the cost of connections into account. For reservations and tickets, contact a travel agent or *Icelandair* (phone: 800-223-5500 or 212-967-8888).

Intra-European Fares – The cost of the round trip across the Atlantic is not the only expense to consider, for flights between European cities can be quite expensive. But discounts have recently been introduced on routes between some European cities, and other discounts do exist.

Recent Common Market moves toward airline deregulation are expected to lead gradually to a greater number of budget fares. In the meantime, however, the high cost of fares between most European cities can be avoided by careful use of stopover rights on the higher-priced transatlantic tickets — first class, business class, and full-fare economy. If your ticket doesn't allow stopovers, ask about excursion fares such as PEX and Super PEX, APEX for round trips, and other excursion fares for one-way trips. If you are able to comply with applicable restrictions and can use them, you may save as much as 35% to 50% off full-fare economy. Note that these tickets, which once could be bought only after arrival in Europe, now are sold in the US and can be bought before departure.

Both *Air France* and its subsidiary, *Air Inter* (a major French domestic airline), offer discount fares for round-trip travel within France. These special fares usually require instant purchase (the passenger must pay for the ticket at time of reservation). Discounts are also offered to senior citizens, French military personnel, and students, as well as family members traveling together.

For travel within France, *Air Inter* offers a France Pass, which allows purchasers to fly *Air Inter* to unlimited destinations in 7 days (consecutive or not) within a 30-day period. Travelers can use this pass to reach 30 cities in France on *Air Inter.* During the summer high season, this pass costs $250. Reservations for specific flight dates need not be made in advance, and pass holders have the flexibility to spend as much time as they wish (within the 30-day validity period) at each destination. This pass is available from *Jet Vacations* (phone: 800-538-0999). Another French domestic airline, *Air Littoral,* also offers a See France Pass. Pass holders can have unlimited travel on *Air Littoral,* which reaches 20 cities in France. A 7-day pass costs $229; a 10-day pass, $279.

Taxes and Other Fees – Travelers who have shopped for the best possible flight at the lowest possible price should be warned that a number of extras will be added to that price and collected by the airline or travel agent who issues the ticket. These taxes *usually* (but not always) are included in the prices quoted by airline reservations clerks.

The $6 International Air Transportation Tax is a departure tax paid by all passengers flying from the US to a foreign destination. A $10 US Federal Inspection Fee is levied on all air and cruise passengers who arrive in the US from outside North America. Still another fee is charged by some airlines to cover more stringent security procedures, prompted by recent terrorist incidents. The 8% federal US Transportation Tax applies to travel within the US or US territories, as well as to passengers flying between US cities en route to a foreign destination if the trip includes a stopover of more than 12 hours at a US point. Someone flying from Los Angeles to New York and stopping in New York for more than 12 hours before boarding a flight to Paris, for instance, would pay the 8% tax on the domestic portion of the trip.

Reservations – For those who don't have the time or patience to investigate personally all possible air departures and connections for a proposed trip, a travel agent can be of inestimable help. A good agent should have all the information on which flights go where and when, and which categories of tickets are available on each. Most have computerized reservation links with the major carriers, so that a seat can be reserved and confirmed in minutes. An increasing number of agents also possess fare-comparison computer programs, so they often are very reliable sources of detailed competitive price data. (For more information, see *How to Use a Travel Agent,* in this section.)

When making reservations through a travel agent, ask the agent to give the airline your home phone number, as well as your daytime business phone number. All too often the agent uses the agency number as the official contact for changes in flight plans. Especially during the winter, weather conditions hundreds or even thousands of miles away can wreak havoc with flight schedules. Aircraft are constantly in use, and a plane delayed in the Orient or on the West Coast can miss its scheduled flight from the East Coast the next morning. The airlines are fairly reliable about getting this sort of information to passengers if they can reach them; diligence does little good at 10 PM if the airline has only the agency's or an office number.

Reconfirmation is strongly recommended for all international flights, and in the case of flights to Paris, it is a good idea to confirm your round-trip reservations — especially the return leg — as well as any point-to-point flights within Europe. Some (though increasingly fewer) reservations to and from international destinations are automatically canceled after a required reconfirmation period (typically 72 hours) has passed — even if you have a confirmed, fully paid ticket in hand. It always is wise to call ahead to make sure that the airline did not slip up in entering your original reservation, or in registering any changes you may have made since, and that it has your seat reservation and/or special meal request in the computer. If you look at the printed information on the ticket, you'll see the airline's reconfirmation policy stated explicitly. Don't be lulled into a false sense of security by the "OK" on your ticket next to the number and time of the return flight. This only means that a reservation has been entered; a reconfirmation still may be necessary. If in doubt — call.

If you plan not to take a flight on which you hold a confirmed reservation, by all means inform the airline. Because the problem of "no-shows" is a constant expense for airlines, they are allowed to overbook flights, a practice that often contributes to the threat of denied boarding for a certain number of passengers (see "Getting Bumped," below).

Seating – For most types of tickets, airline seats usually are assigned on a first-come, first-served basis at check-in, although some airlines make it possible to reserve a seat at the time of ticket purchase. Always check in early for your flight, even with advance seat assignments. A good rule of thumb for international flights is to arrive at the airport *at least* 2 hours before the scheduled departure to give yourself plenty of time in case there are long lines.

Most airlines furnish seating charts, which make choosing a seat much easier, but there are a few basics to consider. You must decide whether you prefer a window, aisle, or middle seat. On flights where smoking is permitted, you also should specify if you prefer the smoking or nonsmoking section. There is a useful quarterly publication called the *Airline Seating Guide* that publishes seating charts for most major US airlines and many foreign carriers as well. Your travel agent should have a copy, or you can buy the US edition for $39.95 per year and the international edition for $44.95. Order from Carlson Publishing Co., Box 888, Los Alamitos, CA 90720 (phone: 800-728-4877 or 213-493-4877).

Simply reserving an airline seat in advance, however, actually may guarantee very little. Most airlines require that passengers arrive at the departure gate at least 45 minutes (sometimes more) ahead of time to hold a seat reservation. Some US airlines may cancel seat assignments and may not honor reservations of passengers not "checked in" 45 minutes before the scheduled departure time, and they *ask* travelers to check in at least 2 hours before all international flights. It pays to read the fine print on your ticket carefully and plan ahead.

A far better strategy is to visit an airline ticket office (or one of a select group of travel agents) to secure an actual boarding pass for your specific flight. Once this has been issued, airline computers show you as checked in, and you effectively own the seat you have selected (although some carriers may not honor boarding passes of passengers arriving at the gate less than 10 minutes before departure). This also is good — but not foolproof — insurance against getting bumped from an overbooked flight and is, therefore, an especially valuable tactic at peak travel times.

Smoking – For information on airplane smoking regulations, there is a wallet-size guide that notes in detail the rights of smokers and nonsmokers according to current US regulations. It is available by sending a self-addressed, stamped envelope to ASH (Action on Smoking and Health), Airline Card, 2013 H St. NW, Washington, DC 20006 (phone: 202-659-4310).

Meals – If you have specific diet requirements, be sure to let the airline know well before departure time. The available meals include vegetarian, seafood, kosher, Muslim, Hindu, high-protein, low-calorie, low-cholesterol, low-fat, low-sodium, diabetic, bland, and children's menus. There is no extra charge for this option. It usually is necessary to request special meals when you make your reservations — check-in time is too late. It's also wise to reconfirm that your request for a special meal has made its way into the airline's computer — the time to do this is 24 hours before departure. (Note that special meals generally are not available on intra-European flights on small local carriers. If this poses a problem, try to eat before you board, or bring a snack with you.)

Baggage – When you fly on a US airline or on a major international carrier such as *Air France,* US baggage regulations will be in effect. Though airline baggage allowances vary slightly, in general all passengers are allowed to carry on board, without charge, one piece of luggage that will fit easily under a seat of the plane or in an overhead bin and whose combined dimensions (length, width, and depth) do not exceed 45 inches. A reasonable amount of reading material, camera equipment, and a handbag also are allowed. In addition, all passengers are allowed to check two bags in the cargo hold: one usually not to exceed 62 inches when length, width, and depth are combined, the other not to exceed 55 inches in combined dimensions. Generally no single bag may weigh more than 70 pounds.

Airline Clubs – US carriers often have clubs for travelers who pay for membership. These clubs are not solely for first class passengers, although a first class ticket *may* entitle a passenger to lounge privileges. Membership (which, by law, requires a fee) entitles the traveler to use the private lounges at airports along their route, to refreshments served in these lounges, and to check-cashing privileges at most of their counters. Extras include special telephone numbers for individual reservations, embossed luggage tags, and a membership card for identification. Airlines serving Paris that offer membership in such clubs include the following:

> *American:* The *Admiral's Club.* Single yearly membership $175 for the first year; $125 yearly thereafter; spouse an additional $70 per year.

British Airways: The *Executive Club.* Single yearly membership £125 (about $200 at press time). No discounted rate for spouse.

Continental: The *President's Club.* Single yearly membership $140 for the first year; $90 yearly thereafter; spouse an additional $25 per year.

Delta: The *Crown Club.* Single yearly membership $150; spouse an additional $50 per year.

Northwest: The *World Club.* Single yearly membership $150 (plus a onetime $25 initiation fee); spouse an additional $45 per year; 3-year and lifetime memberships also available.

TWA: The *Ambassador Club.* Single yearly membership $150, spouse an additional $25; lifetime memberships also available.

United: The *Red Carpet Club.* Single yearly membership $200 for the first year; $100 yearly thereafter; spouse an additional $50 per year; 3-year and lifetime memberships also available.

USAir: The *USAir Club.* Single yearly membership $125; spouse an additional $25 per year.

Note that such companies do not have club facilities in all airports. Other airlines also offer a variety of special services in many airports.

CHARTER FLIGHTS: By booking a block of seats on a specially arranged flight, charter operators offer travelers air transportation for a substantial reduction over the full coach or economy fare. These operators may offer air-only charters (selling transportation alone) or charter packages (the flight plus a combination of land arrangements such as accommodations, meals, tours, or car rentals). Charters are especially attractive to people living in smaller cities or out-of-the-way places, because they frequently leave from nearby airports, saving travelers the inconvenience and expense of getting to a major gateway.

From the consumer's standpoint, charters differ from scheduled airlines in two main respects: You generally need to book and pay in advance, and you can't change the itinerary or the departure and return dates once you've booked the flight. In practice, however, these restrictions don't always apply. Today, although most charter flights still require advance reservations, some permit last-minute bookings (when there are unsold seats available), and some even offer seats on a standby basis.

Though charters almost always are round-trip, and it is unlikely that you would be sold a one-way seat on a round-trip flight, on rare occasions one-way tickets on charters are offered. Although it may be possible to book a one-way charter in the US, giving you more flexibility in scheduling your return, note that US regulations pertaining to charters may be more permissive than the charter laws of other countries. For example, if you want to book a one-way foreign charter back to the US, you may find advance booking rules in force.

Some things to keep in mind about charter travel:

1. It cannot be repeated often enough that if you are forced to cancel your trip, you can lose much (and possibly all) of your money unless you have cancellation insurance, which is a *must* (see *Insurance,* in this section). Frequently, if the cancellation occurs far enough in advance (often 6 weeks or more), you may forfeit only a $25 or $50 penalty. If you cancel only 2 or 3 weeks before the flight, there may be no refund at all unless you or the operator can provide a substitute passenger.

2. Charter flights may be canceled by the operator up to 10 days before departure for any reason, usually underbooking. Your money is returned in this event, but there may be too little time for you to make new arrangements.

3. Most charters have little of the flexibility of regularly scheduled flights regarding refunds and the changing of flight dates; if you book a return flight, you must be on it or lose your money.

4. Charter operators are permitted to assess a surcharge, if fuel or other costs warrant it, of up to 10% of the airfare up to 10 days before departure.
5. Because of the economics of charter flights, your plane almost always will be full, so you will be crowded, though not necessarily uncomfortable. (There is, however, a new movement among charter airlines to provide flight accommodations that are more comfort-oriented, so this situation may change in the near future.)

To avoid problems, *always* choose charter flights with care. When you consider a charter, ask your travel agent who runs it and carefully check the company. The Better Business Bureau in the company's home city can report on how many complaints, if any, have been lodged against it in the past. Protect yourself with trip cancellation and interruption insurance, which can help safeguard your investment if you or a traveling companion is unable to make the trip and must cancel too late to receive a full refund from the company providing your travel services. (This is advisable whether you're buying a charter flight alone or a tour package for which the airfare is provided by charter or scheduled flight.)

Bookings – If you do take a charter, read the contract's fine print carefully and pay particular attention to the following:

Instructions concerning the payment of the deposit and its balance and to whom the check is to be made payable. Ordinarily, checks are made out to an escrow account, which means the charter company can't spend your money until your flight has safely returned. This provides some protection for you. To ensure the safe handling of your money, make out your check to the escrow account, the number of which must appear by law on the brochure, though all too often it is on the back in fine print. Write the details of the charter, including the destination and dates, on the face of the check; on the back, print "For Deposit Only." Your travel agent may prefer that you make out your check to the agency, saying that it will then pay the tour operator the fee minus commission. It is perfectly legal to write the check as we suggest, however, and if your agent objects too vociferously (he or she should trust the tour operator to send the proper commission), consider taking your business elsewhere. If you don't make your check out to the escrow account, you lose the protection of that escrow should the trip be canceled. Furthermore, recent bankruptcies in the travel industry have served to point out that even the protection of escrow may not be enough to safeguard a traveler's investment. More and more, insurance is becoming a necessity. The charter company should be bonded (usually by an insurance company), and if you want to file a claim against it, the claim should be sent to the bonding agent. The contract will set a time limit within which a claim must be filed.

Specific stipulations and penalties for cancellations. Most charters allow you to cancel up to 45 days in advance without major penalty, but some cancellation dates are 50 to 60 days before departure.

Stipulations regarding cancellation and major changes made by the charterer. US rules say that charter flights may not be canceled within 10 days of departure except when circumstances — such as natural disasters or political upheavals — make it impossible to fly. Charterers may make "major changes," however, such as in the date or place of departure or return, but you are entitled to cancel and receive a full refund if you don't wish to accept these changes. A price increase of more than 10% at any time up to 10 days before departure is considered a major change; no price increase at all is allowed during the last 10 days immediately before departure.

Among the charter operators flying between the US and France is *Air France*'s subsidiary, *Air Charter,* which offers spring and summer service between New York and Paris; the booking agent is *Jet Vacations* (888 Seventh Ave., New York, NY 10106; phone: 800-JET-0999 or 212-247-0999). Other charter operators serving Paris include *Amber Tours* (7337 W. Washington St., Indianapolis, IN 46251; phone: 800-225-9920) and *American Trans Air* (PO Box 51609, Indianapolis, IN 46251; phone: 317-243-4150).

For the full range of possibilities at the time you plan to travel, you may want to subscribe to the travel newsletter *Jax Fax*, which regularly features a list of charter companies and packagers offering seats on charter flights and may be a source for other charter flights to Paris. For a year's subscription, send a check or money order for $12 to *Jax Fax* (397 Post Rd., Darien, CT 06820; phone: 203-655-8746).

DISCOUNTS ON SCHEDULED FLIGHTS: Promotional fares often are called discount fares because they cost less than what used to be the standard airline fare — full-fare economy. Nevertheless, they cost the traveler the same whether they are bought through a travel agent or directly from the airline. Tickets that cost less if bought from some outlet other than the airline do exist, however. While it is likely that the vast majority of travelers flying to Paris in the near future will be doing so on a promotional fare or charter rather than on a "discount" air ticket of this sort, it still is a good idea for cost-conscious consumers to be aware of the latest developments in the budget airfare scene. Note that the following discussion makes clear-cut distinctions among the types of discounts available based on how they reach the consumer; in actual practice, the distinctions are not nearly so precise.

Net Fare Sources – The newest notion for reducing the costs of travel services comes from travel agents who offer individual travelers "net" fares. Defined simply, a net fare is the bare minimum amount at which an airline or tour operator will carry a prospective traveler. It doesn't include the amount that normally would be paid to the travel agent as a commission. Traditionally, such commissions amount to about 10% on domestic fares and from 10% to 20% on international fares — not counting significant additions to these commission levels that are paid retroactively when agents sell more than a specific volume of tickets or trips for a single supplier. At press time, at least one travel agency in the US was offering travelers the opportunity to purchase tickets and/or tours for a net price. Instead of making its income from individual commissions, this agency assesses a fixed fee that may or may not provide a bargain for travelers; it requires a little arithmetic to determine whether to use the services of a net travel agent or those of one who accepts conventional commissions. One of the potential drawbacks of buying from agencies selling travel services at net fares is that some airlines refuse to do business with them, thus possibly limiting your flight options.

Travel Avenue is a fee-based agency that rebates its ordinary agency commission to the customer. For domestic flights, they will find the lowest retail fare, then rebate 7% to 10% (depending on the airline selected) of that price minus a $10 ticket-writing charge. The rebate percentage for international flights varies from 5% to 16% (again depending on the airline), and the ticket-writing fee is $25. The ticket-writing charge is imposed per ticket; if the ticket includes more than eight separate flights, an additional $10 or $25 fee is charged. Customers using free flight coupons pay the ticket-writing charge, plus an additional $5 coupon processing fee.

Travel Avenue will rebate its commissions on all tickets, including heavily discounted fares and senior citizen passes. Available 7 days a week, reservations should be made far enough in advance to allow the tickets to be sent by first class mail, since extra charges accrue for special handling. It's possible to economize further by making your own airline reservation, then asking *Travel Avenue* only to write/issue your ticket. For travelers outside the Chicago area, business may be transacted by phone and purchases charged to a credit card. For further information, contact *Travel Avenue* at 641 W. Lake St., Suite 201, Chicago, IL 60606-1012 (phone: 312-876-1116 in Illinois; 800-333-3335 elsewhere in the US).

Consolidators and Bucket Shops – Other vendors of travel services can afford to sell tickets to their customers at an even greater discount because the airline has sold the tickets to them at a substantial discount (usually accomplished by sharply increasing commissions to that vendor), a practice in which many airlines indulge, albeit discreetly, preferring that the general public not know they are undercutting their own "list" prices. Airlines anticipating a slow period on a particular route sometimes sell off a certain portion of their capacity to a wholesaler or consolidator. The wholesaler sometimes is a charter operator who resells the seats to the public as though they were charter seats, which is why prospective travelers perusing the brochures of charter operators with large programs frequently see a number of flights designated as "scheduled service." As often as not, however, the consolidator, in turn, sells the seats to a travel agency specializing in discounting. Airlines also can sell seats directly to such an agency, which thus acts as its own consolidator. The airline offers the seats either at a net wholesale price, but without the volume-purchase requirement that would be difficult for a modest retail travel agency to fulfill, or at the standard price, but with a commission override large enough (as high as 50%) to allow both a profit and a price reduction to the public.

Travel agencies specializing in discounting sometimes are called "bucket shops," a term fraught with connotations of unreliability in this country. But in today's highly competitive travel marketplace, more and more conventional travel agencies are selling consolidator-supplied tickets, and the old bucket shops' image is becoming respectable. Agencies that specialize in discounted tickets exist in most large cities, and usually can be found by studying the smaller ads in the travel sections of Sunday newspapers.

Before buying a discounted ticket, whether from a bucket shop or a conventional, full-service travel agency, keep the following considerations in mind: To be in a position to judge how much you'll be saving, first find out the "list" prices of tickets to your destination. Then, do some comparison shopping among agencies. Also bear in mind that a ticket that may not differ much in price from one available directly from the airline may, however, allow the circumvention of such things as the advance purchase requirement. If your plans are less than final, be sure to find out about any other restrictions, such as penalties for canceling a flight or changing a reservation. Most discount tickets are non-endorsable, meaning that they can be used only on the airline that issued them, and they usually are marked "nonrefundable" to prevent their being cashed for a list price refund.

A great many bucket shops are small businesses operating on a thin margin, so it's a good idea to check the local Better Business Bureau for any complaints registered against the one with which you're dealing — before parting with any money. If you still do not feel reassured, consider buying discounted tickets only through a conventional travel agency, which can be expected to have found its own reliable source of consolidator tickets — some of the largest consolidators, in fact, sell only to travel agencies.

A few bucket shops require payment in cash or by certified check or money order, but if credit cards are accepted, use that option. Note, however, if buying from a charter operator selling seats for both scheduled and charter flights, that the scheduled seats are not protected by the regulations — including the use of escrow accounts — governing the charter seats. Well-established charter operators, nevertheless, may extend the same protections to their scheduled flights, and when this is the case, consumers should be sure that the payment option selected directs their money into the escrow account.

Among the numerous consolidators offering discount fares to Paris are the following:

Bargain Air (655 Deep Valley Dr., Suite 355, Rolling Hills, CA 90274; phone: 800-347-2345 or 213-377-2919).

Maharaja/Consumer Wholesale (393 Fifth Ave., 2nd Floor, New York, NY 10016; phone: 212-213-2020 in New York; 800-223-6862 elsewhere in the US).

TFI Tours International (34 W. 37th St., 12th Floor, New York, NY 10001; phone: 212-736-1140).

Travac Tours and Charters (989 Sixth Ave., New York, NY 10018; phone: 212-563-3303).

25 West Tours (2490 Coral Way, Miami, FL 33145; phone: 305-856-0810; 800-423-6954 in Florida; 800-252-5052 elsewhere in the US).

Unitravel 1177 N. Warson Rd., St. Louis, MO 63132; phone: 314-569-0900 in Missouri; 800-325-2222 elsewhere in the US).

The newsletter *Jax Fax* (see "Charter Flights," above) is also a good source of information on consolidators.

■**Note:** Although rebating and discounting are becoming increasingly common, there is some legal ambiguity concerning them. Strictly speaking, it is legal to discount domestic tickets, but not international tickets. On the other hand, the law that prohibits discounting, the Federal Aviation Act of 1958, is ignored consistently these days, in part because consumers benefit from the practice and in part because many illegal arrangements are indistinguishable from legal ones. Since the line separating the two is so fine that even the authorities can't always tell the difference, it is unlikely that most consumers would be able to do so, and in fact it is not illegal to *buy* a discounted ticket. If the issue of legality bothers you, ask the agency whether any ticket you're about to buy would be permissible under the above-mentioned act.

OTHER DISCOUNT TRAVEL SOURCES: An excellent source of information on economical travel opportunities is the *Consumer Reports Travel Letter,* published monthly by Consumers Union. It keeps abreast of the scene on a wide variety of fronts, including package tours, rental cars, insurance, and more, but it is especially helpful for its comprehensive coverage of airfares, offering guidance on all the options from scheduled flights on major or low-fare airlines to charters and discount sources. For a year's subscription, send $37 ($57 for 2 years) to *Consumer Reports Travel Letter* (PO Box 53629, Boulder, CO 80322-3629; phone: 800-999-7959). For information on other travel newsletters, see *Sources and Resources,* in this section.

Last-Minute Travel Clubs – Still another way to take advantage of bargain airfares is open to those who have a flexible schedule. A number of organizations, usually set up as last-minute travel clubs and functioning on a membership basis, routinely keep in touch with travel suppliers to help them dispose of unsold inventory at discounts of between 15% and 60%. A great deal of the inventory consists of complete tour packages and cruises, but some clubs offer air-only charter seats and, occasionally, seats on scheduled flights.

Members generally pay an annual fee and receive a toll-free hotline number to call for information on imminent trips. In some cases, they also receive periodic mailings with information on bargain travel opportunities for which there is more advance notice. Despite the suggestive names of the clubs providing these services, last-minute travel does not necessarily mean that you cannot make plans until literally the last minute. Trips can be announced as little as a few days or as much as 2 months before departure, but the average is from 1 to 4 weeks' notice.

Among the organizations regularly offering such discounted travel opportunities to Paris are the following:

Discount Club of America (61-33 Woodhaven Blvd., Rego Park, NY 11374; phone: 800-321-9587 or 718-335-9612). Annual fee: $39 per family.

Encore Short Notice (4501 Forbes Blvd., Lanham, MD 20706; phone: 800-242-9913). Annual fee: $48 per family.

Last Minute Travel (1249 Boylston St., Boston MA 02215; phone: 800-LAST-MIN or 617-267-9800). No fee.

Traveler's Advantage (3033 S. Parker Rd., Suite 1000, Aurora, CO 80014; phone: 800-548-1116). Annual fee: $49 per family.

Worldwide Discount Travel Club (1674 Meridian Ave., Miami Beach, FL 33139; phone: 305-534-2082). Annual fee: $40 per person; $50 per family.

Generic Air Travel – Organizations that apply the same flexible-schedule idea to air travel only and sell tickets at literally the last minute also exist. The service they provide sometimes is known as "generic" air travel, and it operates somewhat like an ordinary airline standby service, except that the organizations running it offer seats on not one but several scheduled and charter airlines.

One pioneer of generic flights is *Airhitch* (2790 Broadway, Suite 100, New York, NY 10025; phone: 212-864-2000), which arranges flights to Paris from various US gateways. Prospective travelers register by paying a fee (applicable toward the fare) and stipulate a range of acceptable departure dates and their desired destination, along with alternate choices. The week before the date range begins, they are notified of at least two flights that will be available during the time period, agree on one, and remit the balance of the fare to the company. If they do not accept any of the suggested flights, they lose their deposit; if, through no fault of their own, they do not ultimately get on any agreed-on flight, all of their money is refunded. Return flights are arranged the same way.

Bartered Travel Sources – Suppose a hotel buys advertising space in a newspaper. As payment, the hotel gives the publishing company the use of a number of hotel rooms in lieu of cash. This is barter, a common means of exchange among hotels, airlines, car rental companies, cruise lines, tour operators, restaurants, and other travel service companies. When a bartering company finds itself with empty airline seats (or excess hotel rooms, or cruise ship cabin space, and so on) and offers them to the public, considerable savings can be enjoyed.

Bartered-travel clubs often offer discounts of up to 50% to members who pay an annual fee (approximately $50 at press time) which entitles them to select from the flights, cruises, hotel rooms, or other travel services that the club obtained by barter. Members usually present a voucher, club credit card, or scrip (a dollar-denomination voucher negotiable only for the bartered product) to the hotel, which in turn subtracts the dollar amount from the bartering company's account.

Selling bartered travel is a perfectly legitimate means of retailing. One advantage to club members is that they don't have to wait until the last minute to obtain flight or room reservations.

Among the companies specializing in bartered travel, several that frequently offer members travel services to Paris include the following:

IGT (In Good Taste) Services (1111 Lincoln Rd., 4th Floor, Miami Beach, FL 33139; phone: 800-444-8872 or 305-534-7900). Annual fee: $48 per family.

Travel Guide (18210 Redmond Way, Redmond, WA 98052; phone: 206-885-1213). Annual fee: $48 per family.

Travel World Leisure Club (225 W. 34th St., Suite 2203, New York, NY 10122; phone: 800-444-TWLC or 212-239-4855). Annual fee: $50 per family.

On Arrival

FROM THE AIRPORT TO THE CITY: Paris's airports for both domestic and international flights are Charles de Gaulle, which is located 17 miles (27 km) northeast of the city, and Orly, which is located 10 miles (16 km) south of the city.

Taxi – From the airport, it is about 45 minutes from central Paris by taxi; the fare is about 200F (about $34). There is an extra charge of about 3.5F (60¢) for each bag.

Public Transportation – The *RER* (suburban train) runs between the city and Charles de Gaulle Airport. Take the *B* train; you can buy a train ticket, which costs about 30F ($5), at the airport.

CAR RENTAL: While cars are useful for day trips outside Paris, they are usually more trouble than they are worth for touring within the city.

Renting a car in Paris is not inexpensive, but it is possible to economize by determining your own needs and then shopping around among the car rental companies until you find the best deal. It might be less expensive to rent a car in the center of Paris rather than at the airport. Ask about special rates or promotional deals, such as weekend or weekly rates, bonus coupons for airline tickets, or 24-hour rates that include gas and unlimited mileage.

Renting from the US – Travel agents can arrange foreign rentals for clients, but it is just as easy to call and rent a car yourself. Listed below are some of the major international rental companies that have representation in Paris and have information and reservations numbers that can be dialed toll-free from the US:

Avis (phone: 800-331-1084). Has representatives at Charles de Gaulle and Orly airports, and 17 other city locations.

Budget (phone: 800-527-0700). Has representatives at Charles de Gaulle and Orly airports, and 16 other city locations.

Dollar Rent-a-Car (known in Europe as *Eurodollar;* phone: 800-800-4000). Has representatives at Charles de Gaulle and Orly airports, and 4 city locations.

Hertz (phone: 800-654-3001). Has representatives at Charles de Gaulle and Orly airports, and 20 other city locations.

National (known in Europe as *Europcar;* phone: 800-CAR-EUROPE). Has representatives at Charles de Gaulle and Orly airports, and 23 other city locations.

It also is possible to rent a car before you go by contacting any number of smaller or less well known US companies that do not operate worldwide. These organizations specialize in European auto travel, including leasing and car purchase in addition to car rental, or actually are tour operators with well-established European car rental programs. These firms, whose names and addresses are listed below, act as agents for a variety of European suppliers, offer unlimited mileage almost exclusively, and frequently manage to undersell their larger competitors by a significant margin.

Auto Europe (PO Box 1097, Camden, ME 04843; phone: 207-236-8235; 800-223-5555 throughout the US; 800-458-9503 in Canada).

Europe by Car (One Rockefeller Plaza, New York, NY 10020; phone: 212-581-3040 in New York State; 800-223-1516 elsewhere in the US; and 9000 Sunset Blvd., Los Angeles, CA 90069; phone: 800-252-9401 or 213-272-0424).

European Car Reservations (349 W. Commercial St., Suite 2950, East Rochester, NY 14445; phone: 800-535-3303).

Foremost Euro-Car (5430 Van Nuys Blvd., Suite 306, Van Nuys, CA 91401; phone: 818-786-1960 or 800-272-3299 in California; 800-423-3111 elsewhere in the US).

Kemwel Group (106 Calvert St., Harrison, NY 10528; phone: 800-678-0678 or 914-835-5555).

Meier's World Travel (6033 W. Century Blvd., Suite 1080, Los Angeles, CA 90045; phone: 800-937-0700). In conjunction with major car rental companies, arranges economical rentals throughout Europe, including Paris.

One of the ways to keep the cost of car rentals down is to deal with a car rental consolidator, such as *Connex International* (23 N. Division St., Peekskill, NY 10566; phone: 800-333-3949 or 914-739-0066). *Connex*'s main business is negotiating with virtually all of the major car rental agencies for the lowest possible prices for its customers. This company arranges rentals throughout Europe, including Paris.

Local Rentals – It long has been common wisdom that the least expensive way to rent a car is to make arrangements in Europe. This is less true today than it used to be. Many medium to large European car rental companies have become the overseas suppliers of stateside companies, and often the stateside agency, by dint of sheer volume, has been able to negotiate more favorable rates for its US customers than the European firm offers its own. Still lower rates may be found by searching out small, strictly local rental companies overseas, whether at less than prime addresses in major cities or in more remote areas, but to find them you must be willing to invest a sufficient amount of vacation time comparing prices on the scene. You also must be prepared to return the car to the location that rented it; drop-off possibilities are likely to be limited.

There is not a wide choice of local car rental companies in Paris; however, the Office du Tourisme de Paris (127 Av. des Champs-Elysées; phone: 47-23-61-72) may be able to supply the names of French car rental companies. The local yellow pages is another good place to begin.

If you are in the mood to splurge on something luxurious, *JKL* (23 Av. de Neuilly, Paris 75106; phone: 47-47-77-00) can deliver a BMW, Mercedes, Jaguar, or Porsche to your hotel. *Deluxe International* (92 *bis* Rue Victor-Hugo, Levallois-Perret 92300; phone: 45-79-92-64) specializes in chauffeured Mercedes for business executives and shopping trips.

Requirements – Whether you decide to rent a car in advance from a large international rental company with European branches or wait to rent from a local company, you should know that renting a car is rarely as simple as signing on the dotted line and roaring off into the night. To drive in Paris, you need certain documents (see below), and will have to convince the renting agency that (1) you are personally creditworthy, and (2) you will bring the car back at the stated time. This will be easy if you have a major credit card; most rental companies accept credit cards in lieu of a cash deposit, as well as for payment of your final bill. If you prefer to pay in cash, leave your credit card imprint as a "deposit," then pay your bill in cash when you return the car.

If you are planning to rent a car once you're in France, *Avis, Budget, Hertz,* and other US rental companies usually *will* rent to travelers paying in cash and leaving either a credit card imprint or a substantial amount of cash as a deposit. This is not necessarily standard policy, however, as other international chains, and a number of local and regional European companies will *not* rent to an individual who doesn't have a valid credit card. In this case, you may have to call around to find a company that accepts cash.

Also keep in mind that although the minimum age to drive a car in France is 18, the minimum age to rent a car is set by the rental company. (Restrictions vary from company to company, as well as at different locations.) Many firms have a minimum age requirement of 21, some raise that to 23 or 25, and for some models of cars it rises to 30. The upper age limit at many companies is between 69 and 75; others have no upper limit or may make drivers above a certain age subject to special conditions.

Don't forget that all car rentals are subject to value added tax. This tax rarely is included in the rental price that's advertised or quoted, but it always must be paid — whether you pay in advance in the US or pay it when you drop off the car. In France, the VAT rate on car rentals is 12%.

Driving documents – A valid driver's license from his or her own state of residence is required for a US citizen to drive in France. In addition, an International Driving Permit (IDP), which is a translation of the US license in 9 languages, may be required if you plan to rent a car from a local firm.

You can obtain your IDP, before you leave, from most branches of the *American Automobile Association (AAA)*. Applicants must be at least 18 years old, and the application must be accompanied by two passport-size photos (some *AAA* branches have a photo machine available), a valid US driver's license, and a fee of $10. The IDP is good for 1 year and must be accompanied by your US license to be valid.

Proof of liability insurance also is required and is a standard part of any car rental contract. (To be sure of having the appropriate coverage, let the rental staff know in advance about any national borders you plan to cross.) Car rental companies also make provisions for breakdowns, emergency service, and assistance; ask for a number to call when you pick up the vehicle.

Rules of the road – Contrary to first impressions, rules of the road do exist in Paris. Driving in France is on the right side of the road, as in most of Europe. Passing is on the left; the left turn signal must be flashing before and while passing, and the right indicator must be used when pulling back to the right. In most larger cities, such as Paris, honking is forbidden (except to avoid accidents); flash your headlights instead. Also, don't be intimidated by tailgaters — everyone does it.

According to law, those coming from the right at intersections have the right of way, as in the US, and pedestrians, provided they are in marked crosswalks, have priority over all vehicles. In many areas, though, signposting is meager, and traffic at intersections converges from all directions, resulting in a proceed-at-your-own-risk flow.

In the city, speed limits usually are 80 kph (about 50 mph). Outside the city, the speed limit is 130 kph (about 80 mph) on toll motorways, 110 kph (about 68 mph) on dual carriageways (similar to divided highways in the US).

■**Note:** Finding a parking spot in Paris used to be a major hassle. There were controlled parking zones in the major thoroughfares in the city, and anyone who parked in those areas risked having their cars clamped or even their trunks and doors blown away by overzealous security forces. However, in the past few years the government has undertaken a major project to improve this situation. There is now underground parking (with signs that say "Parking") at all the major tourist attractions, and plenty of *parcomètres* on the street.

Gasoline – In France, gasoline is sold by the liter, which is slightly more than 1 quart; approximately 3.8 liters equal 1 US gallon. Regular or leaded gas generally is sold in two grades — called *super* and *ordinaire*. Similarly, unleaded gas is also available in two grades — called *essence sans plomb super* and *essence sans plomb*. Diesel (called "gasoil") also is widely available. Unleaded gas is common in Paris, but still a rarity in some parts of France, at least until all European gas stations sell unleaded, your safest bet if you're planning to drive outside the city is to rent a car that takes leaded gasoline.

Gas prices everywhere rise and fall depending on the world supply of oil, and an American traveling overseas is further affected by the prevailing rate of exchange, so it is difficult to say exactly how much fuel will cost when you travel. It is not difficult to predict, however, that gas prices will be much higher in France than you are accustomed to paying in the US.

Package Tours

If the mere thought of buying a package for visiting Paris conjures up visions of a march through the city in lockstep with a horde of frazzled fellow travelers, remember that packages have come a long way. For one thing, not all packages necessarily are escorted tours, and the one you buy does not have to include any organized touring at all — nor will it necessarily include traveling companions. If it does, however, you'll find that people of all sorts — many just like yourself — are taking advantage of packages today because they are economical and convenient, save you an immense amount of planning time, and exist in such variety that it's virtually impossible not to find one that suits at least the majority of your travel preferences. Given the high cost of travel these days, packages have emerged as a particularly wise buy.

In essence, a package is just an amalgam of travel services that can be purchased in a single transaction. A Paris package (tour or otherwise) may include any or all of the following: round-trip transatlantic transportation, transfers between the airport and the hotel, local transportation (and/or car rentals), accommodations, some or all meals, sightseeing, entertainment, taxes, tips, escort service, and a variety of incidental features that might be offered as options at additional cost. Its principal advantage is that it saves money: The cost of the combined arrangements invariably is well below the price of all of the same elements if bought separately, and, particularly if transportation is provided by charter or discount flight, the whole package could cost less than just a round-trip economy airline ticket on a regularly scheduled flight. A package provides more than economy and convenience: It releases the traveler from having to make individual arrangements for each separate element of a trip.

Tour programs generally can be divided into two categories — "escorted" (or locally hosted) and "independent." An escorted tour means that a guide will accompany the group from the beginning of the tour through to the return flight; a locally hosted tour means that the group will be met upon arrival at each location by a different local host. On independent tours (which are the ones generally available for visiting cities, such as Paris), there usually is a choice of hotels, meal plans, and sightseeing trips in each city, as well as a variety of special excursions. The independent plan is for travelers who do not want a totally set itinerary, but who do prefer confirmed hotel reservations. Always bring along complete contact information for your tour operator in case a problem arises, although US tour operators often have European affiliates who can give additional assistance or make other arrangements on the spot.

To determine whether a package — or, more specifically, *which* package — fits your travel plans, start by evaluating your interests and needs, deciding how much and what you want to spend, see, and do. Gather whatever package tour information is available for your schedule. Be sure that you take the time to read the brochure *carefully* to determine precisely what is included. Keep in mind that travel brochures are written to entice you into signing up for a package tour. Often the language is deceptive and devious. For example, a brochure may quote the lowest prices for a package tour based on facilities that are unavailable during the off-season, undesirable at any season, or just plain nonexistent. Information such as "breakfast included" (as it often is in packages to France) or "plus tax" (which can add up) should be taken into account. Note, too, that the prices quoted in brochures almost always are based on double occupancy: The rate listed is for each of two people sharing a double room, and if you travel alone, the supplement for single accommodations can raise the price considerably (see *Hints for Single Travelers,* in this section).

In this age of erratic airfares, the brochure most often will *not* include the price of an airline ticket in the price of the package, though sample fares from various gateway cities usually will be listed separately, to be added to the price of the ground arrangements. Before figuring your actual cost, check the latest fares with the airlines, because the samples invariably are out of date by the time you read them. If the brochure gives more than one category of sample fares per gateway city — such as an individual tour-basing fare, a group fare, an excursion, APEX, or other discount ticket — your travel agent or airline tour desk will be able to tell you which one applies to the package you choose, depending on when you travel, how far in advance you book, and other factors. (An individual tour-basing fare is a fare computed as part of a package that includes land arrangements, thereby entitling a carrier to reduce the air portion almost to the absolute minimum. Though it always represents a savings over full-fare coach or economy, lately the individual tour-basing fare has not been as inexpensive as the excursion and other discount fares that also are available to individuals. The group fare usually is the least expensive fare, and it is the tour operator, not you, who makes up the group.) When the brochure does include round-trip transportation in the package price, don't forget to add the cost of round-trip transportation from your home to the departure city to come up with the total cost of the package.

Finally, read the general information regarding terms and conditions and the responsibility clause (usually in fine print at the end of the descriptive literature) to determine the precise elements for which the tour operator is — and is not — liable. Here the tour operator frequently expresses the right to change services or schedules as long as equivalent arrangements are offered. This clause also absolves the operator of responsibility for circumstances beyond human control, such as floods, or injury to you or your property. While reading, ask the following questions:

1. Does the tour include airfare or other transportation, sightseeing, meals, transfers, taxes, baggage handling, tips, or any other services? Do you want all these services?
2. If the brochure indicates that "some meals" are included, does this mean a welcoming and farewell dinner, two breakfasts, or every evening meal?
3. What classes of hotels are offered? If you will be traveling alone, what is the single supplement?
4. Does the tour itinerary or price vary according to the season?
5. Are the prices guaranteed; that is, if costs increase between the time you book and the time you depart, can surcharges unilaterally be added?
6. Do you get a full refund if you cancel? If not, be sure to obtain cancellation insurance.
7. Can the operator cancel if too few people join? At what point?

One of the consumer's biggest problems is finding enough information to judge the reliability of a tour packager, since individual travelers seldom have direct contact with the firm putting the package together. Usually, a retail travel agent is interposed between customer and tour operator, and much depends on his or her candor and cooperation. So ask a number of questions about the tour you are considering. For example:

- Has the travel agent ever used a package provided by this tour operator?
- How long has the tour operator been in business? Check the Better Business Bureau in the area where the tour operator is based to see if any complaints have been filed against it.
- Is the tour operator a member of the *United States Tour Operators Association* (*USTOA*; 211 E. 51st St., Suite 12B, New York, NY 10022; phone: 212-944-5727)? *USTOA* will provide a list of its members upon request; it also offers a useful brochure, *How to Select a Package Tour.*
- How many and which companies are involved in the package?
- If air travel is by charter flight, is there an escrow account in which deposits will be held; if so, what is the name of the bank?

This last question is very important. US law requires that tour operators place every charter passenger's deposit and subsequent payment in a proper escrow account (see "Charter Flights," above).

■ **A word of advice:** Purchasers of vacation packages who feel they're not getting their money's worth are more likely to get a refund if they complain in writing to the operator — and bail out of the whole package immediately. Alert the tour operator or resort manager to the fact that you are dissatisfied, that you will be leaving for home as soon as transportation can be arranged, and that you expect a refund. They may have forms to fill out detailing your complaint; otherwise, state your case in a letter. Even if difficulty in arranging immediate transportation home detains you, your dated, written complaint should help in procuring a refund from the operator.

SAMPLE PACKAGES: Generally speaking, escorted tours cover whole countries or sections of countries. For stays that feature Paris only, you would be looking at an independent city package, sometimes known at a "stay-put" program. Basically the city package includes round-trip transfer between airport and hotel, a choice of hotel accommodations (usually including breakfast) in several price ranges, plus any number of other features you may not need or want but would lose valuable time arranging if you did. Common package features are 1 or 2 half-day guided tours of the city; a boat cruise; passes for unlimited local travel by bus or train; discount cards for shops, museums, and restaurants; temporary membership in and admission to clubs, discotheques, or other nightspots; and car rental for some or all of your stay. Other features may include anything from a souvenir travel bag to a tasting of local wines, dinner, and a show. The packages usually are a week long — although 4-day and 14-day packages also are available, and most packages can be extended by extra days — and often are hosted; that is, a representative of the tour company may be available at a local office or even in the hotel to answer questions, handle problems, and assist in arranging activities and option excursions.

Among companies offering tour packages in Paris are the following:

American Express Travel Related Services (offices throughout the US; phone: 800-241-1700 for information and local branch offices). Offers individual city packages.

American Media Tours (16 W. 32nd St., Suite PH, New York, NY 10001; phone: 800-969-6344 or 212-465-1630). Offers hotel and air packages in Paris, which include one- or half-day excursions.

Cityrama (347 Fifth Ave., Suite 709, New York, NY 10016-5098; phone: 800-225-2595 or 212-683-8120). An associate of *Gray Line,* it offers motorcoach tours of Paris and surrounding areas.

Contiki Holidays (1432 E. Katella Ave., Anaheim, CA 92805; phone: 800-624-0611, 714-937-0611, or 800-626-0611). This agency specializes in travel for those 18 to 35 years old. It offers 11- to 37-day motorcoach tours in Europe that include excursions in Paris.

Dailey-Thorp Travel (315 W. 57th St., New York, NY 10019; phone: 212-307-1555). This music and opera specialist offers 11- and 13-day opera tours in Europe, including a performance of *Die Zauberflöte* (The Magic Flute) in Paris.

Globus Gateway (95-25 Queens Blvd., Rego Park, NY 11374; phone: 800-221-0090 or 718-268-7000; and 150 S. Los Robles Ave., Pasadena, CA 91101; phone: 818-449-2019 in California, 800-556-5454 elsewhere in the western US). This luxury tour operator offers 12- to 23-day escorted trips in Europe that include excursions in Paris. If you prefer to travel on your own, there is a 9-day independent city package in Paris.

Insight International Tours (745 Atlantic Ave., Suite 720, Boston, MA 02111; phone: 800-582-8380 or 617-426-6666). It offers 4- to 38-day escorted tours in Great Britain and other European countries, all of which include 1- or 2-day excursions in Paris. It can also arrange independent programs.

Marsans International (19 W. 34th St., Suite 302, New York, NY 10001; phone: 212-239-3880 in New York State; 800-223-6114 elsewhere in the US). Offers independent city packages.

Saga Holidays (120 Boylston St., Boston, MA 02116-9719; phone: 800-343-0273 or 617-451-6808). This company specializes in travelers who are over 60 or those who are between 50 and 59 accompanying a traveler who is over 60. It offers an 18-day trip that covers Paris, London, Brussels, and Heidelberg, among óther cities. There's also a 19-day trip to France, Spain, and Portugal and a 15-day tour of France, both of which include excursions in Paris.

SuperCities (7855 Haskell Ave., Van Nuys, CA 91406; phone: 800-633-3000 or 818-988-7844). Offers 2- and 3-night packages. This tour operator is a wholesaler, so use a travel agent.

Travcoa (PO Box 2630, Newport Beach, CA 92658-2630; phone: 800-992-2004). Offers 13- to 30-day trips to different areas in France, all of which include 1 or 2-day excursions in the capital city; some also include a ballooning adventure in the itinerary.

Travel Bound (599 Broadway, Penthouse, New York, NY 10012; phone: 800-456-8656 or 212-334-1350). Offers flexible city packages, depending on arrangements desired. This tour operator is a wholesaler, so use a travel agent.

Many of the major air carriers maintain their own tour departments or subsidiaries to stimulate vacation travel to the cities they serve. In all cases, the arrangements may be booked through a travel agent or directly with the company.

American Airlines FlyAAway Vacations (Southern Reservation Center, Mail Drop 1000, Box 619619, Dallas/Fort Worth Airport, TX 75261-9619; phone: 800-321-2121).

British Airways Holidays (65-70 Astoria Blvd., Jackson Heights, NY 11370; phone: 800-AIRWAYS).

Delta's Dream Vacations (PO Box 1525, Fort Lauderdale, FL 33302; phone: 800-872-7786).

KLM's Vacation Center (3755 W. Alabama St., Suite 750, Houston, TX 77098; phone: 800-777-1668).

Northwest WorldVacations (5130 Highway 101, Minnetonka, MN; phone: 800-727-1400).

TWA Getaway (10 E. Stow Rd., Marlton, NJ 08053; phone: 800-GETAWAY).

■ **Note:** Frequently, the best city packages are offered by the hotels, which are trying to attract guests during the weekends, when business travel drops off, and during other off periods. These packages are often advertised in the local newspapers and sometimes in the travel sections of big metropolitan papers, such as *The New York Times*. It's worth asking about packages, especially family and special-occasion offerings, when you call to make a hotel reservation. Calling several hotels can garner you a variety of options from which to choose.

Preparing

How to Use a Travel Agent

 A reliable travel agent remains the best source of service and information for planning a trip abroad, whether you have a specific itinerary and require an agent only to make reservations or you need extensive help in sorting through the maze of airfares, tour offerings, hotel packages, and the scores of other arrangements that may be involved in a trip to Paris.

Know what you want from a travel agent so that you can evaluate what you are getting. It is perfectly reasonable to expect your agent to be a thoroughly knowledgeable travel specialist, with information about your destination and, even more crucial, a command of current airfares, ground arrangements, and other wrinkles in the travel scene.

Most travel agents work through computer reservations systems (CRS). These are used to assess the availability and cost of flights, hotels, and car rentals, and through them they can book reservations. Despite reports of "computer bias," in which a computer may favor one airline over another, the CRS should provide agents with the entire spectrum of flights available to a given destination, as well as the complete range of fares, in considerably less time than it takes to telephone the airlines individually — and at no extra charge to the client.

Make the most intelligent use of a travel agent's time and expertise; understand the economics of the industry. As a client, traditionally you pay nothing for the agent's services; with few exceptions, it's all free, from hotel bookings to advice on package tours. Any money the travel agent makes on the time spent arranging your itinerary — booking hotels or flights, or suggesting activities — comes from commissions paid by the suppliers of these services — the airlines, hotels, and so on. These commissions generally run from 10% to 15% of the total cost of the service, although suppliers often reward agencies that sell their services in volume with an increased commission, called an override. In most instances, you'll find that travel agents make their time and experience available to you at no cost, and you do not pay more for an airline ticket, package tour, or other product bought from a travel agent than you would for the same product bought directly from the supplier.

Exceptions to the general rule of free service by a travel agent are the agencies beginning to practice net pricing. In essence, such agencies return their commissions and overrides to their customers and make their income by charging a flat fee per transaction instead (thus adding a charge after a reduction for the commissions has been made). Net fares and fees are a growing practice, though hardly widespread.

Even a conventional travel agent sometimes may charge a fee for special services. These chargeable items may include long-distance telephone or cable costs incurred in making a booking, for reserving a room in a place that does not pay a commission (such as a small, out-of-the-way hotel), or for special attention such as planning a highly personalized itinerary. A fee also may be assessed in instances of deeply discounted airfares.

Choose a travel agent with the same care with which you would choose a doctor or lawyer. You will be spending a good deal of money on the basis of the agent's judgment, so you have a right to expect that judgment to be mature, informed, and interested. At the moment, unfortunately, there aren't many standards within the travel agent industry to help you gauge competence, and the quality of individual agents varies enormously.

At present, only nine states have registration, licensing, or other forms of travel agent–related legislation on their books. Rhode Island licenses travel agents; Florida, Hawaii, Iowa, and Ohio register them; and California, Illinois, Oregon, and Washington have laws governing the sale of transportation or related services. While state licensing of agents cannot absolutely guarantee competence, it can at least ensure that an agent has met some minimum requirements.

Perhaps the best way to find a travel agent is by word of mouth. If the agent (or agency) has done a good job for your friends over a period of time, it probably indicates a certain level of commitment and competence. Always ask for the name of the company *and* for the name of the specific agent with whom your friends dealt, for it is that individual who will serve you, and quality can vary widely within a single agency. There are some superb travel agents in the business, and they can facilitate vacation or business arrangements.

Entry Requirements and Documents

A valid US passport is the only document a US citizen needs to enter France, and then to re-enter the US. As a general rule, a US passport entitles the bearer to remain in France for up to 6 months as a tourist. A resident alien of the US should inquire at the nearest French consulate (see *The French Embassy and Consulates in the US,* in this section, for addresses) to find out what documents are needed to enter France; similarly, a US citizen intending to work, study, or reside in France should also get in touch with the consulate, because a visa will then be required.

Vaccination certificates are required only if the traveler is entering from an area of contagion — which the US is not — as defined by the World Health Organization.

DUTY AND CUSTOMS: As a general rule, the requirements for bringing the majority of items *into France* is that they must be in quantities small enough not to imply commercial import. Among the items that may be taken into the country duty-free are 200 cigarettes or 50 cigars, 2 liters of wine, and 1 liter of liquor with over 22% alcohol or 2 liters of liquor with under 22% alcohol. Personal effects and sports equipment appropriate for a pleasure trip also are allowed.

If you are bringing along a computer, camera, or other electronic equipment for your own use that you will be taking back to the US, you should register the item with the US Customs Service in order to avoid paying duty both entering and returning from France. (Also see *Customs and Returning to the US,* in this section.) For information on this procedure, as well as for a variety of pamphlets on US Customs regulations, contact the local office of the US Customs Service or the central office, PO Box 7407, Washington, DC 20044 (phone: 202-566-8195).

Additional information regarding French customs regulations is available from the French Government Tourist Office and the French embassy and consulates. See *Tourist Information Offices* and *The French Embassy and Consulates in the US,* both in this section, for addresses.

■**One rule to follow:** When passing through customs, it is illegal not to declare dutiable items; penalties range from stiff fines and seizure of the goods to prison terms. So don't try to sneak anything through — it just isn't worth it.

Insurance

 It is unfortunate that most decisions to buy travel insurance are impulsive and usually are made without any real consideration of the traveler's existing policies. Therefore, the first person with whom you should discuss travel insurance is your own insurance broker, not a travel agent or the clerk behind the airport insurance counter.

TYPES OF INSURANCE: To make insurance decisions intelligently, however, you first should understand the basic categories of travel insurance and what they cover. There are seven basic categories of travel insurance:

1. Baggage and personal effects insurance
2. Personal accident and sickness insurance
3. Trip cancellation and interruption insurance
4. Default and/or bankruptcy insurance
5. Flight insurance (to cover injury or death)
6. Automobile insurance (for driving your own or a rented car)
7. Combination policies

Baggage and Personal Effects Insurance – Ask your insurance agent if baggage and personal effects are included in your current homeowner's policy, or if you will need a special floater to cover you for the duration of a trip. The object is to protect your bags and their contents in case of damage or theft anytime during your travels, not just while you're in flight and covered by the airline's policy. Furthermore, only limited protection is provided by the airline and baggage liability varies from carrier to carrier. For most international flights, including domestic portions of international flights, the airline's liability limit is approximately $9.07 per pound or $20 per kilo (which comes to about $360 per 40-pound suitcase) for checked baggage and up to $400 per passenger for unchecked baggage. These limits should be specified on your airline ticket, but to be awarded any amount, you'll have to provide an itemized list of lost property, and if you're including new and/or expensive items, be prepared for a request that you back up your claim with sales receipts or other proof of purchase.

If you are carrying goods worth more than the maximum protection offered by the airline, consider excess value insurance. Additional coverage is available from insurance companies at an average, currently, of $1 to $2 per $100 worth of coverage, up to a maximum of $5,000. This insurance can also be purchased at some airline counters when you check in, though you should arrive early enough to fill out the necessary forms and to avoid holding up other passengers.

Major credit card companies also provide coverage for lost or delayed baggage — and this coverage often is over and above what the airline will pay. The basic coverage usually is automatic for all cardholders who use the credit card to purchase tickets, but to qualify for additional coverage, cardholders generally must enroll.

Additional baggage and personal effects insurance also is included in certain of the combination travel insurance policies discussed below.

■**A note of warning:** Be sure to read the fine print of any excess value insurance policy; there often are specific exclusions, such as cash, tickets, furs, gold and silver objects, art, and antiques. Insurance companies ordinarily will pay only the depreciated value of the goods rather than their replacement value. The best way to protect your property is to take photos of your valuables, and keep a record of the serial numbers of such items as cameras, typewriters, laptop computers, radios, and so on. If an airline loses your luggage, you will be asked to fill out a Property Irregularity Report before you leave the airport. Also report the loss to the police (since the insurance company will check with the police when processing your claim).

Personal Accident and Sickness Insurance – This covers you in case of illness during your trip or death in an accident. Most policies insure you for hospital and doctor's expenses, lost income, and so on. In most cases, it is a standard part of existing health insurance policies, though you should check with your broker to be sure that your policy will pay for any medical expenses incurred abroad. If not, take out a separate vacation accident policy or an entire vacation insurance policy that includes health and life coverage.

Two examples of such comprehensive health and life insurance coverage are the travel insurance packages offered by *Wallach & Co:*

> *HealthCare Global:* This insurance package, which can be purchased for periods of 10 to 180 days, is offered for two age groups: Men and women up to age 75 receive $25,000 medical insurance and $50,000 accidental injury or death benefit; those from ages 76 to 84 are eligible for $12,500 medical insurance and $25,000 injury or death benefit. For either policy, the cost for a 10-day period is $25.
>
> *HealthCare Abroad:* This program is available to individuals up to age 75. For $3 per day (minimum 10 days, maximum 90 days), policy holders receive $100,000 medical insurance and $25,000 accidental injury or death benefit.

Both of these basic programs also may be bought in combination with trip cancellation and baggage insurance at extra cost. For further information, write to *Wallach & Co.,* 243 Church St. NW, Suite 100-D, Vienna, VA 22180 (phone: 703-281-9500 in Virginia; 800-237-6615 elsewhere in the US).

Trip Cancellation and Interruption Insurance – Most charter and package tour passengers pay for their travel well before departure. The disappointment of having to miss a vacation because of illness or any other reason pales before the awful prospect that not all (and sometimes none) of the money paid in advance might be returned. So cancellation insurance for any package tour is a must.

Although cancellation penalties vary (they are listed in the fine print of every tour brochure, and before you purchase a package tour you should know exactly what they are), rarely will a passenger get more than 50% of this money back if forced to cancel within a few weeks of scheduled departure. Therefore, if you book a package tour or charter flight, you should have trip cancellation insurance to guarantee full reimbursement or refund should you, a traveling companion, or a member of your immediate family get sick, forcing you to cancel your trip or *return home early.*

The key here is *not* to buy just enough insurance to guarantee full reimbursement for the cost of the package or charter in case of cancellation. The proper amount of coverage should be sufficient to reimburse you for the cost of having to catch up with a tour after its departure or having to travel home at the full economy airfare if you have to forgo the return flight of your charter. There usually is quite a discrepancy between a charter fare and the amount charged to travel the same distance on a regularly scheduled flight at full economy fare.

Trip cancellation insurance is available from travel agents and tour operators in two forms: as part of a short-term, all-purpose travel insurance package (sold by the travel agent); or as specific cancellation insurance designed by the tour operator for a specific charter tour. Generally, tour operators' policies are less expensive, but also less inclusive. Cancellation insurance also is available directly from insurance companies or their agents as part of a short-term, all-inclusive travel insurance policy.

Before you decide on a policy, read each one carefully. (Either type can be purchased from a travel agent when you book the charter or package tour.) Be certain that your policy includes enough coverage to pay your fare from the farthest destination on your itinerary should you have to miss the charter flight. Also, be sure to check the fine print for stipulations concerning "family members" and "pre-existing medical conditions," as well as allowances for living expenses if you must delay your return due to bodily injury or illness.

Default and/or Bankruptcy Insurance – Although trip cancellation insurance usually protects you if *you* are unable to complete — or begin — your trip, a fairly recent innovation is coverage in the event of default and/or bankruptcy on the part of the tour operator, airline, or other travel supplier. In some travel insurance packages, this contingency is included in the trip cancellation portion of the coverage; in others, it is a separate feature. Either way, it is becoming increasingly important. Whereas sophisticated travelers long have known to beware of the possibility of default or bankruptcy when buying a charter flight or tour package, in recent years more than a few respected airlines unexpectedly have revealed their shaky financial condition, sometimes leaving hordes of stranded ticket holders in their wake. Moreover, the value of escrow protection of a charter passenger's funds lately has been unreliable. While default/bankruptcy insurance will not ordinarily result in reimbursement in time to pay for new arrangements, it can ensure that you will get your money back, and even independent travelers buying no more than an airplane ticket may want to consider it.

Flight Insurance – Airlines have carefully established limits of liability for injury to or the death of passengers on international flights. For all international flights to, from, or with a stopover in the US, all carriers are liable for up to $75,000 per passenger. For all other international flights, the liability is based on where you purchase the ticket: If booked in advance in the US, the maximum liability is $75,000; if arrangements are made abroad, the liability is $10,000. But remember, these liabilities are not the same thing as insurance policies; every penny that an airline eventually pays in the case of injury or death may be subject to a legal battle.

But before you buy last-minute flight insurance from an airport vending machine, consider the purchase in light of your total existing insurance coverage. A careful review of your current policies may reveal that you already are amply covered for accidental death. Be aware that airport insurance, the kind typically bought at a counter or from a vending machine, is among the most expensive forms of life insurance coverage, and that even within a single airport, rates for approximately the same coverage vary widely.

If you buy your plane ticket with a major credit card, you generally receive automatic insurance coverage at no extra cost. Additional coverage usually can be obtained at extremely reasonable prices, but a cardholder must sign up for it in advance.

Automobile Insurance – Public liability and property damage (third-party) insurance is compulsory in Europe, and whether you drive your own or a rental car you must carry insurance. Car rentals in France usually include public liability, property damage, fire, and theft coverage and, sometimes (depending on the car rental company), collision damage coverage with a deductible.

In your car rental contract, you'll see that for about $11 to $13 a day, you may buy optional collision damage waiver (CDW) protection. (If partial coverage with a deductible is included in the rental contract, the CDW will cover the deductible in the event of an accident, and can cost as much as $25 per day.) If you do not accept the CDW coverage, you may be liable for as much as the full retail value of the rental car if it is damaged or stolen; by paying for the CDW, you are relieved of all responsibility for any damage to the car. Before agreeing to this coverage, however, check with your own broker about your existing personal auto insurance policy. It very well may cover your entire liability exposure without any additional cost, or you automatically may be covered by the credit card company to which you are charging the cost of your rental. To find out the amount of rental car insurance provided by major credit cards, contact the issuing institutions.

You also should know that an increasing number of the major international car rental companies automatically are including the cost of the CDW in their basic rates. Car rental prices have increased to include this coverage, although rental company ad campaigns may promote this as a new, improved rental package "benefit." The disadvantage of this inclusion is that you may not have the option to turn down the CDW — even if you already are adequately covered by your own insurance policy or through a credit card company.

Your rental contract (with the appropriate insurance box checked off), as well as proof of your personal insurance policy, if applicable, are required as proof of insurance. If you will be driving your own car in France, you must carry an International Insurance Certificate (called a Green Card), available through insurance brokers in the US.

Combination Policies – Short-term insurance policies, which may include a combination of any or all of the types of insurance discussed above, are available through retail insurance agencies, automobile clubs, and many travel agents. These combination policies are designed to cover you for the duration of a single trip.

Companies offering policies of this type include the following:

Access America International (600 Third Ave., PO Box 807, New York, NY 10163; phone: 800-284-8300 or 212-490-5345).

Carefree Travel Insurance (Arm Coverage, PO Box 310, Mineola, NY 11501; phone: 800-645-2424 or 516-294-0220).

NEAR Services (450 Prairie Ave., Suite 101, Calumet City, IL 60409; phone: 708-868-6700 in the Chicago area; 800-654-6700 elsewhere in the US and Canada).

Tele-Trip Co. (PO Box 31685, 3201 Farnam St., Omaha, NE 68131; phone: 402-345-2400 in Nebraska; 800-228-9792 elsewhere in the US).

Travel Assistance International (1333 15th St. NW, Suite 400, Washington, DC 20005; phone: 202-331-1609 in Washington, DC; 800-821-2828 elsewhere in the US).

Travel Guard International (1145 Clark St., Stevens Point, WI 54481; phone: 715-345-0505 in Wisconsin; 800-826-1300 elsewhere in the US).

Travel Insurance PAK c/o *The Travelers Companies* (One Tower Sq., Hartford, CT 06183-5040; phone: 203-277-2319 in Connecticut; 800-243-3174 elsewhere in the US).

WorldCare Travel Assistance Association (605 Market St., Suite 1300, San Francisco, CA 94105; phone: 800-666-4993 or 415-541-4991).

Hints for Handicapped Travelers

From 40 to 50 million people in the US have some sort of disability, and over half this number are physically handicapped. Like everyone else today, they — and the uncounted disabled millions around the world — are on the move. More than ever before, they are demanding facilities they can use comfortably, and they are being heard.

During the past several years, the city of Paris has spent a tremendous effort in making the city more accessible for the handicapped. Most of the major hotels are accessible to wheelchairs, and some are equipped with special handles and bars in the rooms. The major museums (including the *Louvre*) and other attractions are also equipped with ramps for wheelchair visitors. The French Government Tourist Office (see *Tourist Information Offices,* in this section) in the US distributes two pamphlets called the *Paris Hotel Guide* and *Paris Guide to Monuments and Museums* that list wheelchair accessibility. Generally, you can get around Paris well enough to thoroughly enjoy its varied delights.

PLANNING: Collect as much information as you can about facilities for travelers with your sort of disability in Paris. Make your travel arrangements well in advance and specify to all services involved the exact nature of your condition or restricted mobility. The best way to find out is to write or call the local tourist authority or hotel and ask specific questions. If you require a corridor of a certain width to maneuver a wheelchair or if you need handles on the bathroom walls for support, ask the hotel manager. A travel agent or the local chapter or national office of the organization that deals with your particular disability will supply the most up-to-date information on the subject. The following organizations offer general information on access:

ACCENT on Living (PO Box 700, Bloomington, IL 61702; phone: 309-378-2961). This information service for persons with disabilities provides a free list of travel agencies specializing in arranging trips for the disabled; for a copy send a self-addressed, stamped envelope. It also offers a wide range of publications, including a quarterly magazine ($8 per year; $14 for 2 years) for persons with disabilities.

Comité National Français de Liaison pour la Réadaptation des Handicapés (38 Bd. Raspail, Paris 75007; phone: 45-48-90-13). This organization provides extensive information about accessibility and transportation for the handicapped within the city of Paris.

Mobility International USA (*MIUSA;* PO Box 3551, Eugene, OR 97403; phone: 503-343-1284; both voice and TDD). This US branch of *Mobility International,* a nonprofit British organization with affiliates worldwide, offers members advice and assistance — including information on accommodations and other travel services, and publications applicable to the traveler's disability. It also offers a quarterly newsletter and a comprehensive sourcebook, *A World of Options for the 90s: A Guide to International Education Exchange, Community Service and Travel for Persons with Disabilities* ($14 for members; $16 for non-members). Membership includes the newsletter and is $20 a year; subscription to the newsletter alone is $10 annually.

National Rehabilitation Information Center (8455 Colesville Rd., Suite 935, Silver Spring, MD 20910; phone: 301-588-9284). A general information, resource, research, and referral service.

Paralyzed Veterans of America (*PVA;* PVA/ATTS Program, 801 18th St. NW, Washington, DC 20006; phone: 202-416-7708 in Washington, DC; 800-424-8200 elsewhere in the US). The members of this national service organization all are veterans who have suffered spinal cord injuries, but it offers advocacy services and information to all persons with a disability. *PVA* also sponsors *Access to the Skies,* a program that coordinates the efforts of the national and international air travel industry in providing airport and airplane access for the disabled. Members receive several helpful publications, as well as regular notification of conferences on subjects of interest to the disabled traveler.

Royal Association for Disability and Rehabilitation (*RADAR;* 25 Mortimer St., London W1N 8AB, England; phone: 44-71-637-5400). Offers a number of publications for the handicapped. Their comprehensive guide, *Holidays and Travel*

Abroad 1991/92 — A Guide for Disabled People, focuses on international travel. This publication can be ordered by sending payment in British pounds to *RADAR.* As we went to press, it cost just over £6; call for current pricing before ordering.

Society for the Advancement of Travel for the Handicapped (*SATH;* 26 Court St., Penthouse, Brooklyn, NY 11242; phone: 718-858-5483). To keep abreast of developments in travel for the handicapped as they occur, you may want to join *SATH,* a nonprofit organization whose members include consumers, as well as travel service professionals who have experience (or an interest) in travel for the handicapped. For an annual fee of $45 ($25 for students and travelers who are 65 and older), members receive a quarterly newsletter and have access to extensive information and referral services. *SATH* also offers a useful publication, *Travel Tips for the Handicapped* (a series of informative fact sheets); to order, send a self-addressed, #10 envelope and $1.

Travel Information Service (Moss Rehabilitation Hospital, 1200 W. Tabor Rd., Philadelphia, PA 19141-3099; phone: 215-456-9600 for voice; 215-456-9602 for TDD). This service assists physically handicapped people in planning trips and supplies detailed information on accessibility for a nominal fee.

Blind travelers should contact the *American Foundation for the Blind* (15 W. 16th St., New York, NY 10011; phone: 212-620-2147 in New York State; 800-232-5463 elsewhere in the US) and *The Seeing Eye* (Box 375, Morristown, NJ 07963-0375; phone: 201-539-4425); both provide useful information on resources for the visually impaired. *Note:* In France, Seeing Eye dogs must be accompanied by a certificate of inoculation against rabies, issued within the previous year and certified by the attending veterinarian. *The American Society for the Prevention of Cruelty to Animals (ASPCA,* Education Dept., 441 E. 92 St., New York, NY 10128; phone: 212-876-7700) offers a useful booklet, *Traveling With Your Pet,* which lists inoculation and other requirements by country. It is available for $5 (including postage and handling).

In addition, there are a number of publications — from travel guides to magazines — of interest to handicapped travelers. Among these are the following:

Access to the World, by Louise Weiss, offers sound tips for the disabled traveler. Published by Facts on File (460 Park Ave. S., New York, NY 10016; phone: 212-683-2244 in New York State; 800-322-8755 elsewhere in the US; 800-443-8323 in Canada), it costs $16.95. Check with your local bookstore; it also can be ordered by phone with a credit card.

The Diabetic Traveler (PO Box 8223 RW, Stamford, CT 06905; phone: 203-327-5832) is a useful quarterly newsletter. Each issue highlights a single destination or type of travel and includes information on general resources and hints for diabetics. A 1-year subscription costs $15. When subscribing, ask for the free fact sheet including an index of special articles; back issues are available for $4 each.

Guide to Traveling with Arthritis, a free brochure available by writing to the Upjohn Company (PO Box 307-B, Coventry, CT 06238), provides lots of good, commonsense tips on planning your trip and how to be as comfortable as possible when traveling by car, bus, train, cruise ship, or plane.

Handicapped Travel Newsletter is regarded as one of the best sources of information for the disabled traveler. It is edited by wheelchair-bound Vietnam veteran Michael Quigley, who has traveled to 93 countries around the world. Issued every 2 months (plus special issues), a subscription is $10 per year. Write to *Handicapped Travel Newsletter,* PO Box 269, Athens, TX 75751 (phone: 214-677-1260).

Handi-Travel: A Resource Book for Disabled and Elderly Travellers, by Cinnie

Noble, is a comprehensive travel guide full of practical tips for those with disabilities affecting mobility, hearing, or sight. To order this book, send $12.95, plus shipping and handling, to the *Canadian Rehabilitation Council for the Disabled*, 45 Sheppard Ave. E., Suite 801, Toronto, Ontario M2N 5W9, Canada (phone: 416-250-7490; both voice and TDD).

The Itinerary (PO Box 2012, Bayonne, NJ 07002-2012; phone: 201-858-3400). This bimonthly travel magazine for people with disabilities includes information on accessibility, listings of tours, news of adaptive devices, travel aids, and special services, as well as numerous general travel hints. A subscription costs $10 a year.

The Physically Disabled Traveler's Guide, by Rod W. Durgin and Norene Lindsay, rates accessibility of a number of travel services and includes a list of organizations specializing in travel for the disabled. It is available for $9.95, plus shipping and handling, from Resource Directories, 3361 Executive Pkwy., Suite 302, Toledo, OH 43606 (phone: 419-536-5353 in the Toledo area; 800-274-8515 elsewhere in the US).

Ticket to Safe Travel offers useful information for travelers with diabetes. A reprint of this article is available free from local chapters of the *American Diabetes Association*. For the nearest branch, contact the central office at 505 Eighth Ave., 21st Floor, New York, NY 10018 (phone: 212-947-9707 in New York State; 800-232-3472 elsewhere in the US).

Travel for the Patient with Chronic Obstructive Pulmonary Disease, a publication of the George Washington University Medical Center, provides some sound practical suggestions for those with emphysema, chronic bronchitis, asthma, or other lung ailments. To order, send $2 to Dr. Harold Silver, 1601 18th St. NW, Washington, DC 20009 (phone: 202-667-0134).

Traveling Like Everybody Else: A Practical Guide for Disabled Travelers, by Jacqueline Freedman and Susan Gersten, offers the disabled tips on traveling by car, cruise ship, and plane, as well as lists of accessible accommodations, tour operators specializing in tours for disabled travelers, and other resources. It is available for $11.95, plus postage and handling, from Modan Publishing, PO Box 1202, Bellmore, NY 11710 (phone: 516-679-1380).

Travel Tips for Hearing-Impaired People, a free pamphlet for deaf and hearing-impaired travelers, is available from the *American Academy of Otolaryngology* (One Prince St., Alexandria, VA 22314; phone: 703-836-4444). For a copy, send a self-addressed, stamped, business-size envelope to the academy.

Travel Tips for People with Arthritis, a free 31-page booklet published by the *Arthritis Foundation*, provides helpful information regarding travel by car, bus, train, cruise ship, or plane, planning your trip, and medical considerations, and includes listings of helpful resources, such as associations and travel agencies that operate tours for disabled travelers. For a copy, contact your local *Arthritis Foundation* chapter, or write to the national office, PO Box 19000, Atlanta, GA 30326 (phone: 404-872-7100).

A few more basic resources to look for are *Travel for the Disabled*, by Helen Hecker ($9.95), and by the same author, *Directory of Travel Agencies for the Disabled* ($19.95). *Wheelchair Vagabond*, by John G. Nelson, is another useful guide for travelers confined to a wheelchair (hardcover, $14.95; paperback, $9.95). All three are published by Twin Peaks Press, PO Box 129, Vancouver, WA 98666 (phone: 800-637-CALM or 206-694-2462).

Another good source of information is the French Government Tourist Office, although brochures specifically for the handicapped may not be in English. (For the addresses of this agency's US branches, see *Tourist Information Offices*, in this section.)

Two organizations based in Great Britain offer information for handicapped persons traveling throughout Europe, including France. *Tripscope* (63 Esmond Rd., London W4 1JE, UK; phone: 44-81-994-9294) is a telephone-based information and referral service (not a booking agent) that can help with transportation options for journeys throughout Europe. It may, for instance, be able to recommend outlets leasing small family vehicles adapted to accommodate wheelchairs. *Tripscope* also provides information on cassettes for blind or visually impaired travelers, and accepts written requests for information from those with speech impediments. And for general information, there's *Holiday Care Service* (2 Old Bank Chambers, Station Rd., Horley, Surrey RH6 9HW, UK; phone: 44-293-774535), a first-rate, free advisory service on accommodations, transportation, and holiday packages throughout Europe for disabled visitors.

Regularly revised hotel and restaurant guides use the symbol of access (a person in a wheelchair; see the symbol at the beginning of this section) to point out accommodations suitable for wheelchair-bound guests. The red *Michelin Guide to France* (Michelin; $19.95), found in general and travel bookstores, is one such publication.

PLANE: The US Department of Transportation (DOT) has ruled that US airlines must accept all passengers with disabilities. As a matter of course, US airlines were pretty good about accommodating handicapped passengers even before the ruling, although each airline has somewhat different procedures. Foreign airlines also generally are good about accommodating the disabled traveler, but again, policies vary from carrier to carrier. Ask for specifics when you book your flight.

Disabled passengers always should make reservations well in advance and should provide the airline with all relevant details of their conditions. These details include information on mobility and equipment that you will need the airline to supply — such as a wheelchair for boarding or portable oxygen for in-flight use. Be sure that the person to whom you speak fully understands the degree of your disability — the more details provided, the more effective help the airline can give you.

On the day before the flight, call back to make sure that all arrangements have been prepared, and arrive early on the day of the flight so that you can board before the rest of the passengers. It's a good idea to bring a medical certificate with you, stating your specific disability or the need to carry particular medicine.

Because most airports have jetways (corridors connecting the terminal with the door of the plane), a disabled passenger usually can be taken as far as the plane, and sometimes right onto it, in a wheelchair. If not, a narrow boarding chair may be used to take you to your seat. Your own wheelchair, which will be folded and put in the baggage compartment, should be tagged as escort luggage to assure that it's available at planeside upon landing rather than in the baggage claim area. Travel is not quite as simple if your wheelchair is battery-operated: Unless it has non-spillable batteries, it might not be accepted on board, and you will have to check with the airline ahead of time to find out how the batteries and the chair should be packaged for the flight. Usually people in wheelchairs are asked to wait until other passengers have disembarked. If you are making a tight connection, be sure to tell the attendant.

Passengers who use oxygen may not use their personal supply in the cabin, though it may be carried on the plane as cargo when properly packed and labeled. If you will need oxygen during the flight, the airline will supply it to you (there is a charge) provided you have given advance notice — 24 hours to a few days, depending on the carrier.

Useful information on every stage of air travel, from planning to arrival, is provided in the booklet *Incapacitated Passengers Air Travel Guide.* To receive a free copy, write to the *International Air Transport Association* (Publications Sales Department, 2000 Peel St., Montreal, Quebec H3A 2R4, Canada; phone: 514-844-6311). Another helpful publication is *Air Transportation of Handicapped Persons,* which explains the general guidelines that govern air carrier policies. For a copy of this free booklet, write to the

US Department of Transportation (Distribution Unit, Publications Section, M-443-2, Washington, DC 20590) and ask for "Free Advisory Circular #AC-120-32."

Among the major carriers serving France, the following airlines have TDD toll-free lines in the US for the hearing-impaired:

American: 800-582-1573 in Ohio; 800-543-1586 elsewhere in the US.
Delta: 800-831-4488.
TWA: 800-252-0622 in California; 800-421-8480 elsewhere in the US.
United: 800-942-8819 in Illinois; 800-323-0170 elsewhere in the US.
USAir: 800-242-1713 in Pennsylvania; 800-245-2966 elsewhere in the US.

GROUND TRANSPORTATION: Perhaps the simplest solution to getting around is to travel with an able-bodied companion who can drive. Another alternative in France is to hire a driver/translator with a car. The organizations listed above may be able to help you make arrangements — another source is your hotel concierge.

If you are accustomed to driving your own hand-controlled car and are determined to rent one, you may have to do some extensive research, as in France it is difficult to find rental cars fitted with hand controls. If agencies do provide hand-controlled cars, they are apt to be offered only on a limited basis in major metropolitan areas, such as Paris, and usually are very much in demand. The best course is to contact the major car rental agencies listed in "Car Rental" in *On Arrival,* in this section, well before your departure (at least 7 days, much earlier preferably); but be forewarned, you still may be out of luck. Other sources for information on vehicles adapted for the handicapped are the organizations discussed above.

The *American Automobile Association (AAA)* publishes a useful booklet, *The Handicapped Driver's Mobility Guide.* Contact the central office of your local *AAA* club for availability and pricing, which may vary at different branch offices.

Although taxis and public transportation also are available in France, accessibility for the disabled varies and may be limited in rural areas, as well as in some cities. Check with a travel agent or the French Government Tourist Office for information.

TOURS: Programs designed for the physically impaired are run by specialists, and the following travel agencies and tour operators specialize in making group and individual arrangements for travelers with physical or other disabilities:

Access: The Foundation for Accessibility by the Disabled (PO Box 356, Malverne, NY 11565; phone: 516-887-5798). A travelers' referral service that acts as an intermediary with tour operators and agents worldwide, and provides information on accessibility at various locations.

Accessible Journeys (412 S. 45th St., Philadelphia, PA 19104; phone: 215-747-0171). Arranges for medical professional traveling companions — registered or licensed practical nurses, therapists, or doctors (all are experienced travelers). Several prospective companions' profiles and photos are sent to the client for perusal, and if one is acceptable, the "match" is made. The client usually pays all travel expenses for the companion, plus a certain amount in "earnings" to replace wages the companion would be making at his or her usual job.

Accessible Tours/Directions Unlimited (720 N. Bedford Rd., Bedford Hills, NY 10507; phone: 914-241-1700 in New York State; 800-533-5343 elsewhere in the continental US). Arranges group or individual tours for disabled persons traveling in the company of able-bodied friends or family members. Accepts the unaccompanied traveler if completely self-sufficient.

Evergreen Travel Service (4114 198th St. SW, Suite 13, Lynnwood, WA 98036-6742; phone: 206-776-1184 or 800-435-2288 throughout the continental US and Canada). It offers worldwide programs for the disabled (Wings on Wheels Tours) and the sight-impaired/blind (White Cane Tours).

Flying Wheels Travel (143 W. Bridge St., Box 382, Owatonna, MN 55060; phone: 507-451-5005 or 800-535-6790). Handles both tours and individual arrangements.

Guided Tour (613 W. Cheltenham Ave., Suite 200, Melrose Park, PA 19126-2414; phone: 215-782-1370). Arranges tours for people with developmental and learning disabilities and sponsors separate tours for members of the same population who also are physically disabled or who simply need a slower pace.

Handi-Travel (First National Travel Ltd., Thornhill Sq., 300 John St., Suite 405, Thornhill, Ontario L3T 5W4, Canada; phone: 416-731-4714). Handles individual arrangements.

USTS Travel (11 E. 44th St., New York, NY 10017; phone: 800-487-8787 or 212-687-5121). Travel agent and registered nurse Mary Ann Hamm designs trips for individual travelers requiring all types of kidney dialysis and handles arrangements for the dialysis.

Whole Person Tours (PO Box 1084, Bayonne, NJ 07002-1084; phone: 201-858-3400). Handicapped owner Bob Zywicki travels the world with his wheelchair and offers a lineup of escorted tours (many conducted by him) for the disabled. Call for current itinerary at the time you plan to travel. *Whole Person Tours* also publishes *The Itinerary,* a bimonthly newsletter for disabled travelers (see the publication source list above).

Travelers who would benefit from being accompanied by a nurse or physical therapist also can hire a companion through *Traveling Nurses' Network,* a service provided by Twin Peaks Press (PO Box 129, Vancouver, WA 98666; phone: 800-637-CALM or 206-694-2462). For a $10 fee, clients receive the names of three nurses, whom they can then contact directly; for a $125 fee, the agency will make all the hiring arrangements for the client. Travel arrangements also may be made in some cases — the fee for this further service is determined on an individual basis.

A similar service is offered by *MedEscort International* (ABE International Airport, PO Box 8766, Allentown, PA 18105; phone: 800-255-7182 in the continental US; elsewhere, call 215-791-3111). The service arranges for clients to be accompanied by a nurse, paramedic, respiratory therapist, or physician. The fees are based on the disabled traveler's needs. *MedEscort* also can assist in making travel arrangements.

Hints for Single Travelers

Just about the last trip in human history on which the participants were neatly paired was the voyage of Noah's Ark. Ever since, passenger lists and tour groups have reflected the same kind of asymmetry that occurs in real life, as countless individuals set forth to see the world unaccompanied (or unencumbered, depending on your outlook) by spouse, lover, friend, companion, or relative.

The truth is that the travel industry is not very fair to people who vacation by themselves. People traveling alone almost invariably end up paying more than individuals traveling in pairs. Most travel bargains, including package tours, accommodations, resort packages, and cruises, are based on *double-occupancy* rates. The single traveler will have to pay a surcharge, called a single supplement, for exactly the same package. In extreme cases, this can add as much as 30% to 55% to the basic per-person rate.

The obvious, most effective alternative is to find a traveling companion. Even special "singles' tours" that promise no supplements usually are based on people sharing double rooms. Perhaps the most recent innovation along these lines is the creation of organizations that "introduce" the single traveler to other single travelers. Some charge fees, while others are free, but the basic service offered is the same: to match an unattached person with a compatible travel mate, often as part of the company's own package tours. Among such organizations are the following:

Jane's International (2603 Bath Ave., Brooklyn, NY 11214; phone: 718-266-2045). This service puts potential traveling companions in touch with one another. No age limit, no fee.

Odyssey Network (118 Cedar St., Wellesley, MA 02181; phone: 617-237-2400). Originally founded to match single women travelers, this company now includes men in its enrollment. *Odyssey* offers a quarterly newsletter for members who are seeking a travel companion, and occasionally organizes small group tours. A newsletter subscription is $50.

Partners-in-Travel (PO Box 491145, Los Angeles, CA 90049; phone: 213-476-4869). Members receive a list of singles seeking traveling companions; prospective companions make contact through the agency. The membership fee is $40 per year and includes a chatty newsletter (6 issues per year).

Travel Companion Exchange (PO Box 833, Amityville, NY 11701; phone: 516-454-0880). This group publishes a newsletter for singles and a directory of individuals looking for travel companions. On joining, members fill out a lengthy questionnaire and write a small listing (much like an ad in a personal column). Based on these listings, members can request copies of profiles and contact prospective traveling companions. It is wise to join well in advance of your planned vacation so that there's enough time to determine compatibility and plan a joint trip. Membership fees, including the newsletter, are $36 for 6 months or $60 a year for a single-sex listing; $66 and $120, respectively, for a complete listing. Subscription to the newsletter alone costs $24 for 6 months or $36 per year.

In addition, a number of tour packagers cater to single travelers. These companies offer packages designed for individuals interested in vacationing with a group of single travelers or in being matched with a traveling companion. Among these agencies are the following:

Singles in Motion (545 W. 236th St., Suite 1D, Riverdale, NY 10463; phone: 212-884-4464). Recent itineraries include an 11-day southern France program that also takes in Paris, and an 8-day Paris and London city package.

Singleworld (401 Theodore Fremd Ave., Rye, NY 10580; phone: 914-967-3334 or 800-223-6490 in the continental US). It offers its own package tours for singles, with departures categorized by age group — 35 or younger — or for all ages. Recent offers include a 14-day escorted tour of England, France, and Italy, with a stay in Paris.

Student Travel International (STI) (8619 Reseda Blvd., Suite 103, Northridge, CA 91324; phone: 800-525-0525). Specializes in travel for 18- to 30-year-olds. Itineraries include 14- to 63-day European escorted tours, with excursions in Paris.

A good book for single travelers is *Traveling On Your Own,* by Eleanor Berman, which offers tips on traveling solo and includes information on trips for singles, ranging from outdoor adventures to educational programs. Available in bookstores, it also can be ordered by sending $12.95, plus postage and handling, to Random House, Order Dept., 400 Hahn Rd., Westminster, MD 21157 (phone: 800-733-3000).

Single travelers also may want to subscribe to *Going Solo,* a newsletter that offers helpful information on going on your own. Issued eight times a year, a subscription costs $36. Contact Doerfer Communications, PO Box 1035, Cambridge, MA 02238 (phone: 617-876-2764).

WOMEN AND STUDENTS: Two specific groups of single travelers deserve special mention: women and students. Countless women travel by themselves in Paris, and such an adventure need not be feared. One lingering inhibition many female travelers still harbor is that of eating alone in public places. The trick here is to relax and enjoy your meal and surroundings; while you may run across the occasional unenlightened waiter, a woman dining solo is no longer uncommon.

Studying Abroad – A large number of single travelers are students. Travel *is* education. Travel broadens a person's knowledge and deepens his or her perception of the world in a way no media or "armchair" experience ever could. In addition, to study a country's language, art, culture, or history in one of its own schools is to enjoy the most productive method of learning.

By "student" we do not necessarily mean a person who wishes to matriculate at a foreign university to earn a degree. Nor do we necessarily mean a younger person. A student is anyone who wishes to include some sort of educational program in a trip to Paris.

There are many benefits for students abroad, and the way to begin to discover them is to consult the *Council on International Educational Exchange (CIEE)*, the US sponsor of the International Student Identity Card (ISIC), which permits reductions on airfare, other transportation, and entry fees to most museums and other exhibitions. The organization also is the source of the Federation of International Youth Travel Organizations (FIYTO) card, which provides many of the same benefits. For further information and applications, write to *CIEE* at one of the following addresses: 205 E. 42nd St., New York, NY 10017 (phone: 212-661-1414); 312 Sutter St., Suite 407, San Francisco, CA 94108 (phone: 415-421-3473); and 919 Irving St., Suite 102, San Francisco, CA 94122 (phone: 415-566-6222). Mark the letter "Attn. Student ID."

CIEE also offers a free, informative, annual, 64-page *Student Travel Catalog,* which covers all aspects of youth travel abroad for vacation trips, jobs, or study programs, and also includes a list of other helpful publications. It also sells *Work, Study, Travel Abroad: The Whole World Handbook,* an informative, chatty guide on study programs, work opportunities, and travel hints, with a particularly good section on France. It is available for $10.95, plus shipping and handling. The publications are available from the Information and Student Services Department at the New York address given above.

CIEE also sponsors charter flights to Europe that are open to students and non-students of any age. For example, flights between New York and Paris (with budget-priced add-ons available from Chicago, Cleveland, Miami, Minneapolis, Phoenix, Portland, Salt Lake City, San Diego, Seattle, and Spokane) arrive and depart at least three times a week from Kennedy (JFK) Airport during the high season.

Students and singles in general should keep in mind that youth hostels exist throughout France, including several in Paris. They always are inexpensive, generally clean and well situated, and they are a sure place to meet other people traveling alone. Hostels are run by the hosteling associations of 68 countries that make up the *International Youth Hostel Federation (IYHF);* membership in one of the national associations affords access to the hostels of the rest. To join the American affiliate, *American Youth Hostels (AYH),* contact the national office (PO Box 37613, Washington, DC 20013-7613; phone: 202-783-6161), or the local *AYH* council nearest you.

Those who go abroad without an *AYH* card may purchase a youth hostel International Guest Card (for the equivalent of about $18), and obtain information on local youth hostels by contacting the *Fédération Unie des Auberges de Jeunesse* (27 Rue Pajol, Paris 75018; phone: 46-07-00-01). This association also provides information on hostels throughout France.

Student Travel International (STI; address above) specializes in European travel for students. It offers 14- to 63-day European motorcoach tours including Paris.

Opportunities for study range from summer or academic-year courses in the language and civilization of France, designed specifically for foreigners (including those whose school days are well behind them), to long-term university attendance by those intending to take a degree.

Complete details on more than 3,000 courses available abroad (including at French universities) and suggestions on how to apply are contained in two books published by the *Institute of International Education* (IIE Books, 809 UN Plaza, New York, NY 10017; phone 212-883-8200): *Vacation Study Abroad* ($24.95, plus shipping and handling) and *Academic Year Abroad* ($31.95, plus shipping and handling). IIE Books also offers a free pamphlet called *Basic Facts on Study Abroad.*

The *National Registration Center for Study Abroad* (*NRCSA;* PO Box 1393, Milwaukee, WI 53201; phone: 414-278-0631) also offers a publication called *Worldwide Classroom: Study Abroad and Learning Vacations in 40 Countries: 1991–1992,* available for $8, which includes information on over 160 schools and cultural centers, including in Paris, that offer courses for Americans, with the primary focus on foreign language and culture.

Those who are interested in a "learning vacation" abroad also may be interested in *Travel and Learn* by Evelyn Kaye. This guide to educational travel discusses a wide range of opportunities — everything from archaeology to whale watching — and provides information on organizations that offer programs in these areas of interest. The book is available in bookstores for $23.95; or you can send $26 (which includes shipping charges) to Blue Penguin Publications (147 Sylvan Ave., Leonia, NJ 07605; phone: 800-800-8147 or 201-461-6918). *Learning Vacations* by Gerson G. Eisenberg also provides extensive information on seminars, workshops, courses, and so on — in a wide variety of subjects. Available in bookstores, it also can be ordered from Peterson's Guides (PO Box 2123, Princeton, NJ 08543-2123; phone: 609-243-9111) for $11.95, plus shipping and handling.

If you are interested in a home-stay travel program, in which you learn about European culture by living with a family, contact the *Experiment in International Living* (PO Box 676, Brattleboro, VT 05302-0676; phone: 802-257-7751 in Vermont; 800-345-2929 elsewhere in the continental US), which sponsors home-stay educational travel in more than 40 countries, including locations throughout France. The organization aims its programs at high school or college students.

Another organization specializing in travel as an educational experience is the *American Institute for Foreign Study* (*AIFS;* 102 Greenwich Ave., Greenwich, CT 06830; phone: 800-727-AIFS, 203-869-9090, or 203-863-6087). Although it does not specialize in travel to France, approximately a third of the participants in its hundred-some programs around the world — tours, academic year, and summer programs — choose to study in France. The programs at the University of Paris are among the most favored by those studying French. Students can enroll for the full academic year or for any number of semesters. *AIFS* caters primarily to bona fide high school or college students, but its non-credit international learning programs are open to independent travelers of all ages (approximately 20% of *AIFS* students are over 25).

Hints for Older Travelers

Special discounts and more free time are just two factors that have given Americans over age 65 a chance to see the world at affordable prices. Senior citizens make up an ever-growing segment of the travel population, and the trend among them is to travel more frequently and for longer periods of time.

PLANNING: When planning a vacation, prepare your itinerary with one eye on your own physical condition and the other on your interests. One important factor to keep in mind is not to overdo anything and to be aware of the effects that the weather may have on your capabilities.

Older travelers may find the following publications of interest:

Discount Guide for Travelers Over 55, by Caroline and Walter Weintz, is an excellent book for budget-conscious older travelers. It is available by sending $7.95, plus shipping and handling, to Penguin USA (Att. Cash Sales, 120 Woodbine St., Bergenfield, NJ 07621); when ordering, specify the ISBN number: 0-525-48358-6.

Going Abroad: 101 Tips for the Mature Traveler offers tips on preparing for your trip, commonsense precautions en route, and some basic travel terminology. This concise, free booklet is available from *Grand Circle Travel,* 347 Congress St., Boston, MA 02210 (phone: 800-221-2610 or 617-350-7500).

International Health Guide for Senior Citizen Travelers, by Dr. W. Robert Lange, covers such topics as trip preparations, food and water precautions, adjusting to weather and climate conditions, finding a doctor, motion sickness, jet lag, and so on. Also includes a list of resource organizations that provide medical assistance for travelers. It is available for $4.95 postpaid from Pilot Books, 103 Cooper St., Babylon, NY 11702 (phone: 516-422-2225).

Mature Traveler is a monthly newsletter that provides information on travel discounts, places of interest, useful tips, and other topics of interest for travelers 49 and up. To subscribe, send $21.95 to GEM Publishing Group, PO Box 50820, Reno, NV 89513 (phone: 702-786-7419).

Travel Easy: The Practical Guide for People Over 50, by Rosalind Massow, discusses a wide range of subjects — from trip planning, transportation options, and preparing for departure to avoiding and handling medical problems en route. It's available for $6.50 to members of the *American Association of Retired Persons (AARP),* and for $8.95 to non-members; call about current charges for postage and handling. Order from *AARP* Books, c/o Customer Service, Scott, Foresman & Company, 1900 E. Lake Ave., Glenview, IL 60025 (phone: 708-729-3000).

Travel Tips for Older Americans is a useful booklet that provides good, basic advice. This US State Department publication (stock number: 044-000-02270-2) can be ordered by sending a check or money order for $1 to the Superintendent of Documents (US Government Printing Office, Washington, DC 20402) or by calling 202-783-3238 and charging the order to a credit card.

Unbelievably Good Deals & Great Adventures That You Absolutely Can't Get Unless You're Over 50, by Joan Rattner Heilman, offers travel tips for older travelers, including discounts on accommodations and transportation, as well as a list of organizations for seniors. It is available for $7.95, plus shipping and handling, from Contemporary Books, 180 N. Michigan Ave., Chicago, IL 60601 (phone: 312-782-9181).

DISCOUNTS AND PACKAGES: Many hotel chains, airlines, cruise lines, bus companies, car rental companies, and other travel suppliers offer discounts to older travelers. For instance, *TWA* offers those age 62 and over (and one traveling companion per qualifying senior citizen) 10% discounts on flights from the US to Paris. Other airlines also offer discounts for passengers age 60 (or 62) and over, which also may apply to one traveling companion. For information on current prices and applicable restrictions, contact the individual carriers.

Some discounts, however, are extended only to bona fide members of certain senior citizens organizations. Because the same organizations frequently offer package tours to both domestic and international destinations, the benefits of membership are twofold: Those who join can take advantage of discounts as individual travelers and also reap the savings that group travel affords. In addition, because the age requirements for some of these organizations are quite low (or nonexistent), the benefits can begin to accrue early. In order to take advantage of these discounts, you should carry proof of your age (or eligibility). A driver's license, membership card in a recognized senior citizens organization, or a Medicare card should be adequate. Among the organizations dedicated to helping older travelers see the world are the following:

American Association of Retired Persons (*AARP;* 1909 K St. NW, Washington, DC 20049; phone: 202-872-4700). The largest and best known of these organizations. Membership is open to anyone 50 or over, whether retired or not; dues are $5 a year, $12.50 for 3 years, or $35 for 10 years, and include spouse. The *AARP* Travel Experience Worldwide program, available through *American Express Travel Related Services,* offers members travel programs worldwide designed exclusively for older travelers. Members can book these services by calling *American Express* at 800-927-0111 for land and air travel.

Mature Outlook (Customer Service Center, 6001 N. Clark St., Chicago, IL 60660; phone: 800-336-6330). Through its *TravelAlert,* vacation packages are available to members at special savings. Hotel and car rental discounts and travel accident insurance also are available. Membership is open to anyone 50 years of age or older, costs $9.95 a year, and includes a bimonthly newsletter and magazine, as well as information on package tours.

National Council of Senior Citizens (1331 F St., Washington, DC 20005; phone: 202-347-8800). Here, too, the emphasis is on keeping costs low. This nonprofit organization offers members a different roster of package tours each year, as well as individual arrangements through its affiliated travel agency *(Vantage Travel Service).* Although most members are over 50, membership is open to anyone (regardless of age) for an annual fee of $12 per person or couple. Lifetime membership costs $150.

Many travel agencies, particularly the larger ones, are delighted to make presentations to help a group of senior citizens select destinations. A local chamber of commerce should be able to provide the names of such agencies. Once a time and place are determined, an organization member or travel agent can obtain group quotations for transportation, accommodations, meal plans, and sightseeing. Larger groups usually get the best breaks.

Another choice open to older travelers is a trip that includes an educational element. *Elderhostel,* a nonprofit organization, offers programs at educational institutions worldwide, including Paris. The foreign programs generally last about 2 weeks, and include double occupancy accommodations in hotels or student residence halls and all meals. Travel to the programs usually is by designated scheduled flights, and participants can arrange to extend their stay at the end of the program. Elderhostelers must be at least 60 years old (younger if a spouse or companion qualifies), in good health, and not in need of a special diet. For a free catalogue describing the program and current offerings, write to *Elderhostel* (75 Federal St., Boston, MA 02110; phone: 617-426-7788). Those interested in the program also can borrow slides at no charge or purchase an informational videotape for $5.

Hints for Traveling with Children

What better way to encounter the world's variety than in the company of the young, wide-eyed members of your family? Their presence does not have to be a burden or an excessive expense. The current generation of discounts for children and family package deals can make a trip together quite reasonable.

PLANNING: Here are several hints for making a trip with children easy and fun:

1. Children, like everyone else, will derive more pleasure from a trip if they know something about their destination before they arrive. Begin their education about a month before you leave. Using maps, travel magazines, and books, give children a clear idea of where you are going and how far away it is.
2. Children should help to plan the itinerary, and where you go and what you do should reflect some of their ideas. If they already know something about the sites they'll visit, they will have the excitement of recognition when they arrive.
3. Children also will enjoy learning some French phrases — a few basics like *"bonjour!"* ("hello"), *"au revoir"* ("good-bye"), and *"merci"* ("thank you").
4. Familiarize your children with francs. Give them an allowance for the trip, and be sure they understand just how far it will or won't go.
5. Give children specific responsibilities: The job of carrying their own flight bags and looking after their personal things, along with some other light chores, will give them a stake in the journey.
6. Give each child a diary or scrapbook to take along.

One useful resource to which you may want to refer is the *Berlitz Jr. French Phrasebook* instructional series for children. The series combines an illustrated storybook with a lively 60-minute audiocassette. Each book features a character, Teddy, who goes to school and learns to count and spell and speak French phrases. The book/cassette package is available for $19.95, plus shipping and handling, from Macmillan Publishing Company, Front and Brown Sts., Riverside, NJ 08075 (phone: 800-257-5755).

And for parents, *Travel With Your Children* (*TWYCH;* 80 Eighth Ave., New York, NY 10011; phone: 212-206-0688) publishes a newsletter, *Family Travel Times,* that focuses on families with young travelers and offers helpful hints. An annual subscription (10 issues) is $35 and includes a copy of the "Airline Guide" issue (updated every other year), which focuses on the subject of flying with children. This special issue is available separately for $10.

Another newsletter devoted to family travel is *Getaways.* This quarterly publication provides reviews of family-oriented literature, activities, and useful travel tips. To subscribe, send $25 to *Getaways,* Att. Ms. Brooke Kane, PO Box 11511, Washington, DC 20008 (phone: 703-534-8747).

Also of interest to parents traveling with their children is *How to Take Great Trips With Your Kids,* by psychologist Sanford Portnoy and his wife, Joan Flynn Portnoy. The book includes helpful tips from fellow family travelers, tips on economical accommodations and touring by car, recreational vehicle, and train, as well as over 50 games to play with your children en route. It is available for $8.95, plus shipping and handling, from Harvard Common Press, 535 Albany St., Boston, MA 02118 (phone: 617-423-5803).

Another book on family travel, *Travel with Children* by Maureen Wheeler, offers a wide range of practical tips on traveling with children, and includes accounts of the author's family travel experiences. It is available for $10.95, plus shipping and handling, from Lonely Planet Publications, Embarcadero West, 112 Linden St., Oakland, CA 94607 (phone: 415-893-8555).

Also look for the Paris volume of the "Kidding Around" series, published by John Muir Publications. This book starts with an overview of the city, along with some interesting background information, and then is divided into areas, with descriptions of the various attractions in the general order in which you might encounter them. It can be ordered directly from the publisher by sending $9.95, plus shipping, to John Muir Publications, PO Box 613, Santa Fe, NM 87504, or by calling 800-888-7504 or 505-982-4087.

Finally, parents arranging a trip with their children may want to deal with an agency specializing in family travel such as *Let's Take the Kids* (1268 Devon Ave., Los

Angeles, CA 90024; phone: 800-726-4349 or 213-274-7088). In addition to arranging and booking trips for individual families, this group occasionally organizes trips for single-parent families traveling together. They also offer a parent travel network, whereby parents who have been to a particular destination can evaluate it for others.

PLANE: Begin early to investigate all available family discounts and charter flights, as well as any package deals and special rates offered by the major airlines. When you make your reservations, tell the airline that you are traveling with a child. Children ages 2 through 11 generally travel at about a 20% to 30% discount off regular full-fare adult ticket prices on domestic flights. This children's fare, however, usually is much higher than the excursion fare, which may be used by any traveler, regardless of age. An infant under 2 years of age usually can travel free if it sits on an adult's lap. A second infant without a second adult would pay the fare applicable to children ages 2 through 11.

Although some airlines will, on request, supply bassinets for infants, most carriers encourage parents to bring their own safety seat on board, which then is strapped into the airline seat with a regular seat belt. This is much safer — and certainly much more comfortable — than holding the child in your lap. If you do not purchase a seat for your baby, you have the option of bringing the infant restraint along on the off-chance that there might be an empty seat next to yours — in which case some airlines will let you use that seat at no charge for your baby and infant seat. However, if there is no empty seat available, the infant seat no doubt will have to be checked as baggage (and you may have to pay an additional charge), since it generally does not fit under the seat or in the overhead racks.

The safest bet is to pay for a seat — this usually will be the same as fares applicable to children ages 2 through 11. It usually is less expensive to pay for an adult excursion rate than the discounted children's fare.

Be forewarned: Some safety seats designed primarily for use in cars do not fit into plane seats properly. Although nearly all seats manufactured since 1985 carry labels indicating whether they meet federal standards for use aboard planes, actual seat sizes may vary from carrier to carrier. At the time of this writing, the FAA was in the process of reviewing and revising the federal regulations regarding infant travel and safety devices — it was still to be determined if children should be *required* to sit in safety seats and whether the airlines will have to provide them.

If using one of these infant restraints, you should try to get bulkhead seats, which will provide extra room to care for your child during the flight. You also should request a bulkhead seat when using a bassinet — again, this is not as safe as strapping the child in. On some planes bassinets hook into a bulkhead wall; on others it is placed on the floor in front of you. (Note that bulkhead seats often are reserved for families traveling with small children.) As a general rule, babies should be held during takeoff and landing.

Request seats on the aisle if you have a toddler or if you think you will need to use the bathroom frequently. Carry onto the plane all you will need to care for and occupy your children during the flight — formula, diapers, a sweater, books, favorite stuffed animals, and so on. Dress your baby simply, with a minimum of buttons and snaps, because the only place you may have to change a diaper is at your seat or in a small lavatory.

On US carriers, you also can ask for a hot dog or hamburger instead of the airline's regular dinner if you give at least 24 hours' notice. Some, but not all, airlines have baby food aboard, and the flight attendant can warm a bottle for you. While you should bring along toys from home, also ask about children's diversions. Some carriers have terrific free packages of games, coloring books, and puzzles.

When the plane takes off and lands, make sure your baby is nursing or has a bottle, pacifier, or thumb in its mouth. This sucking will make the child swallow and help to clear stopped ears. A piece of hard candy will do the same thing for an older child.

Parents traveling by plane with toddlers, children, or teenagers may want to consult *When Kids Fly,* a free booklet published by Massport (Public Affairs Department, 10 Park Plaza, Boston, MA 02116-3971; phone: 617-973-5600), which includes helpful information on airfares for children, infant seats, what to do in the event of overbooked or canceled flights, and so on.

■**Note:** Newborn babies, whose lungs may not be able to adjust to the altitude, should not be taken aboard an airplane. And some airlines may refuse to allow a pregnant woman in her 8th or 9th month to fly. Check with the airline ahead of time, and carry a letter from your doctor stating that you are fit to travel — and indicating the estimated date of birth.

ACCOMMODATIONS AND MEALS: Often a cot for a child will be placed in a hotel room at little or no extra charge. If you wish to sleep in separate rooms, special rates sometimes are available for families; some places do not charge for children under a certain age. In many of the larger chain hotels, the staffs are more used to children. These hotels also are likely to have swimming pools or gamerooms — both popular with most youngsters. Apartments, condominiums, and other rental options offer families privacy, flexibility, some kitchen facilities, and often lower costs.

Most better hotels will try to arrange for a sitter for the times you will want to be without the children — for an evening's entertainment or a particularly rigorous stint of sightseeing.

At mealtime, don't deny yourself or your children the delights of a new style of cooking. Children like to know what kind of food to expect, so the family can have the pleasure of looking up French dishes before leaving. Encourage your children to try new things, although sometimes you can find American-style food in Paris — even *McDonald's.*

Things to Remember
1. Pace the days with children in mind. Break the touring time into half-day segments, with running around or "doing" time built in.
2. Don't forget that a child's attention span is far shorter than an adult's. Children don't have to see every sight or all of any sight to learn something from their trip; watching, playing with, and talking to other children can be equally enlightening.
3. Let your children lead the way sometimes; their perspective is different from yours, and they may lead you to things you would never have noticed on your own.
4. Remember the places that children love to visit: aquariums, zoos, amusement parks, beaches, and so on. Among the activities that may pique their interest are bicycling, snorkeling, boat trips, horseback riding, visiting children's museums, and viewing natural habitat exhibits. Children's favorites in Paris include the *Parc Zoölogique de Paris* in the Bois de Vincennes, the *Jardin d'Acclimatation* (Children's Amusement Park) in the Bois de Boulogne, and the *Parc Océanique Cousteau.*

Staying Healthy

The surest way to return home in good health is to be prepared for medical problems that might occur while on vacation. Below, we've outlined some things about which you need to think before you go.

Older travelers or anyone suffering from a chronic medical condition, such as diabetes, high blood pressure, cardiopulmonary disease, asthma, or ear, eye, or sinus trouble, should consult a physician before leaving home. Those with conditions requiring special consideration when traveling should think about seeing, in addition to their regular physician, a specialist in travel medicine. For a referral in a particular community, contact the nearest medical school or ask a local doctor to recommend such a specialist. Dr. Leonard Marcus, a member of the *American Committee on Clinical Tropical Medicine and Travelers' Health,* provides a directory of more than 100 travel doctors across the country. For a copy, send a 9-by-12-inch self-addressed, stamped envelope to Dr. Marcus at 148 Highland Ave., Newton, MA 02165 (phone: 617-527-4003).

FIRST AID: Put together a compact, personal medical kit including Band-Aids, first-aid cream, antiseptic, nose drops, insect repellent, aspirin, an extra pair of prescription glasses or contact lenses (and a copy of your prescription for glasses or contact lenses), sunglasses, over-the-counter remedies for diarrhea, indigestion, and motion sickness, a thermometer, and a supply of those prescription medicines you take regularly.

In a corner of your kit, keep a list of all the drugs you have brought and their purpose, as well as duplicate copies of your doctor's prescriptions (or a note from your doctor). As brand names may vary in different countries, it's a good idea to ask your doctor for the generic name of any drugs you use so that you can ask for their equivalent should you need a refill.

It also is a good idea to ask your doctor to prepare a medical identification card that includes such information as your blood type, your social security number, any allergies or chronic health problems you have, and your medical insurance information. Considering the essential contents of your medical kit, keep it with you, rather than in your checked luggage.

HELPFUL PUBLICATIONS: Practically every phase of health care — before, during, and after a trip — is covered in *The New Traveler's Health Guide,* by Drs. Patrick J. Doyle and James E. Banta. It is available for $4.95, plus postage and handling, from Acropolis Books Ltd., 13950 Park Center Rd., Herndon, VA 22071 (phone: 800-451-7771 or 703-709-0006).

The *Traveling Healthy Newsletter,* which is published six times a year, also is brimming with health-related travel tips. For a year's subscription, which costs $24, contact Dr. Karl Neumann (108-48 70th Rd., Forest Hills, NY 11375; phone: 718-268-7290). Dr. Neumann also is the editor of the useful free booklet *Traveling Healthy,* which is available by writing to the *Travel Healthy Program* (PO Box 10208, New Brunswick, NJ 08906-9910; phone: 215-732-4100).

For more information regarding preventive health care for travelers, contact the *International Association for Medical Assistance to Travelers* (*IAMAT;* 417 Center St., Lewiston, NY 14092; phone: 716-754-4883). The Centers for Disease Control also publishes an interesting booklet, *Health Information for International Travel.* To order send a check or money order for $5 to the Superintendent of Documents (US Government Printing Office, Washington, DC 20402), or charge it to your credit card by calling 202-783-3238. For information on vaccination requirements, disease outbreaks, and other health information pertaining to traveling abroad, you also can call the Centers for Disease Control's 24-hour International Health Requirements and Recommendations Information Hotline: 404-332-4559.

On the Road

Credit and Currency

 It may seem hard to believe, but one of the greatest (and least understood) costs of travel is money itself. So your one single objective in relation to the care and retention of travel funds is to make them stretch as far as possible. Herewith, a primer on making money go as far as possible overseas.

CURRENCY: The basic unit of French currency is the French *franc* (abbreviated F). This is distributed in coin denominations of 1, 2, and 10 francs, and 50 centimes (100 centimes equal 1 franc). Paper money is issued in bills of 20, 50, 100, and 500 francs. The value of French currency in relation to the US dollar fluctuates daily, affected by a wide variety of phenomena. At press time, the franc was being exchanged at a rate of about 6 francs to $1 US.

Visitors are allowed to bring no more than 50,000F (or its equivalent in US currency) into France. To avoid problems anywhere along the line, it's advisable to fill out any customs forms provided when leaving the US on which you can declare all money you are taking with you — cash, traveler's checks, and so on. US law requires that anyone taking more than $10,000 into or out of the US must report this fact on customs form No. 4790, which is available from US Customs. If taking over $10,000 out of the US, you must report this *before* leaving the US; if returning with such an amount, you should include this information on your customs declaration. Although travelers usually are not questioned by customs officials about currency when entering or leaving, the sensible course is to observe all regulations just to be on the safe side.

In Paris, as in the rest of France, you will find the official rate of exchange posted in banks, airports, money exchange houses, and some shops. As a general rule, expect to get more local currency for your US dollar at banks than at any other commercial establishment. Exchange rates do change from day to day, and most banks offer the same (or very similar) exchange rates. (In a pinch, the convenience of cashing money in your hotel — sometimes on a 24-hour basis — *may* make up for the difference in the exchange rate.) Don't try to bargain in banks or hotels — no one will alter the rates for you.

Money exchange houses *(bureaus de change)* are financial institutions that charge a fee for the service of exchanging dollars into local currency. When considering alternatives, be aware that although the rate varies among these establishments, the rates of exchange offered are bound to be slightly less favorable than the terms offered at nearby banks — again, don't be surprised if you get fewer francs for your dollar than the rate published in the papers.

That said, however, the following rules of thumb are worth remembering:

Rule number one: Never (repeat: *never*) exchange dollars for foreign currency at hotels, restaurants, or retail shops. If you do, you are sure to lose a significant amount of your US dollar's buying power. If you do come across a storefront exchange counter offering what appears to be an incredible bargain, there's too much counterfeit specie in circulation to take the chance. (see Rule number three, below.)

Rule number two: Estimate your needs carefully; if you overbuy you lose twice — buying and selling back. Every time you exchange money, someone is making a profit, and rest assured it isn't you. Use up foreign notes before leaving, saving just enough for last-minute incidentals, and tips.

Rule number three: Don't buy money on the black market. The exchange rate may be better, but it is a common practice to pass off counterfeit bills to unsuspecting foreigners who aren't familiar with the local currency. It's usually a sucker's game, and you almost always are the sucker; it also can land you in jail.

Rule number four: Learn the local currency quickly and keep abreast of daily fluctuations in the exchange rate. These are listed in the English-language *International Herald Tribune* daily for the preceding day, as well as in every major newspaper in Europe. Rates change to some degree every day. For rough calculations, it is quick and safe to use round figures, but for purchases and actual currency exchanges, carry a small pocket calculator to help you compute the exact rate. Inexpensive calculators specifically designed to convert currency amounts quickly for travelers are widely available.

When changing money, don't be afraid to ask how much commission you're being charged, and the exact amount of the prevailing exchange rate. In fact, in any exchange of money for goods or services, you should work out the rate before making any payment.

TRAVELER'S CHECKS: It's wise to carry traveler's checks instead of (or in addition to) cash, since it's possible to replace them if they are stolen or lost. Issued in various denominations and available in both US dollars and French francs, with adequate proof of identification (credit cards, driver's license, passport), traveler's checks are as good as cash in most hotels, restaurants, stores, and banks. Don't assume, however, that restaurants, small shops, and other establishments are going to be able to change checks of large denominations.

Although traveler's checks are available in foreign currencies such as French francs, the exchange rates offered by the issuing companies in the US generally are far less favorable than those available from banks both in the US and abroad. Therefore, it usually is better to carry the bulk of your travel funds abroad in US dollar–denomination traveler's checks.

Every type of traveler's check is legal tender in banks around the world, and each company guarantees full replacement if checks are lost or stolen. After that the similarity ends. Some charge a fee for purchase, others are free; you can buy traveler's checks at almost any bank, and some are available by mail. Most important, each traveler's check issuer differs slightly in its refund policy — the amount refunded immediately, the accessibility of refund locations, the availability of a 24-hour refund service, and the time it will take for you to receive replacement checks. For instance, *American Express* guarantees replacement of lost or stolen traveler's checks in under 3 hours at any *American Express* office — other companies may not be as prompt. In Paris, the *American Express* offices are located at 11 Place du Marché (phone: 39-76-50-39), 11 Rue Scribe (phone: 47-77-77-07), and 5 Rue de Chaillot (phone: 47-23-61-20). Travelers should keep in mind that *American Express*'s 3-hour policy is based on the traveler being able to provide the serial numbers of the lost checks. Without these numbers, refunds can take much longer.

We cannot overemphasize the importance of knowing how to replace lost or stolen checks. All of the traveler's check companies have agents around the world, both in their own name and at associated agencies (usually, but not necessarily, banks), where refunds can be obtained during business hours. Most of them also have 24-hour toll-free telephone lines, and some will even provide emergency funds to tide you over on a Sunday.

Be sure to make a photocopy of the refund instructions that will be given you at the time of purchase. To avoid complications should you need to replace lost checks (and to speed up the process), keep the purchase receipt and an accurate list, by serial number, of the checks that have been spent or cashed. Always keep these records separate from the checks and the original records themselves (you may want to give them to a traveling companion to hold).

Following is a list of the major companies issuing traveler's checks and the numbers to call in the event that loss or theft makes replacement necessary:

    American Express: The company advises travelers in Europe to call 44-273-571600 (in Brighton, England), collect. Another (slower) option is to call 801-968-8300 (in the US), collect or contact the nearest *American Express* office (see above for the Paris address).

    Bank of America: In France and elsewhere worldwide, call 415-624-5400 or 415-622-3800, collect.

    Citicorp: In France and elsewhere worldwide, call 813-623-1709 or 813-626-4444, collect.

    MasterCard: In France, call the New York office at 212-974-5696, collect.

    Thomas Cook MasterCard: In France, call 609-987-7300 (in the US) or 44-733-502995 (in England), collect, and they will direct you to the nearest branch of *Thomas Cook* or *Wagons-Lits,* their nearest European agent.

    Visa: In France, call 415-574-7111, collect. In Europe, you also can call this London number collect: 44-71-937-8091.

CREDIT CARDS: Some establishments you encounter during the course of your travels may not honor any credit cards and some may not honor all cards, so there is a practical reason to carry more than one. Most US credit cards, including the principal bank cards, are honored in France; however, keep in mind that some cards may be issued under different names in Europe. For example, *MasterCard* may go under the name *Access* or *Eurocard,* and *Visa* often is called *Carte Bleue* — wherever these equivalents are accepted, *MasterCard* and *Visa* may be used. The following is a list of credit cards that enjoy wide international acceptance:

    American Express: For information call 800-528-4800 in the US; to report a lost or stolen *American Express* card in Paris, contact the local *American Express* office (see address above) or call 212-477-5700, collect.

    Carte Blanche: For medical, legal, and travel assistance in France, call 214-680-6480, collect. For information call 800-525-9135 in the US; to report a lost or stolen *Carte Blanche* card in France, call 303-790-2433, collect.

    Diners Club: For medical, legal, and travel assistance in France, call 214-680-6480, collect. For information call 800-525-9135 in the US; to report a lost or stolen *Diners Club* card in France, call 303-790-2433, collect.

    Discover Card: For information call 800-DISCOVER in the US; to report a lost or stolen *Discover* card, in France call 302-323-7652, collect.

    MasterCard: For 24-hour emergency lost card service, call 314-275-6690, collect, from abroad.

    Visa: For 24-hour emergency lost card service in France, call 415-574-7700, collect.

SENDING MONEY ABROAD: If you have used up your traveler's checks, cashed as many emergency personal checks as your credit card allows, drawn on your cash advance line to the fullest extent, and still need money, have it sent to you via one of the following services:

American Express (phone: 800-543-4080). Offers a service called "Moneygram," completing money transfers in anywhere from 15 minutes to 5 days. The sender can go to any *American Express* office in the US and transfer money by presenting cash, a personal check, money order, or credit card — *Discover, MasterCard, Visa,* or *American Express Optima Card* (no other *American Express* or other credit cards are accepted). *American Express Optima* cardholders also can arrange for this transfer over the phone. To collect at the other end, the receiver must show identification (passport, driver's license, or other picture ID) at the *American Express* office in Paris and present a passport as identification. For further information on this service, call 800-543-4080.

Western Union Telegraph Company (phone: 800-325-4176 throughout the US). A friend or relative can go, cash in hand, to any *Western Union* office in the US, where, for a *minimum* charge of $15 (it rises with the amount of the transaction), the funds will be transferred to a representative of *Western Union* in Paris. (There are 2 in Paris.) When the money arrives, you will not be notified — you must go to the bank to inquire. Transfers generally take only about 15 minutes. The funds will be turned over in local currency, based on the rate of exchange in effect on the day of receipt. For a higher fee, the US party to this transaction may call *Western Union* with a *MasterCard* or *Visa* number to send up to $2,000.

If you are literally down to your last franc, the nearest US consulate (see *Medical and Legal Aid and Consular Services,* in this section) will let you call home to set these matters in motion.

CASH MACHINES: Automatic teller machines (ATMs) are increasingly common worldwide. If your bank participates in one of the international ATM networks (most do), the bank will issue you a "cash card" along with a personal identification code or number (also called a PIC or PIN). You can use this card at any ATM in the same electronic network to check your account balances, transfer monies between checking and savings accounts, and — most important for a traveler — withdraw cash instantly. Network ATMs generally are located in banks, commercial and transportation centers, and near major tourist attractions.

Some financial institutions offer exclusive automatic teller machines for their own customers only at bank branches. At the time of this writing, there is only one international network of ATMs in France, *Cirrus,* which has over 55,000 ATMs in more than 22 countries, including 15 in Paris. *MasterCard* holders also may use their cards to draw cash against their credit lines. For a free booklet listing the locations of these machines and further information on the *Cirrus* network, call 800-4-CIRRUS.

Accommodations

Paris is commonly thought of as an expensive town, abounding with 4-star palace hotels available to those who can pay $300 a night. However, if you are willing to spend some time investigating before you travel, it is not difficult to find a relatively wide choice of establishments that are more affordable. At the lower end of the price scale, you will not necessarily have to forgo charm. While a fair number of inexpensive establishments are simply no-frills, "generic" places to spend the night, even the sparest room may have the cachet of once having been the nightly retreat of a monk or nun. And some of the most delightful places to stay are the smaller, less expensive, often family-run small inns. For more information, see *Best in Town* in THE CITY.

Time Zones, Business Hours, and Public Holidays

 TIME ZONES: The countries of Europe fall into three time zones. Greenwich Mean Time — the time in Greenwich, England, at longitude 0°0′ — is the base from which all other time zones are measured. Areas in zones west of Greenwich have earlier times and are called Greenwich Minus; those to the east have later times and are called Greenwich Plus. For example, New York City — which falls into the Greenwich Minus 5 time zone — is 5 hours earlier than Greenwich, England.

France is in the Greenwich Plus 1 time zone (or Central European Time) — which means that the time is 1 hour later than it is in Greenwich, England, and when it is noon in Paris, it is 6 AM in New York.

As do most Western European nations, France moves its clocks ahead an hour in late spring and an hour back in the fall, although the date of the change tends to be about a week earlier (in spring) and a week later (in fall) than the dates we have adopted in the US. For about 2 weeks a year, then, the time difference between the US and France is 1 hour more or less than usual.

French and other European timetables use a 24-hour clock to denote arrival and departure times, which means that hours are expressed sequentially from 1 AM. By this method, 9 AM is recorded as 0900, noon as 1200, 1 PM as 1300, 6 PM as 1800, midnight as 2400, and so on. For example, the departure of a train at 7 AM will be announced as "0700"; one leaving at 7 PM will be noted as "1900."

BUSINESS HOURS: In Paris, as throughout France, most businesses and shops are open Mondays through Fridays from 9 AM to 1 or 2 PM, then from 3 or 4 PM until 7 or 8 PM, although more and more businesses now are open through midday and close at 5 PM. Many shops also are open on Saturday mornings. Major department stores and shopping centers generally stay open through midday and are open Mondays through Saturdays from 9:30 AM to 6:30 PM.

Weekday banking hours in Paris are from 9 AM to 4:30 PM, usually without a break for lunch.

Restaurant hours are similar to those in the US. Most restaurants are open all week during the high season and close 1 day each week during the off-season — the day varies from restaurant to restaurant.

PUBLIC HOLIDAYS: In Paris, as in the rest of France, the public holidays (and their dates this year) are as follows:

New Year's Day (January 1)
Good Friday (April 17)
Easter Monday (April 20)
Labor Day or May Day (May 1)
End of World War II (May 8)
Whitmonday (June 7)
Bastille Day (July 14)
Assumption Day (August 15)
All Saints' Day (November 1)
Christmas Day (December 25)

Mail and Electricity

 MAIL: The main post office, located at 52 Rue du Louvre, 1er (phone: 42-33-71-60), is the only post office that is open 24 hours. Other post offices are open Mondays through Fridays from 9 AM to 6 PM; Saturdays from 9 AM to noon. Postal rates change frequently; stamps *(timbres)* can be bought at the post office and at authorized tobacconists *(bureaus de tabac)* and at some hotels.

Be advised that delivery from France can be erratic (postcards often are given lowest priority, so don't use them for important messages). Airmail letters from France to the US usually takes at least 4 to 7 days.

If your correspondence is important, you may want to send it via a special courier service: *DHL International* (59 Av. d'Iéna, 16e; phone: 45-01-91-00 or 48-63-70-00); *Federal Express* (*Copyshop,* 44 Rue du Colisée, 8e; phone: 40-85-38-88). The cost is considerably higher than sending something via the postal services — but the assurance of its timely arrival may be worth it.

If you're mailing to an address within France, a good way to ensure or speed delivery is to use the postal code. And since small towns in France may have similar names, the postal code always should be specified — delivery of a letter may depend on it. If you do not know the correct postal code, call the French Government Tourist Office (see *Tourist Information Offices,* in this section, for telephone numbers) — they should be able to look it up for you.

There are several places that will receive and hold mail for travelers in France. Mail sent to you at a hotel and clearly marked "Guest Mail, Hold for Arrival" is one safe approach. French post offices, including the main Paris office, also will extend this service to you if the mail is addressed to the equivalent of US general delivery — called *poste restante.* Address the mail to Poste restante, 52 Rue du Louvre, Paris 75100. Call 42-33-71-60 to inquire about mail. Also, don't forget to take your passport with you when you go to collect it. Most French post offices require formal identification before they will release anything; there also may be a small charge for picking up your mail.

If you are an *American Express* customer (a cardholder, a carrier of *American Express* traveler's checks, or traveling on an *American Express Travel Service* tour) you can have mail sent to its office in Paris. Letters are held free of charge — registered mail and packages are not accepted. You must be able to show an *American Express* card, traveler's checks, or a voucher proving you are on one of the company's tours to avoid paying for mail privileges. Those who aren't clients must pay a nominal charge each time they inquire if they have received mail, whether or not they actually have a letter. Mail should be addressed to you, care of *American Express,* and should be marked "Client Mail Service."

While US embassies and consulates abroad will not under ordinary circumstances accept mail for tourists, they *may* hold mail for US citizens in an emergency situation, especially if the papers sent are important. It is best to inform them either by separate letter or cable, or by phone (particularly if you are in the country already), that you will be using their address for this purpose.

ELECTRICITY: The US runs on 110-volt, 60-cycle alternating current; Paris (and the rest of France) runs on 220- or 230-volt, 50-cycle alternating current. (Some large tourist hotels also offer 110-volt currency for your convenience; if not, they usually have convertors available.) The difference between US and French voltage means that, without a converter, at 220 volts the motor of a US appliance used overseas would run at twice the speed at which it's meant to operate and would quickly burn out.

Medical and Legal Aid and Consular Services

 MEDICAL AID ABROAD: Nothing ruins a vacation or business trip more effectively than sudden injury or illness. Medical institutes in France, especially in the larger cities, generally provide the same basic specialties and services that are available in the US.

Before you go, be sure to check with your insurance company about the applicability of your hospitalization and major medical policies while you're abroad; many policies do not apply, and others are not accepted in France. Older travelers should know that Medicare does not make payments outside the US.

If a bona fide emergency occurs, the fastest way to get attention may be to take a taxi to the emergency room of the nearest hospital. In Paris go to the *American Hospital* (63 Bd. Victor-Hugo, Neuilly 92202; phone: 46-41-25-25; for an ambulance, call 43-78-26-26). It is a major hospital with advanced equipment and technology to deal with acute medical situations, and all of the staff speak English. An alternative is to dial the free national "emergency" number — 17 in France — used to summon the police, fire engines, or an ambulance.

France has socialized medicine, and all hospitals are public facilities *(hôpitaux publiques).* However, there also are some private clinics *(cliniques privées),* which are like small hospitals, that can also provide medical aid for less serious cases. Medical service for French residents is generally free, but foreign travelers will have to pay full fees for such service, which, depending on your coverage, may or may not be reimbursed by your insurance company.

If a doctor is needed for something less than an emergency, there are several ways to find one. If you are staying in a hotel or at a resort, ask for help in reaching a doctor or other emergency services, or for the house physician, who may visit you in your room or ask you to visit an office. Travelers staying at a hotel of any size probably will find that the doctor on call speaks at least a modicum of English — if not, request one who does.

Dialing the nationwide emergency number (17) also may be of help in locating a physician. It also usually is possible to obtain a referral through a US consulate (see addresses and phone numbers below) or directly through a hospital, especially if it is an emergency.

If you have a minor medical problem, a pharmacist might offer some help. There are a number of 24-hour drugstores *(les pharmacies)* in Paris. One 24-hour drugstore is *Pharmacie Derhy* (84 Av. des Champs-Elysées, Paris 75008; phone: 45-62-02-41).

Bring along a copy of any prescription you may have from your doctor in case you should need a refill. In the case of minor complaints, French pharmacists may do some prescribing and *may* fill a foreign prescription; however, do not count on this. In most cases, you will need a local doctor to rewrite the prescription. Even in an emergency, a traveler will more than likely be given only enough of a drug to last until a local prescription can be obtained.

Emergency assistance also is available from the various medical programs designed for travelers who have chronic ailments or whose illness requires them to return home:

> *International Association for Medical Assistance to Travelers (IAMAT;* 417 Center St., Lewiston, NY 14092; phone: 716-754-4883). Entitles members to the services of participating doctors around the world, as well as clinics and hospitals in various locations. Participating physicians agree to adhere to a basic charge

of around $40 to see a patient referred by *IAMAT*. To join, simply write to *IAMAT;* in about 3 weeks you will receive a membership card, the booklet of members, and an inoculation chart. A nonprofit organization, *IAMAT* appreciates donations; with a donation of $25 or more, you will receive a set of worldwide climate charts detailing weather and sanitary conditions. (Delivery can take up to 5 weeks, so plan ahead.)

International SOS Assistance (PO Box 11568, Philadelphia, PA 19116; phone: 800-523-8930 or 215-244-1500). Subscribers are provided with telephone access — 24 hours a day, 365 days a year — to a worldwide, monitored, multilingual network of medical centers. A phone call brings assistance ranging from a telephone consultation to transportation home by ambulance or aircraft, or, in some cases, transportation of a family member to wherever you are hospitalized. Individual rates are $35 for 2 weeks of coverage ($3.50 for each additional day), $70 for 1 month, or $240 for 1 year; couple and family rates also are available.

Medic Alert Foundation (2323 N. Colorado, Turlock, CA 95380; phone: 800-ID-ALERT or 209-668-3333). If you have a health condition that may not be readily perceptible to the casual observer — one that might result in a tragic error in an emergency situation — this organization offers identification emblems specifying such conditions. The foundation also maintains a computerized central file from which your complete medical history is available 24 hours a day by phone (the telephone number is clearly inscribed on the emblem). The onetime membership fee (between $25 and $45) is based on the type of metal from which the emblem is made — the choices range from stainless steel to 10K gold-filled.

TravMed (PO Box 10623, Baltimore, MD 21204; phone: 800-732-5309 or 301-296-5225). For $3 per day, subscribers receive comprehensive medical assistance while abroad. Major medical expenses are covered up to $100,000, and special transportation home or of a family member to wherever you are hospitalized is provided at no additional cost.

■ **Note:** Those who are unable to take a reserved flight due to personal illness or who must fly home unexpectedly due to a family emergency should be aware that airlines may offer a discounted airfare (or arrange a partial refund) if the traveler can demonstrate that his or her situation is indeed a legitimate emergency. Your inability to fly or the illness or death of an immediate family member usually must be substantiated by a doctor's note or the name, relationship, and funeral home from which the deceased will be buried. In such cases, airlines often will waive certain advance purchase restrictions or you may receive a refund check or voucher for future travel at a later date. Be aware, however, that this bereavement fare may not necessarily be the least expensive fare available and, if possible, it is best to have a travel agent check all possible flights through a computer reservations system (CRS).

 LEGAL AID AND CONSULAR SERVICES: There is one crucial place to keep in mind when outside the US, namely, the US Embassy (2 Av. Gabriel, Paris 75008; phone: 42-96-12-02) and Consulate (2 Rue St.-Florentin, Paris 75001; phone: 42-61-80-75).

If you are injured or become seriously ill, or if you encounter legal difficulties, the consulate is the first place to turn, although its powers and capabilities are limited. It will direct you to medical assistance and notify your relatives if you are ill; it can advise you of your rights and provide a list of lawyers if you are arrested, but it cannot interfere with the local legal process.

For questions about US citizens arrested abroad, how to get money to them, and other useful information, call the *Citizens' Emergency Center* of the Office of Special Consular Services in Washington, DC, at 202-647-5225. (For further information about this invaluable hotline, see below.)

A consulate exists to aid US citizens in serious matters, such as illness, destitution, and the above legal difficulties. It is not there to aid in trivial situations, such as canceled reservations or lost baggage, no matter how important these matters may seem to the victimized tourist. If you should get sick, the US consul can provide names of doctors, dentists, local hospitals, and clinics; the consul also will contact family members in the US and help arrange special ambulance service for a flight home. In a situation involving "legitimate and proven poverty" of an US citizen stranded abroad without funds, the consul will contact sources of money (such as family or friends in the US), apply for aid to agencies in foreign countries, and in the last resort — which is *rarely* — arrange for repatriation at government expense, although this is a loan that must be repaid. And in case of natural disasters or civil unrest, consulates around the world handle the evacuation of US citizens if it becomes necessary.

As mentioned above, the US State Department operates a *Citizens' Emergency Center,* which offers a number of services to US citizens abroad and their families at home. In addition to giving callers up-to-date information on trouble spots, the center will contact authorities abroad in an attempt to locate a traveler or deliver an urgent message. In case of illness, death, arrest, destitution, or repatriation of an US citizen on foreign soil, it will relay information to relatives at home if the consulate is unable to do so. Travel advisory information is available 24 hours a day to people with touch-tone phones (phone: 202-647-5225). Callers with rotary phones can get information at this number from 8:15 AM to 10 PM (eastern standard time) on weekdays, 9 AM to 3 PM Saturdays. In the event of an emergency, this number also may be called during these hours. For emergency calls only, at all other times, call 202-634-3600 and ask for the duty officer.

Drinking and Drugs

 DRINKING: It is more than likely that some of the warmest memories of a trip to Paris will be moments of conviviality shared over a drink in a neighborhood bar or sunlit café. Visitors will find that liquor, wine, and brandies in France are distilled to the same proof and often are the same labels as those found at home.

French bars and cafés open at about 11 AM or earlier to serve coffee and breakfast; most remain open until 3 or 4 AM. In France, there is no established minimum drinking age. In this world-famous wine country, young people are introduced to the national treasure at an early age.

As in the US, national taxes on alcohol affect the prices of liquor in France, and as a general rule, mixed drinks — especially imported liquors such as whiskey and gin — are more expensive than at home. If you like a drop before dinner, a good way to save money is to buy a bottle of your favorite brand at the airport before leaving the US and enjoy it in your hotel before setting forth.

Visitors to France may bring in 2 liters of wine and 1 liter of liquor over 22% proof or 2 liters of liquor under 22% proof per person duty-free. If you are buying any quantity of alcohol (such as a case of wine) in France and traveling through other European countries on your route back to the US, you will have to pass through customs and pay duty at each border crossing, so you might want to arrange to have it shipped home. Whether bringing it with you or shipping, you will have to pay US import duties on any quantity over the allowed 1 liter (see *Customs and Returning to the US,* in this section).

DRUGS: Illegal narcotics are as prevalent in France as in the US, but the moderate legal penalties and vague social acceptance that marijuana has gained in the US have no equivalents in France. Due to the international war on drugs, enforcement of drug laws is becoming increasingly strict throughout the world. Local European narcotics officers and customs officials are renowned for their absence of understanding and lack of a sense of humor — especially where foreigners are involved.

Opiates and barbiturates, and other increasingly popular drugs — "white powder" substances like heroin, cocaine, and "crack" (the cocaine derivative) — continue to be of major concern to narcotics officials. Most European countries — including France — have toughened laws regarding illegal drugs and narcotics, and it is important to bear in mind that the type or quantity of drugs involved is of minor importance. Particularly for foreigners, the maximum penalties may be imposed for possessing even *traces* of illegal drugs. There is a high conviction rate in these cases, and bail for foreigners is rare. Persons arrested are subject to the laws of the country they are visiting, and there isn't much that the US consulate can do for drug offenders beyond providing a list of lawyers. The best advice we can offer is this: Don't carry, use, buy, or sell illegal drugs.

Those who carry medicines that contain a controlled drug should be sure to have a current doctor's prescription with them. Ironically, travelers can get into almost as much trouble coming through US customs with over-the-counter drugs picked up abroad that contain substances that are controlled in the US. Cold medicines, pain relievers, and the like often have codeine or codeine derivatives that are illegal, except by prescription, in the US. Throw them out before leaving for home.

■ **Be forewarned:** US narcotics agents warn travelers of the increasingly common ploy of drug dealers asking travelers to transport a "gift" or other package back to the US. Don't be fooled into thinking that the protection of US law applies abroad — accused of illegal drug trafficking, you will be considered guilty until you prove your innocence. In other words, do not, under any circumstances, agree to take anything across the border for a stranger.

Tipping

In Paris, as throughout France and most of the rest of Europe, you will find the custom of including some kind of service charge on the bill for a meal more common than in North America. This can confuse Americans unfamiliar with the custom. On the one hand, many a traveler, unaware of this policy, has left many a superfluous tip. On the other hand, travelers aware of this policy may make the mistake of assuming that it takes care of everything. It doesn't. While "service included" in theory eliminates any question about how much and whom to tip, in practice there still are occasions when on-the-spot tips are appropriate. Among these are tips to show appreciation for special services, as well as tips meant to say "thank you" for services rendered. So keep a pocketful of 10F bills (or coins) ready, and hand these out like dollar bills.

In French restaurants, the service charge is usually calculated in the prices listed; if not (evidenced by the phrase *service non-compris*), it will be added to the final bill. For the most part, if you see a notation at the bottom of the menu without a percentage figure, the charge should be included in the price; if a percentage figure is indicated, the service charge has not yet been added. To further confuse the issue, not every restaurant notes what its policy is. If you are at all unsure, ask a waiter.

This service charge generally is 15%. In the rare instance where it isn't added, a 15% tip to the waiter — just as in the US — usually is a safe figure, although one should never hesitate to penalize poor service or reward excellent and efficient attention by leaving less or more. If the service charge has been added, no further gratuity is expected — though it's a common practice in Europe to leave a few extra coins on the table. The emphasis is on *few,* and the current equivalent of $1 usually is quite adequate.

Although it's not necessary to tip the maître d' of most restaurants — unless he has been especially helpful in arranging a special party or providing a table (slipping him something in a crowded restaurant *may* get you seated sooner or procure a preferred table) — when tipping is desirable or appropriate, the least amount should be the local equivalent of $5. In the finest restaurants, where a multiplicity of servers are present, plan to tip 5% to the captain. The sommelier (wine waiter) is entitled to a gratuity of approximately 10% of the price of the bottle.

As in restaurants, visitors usually will find a service charge of 10% to 15% included in their final bill at most Paris hotels. No additional gratuities are required — or expected — beyond this billed service charge. It is unlikely, however, that a service charge will be added to bills in small family-run guesthouses or other modest establishments. In these cases, guests should let their instincts be their guide; no tipping is expected by members of the family who own the establishment, but it is a nice gesture to leave something for others — such as a dining room waiter or a maid — who may have been helpful. A gratuity of around $1 per night is adequate in most cases.

If a hotel does not automatically add a service charge, it is perfectly proper for guests to ask to have an extra 10% to 15% added to their bill, to be distributed among those who served them. This may be an especially convenient solution in a large hotel, where it's difficult to determine just who out of a horde of attendants actually performed particular services.

For those who prefer to distribute tips themselves, a chambermaid generally is tipped at the rate of approximately $1 per day. Tip the concierge or hall porter for specific services only, with the amount of such gratuities dependent on the level of service provided. For any special service you receive in a hotel, a tip is expected — the current equivalent of $1 being the minimum for a small service.

Bellhops, doormen, and porters at hotels and transportation centers generally are tipped at the rate of $1 per piece of luggage, along with a small additional amount if a doorman helps with a cab or car. Once upon a time, taxi drivers in Europe would give you a rather odd look if presented with a tip for a fare, but times have changed, and 10% to 15% of the amount on the meter is now a standard gratuity.

Miscellaneous tips: Tipping ushers in a movie house, theater, or concert hall used to be the rule, but is becoming less common — the best policy is to check what other patrons are doing and follow suit. Most of the time, the program is not free, and in lieu of a tip it is common practice to purchase a program from the person who seats you. Sightseeing tour guides also should be tipped. If you are traveling in a group, decide together what you want to give the guide and present it from the group at the end of the tour. If you have been individually escorted, the amount paid should depend on the degree of your satisfaction, but it should not be less than 10% of the total tour price. Museum and monument guides also usually are tipped, and it is a nice touch to tip a caretaker who unlocks a small church or turns on the lights in a chapel.

In barbershops and beauty salons, tip as you would at home, keeping in mind that the percentages vary according to the type of establishment — 10% in the most expensive salons; 15% to 20% in less expensive establishments. (As a general rule, the person who washes your hair should get an additional small tip.) The washroom attendants in these places, or wherever you see one, should get a small tip — they usually set out a little plate with a coin already on it indicating the suggested denomination. Don't forget service station attendants, for whom a tip of around 50¢ for cleaning the windshield or other attention is not unusual.

Tipping always is a matter of personal preference. In the situations covered above, as well as in any others that arise where you feel a tip is expected or due, feel free to express your pleasure or displeasure. Again, never hesitate to reward excellent and efficient attention and to penalize poor service. Give an extra gratuity and a word of thanks when someone has gone out of his or her way for you. Either way, the more personal the act of tipping, the more appropriate it seems. And if you didn't like the service — or the attitude — don't tip.

Duty-Free Shopping and Value Added Tax

DUTY-FREE SHOPS: Note that at the time of this writing, because of the newly integrated European economy, there was some question as to the fate and number of duty-free shops that would be maintained at international airports in member countries of the European Economic Community (EEC). It appears, however, that those traveling between EEC countries and any country *not* a member of the Common Market will still be entitled to buy duty-free items. Since the United States is not a Common Market member, duty-free purchases by US travelers will, presumably, remain as they have been even after the end of 1992.

If common sense says that it always is less expensive to buy goods in an airport duty-free shop than to buy them at home or in the streets of a foreign city, travelers should be aware of some basic facts. Duty-free, first of all, does not mean that the goods travelers buy will be free of duty when they return to the US. Rather, it means that the shop has paid no import tax in acquiring goods of foreign make, because the goods are not to be used in the country where the shop is located. This is why duty-free goods are available only in the restricted, passengers-only area of international airports or are delivered to departing passengers on the plane. In a duty-free store, travelers save money only on goods of foreign make because they are the only items on which an import tax would be charged in any other store. There usually is no saving on locally made items, although in countries such as France that impose value added taxes (see below) that are refundable to foreigners, the prices in airport duty-free shops are minus this tax, sparing travelers the often cumbersome procedures they otherwise have to follow to obtain a VAT refund.

Beyond this, there is little reason to delay buying locally made merchandise and/or souvenirs until reaching the airport. In fact, because airport duty-free shops usually pay high rents, the locally made goods they sell may well be more expensive than they would be in downtown stores. The real bargains are foreign goods, but — let the buyer beware — not all foreign goods automatically are less expensive in an airport duty-free shop. You can get a good deal on even small amounts of perfume, costing less than the usually required minimum purchase, tax-free. Other fairly standard bargains include spirits, smoking materials, cameras, clothing, watches, chocolates, and other food and luxury items — but first be sure to know what these items cost elsewhere. Terrific savings do exist (they are the reason for such shops, after all), but so do overpriced items that an unwary shopper might find equally tempting. In addition, if you wait to do your shopping at airport duty-free shops, you will be taking the chance that the desired item is out of stock or unavailable.

Duty-free shops are located in most major international airports throughout Europe, including Paris.

VALUE ADDED TAX: Commonly abbreviated as VAT, this is a tax levied by various European countries, including France, and added to the purchase price of most goods and services. The standard VAT (known as TVA in France) is 18.6% on most purchases, with a higher rate of 22% applying to luxury goods such as watches, jewelry, furs, glass, and cameras. However, the rate will likely be changed in 1992 when the Economic Community comes into effect. At press time, discussions are still being held to decide on one uniform VAT for all EC members.

The tax is intended for residents (and already is included in the price tag), but visitors are also required to pay it unless they have purchases shipped by the store directly to an address abroad. If visitors pay the tax and take purchases with them, however, they generally are entitled to a refund.

In order to qualify for a refund, you must purchase a minimum of 1,200F (about $200 US at press time) at one store — purchases from several stores cannot be combined. In most cases, stores will provide the appropriate refund forms on request. If the store does not have this form, it can be obtained at the refund office at the airport, which also can provide information on the procedure for submitting the paperwork to obtain the refund. Visitors leaving France must have all of their receipts for purchases and refund vouchers stamped by customs; as customs officials may well ask to see the merchandise, it's a good idea not to pack it in the bottom of your suitcase. A copy of that form must be sent back to the store at the airport, and you can arrange with the store owner whether you wish to have the refund credited to your credit card or have a check sent to you.

A VAT refund by dollar check or by credit to a credit card account is relatively hassle-free. If it arrives in the form of a foreign currency check and if the refund is less than a significant amount, charges imposed by US banks for converting foreign currency refund checks — which can run as high as $15 or more — could make the whole exercise hardly worth your while.

Far less costly is sending your foreign currency check (after endorsing it) to *Ruesch International,* which will covert it to a check in US dollars for a $2 fee (deducted from the dollar check). Other services include commission-free traveler's checks and foreign currency, which can be ordered by mail. Contact *Ruesch International* at one of the following address: 191 Peachtree St., Atlanta, GA 30303 (phone: 404-222-9300); 3 First National Plaza, Suite 2020, Chicago, IL 60602 (phone: 312-332-5900); 1925 Century Park E., Suite 240, Los Angeles, CA 90067 (phone: 213-277-7800); 608 Fifth Ave., "Swiss Center," New York, NY 10020 (phone: 212-977-2700); and 1350 Eye St. NW, 10th Floor and street level, Washington, DC 20005 (phone: 800-424-2923 or 202-408-1200).

■ **Buyer Beware:** You may come across shops *not* at airports that call themselves duty-free shops. These require shoppers to show a foreign passport but are subject to the same rules as other stores, including paying import duty on foreign items. What "tax-free" means in the case of these establishments is something of an advertising strategy: They are announcing loud and clear that they do, indeed, offer the VAT refund service — sometimes on the spot (minus a fee for higher overhead). Prices may be no better at these stores, and could be even higher due to this service.

Customs and Returning to the US

 Whether you return to the United States by air or sea, you must declare to the US Customs official at the point of entry everything you have bought or acquired while in Europe. The customs check can go smoothly, lasting only a few minutes, or can take hours, depending on the officer's instinct. To speed up the process, keep all your receipts handy and try to pack your purchases together in an accessible part of your suitcase. It might save you from unpacking all your belongings.

DUTY-FREE ARTICLES: In general, the duty-free allowance for US citizens returning from abroad is $400. This duty-free limit covers purchases that accompany you and are for personal use. This limit includes items used or worn while abroad, souvenirs for friends, and gifts received during the trip. A flat 10% duty based on the "fair retail value in country of acquisition" is assessed on the next $1,000 worth of merchandise brought in for personal use or gifts. Amounts above those two levels are dutiable at a variety of rates. The average rate for typical tourist purchases is about 12%, but you can find out about specific items by consulting *Tariff Schedules of the United States* in a library or at any US Customs Service office.

Families traveling together may make a joint declaration to customs, which permits one member to exceed his or her duty-free exemption to the extent that another falls short. Families also may pool purchases dutiable at the flat rate. A family of three, for example, would be eligible for up to a total of $3,000 at the 10% flat duty rate (after each member had used up his or her $400 duty-free exemption) rather than three separate $1,000 allowances. This grouping of purchases is extremely useful when considering the duty on a high-tariff item, such as jewelry or a fur coat.

Personal exemptions can be used once every 30 days; in order to be eligible, an individual must have been out of the country for more than 48 hours. If any portion of the exemption has been used once within any 30-day period or if your trip is less than 48 hours long, the duty-free allowance is cut to $25.

There are certain articles, however, that are duty-free only up to certain limits. The $25 allowance includes the following: 10 cigars (not Cuban), 60 cigarettes, and 4 ounces of perfume. Individuals eligible for the full $400 duty-free limit are allowed 1 carton of cigarettes (200), 100 cigars, and 1 liter of liquor or wine if the traveler is over 21. Alcohol above this allowance is liable for both duty and an Internal Revenue tax. Antiques, if they are 100 or more years old and you have proof from the seller of that fact, are duty-free, as are paintings and drawings if done entirely by hand.

To avoid paying duty twice, register the serial numbers of foreign-made watches and electronic equipment with the nearest US Customs bureau before departure; receipts of insurance policies also should be carried for other foreign-made items. (Also see the note at the end of *Entry Requirements and Documents,* in this section.)

Gold, gold medals, bullion, and up to $10,000 in currency or negotiable instruments may be brought into the US without being declared. Sums over $10,000 must be declared in writing.

The allotment for individual "unsolicited" gifts mailed from abroad (no more than one per day per recipient) is $50 retail value per gift. These gifts do not have to be declared and are not included in your duty-free exemption (see below). Although you should include a receipt for the purchases with each package, the examiner is empowered to impose a duty based on his or her assessment of the value of the goods. The duty owed is collected by the US Postal Service when the package is delivered (also see below). More information on mailing packages home from abroad is contained in the US Customs Service pamphlet *Buyer Beware, International Mail Imports* (see below for where to write for this and other useful brochures).

CLEARING CUSTOMS: This is a simple procedure. Forms are distributed by airline or ship personnel before arrival. (Note that a $5-per-person service charge — called a user fee — is collected by airlines to help cover the cost of customs checks, but this is included in the ticket price.) If your purchases total no more than the $400 duty-free limit, you need only fill out the identification part of the form and make an oral declaration to the customs inspector. If entering with more than $400 worth of goods, you must submit a written declaration.

Customs agents are businesslike, efficient, and not unkind. During the peak season, clearance can take time, generally because of the strain imposed by a number of jumbo jets simultaneously discharging their passengers, not because of unwarranted zealousness on the part of the customs people.

Efforts to streamline procedures used to include the so-called Citizens' Bypass Program, which allowed US citizens whose purchases were within their duty-free allowance to go to the "green line," where they simply showed their passports to the customs inspector. Although at the time of this writing this procedure still is being followed at some international airports in the US, most airports have returned to an earlier system. US citizens arriving from overseas now have to go through a passport check by the Immigration & Naturalization Service (INS) before recovering their baggage and proceeding to customs. (This additional wait will delay clearance on re-entry into the US, although citizens will not be on the same line as foreign visitors.) Although all passengers have to go through this passport inspection, those entering with purchases within the duty-free limit may be spared a thorough customs inspection. Inspectors still retain the right to search any luggage they choose, however, so don't do anything foolish.

It is illegal not to declare dutiable items; not to do so, in fact, constitutes smuggling, and the penalty can be anything from stiff fines and seizure of the goods to prison sentences. It simply isn't worth doing. Nor should you go along with the suggestions of foreign merchants who offer to help you secure a bargain by deceiving customs officials in any way. Such transactions frequently are a setup, using the foreign merchant as an agent of US customs. Another agent of US customs is TECS, the Treasury Enforcement Communications System, a computer that stores all kinds of pertinent information on returning citizens. There is a basic rule to buying goods abroad, and it should never be broken: *If you can't afford the duty on something, don't buy it.* Your list or verbal declaration should include all items purchased abroad, as well as gifts received abroad, purchases made at the behest of others, the value of repairs, and anything brought in for resale in the US.

Do not include in the list items that do not accompany you, i.e., purchases that you have mailed or had shipped home. These are dutiable in any case, even if for your own use and even if the items that accompany your return from the same trip do not exhaust your duty-free exemption. It is a good idea, if you have accumulated too much while abroad, to mail home any personal effects (made and bought in the US) that you no longer need rather than your foreign purchases. These personal effects pass through US Customs as "American goods returned" and are not subject to duty.

If you cannot avoid shipping home your foreign purchases, however, the US Customs Service suggests that the package be clearly marked "Not for Sale," and that a copy of the bill of sale be included. The US Customs examiner usually will accept this as indicative of the article's fair retail value, but if he or she believes it to be falsified or feels the goods have been seriously undervalued, a higher retail value may be assigned.

FORBIDDEN ITEMS: Narcotics, plants, and many types of food are not allowed into the US. Drugs are totally illegal, with the exception of medication prescribed by a physician. It's a good idea not to travel with too large a quantity of any given prescription drug (although, in the event that a pharmacy is not open when you need it, bring along several extra doses) and to have the prescription on hand in case any question arises either abroad or when re-entering the US.

Any sculpture that is part of an architectural structure, any authentic archaeological find, or other artifacts may not be exported from France without the permission of Safico (Service for Financial and Commercial Authorization); for information on items that might fall into this category, contact Safico (42 Rue de Clichy, Paris 75436; phone: 42-81-91-44) or the French customs information center in Paris (phone: 40-24-99-00). If you do not obtain prior permission of the proper regulatory agencies, such items will be confiscated at the border, and you will run the risk of being fined or imprisoned.

Tourists have long been forbidden to bring into the US foreign-made, US-trade-marked articles purchased abroad (if the trademark is recorded with customs) without written permission. It's now permissible to enter with one such item in your possession as long as it's for personal use.

The US Customs Service implements the rigorous Department of Agriculture regulations concerning the importation of vegetable matter, seeds, bulbs, and the like. Living vegetable matter may not be imported without a permit, and everything must be inspected, permit or not. Approved items (which do not require a permit) include dried bamboo and woven items made of straw; beads made of most seeds (but not jequirity beans — the poisonous scarlet and black seed of the rosary pea); cones of pine and other trees; roasted coffee beans; most flower bulbs; flowers (without roots); dried or canned fruits, jellies, or jams; polished rice, dried beans and teas; herb plants (not witchweed); nuts (but not acorns, chestnuts, or nuts with outer husks); dried lichens, mushrooms, truffles, shamrocks, and seaweed; and most dried spices.

Other processed foods and baked goods usually are okay. Regulations on meat products generally depend on the country of origin and manner of processing. As a rule, commercially canned meat, hermetically sealed and cooked in the can so that it can be stored without refrigeration, is permitted, but not all canned meat fulfills this requirement. Be careful when buying European-made pâté, for instance. Goose liver pâté in itself is acceptable, but the pork fat that often is part of it, either as an ingredient or a rind, may not be. Even canned pâtés may not be admitted for this reason. (The imported ones you see in US stores have been prepared and packaged according to US regulations.) So before stocking up on a newfound favorite, it pays to check in advance — otherwise you might have to leave it behind.

The US Customs Service also enforces federal laws that prohibit the entry of articles made from the furs or hides of animals on the endangered species list. Beware of shoes, bags, and belts made of crocodile and certain kinds of lizard, and anything made from tortoiseshell; this also applies to preserved crocodiles, lizards, and turtles sometimes sold in gift shops. And if you're shopping for big-ticket items, beware of fur coats made from the skins of spotted cats. They are sold in Europe, but they will be confiscated upon your return to the US, and there will be no refund. For information about other animals on the endangered species list, contact the Department of the Interior, US Fish and Wildlife Service (Publications Unit, 4401 N. Fairfax Dr., Room 130, Arlington, VA 22203; phone: 703-358-1711), and ask for the free publication *Facts About Federal Wildlife Laws.*

Also note that some foreign governments prohibit the export of items made from certain species of wildlife, and the US honors any such restrictions. Before you go shopping in any foreign country, check with the US Department of Agriculture (G110 Federal Bldg., Hyattsville, MD 20782; phone: 301-436-8413) and find out what items are prohibited by the country you will be visiting.

The US Customs Service publishes a series of free pamphlets with customs information. It includes *Know Before You Go,* a basic discussion of customs requirements pertaining to all travelers; *Buyer Beware, International Mail Imports; Travelers' Tips on Bringing Food, Plant, and Animal Products into the United States; Importing a Car; GSP and the Traveler; Pocket Hints; Currency Reporting; Pets, Wildlife, US Customs; Customs Hints for Visitors (Nonresidents);* and *Trademark Information for Travelers.* For the entire series or individual pamphlets, write to the US Customs Service (PO Box 7407, Washington, DC 20044) or contact any of the seven regional offices — in Boston, Chicago, Houston, Long Beach (California), Miami, New Orleans, and New York. The US Customs Service has a tape-recorded message whereby callers using touch-tone phones can get more information on various topics; the number is 202-566-8195. These pamphlets provide great briefing material, but if you still have questions when you're in Europe, contact the nearest US consulate.

Sources and Resources

Tourist Information Offices

 North American branches of the French Government Tourist Office generally are the best sources of travel information, and most of their many, varied publications are free for the asking. For the best results, request general information on specific provinces or cities, as well as publications relating to your particular areas of interest: accommodations, restaurants, special events, sports, guided tours, and facilities for specific sports. There is no need to send a self-addressed, stamped envelope with your request, unless specified. Following are the tourist information offices located in the US and Canada:

Chicago: 645 N. Michigan Ave., Suite 630, Chicago, IL 60611-2836 (phone: 312-337-6301).

Dallas: 2305 Cedar Springs Rd., Suite 205, Dallas, TX 75201 (phone: 214-720-4010).

Los Angeles: 9454 Wilshire Blvd., Suite 303, Beverly Hills, CA 90212-2967 (phone: 213-271-6665).

New York City: 610 Fifth Ave., New York, NY 10020-2452 (requests by mail only); walk-in office on street level: 628 Fifth Ave., New York, NY 10020 (phone: 212-757-1125).

The French Embassy and Consulates in the US

The French government maintains an embassy and a number of consulates in the US. One of their primary functions is to provide visas for certain resident aliens (depending on their country of origin) and for Americans planning to visit for longer than 6 months, or to study, reside, or work in France. Consulates also are empowered to sign official documents and to notarize copies or translations of US documents, which may be necessary for those papers to be considered legal abroad.

The French Embassy is located at 4101 Reservoir Rd. NW, Washington, DC 20007-2176 (phone: 202-944-6000). Listed below are the French consulates in the US. In general, these offices are open 9 AM to 1 PM, Mondays through Fridays — call ahead to be sure.

French Consulates in the US

Boston: *For visa applications:* 20 Park Plaza (in the Statler Office Bldg.), Suite 1123, Boston, MA 02116 (phone: 617-451-6755/6). *All other business:* 3 Commonwealth Ave., Boston, MA 02116 (phone: 617-266-9413).

Chicago: Olympia Center, 737 N. Michigan Ave., Suite 2020, Chicago, IL 60611 (phone: 312-787-5359, 312-787-5360, or 312-787-5361; recorded visa information: 312-787-7889).

Houston: 2727 Allen Pkwy., Suite 976, Houston, TX 77019 (phone: 713-528-2181).
Los Angeles: 10990 Wilshire Blvd., Suite 300, Los Angeles, CA 90024 (phone: 213-479-4426).
Miami: 1 Biscayne Tower, Suite 1710, 2 S. Biscayne Blvd., Miami, FL 33131 (phone: 305-372-9798).
New Orleans: 3305 St. Charles Ave., New Orleans, LA 70115 (phone: 504-897-6381/2).
New York City: *Main office and to apply by mail for a visa:* 934 Fifth Ave., New York, NY 10021 (phone: 212-606-3688; recorded visa information: 212-606-3680).
San Francisco: 540 Bush St., San Francisco, CA 94108 (phone: 415-397-4330).

Theater and Special Event Tickets

 As you read this book, you will learn about events that spark your interest — everything from music festivals and special theater seasons to sporting championships — along with telephone numbers and addresses to which to write for descriptive brochures, reservations, or tickets. The French Government Tourist Office can supply information on these and other special events and festivals that take place in Paris and the rest of France, though they cannot in all cases provide the actual program or detailed information on ticket prices.

Since many of these occasions often are fully booked well in advance, think about having your reservation in hand before you go. In some cases, tickets may be reserved over the phone and charged to a credit card, or you can send an international money order or foreign draft. If you do write, remember that any request from the US should be accompanied by an International Reply Coupon to ensure a response (send two of them for an airmail response). These international coupons, money orders, and drafts are available at US post offices.

For further information, write for the *European Travel Commission*'s extensive list of events scheduled for the entire year for its 24 member countries (including France). For a free copy, send a self-addressed, stamped, business-size (4 x 9½) envelope to "European Events," *European Travel Commission,* PO Box 1754, New York, NY 10185.

Books, Newspapers, Magazines, and Newsletters

BOOKS: Throughout GETTING READY TO GO, numerous books and brochures have been recommended as good sources of further information on a variety of topics.

Suggested Reading – The list below is made up of books we have seen and think worthwhile; it is by no means complete — but meant merely to start you on your way. These titles include some informative guides to special interests, solid fictional tales, and books that call your attention to things you might not notice otherwise.

Travel
Birnbaum's France 1992, edited by Stephen Birnbaum and Alexandra Mayes Birnbaum (HarperCollins; $17).
French Country Welcome: Bed & Breakfast Guide, Official Guidebook 1991 Edition (Fédération Nationale des Gîtes de France; $21.50).
A Little Tour in France by Henry James (Weidenfeld & Nicolson; $24.95).

Fiction

A Day in the Country and Other Stories by Guy de Maupassant (Oxford University Press; $4.95).

Don Juan and Other Plays by Molière (Oxford University Press; $3.95).

Les Misérables by Victor Hugo (Fawcett; $3.95).

The Murders in the Rue Morgue by Edgar Allan Poe (available in various paperback collections of Poe stories).

Remembrance of Things Past by Marcel Proust (Random House; $52.85).

A Tale of Two Cities by Charles Dickens (Random House; $7.95).

The Three Musketeers by Alexandre Dumas (Penguin; $5.95)

History

The Days of the French Revolution by Christopher Hibbert (Morrow Quill Paperbacks; $12.95).

France, 1814–1940 by J. P. Bury (Routledge, Chapman, & Hall; $15.95).

France: The Tragic Years by Sisley Huddleston (Devin; $9.95).

France under the German Occupation, 1940–1944: An Annotated Bibliography by Donna Evleth (Greenwood Publishing Group; $45).

A Short History of France from Early Times to 1972 by J. H. Jackson (Cambridge University Press; $10.95).

A Traveller's History of France by Robert Cole (Interlink Publishing Group; $10.95).

The United States & the Making of Postwar France, 1945–1954 by Irwin M. Hall (Cambridge University Press; $47.50).

Culture

Between Meals: An Appetite for Paris by A. J. Liebling (North Point Press; $10.95).

France by Donna Bailey & Anna Sproule (Steck-Vaughn Co.; $13.28).

The Paris Edition 1927–1934 by Waverly Root (North Point Press; $9.95).

Food & Wine

Food Lover's Guide to Paris by Patricia Wells (Workman Press; $12.95).

The Food of France by Waverly Root (Random House; $10.95).

France: The Beautiful Cookbook by Elisabeth Scotto, Marianne Comolli, and Michele Carles (Collin Publishing; $39.95).

Lichine's Guide to Wines by Alexis Lichine (Random House; $18.95).

Menu French: The A to Z of French Food edited by G. de Temmerman and D. Chédorge (Editions Scribo; $21).

Michelin Green Guide to Paris (Michelin; $19.95).

Michelin Red Guide to France (Michelin; $19.95).

Autobiography and Biography

The French Revolution and the Tragedy of Marie Antoinette by Edmund Burke (Foundation for Classical Reprints; $287).

The Last Days of Marie Antoinette: An Historical Sketch by Ronald Charles Sutherland Gower (AMS Press; $22.50).

Napoleon by Steven Englund (Lyceum; $8.95).

Napoleon Bonaparte by J. M. Thompson (Basil Blackwell; $29.95).

Napoleon's Memoirs translated by Somerset DeChair (Dunfour; $18.95).

Art

Art & Architecture in France 1500–1700 by Anthony Blunt (Penguin; $21.95).

Impressionism by Phoebe Pool (Thames-Hudson; $14.95).

Lives of the Artists by Giorgio Vasari (Penguin Classics; published in two volumes, $5.95 each).

The Story of Art by E. H. Gombrich (Prentice Hall; $36.67).

A source of cultural information is *Do's and Taboos Around the World,* compiled by the Parker Pen Company and edited by Roger E. Axtell. It focuses on protocol, customs, etiquette, hand gestures and body language, gift giving, the dangers of using US jargon, and so on, and can be fun to read even if you're not going anyplace. It's available for $10.95 in bookstores or through John Wiley & Sons, 1 Wiley Dr., Somerset, NJ 08875 (phone: 908-469-4400).

Newspapers and Magazines: A subscription to the *International Herald Tribune* is a good idea for dedicated travelers. This English-language newspaper is written and edited mostly in Paris and is *the* newspaper read most regularly and avidly by Americans abroad to keep up with world news, US news, sports, the stock market (US and foreign), fluctuations in the exchange rate, and an assortment of help-wanted ads, real estate listings, and personals, global in scope. Published 6 days a week (no Sunday paper), it is available at newsstands throughout the US and in cities worldwide. It can be found on most newsstands in France, and larger hotels usually have copies in the lobby for guests—if you don't see a copy, ask the hotel concierge if it is available. A 1-year subscription in the US costs $349. To subscribe, write or call the Subscription Manager, *International Herald Tribune,* 850 Third Ave., 10th Floor, New York, NY 10022 (phone: 800-882-2884 or 212-752-3890).

Among the major US publications that can be bought (generally a day or two after distribution in the US) in many of the larger cities, such as Paris, at hotels, airports, and newsstands, are the *The New York Times, USA Today,* the *Wall Street Journal,* and the *Washington Post.* As with other imports, expect these and other US publications to cost considerably more in France than in the US.

Newsletters: Throughout GETTING READY TO GO we have mentioned specific newsletters that our readers may be interested in consulting for further information. One of the very best sources of detailed travel information is *Consumer Reports Travel Letter.* Published monthly by Consumers Union (PO Box 53629, Boulder, CO 80322-3629; phone: 800-999-7959), it offers comprehensive coverage of the travel scene on a wide variety of fronts. A year's subscription costs $37; 2 years, $57.

In addition, the following travel newsletters provide useful up-to-date information on travel services and bargains:

Entree (PO Box 5148, Santa Barbara, CA 93150; phone: 805-969-5848). This newsletter caters to a sophisticated, discriminating traveler with the means to explore the places mentioned. Subscribers have access to a 24-hour hotline providing information on restaurants and accommodations around the world. Monthly; a year's subscription costs $59.

Travel Smart (Communications House, 40 Beechdale Rd., Dobbs Ferry, NY 10522; phone: 914-693-8300 in New York; 800-327-3633 elsewhere in the US). This monthly covers a wide variety of trips and travel discounts. A year's subscription costs $37.

■**Computer Services:** Anyone who owns a personal computer and a modem can subscribe to a database service providing everything from airline schedules and fares to restaurant listings. Two such services of particular use to travelers are *CompuServe* (5000 Arlington Center Blvd., Columbus, OH 43220; phone: 800-848-8199 or 614-457-8600; $39.95 to join, plus usage fees of $6 to $12.50 per hour) and *Prodigy Services* (445 Hamilton Ave., White Plains, NY 10601; phone: 800-822-6922 or 914-993-8000; $12.95 per month's subscription, plus variable usage fees). Before using any computer bulletin-board services, be sure to take precautions to prevent downloading of a computer "virus." First install one of the programs designed to screen out such nuisances.

Weights and Measures

 When traveling in France, you'll find that just about every quantity, whether it is length, weight, or capacity, will be expressed in unfamiliar terms. In fact, this is true for travel almost everywhere in the world, since the US is one of the last countries to make its way to the metric system. Your trip to Paris may serve to familiarize you with what one day may be the weights and measures at your grocery store.

There are some specific things to keep in mind during your trip. Fruits and vegetables at a market generally are recorded in kilos (kilograms), as are your luggage at the airport and your body weight. (This latter is particularly pleasing to people of significant size, who, instead of weighing 220 pounds, hit the scales at a mere 100 kilos.) A kilo equals 2.2 pounds and 1 pound is .45 kilo. Body temperature usually is measured in degrees centigrade or Celsius rather than on the Fahrenheit scale, so that a normal body temperature is 37C, not 98.6F, and freezing is 0 degrees C rather than 32F.

Gasoline is sold by the liter (approximately 3.8 liters to 1 gallon). Tire pressure gauges and other equipment measure in kilograms per square centimeter rather than pounds per square inch. Highway signs are written in kilometers rather than miles (1 mile equals 1.6 kilometers; 1 kilometer equals .62 mile). And speed limits are in kilometers per hour, so think twice before hitting the gas when you see a speed limit of 100. That means 62 miles per hour.

The tables and conversion factors on the following page should give you all the information you will need to understand any transaction, road sign, or map you encounter during your travels.

APPROXIMATE EQUIVALENTS		
Metric Unit	**Abbreviation**	**US Equivalent**
LENGTH		
meter	m	39.37 inches
kilometer	km	.62 mile
millimeter	mm	.04 inch
CAPACITY		
liter	l	1.057 quarts
WEIGHT		
gram	g	.035 ounce
kilogram	kg	2.2 pounds
metric ton	MT	1.1 ton
ENERGY		
kilowatt	kw	1.34 horsepower

CONVERSION TABLES
METRIC TO US MEASUREMENTS

Multiply:	by:	to convert to:
LENGTH		
millimeters	.04	inches
meters	3.3	feet
meters	1.1	yards
kilometers	.6	miles
CAPACITY		
liters	2.11	pints (liquid)
liters	1.06	quarts (liquid)
liters	.26	gallons (liquid)
WEIGHT		
grams	.04	ounces (avoir.)
kilograms	2.2	pounds (avoir.)

US TO METRIC MEASUREMENTS

LENGTH		
inches	25.	millimeters
feet	.3	meters
yards	.9	meters
miles	1.6	kilometers
CAPACITY		
pints	.47	liters
quarts	.95	liters
gallons	3.8	liters
WEIGHT		
ounces	28.	grams
pounds	.45	kilograms

TEMPERATURE

$$°F = (°C \times 9/5) + 32 \qquad °C = (°F - 32) \times 5/9$$

USEFUL WORDS
AND PHRASES

Useful Words and Phrases

 The French as a nation have a reputation for being snobbish and brusque to tourists, and, unfortunately, many Americans have allowed this stereotype to dissuade them from visiting France. The more experienced traveler, however, knows that on an individual basis, the French people are usually cordial and helpful, especially if you speak a few words of their language. Don't be afraid of misplaced accents or misconjugated verbs — in most cases you will be understood (and possibly corrected) and then advised on the menu or pointed in the right direction. Below is a basic guide to pronunciation, as well as a selection of commonly used words and phrases to speed you on your way.

French words are stressed on the vowel preceding the last consonant in the word, except that a final accented *e* (*é*) is stressed. Final consonants are pronounced only if they precede words beginning with vowels. Vowels preceding nasals (*m, n*) are nasalized (i.e., pronounced with emission of air through the nose) and the *m* or *n* is not pronounced.

French consonants are pronounced almost as in English, with these exceptions:

ch is pronounced like *sh* in *push*
c before *e, i,* or *y* is pronounced *s;* otherwise as *k*
s is pronounced as *z* between vowels
gn is pronounced like *ny* in canyon
g before *e, i,* or *y* is pronounced like *si* in vision; otherwise like *g* in *go*
j is pronounced like *si* in vision
ll following *i* is pronounced like *y* in year
qu is pronounced as *k* (not *kw*)
h is silent

French vowels are different from those in English, but usually can be pronounced intelligibly following these rules:

Final unaccented *e* is silent; it signals that a preceding consonant is pronounced.
é is pronounced like the *a* in *late*
e is pronounced as in *met*
i is pronounced as in *machine*
o is pronounced like *ou* in *ought*
u is pronounced like *i* in *bit* but with the lips rounded
an and *en* are pronounced like the *a* in *father* but nasalized
in is pronounced with the vowel of *met* but nasalized
ai is pronounced like *e* in *met*
au is pronounced like *o* in *cold*
oi and *oy* are pronounced *wa*
ou is pronounced as in *youth*
eu is pronounced like the *e* of *men* but with the lips rounded
Final *er* is pronounced like the *ay* of *delay*

Greetings and Everyday Expressions

Good morning! (Hello!)	*Bonjour!*
Good afternoon, good evening!	*Bonsoir!*
How are you?	*Comment allez-vous?*
Pleased to meet you!	*Enchanté!*
Good-bye!	*Au revoir!*
See you soon!	*A bientôt!*
Good night!	*Bonne nuit!*
Yes!	*Oui!*
No!	*Non!*
Please!	*S'il vous plaît!*
Thank you!	*Merci!*
You're welcome!	*De rien!*
Excuse me!	*Excusez-moi* or *pardonnez-moi!*
It doesn't matter.	*Ca m'est égal.*
I don't speak French.	*Je ne parle pas français.*
Do you speak English?	*Parlez-vous anglais?*
Please repeat.	*Répétez, s'il vous plaît.*
I don't understand.	*Je ne comprends pas.*
Do you understand?	*Vous comprenez?*
My name is . . .	*Je m'appelle . . .*
What is your name?	*Comment vous appelez-vous?*
miss	*mademoiselle*
madame	*madame*
mister/sir	*monsieur*
open	*ouvert*
closed	*fermé*
entrance	*l'entrée*
exit	*la sortie*
push	*poussez*
pull	*tirez*
today	*aujourd'hui*
tomorrow	*demain*
yesterday	*hier*
Help!	*Au secours!*
ambulance	*l'ambulance*
Get a doctor!	*Appelez le médecin!*

Checking In

I have (don't have) a reservation.	*J'ai une (Je n'ai pas de) réservation.*
I would like . . .	*Je voudrais . . .*
a single room	*une chambre pour une personne*
a double room	*une chambre pour deux*
a quiet room	*une chambre tranquille*
with bath	*avec salle de bains*
with shower	*avec douche*
with a view of the Seine	*avec une vue sur la Seine*
with air conditioning	*une chambre climatisée*
with balcony	*avec balcon*

overnight only	*pour une nuit seulement*
a few days	*quelques jours*
a week (at least)	*une semaine (au moins)*
with full board	*avec pension complète*
with half board	*avec demi-pension*
Does that price include breakfast?	*Est-ce que le petit dejeuner est inclus?*
Are taxes included?	*Est-ce que les taxes sont compris?*
Do you accept traveler's checks?	*Acceptez-vous les chèques de voyage?*
Do you accept credit cards?	*Acceptez-vous les cartes de crédit?*

Eating Out

ashtray	*un cendrier*
bottle	*une bouteille*
(extra) chair	*une chaise (en sus)*
cup	*une tasse*
fork	*une fourchette*
knife	*un couteau*
spoon	*une cuillère*
napkin	*une serviette*
plate	*une assiette*
table	*une table*

beer	*bière*
coffee	*café*
black coffee	*café noir*
coffee with milk	*café au lait*
cream	*crème*
fruit juice	*jus de fruit*
lemonade	*citron pressé*
milk	*lait*
mineral water (non-carbonated)	*l'eau minérale*
mineral water (carbonated)	*l'eau gazeuse*
orangeade	*orange pressé*
port	*vin de porto*
sherry	*vin de Xérès*
red wine	*vin rouge*
white wine	*vin blanc*
rosé	*rosé*
tea	*thé*
water	*eau*

cold	*froid*
hot	*chaud*
sweet	*doux*
(very) dry	*(très) sec*

bacon	*bacon*
bread	*pain*
butter	*beurre*

eggs	*oeufs*
soft boiled	*à la coque*
hard boiled	*oeuf dur*
fried	*sur le plat*
scrambled	*brouillé*
poached	*poché*
ham	*jambon*
honey	*miel*
sugar	*sucre*
jam	*confiture*
juice	*jus*
orange	*jus d'orange*
tomato	*jus de tomate*
omelette	*omelette*
pepper	*poivre*
salt	*sel*
Waiter!	*Garçon!*
Waitress!	*Mademoiselle!*
I would like	*Je voudrais*
a glass of	*un verre de*
a bottle of	*une bouteille de*
a half bottle of	*une demie-bouteille*
a liter of	*un litre de*
a carafe of	*une carafe de*
The check, please.	*L'addition, s'il vous plaît.*
Is the service charge included?	*Le service, est-il compris?*
I think there is a mistake in the bill.	*Je crois qu'il y a une erreur dans l'addition.*

Shopping

bakery	*boulangerie*
bookstore	*librairie*
butcher store	*boucherie*
camera shop	*magasin de photographie*
clothing store	*magasin de vêtements*
delicatessen	*charcuterie*
department store	*grand magasin*
drugstore (for medicine)	*pharmacie*
grocery	*épicerie*
jewelry store	*bijouterie*
newsstand	*kiosque à journaux*
notions (sewing supplies) shop	*mercerie*
pastry shop	*pâtisserie*
perfume (and cosmetics) store	*parfumerie*
pharmacy/drugstore	*pharmacie*
shoestore	*magasin de chaussures*

supermarket	*supermarché*
tobacconist	*bureau de tabac*
inexpensive	*bon marché*
expensive	*cher*
large	*grand*
larger	*plus grand*
too large	*trop grand*
small	*petit*
smaller	*plus petit*
too small	*trop petit*
long	*long*
short	*court*
old	*vieux*
new	*nouveau*
used	*d'occasion*
handmade	*fabriqué à la main*
Is it machine washable?	*Est-ce que c'est lavable à la machine?*
How much does this cost?	*Quel est le prix?/Combien?*
What is it made of?	*De quoi est-il fait?*
camel's hair	*poil de chameau*
cotton	*coton*
corduroy	*velours côtelé*
filigree	*filigrane*
lace	*dentelle*
leather	*cuir*
linen	*lin*
silk	*soie*
suede	*suède*
synthetic	*synthétique*
wool	*laine*
brass	*cuivre jaune*
copper	*cuivre*
gold (plated)	*or (plaqué)*
silver (plated)	*argent (plaqué)*
wood	*bois*
May I have a sales tax rebate form?	*Puis-je avoir la forme pour la détaxe?*
May I pay with this credit card?	*Puis-je payer par cette carte de crédit?*
May I pay with a traveler's check?	*Puis-je payer par chèques de voyage?*

Getting around

north	*le nord*
south	*le sud*

east	*l'est*
west	*l'ouest*
right	*droite*
left	*gauche*
Go straight ahead	*tout droit*
far	*loin*
near	*proche*
airport	*l'aéroport*
bus stop	*l'arrêt de bus*
gas station	*station service*
train station	*la gare*
subway	*le métro*
map	*carte*
one-way ticket	*aller simple*
round-trip ticket	*un billet aller et retour*
gate	*porte*
track	*voie*
in first class	*en première*
in second class	*en deuxième*
no smoking	*défense de fumer*
Does this subway/bus go to . . . ?	*Est-ce que ce métro/bus va à . . . ?*
What time does it leave?	*A quelle heure part-il?*
gas	*essence*
regular (leaded)	*ordinaire*
super (leaded)	*super*
unleaded	*sans plomb*
diesel	*diesel*
Fill it up, please.	*De plein, s'il vous plaît.*
the tires	*pneus*
the oil	*huile*
Danger	*Danger*
Caution	*Attention*
Detour	*Détour*
Dead End	*Cul-de-sac*
Do Not Enter	*Défense d'entrer*
No Parking	*Défense de garer*
No Passing	*Défense de dépasser*
No U-turn	*Défense de faire demi-tour*
One way	*Sens unique*
Pay toll	*Péage*
Pedestrian Zone	*Zone piétone*
Reduce Speed	*Ralentissez*
Steep Incline	*Côte à forte inclination*

Stop	*Stop; Arrêt*
Use Headlights	*Allumez les phares*
Yield	*Cédez*
Where is the . . . ?	*Où se trouve . . . ?*
How many kilometers are we from . . . ?	*A combien de kilomètres sommes nous de . . . ?*

Personal Items and Services

aspirin	*aspirine*
Band-Aids	*sparadrap*
barbershop	*coiffeur pour hommes*
bath	*bain*
bathroom	*salle de bain*
beauty shop	*salon de coiffeur*
condom	*préservatif*
dentist	*dentiste*
disposable diapers	*couches*
dry cleaner	*nettoyage à sec*
hairdresser	*coiffeur pour dames*
laundromat	*laundrette* or *blanchisserie automatique*
post office	*bureau de poste*
postage stamps (airmail)	*timbres (par avion)*
razor	*rasoir*
sanitary napkins	*serviettes hygiéniques*
shampoo	*shampooing*
shaving cream	*crème à raser*
shower	*douche*
soap	*savon*
tampons	*tampons*
tissues	*tissus*
toilet	*toilette* or *WC*
toilet paper	*papier hygiénique*
toothbrush	*brosse à dents*
toothpaste	*pâte dentifrice*

| Where is the men's/ladies' room? | *Où est la toilette?* |

Days of the Week

Monday	*lundi*
Tuesday	*mardi*
Wednesday	*mercredi*
Thursday	*jeudi*
Friday	*vendredi*
Saturday	*samedi*
Sunday	*dimanche*

Months

January	*janvier*
February	*février*
March	*mars*
April	*avril*

May	*mai*
June	*juin*
July	*juillet*
August	*août*
September	*septembre*
October	*octobre*
November	*novembre*
December	*décembre*

Numbers

zero	*zéro*
one	*un*
two	*deux*
three	*trois*
four	*quatre*
five	*cinq*
six	*six*
seven	*sept*
eight	*huit*
nine	*neuf*
ten	*dix*
eleven	*onze*
twelve	*douze*
thirteen	*treize*
fourteen	*quatorze*
fifteen	*quinze*
sixteen	*seize*
seventeen	*dix-sept*
eighteen	*dix-huit*
nineteen	*dix-neuf*
twenty	*vingt*
twenty-one	*vingt-et-un*
thirty	*trente*
forty	*quarante*
fifty	*cinquante*
sixty	*soixante*
seventy	*soixante-dix*
eighty	*quatre-vingts*
ninety	*quatre-vingt-dix*
one hundred	*cent*

Colors

black	*noir*
blue	*bleu*
brown	*brun*
gray	*gris*
green	*vert*
orange	*orange*
pink	*rose*
purple	*violet*
red	*rouge*

yellow	*jaune*
white	*blanc*

Writing Reservations Letters

Restaurant/Hotel Name
Street Address
Postal Code, City
France

Dear Sir:

    I would like to reserve a table for (number of) persons for lunch/dinner on (day and month), 199?, at (hour) o'clock.

or

    I would like to reserve a room for (number of) people for (number of) nights.

    Would you be so kind as to confirm the reservation as soon as possible?

    I am very much looking forward to meeting you. (The French usually include a pleasantry such as this.)

    With my thanks,
(Signature, followed by your typed name and address)

Monsieur:

    Je voudrais réserver une table pour (number) personnes pour le déjeuner/dîner du (day and month) 199?, à (time using the 24-hour clock) heures.

or

    Je voudrais réserver une chambre à (number) personne(s) pour (number) nuits.

    Auriez-vous la bonté de bien vouloir me confirmer cette réservation dès que possible?

    J'attends avec impatience la chance de faire votre connaissance.

    Avec tous remerciements,

THE CITY

PARIS

It was Victor Hugo, the great French poet and novelist, who captured the true spirit of his native city when he called it "the heir of Rome, the mundane pilgrim's home away from home." If Rome, for all its earthly exuberance, never lets a visitor forget that it is the spiritual home of the West, Paris — with its supreme joie de vivre and its passion for eating, drinking, and dressing well — belongs unabashedly to the material world.

Like a magnet, Paris always has attracted visitors and exiles from all corners of the earth. At the same time, it remains not so much an international city as a very French one, and a provincial one at that. Paris has its own argot, and each neighborhood retains its peculiar character, so that the great capital is still very much a city of 20 villages.

But parochialism aside — and forgetting about the consummate haughtiness of Parisians (someone once remarked that Parisians don't even like themselves) — the main attraction of the City of Light is its beauty. When you speak of the ultimate European city, it must be Paris, if only for the view from the Place de la Concorde or the Tuileries up the Champs-Elysées toward the Arc de Triomphe, or similarly striking sights beside the Seine. Here is the fashion capital of the world and the center of gastronomic invention and execution. Here the men all seem to swagger with the insouciance of privilege, and even the humblest shopgirl dresses with the care of a haute couture mannequin. Paris is the reason "foreign" means "French" to so many travelers.

Paris is in the north-central part of France, in the rich agricultural area of the Seine River Valley. With a population of over 2 million people, it is France's largest city, an industrial and commercial center, and an important river port. Roughly elliptical in shape, the city has more than doubled in size in the last century. Its limits now are the ring of mid-19th-century fortifications that once were well beyond its boundaries. At its western edge is the vast Bois de Boulogne and to the east the Bois de Vincennes — two enormous parks. Curving through Paris, the Seine divides the city into its northern Right Bank (La Rive Droite) and southern Left Bank (La Rive Gauche). The Right Bank extends from the Bois de Boulogne on the far west, through Place Charles-de-Gaulle (l'Etoile), which surrounds the Arc de Triomphe, and farther east to the Tuileries Gardens and the fabulous *Louvre*. North of the *Louvre* is the area of the Grands Boulevards, centers of business and fashion; farther north is the district of Montmartre, built on a hill and crowned by the domed Basilica of Sacré-Coeur, an area that has attracted great artists (and many of markedly less greatness) since the days of Monet and Renoir.

The Left Bank sweeps from the Eiffel Tower on the west through the Latin Quarter, with its university and bohemian and intellectual community. South of the Latin Quarter is Montparnasse, once inhabited jointly by artists and intellectuals and laborers, now a large urban renewal project that includes a suburban-style shopping center around the Tour Montparnasse.

In the middle of the Seine are two islands, the Ile de la Cité and the Ile St.-Louis, the oldest parts of Paris. It was on the Ile de la Cité (in the 3rd century BC) that Celtic fishermen known as Parisii first built a settlement they named Lutetia, "place surrounded by water." Caesar conquered the city for Rome in 52 BC, and in about AD 300, Paris was invaded by Germanic tribes, the strongest of which were the Franks. In 451, when Attila the Hun threatened to overrun Paris, a holy woman named Geneviève promised to defend the city by praying. She succeeded — the enemy decided to spare the capital — and Geneviève became the patron saint of Paris. Clovis I, the first Christian King of the Franks, made Paris his capital in the 6th century. Relentless Norman sieges, famine, and plague curtailed the city's development, but at the end of the 10th century peace and prosperity came with the triumph of Hugh Capet over the Carolingians. Capet ascended the throne, the first of a long line of Capetian kings, and Paris became the "central jewel of the French crown," a great cultural center and seat of learning.

The Capetian monarchs contributed much to the growth of the city over the next few centuries. A defensive wall was begun in 1180 by Philip Augustus to protect the expanding Right Bank business and trading center, as well as the intellectual quarter around the newly formed university on the Left Bank. He then built a new royal palace, the *Louvre,* just outside these ramparts, but he never lived there. Medieval Paris was a splendid city, a leader in the arts and in the intellectual life of Europe. The Sorbonne attracted such outstanding scholars as Alexander of Hales, Giovanni di Fidanza (St. Bonaventure), Albertus Magnus, and Thomas Aquinas.

The Ile de la Cité remained a warren of narrow streets and wood and plaster houses, but the banks of the Seine continued to be built up in both directions. Renaissance kings, patrons of the arts, added their own architectural and aesthetic embellishments to the flourishing city. Major streets were laid out; some of Paris's most charming squares were constructed; the Pont-Neuf, the first stone bridge spanning the Seine, was completed; and Lenôtre, the royal gardener, introduced proportion, harmony, and beauty with his extraordinary Tuileries.

Louis XIV, who was responsible for many of the most notable Parisian landmarks, including Les Invalides, moved the court to Versailles in the late 17th century. Paris nevertheless continued to blossom, and it was under the Sun King's rule that France and Paris first won international prestige. Visitors were drawn to the city, luxury trades were begun, and the Panthéon, Champ-de-Mars parade ground, and Ecole Militaire were built. In 1785, at age 16, Napoleon Bonaparte graduated from this military school with the notation in his report: "Will go far if circumstances permit!"

French history reflects the conflict between the two extremes of the French character, both equally strong: a tradition of aristocracy and a penchant for revolution. To the French aristocracy we owe magnificent palaces like the *Louvre,* the Luxembourg Palace, and Versailles, with their formal gardens. At the same time, the people of Paris have always been noisily rebellious and independent: from 1358, when the mob rebelled against the dauphin, to the

Fronde in 1648–49, the great French Revolution of 1789, the 1830 and 1848 revolutions that reverberated throughout Europe, the Paris Commune of 1870–71, and finally the student rebellion of 1968, which nearly overthrew the Fifth Republic. The most profound one of all was the French Revolution at the close of the 18th century, the bicentennial of which was celebrated in grand style in 1989.

The excesses of the French court, the consummate luxury of the Versailles of Louis XIV, cost the French people dearly in taxes and oppression. The Parisians, fiercely independent, forced the French king to his knees with their dramatic storming of the Bastille in 1789. Inspired by the ideas of the French and English philosophers of the Enlightenment, just like the American founding fathers in 1776, the French subsequently overthrew their monarchy.

During the Revolution, unruly mobs damaged many of the city's buildings, including Ste.-Chapelle and Notre-Dame, which were not restored until the mid-19th century. Napoleon, who came to power in 1799, was too busy being a conqueror to complete all he planned, though he did manage to restore the *Louvre,* construct the Carrousel Arch and Place Vendôme victory column, and begin work on the Arc de Triomphe and the Madeleine. Though something of a tyrant, Napoleon's conquests spread the new ideas of the Revolution — including the Code Napoléon, a system of laws embodying the ideals of "Liberty, Equality, Fraternity" — to places as far away as Canada and Moscow.

Later in the 19th century, Paris was reorganized and modernized by a great urban planner, Baron Haussmann. He instituted the brilliant system of squares as focal points for marvelous, wide boulevards and roads; he planned the Place de l'Opéra, the Bois de Boulogne and Bois de Vincennes, the railway stations, the boulevards, and the system of 20 *arrondissements* (districts) that make up Paris today. He also destroyed most of the center of the old Cité, displacing 25,000 people.

During the peaceful lull between the Franco-Prussian War and World War I, the city of Paris thrived as never before. These were the days of the Belle Epoque, the heyday of *Maxim's,* the *Folies-Bergère,* and the cancan, whose spirit is captured so well in Offenbach's heady music for *Gaieté Parisienne.* Montmartre, immortalized by Toulouse-Lautrec, was so uninhibited that the foreign press dubbed Paris the "City of Sin."

In the 2 decades before World War II, this free-spirited city attracted politically and socially exiled artists by the dozens: Picasso, Hemingway, Fitzgerald, and Gertrude Stein were just a few. Only in Paris could such avant-garde writers as James Joyce and D. H. Lawrence, and later, Henry Miller, find publishers. And Paris, which witnessed the first Impressionist exhibition in 1874 — introducing Monet, Renoir, Pissarro, and Seurat — heard the first performance of Stravinsky's revolutionary "Sacre du Printemps" (Rite of Spring) in 1913, even though the baffled audience jeered loudly.

As the quintessentially beautiful center of intellectual life and home of the arts, Paris can claim to have earned its City of Light title. Even though it, like other modern cities, is troubled by a rise in crime — at *Maxim's,* for instance, a precautionary bulletproof window has been installed — its beauty and libertarian atmosphere remain. Its supreme talent for civilized living has made the city beloved by the French and foreigners alike. After all, these are the people who made food preparation a fine art, and despite the unfortunate presence of fast-food vendors on the Champs-Elysées, the French passion for haute cuisine remains unrivaled. And as the undisputed capital of fashion, male and female, Paris continues to be the best-dressed city in the world, and the Rue du Faubourg-St.-Honoré remains the standard by which all other shopping streets are measured.

However avant-garde in dress, Parisians are a conservative lot when it comes to any changes in the appearance of their beloved city. When the Eiffel Tower was built in 1889, Guy de Maupassant commented, "I spend all my afternoons on the Eiffel Tower; it's the only place in Paris from which you can't see it." So today's Parisians grumble about the ultramodern *Centre Georges-Pompidou,* a focus for every type of modern art: theater, music, dance, circus, painting, sculpture, photography, and film, and about *Le Forum des Halles,* a sunken glass structure filled with boutiques in what was once *Les Halles,* the bawdy produce market. They also don't seem especially thrilled by the I. M. Pei glass pyramids that form the new entrance to the *Louvre.*

Parisians accept innovations reluctantly because they want their city to remain as it has always been. They love their remarkable heritage inordinately, and perhaps it is this love, together with the irrepressible sense of good living, that has made Paris so eternally attractive to others.

PARIS AT-A-GLANCE

SEEING THE CITY: It's impossible to single out just one perfect Paris panorama; they exist in profusion. The most popular is the bird's-eye view from the top of the Eiffel Tower on the Left Bank; there are several places to have snacks and drinks and enjoy a view (on a clear day) of more than 50 miles. (There also are three restaurants where you can enjoy fine dining.) The tower is open daily, 10 AM to 11 PM; admission charge (Champ-de-Mars; phone: 45-55-91-11). From the top of the towers of Notre-Dame, eager spectators enjoy close-ups of the cathedral's Gothic spires and flying buttresses, along with a magnificent view of the Ile de la Cité and the rest of Paris. Start climbing the steps at the foot of the north tower; admission charge (Rue du Cloître Notre-Dame, 4e; phone: 43-25-42-92). On the Right Bank there's a stunning view from the terrace of Sacré-Coeur. The observatory on Tour Montparnasse also offers a striking panorama, as does the landing at the top of the escalator at the *Centre Georges-Pompidou,* and the observation deck of *Samaritaine,* the 10-floor department store at the foot of the Pont-Neuf.

The most satisfying view, if not the highest, is from the top of the Arc de Triomphe. The arch is the center of Place Charles-de-Gaulle, once Place de l'Etoile (Square of the Star), so called because it is the center of a "star" whose radiating points are the 12 broad avenues, including the Champs-Elysées, planned and built by Baron Haussmann in the mid-19th century. Open daily, 10 AM to 5:30 PM; admission charge (phone: 43-80-31-31).

SPECIAL PLACES: Getting around this sprawling metropolis isn't difficult once you understand the layout of the 20 *arrondissements.* We suggest that visitors orient themselves by taking one of the many excellent sightseeing tours offered by *Cityrama* (4 Pl. des Pyramides, 1er; phone: 42-60-30-14) or *Paris Vision* (214 Rue de Rivoli, 1er; phone: 42-60-31-25). Their bubble-top, double-decker buses are equipped with earphones for simultaneous commentary in English and several other languages. Reserve through any travel agent or your hotel's concierge.

Once you have a better idea of the basic layout of the city, buy a copy of *Paris Indispensable* or *Plan de Paris par Arrondissement* at any bookshop or newsstand. These little lifesavers list streets alphabetically and indicate the nearest métro station on individual maps and an overall plan. Now you're ready to set out by foot (the most rewarding) or by métro (the fastest and surest) to discover Paris for yourself.

Street addresses of the places mentioned throughout the chapter are followed by their *arrondissement* number.

LA RIVE DROITE (THE RIGHT BANK)

Arc de Triomphe and Place Charles-de-Gaulle – This monumental arch (165 feet high, 148 feet wide) was built between 1806 and 1836 to commemorate Napoleon's victories. It underwent a major cleanup and restoration for the bicentennial of the French Revolution. Note the frieze and its 6-foot-high figures, the ten impressive sculptures (especially Rude's *La Marseillaise* on the right as you face the Champs-Elysées), and the arches inscribed with the names of Bonaparte's victories, as well as those of Empire heroes. Beneath the arch is the French Tomb of the Unknown Soldier and its Eternal Flame, which is rekindled each day at 6:30 PM. An elevator (or 284 steps) carries visitors to the top for a magnificent view of the city and the 12 avenues radiating from l'Etoile. Admission charge. Pl. Charles-de-Gaulle (phone: 43-80-31-31).

Champs-Elysées – Paris's legendary promenade, the "Elysian Fields," was swampland until 1616. It has come to be synonymous with everything glamorous in the city, though the "Golden Arches" and shlocky shops recently have replaced much of the old glamour (a commission was formed in 1990 to try to restore some of the old elegance). The Champs-Elysées stretches for more than 2 miles between the Place de la Concorde and the Place Charles-de-Gaulle (l'Etoile). The very broad avenue, lined with rows of plane and horse chestnut trees, shops, cafés, and cinemas, is perfect for strolling, window shopping, and people watching.

The area from the Place de la Concorde to the Rond-Point des Champs-Elysées is a charming park, where Parisians often bring their children. On the north side of the gardens is the Palais de l'Elysée, the official home of the President of the French Republic. Ceremonial events, such as the *Bastille Day Parade* (July 14), frequently take place along the Champs-Elysées.

Grand Palais – Off the Champs-Elysées, on opposite sides of Avenue Winston-Churchill, are the elaborate turn-of-the-century *Grand Palais* and *Petit Palais* (Large Palace and Small Palace), built of glass and stone for the *1900 World Exposition.* With its stone columns, mosaic frieze, and flat glass dome, the *Grand Palais* contains a large area devoted to temporary exhibits, as well as the *Palais de la Découverte* (the Paris science museum and the planetarium). Closed Tuesdays; open Wednesdays until 9:45 PM. Av. Franklin-Roosevelt, 8e (phone: 42-89-54-10).

Petit Palais – Built contemporaneously with the *Grand Palais,* it has exhibits of the city's history, as well as a variety of fine and applied arts and special shows. Closed Mondays. Admission charge. Av. Winston-Churchill, 8e (phone: 42-65-12-73).

Place de la Concorde – This square, surely one of the most magnificent in the world, is grandly situated in the midst of equally grand landmarks: the *Louvre* and the Tuileries on one side, the Champs-Elysées and the Arc de Triomphe on another, the Seine and the Napoleonic Palais Bourbon on a third, and the pillared façade of the

Madeleine on the fourth. Designed by Gabriel for Louis XV, the elegant square was where his unfortunate successor, Louis XVI, lost his head to the guillotine, as did Marie-Antoinette, Danton, Robespierre, Charlotte Corday, and others. It was first named for Louis XV, then called Place de la Révolution by the triumphant revolutionaries. Ornamenting the square, the eight colossal statues representing important French provincial capitals were polished and blasted clean for the bicentennial celebration in 1989. The 3,300-year-old, 75-foot-high obelisk was a gift from Egypt in 1829.

Jardin des Tuileries – Carefully laid out in patterned geometric shapes, with clipped shrubbery and formal flower beds, statues, and fountains, this is one of the finest examples of French garden design (in contrast to an informal English garden, exemplified by the Bois de Boulogne). Along the Seine, between the Place de la Concorde and the *Louvre.*

Orangerie – A museum on the edge of the Tuileries gardens, it displays a series of large paintings of water lilies by Monet called the *Nymphéas* and the collection of Jean Walter and Paul Guillaume, with works by Cézanne, Renoir, Matisse, Picasso, and others. Open 10 AM to 5:15 PM; closed Tuesdays. Admission charge. Pl. de la Concorde and Quai des Tuileries, 1er (phone: 42-97-48-16).

Rue de Rivoli – This charming old street has perfume shops, souvenir stores, boutiques, bookstores, cafés, and such hotels as the *Meurice* and the *Inter-Continental* under its 19th-century arcades. The section facing the Tuileries, from the Place de la Concorde to the *Louvre,* is an especially good place to explore on rainy days.

Louvre – Built on the site of a medieval fortress on the banks of the Seine, this palace was the home of the French kings during the 16th and 17th centuries, until Louis XIV moved the court to Versailles in 1682. In 1793 it became a museum, and now is one of the world's greatest art repositories. It's easy to spend a couple of days here, savoring treasures like the *Venus de Milo, Winged Victory,* the *Mona Lisa,* and the French crown jewels — just a few of the 297,000 pieces in six different collections.

Nor is the outside of this huge edifice to be overlooked. Note especially the Cour Carrée (the courtyard of the old *Louvre*), the southwest corner of which, dating from the mid-1550s, is the oldest part of the palace and a beautiful example of the Renaissance style that François I had so eagerly introduced from Italy. Note, too, the Colonnade, which forms the eastern front of the Cour Carrée, facing the Place du Louvre; fully classical in style, it dates from the late 1660s, not too long before the Sun King left for Versailles. Newer wings of the *Louvre* embrace the palace gardens, in the midst of which stands the Arc de Triomphe du Carrousel, erected by Napoleon. From here, the vista across the Tuileries and the Place de la Concorde and on up the Champs-Elysées to the Arc de Triomphe is one of the most beautiful in Paris — which says a lot. The glass pyramids — designed by I. M. Pei and opened in 1989 — sit center stage in the *Louvre's* grand interior courtyard, and the largest of the intrusive trio now is the museum's main entrance. The controversial structure is the first step of a major expansion; when completed (the target date is 1993), the *Louvre's* underground galleries, shops, and exhibit space will connect the North and South wings, increasing museum exhibition space by almost 80%.

Good guided tours in English, covering the highlights of the *Louvre,* are frequently available, although not every day, so be sure to check in advance. Open from 9:45 AM to 6:30 PM; Wednesdays and Mondays from 9:45 AM to 9:45 PM; closed Tuesdays. Admission charge. Pl. du Louvre, 1er (phone: 40-20-51-51 for recorded information in French and English, or 4(20-50-50 for more detailed information).

Place Vendôme – Just north of the Tuileries is an aristocrat of a square, one of the loveliest in Paris, the octagonal Place Vendôme, designed by Mansart in the 17th century. Its arcades contain world-famous jewelers, perfumers, and banks, the *Ritz* hotel, and the Ministry of Justice. The 144-foot column in the center is covered with bronze from the 1,200 cannons captured at Austerlitz by Napoleon in 1805. Just off

Place Vendôme is the famous Rue du Faubourg-St.-Honoré, one of the oldest streets in Paris, which now holds elegant shops selling the world's most expensive made-to-order items. To the north is the Rue de la Paix, noted for its jewelers.

Opéra – Charles Garnier's imposing rococo edifice stands in its own busy square, its façade decorated with sculpture, including a copy of Carpeaux's *The Dance* (the original is now in the *Musée d'Orsay*). The ornate interior has an impressive grand staircase, a beautiful foyer, lavish marble from every quarry in France, and Chagall's controversially decorated dome. Until a few years ago, the opera house could be seen only by attending a performance (held September–June); now, however, visitors may explore its magnificent interior and enjoy its special exhibitions daily from 11 AM to 4:30 PM, except on the days when there are special performances. Pl. de l'Opéra, 9e (phone: 47-42-57-50).

Opéra de La Bastille – In sharp contrast to Garnier's *Opéra* is the curved glass façade of 20th-century architect Carlos Ott's new Paris opera house. Set against the historic landscape of the Bastille quarter, this austere, futuristic structure houses over 30 acres of multipurpose theaters, shops, and urban promenade. Inaugurated for the bicentennial of the revolution on July 14, 1989, the opera house opened in March 1990 with a production of Berlioz's *Les Troyens*. It looks a lot like the prison-fortress that started the French Revolution. Pl. de la Bastille, 11e (phone: 40-01-17-89).

La Madeleine – Starting in 1764, the Church of St. Mary Magdalene was built and razed twice before the present structure was commissioned by Napoleon in 1806 to honor his armies. The church is based on a Greek temple design, with 65-foot-high Corinthian columns supporting the sculptured frieze. From its portals, the view extends down Rue Royale to Place de la Concorde and over to the dome of Les Invalides. Nearby are some of Paris's most tantalizing food shops. Open from 7:30 AM to 7 PM as well as during concerts (held 4 PM Sundays) and other frequent musical events. Pl. de la Madeleine, 8e (phone: 42-65-52-17).

Sacré-Coeur and Montmartre – Built on the highest of Paris's seven hills, the white-domed Basilica of Sacré-Coeur provides an extraordinary view from its steps, especially at dawn or sunset. The area around the church was the artists' quarter of late-19th- and early-20th-century Paris. The more garish aspects of Montmartre's notoriously frivolous 1890s nightlife, particularly the dancers and personalities at the *Moulin Rouge,* were immortalized by the paintings of Henri de Toulouse-Lautrec. And if the streets look familiar, chances are you've seen them in the paintings of Utrillo; they still look the same. The Place du Tertre is still charming, though often filled with tourists and overly eager, mostly undertalented artists. Go early in the day to see it as it was when Braque, Dufy, Modigliani, Picasso, Rousseau, and Utrillo lived here. Montmartre has the last of Paris's vineyards — and still contains old houses, narrow alleys, steep stairways, and carefree cafés enough to provide a full day's entertainment; at night, this is one of the centers of Paris life. Spare yourself most of the climb to Sacré-Coeur by taking the funicular (as we went to press, it was being replaced by a more modern, glass contraption — bringing the *Louvre's* main pyramid to mind) or the Montmartre bus (marked with an icon of Sacré-Coeur on the front instead of the usual number) from Place St.-Pierre. Butte Montmartre, 18e.

Les Halles – Just northeast of the *Louvre,* this 80-acre area, formerly the *Central Market,* "the Belly of Paris," was razed in 1969. Gone are most of the picturesque early-morning fruit-and-vegetable vendors, butchers in blood-spattered aprons, truckers bringing the freshest produce from all over France. Their places have been usurped by trendy shops and galleries of youthful entrepreneurs and artisans, small restaurants with lots of charm, the world's largest subway station, acres of trellised gardens and playgrounds, and *Le Forum des Halles,* a vast complex of boutiques, ranging from the superchic designer ready-to-wear to more ordinary shops, as well as concert space and movie theaters. Touch-sensitive locator devices, which help visitors find products and services, are placed strategically. A few echoes of the earthy past remain, however, and you can still dine at *Au Pied de Cochon, Le Pharamond,* and *L'Escargot Montorgueil,* or have a drink with the few remaining workmen (before noon) at one of the old brasseries.

Le Centre National d'Art et de Culture Georges-Pompidou (Le Centre Georges-Pompidou) – Better known as "the Beaubourg," after the plateau on which it is built, this stark, 6-level creation of steel and glass, with its exterior escalators and blue, white, and red pipes, created a stir the moment its construction began. Outside, a computerized digital clock ticks off the seconds remaining until the 21st century. This wildly popular museum brings together all the contemporary art forms — painting, sculpture, the plastic arts, industrial design, music, literature, cinema, and theater — under one roof, and that roof offers one of the most exciting views of Paris. The old houses and cobbled, tree-shaded streets and squares vie for attention with galleries, boutiques, and the spectacle provided by jugglers, mimes, acrobats, and magicians in the plaza out front. The scene in the courtyard often rivals the exhibits inside. Open weekdays from noon to 10 PM; 10 AM to 10 PM weekends. Closed Tuesdays; no admission charge on Sundays except for special exhibitions. Rue Rambuteau, at the corner of Rue St.-Martin, 4e (phone: 42-77-12-33).

Le Marais – Northeast of the *Louvre,* a marshland until the 16th century, this district became the height of residential fashion during the 17th century. But as the aristocracy moved on, it fell into disrepair. Recently, after a long period of neglect, the Marais has been enjoying a complete face-lift. Spurred on by the opening of the *Picasso Museum* in the Hôtel du Salé, preservationists have lovingly restored more than a hundred of the magnificent old mansions to their former grandeur. They now are museums of exquisite beauty, with muraled walls and ceilings, and their courtyards are the sites of dramatic and musical presentations during the summer *Festival du Marais.* Among the houses to note are the Palais de Soubise, now the National Archives, and the Hôtels d'Aumont, de Clisson, de Rohan, de Sens, and de Sully (*hôtel* in this sense means private residence or townhouse). The Caisse Nationale des Monuments, housed in the last one, can provide maps of the area, as well as fascinating and detailed tours. It also offers lectures on Saturdays and Sundays. 62 Rue St.-Antoine, 4e (phone: 42-74-22-22).

Place des Vosges – In the Marais district, the oldest square in Paris — and also one of the most beautiful — was completed in 1612 by order of Henri IV, with its houses elegantly "built to a like symmetry." Though many of the houses have been rebuilt inside, their original façades remain, and the recently restored square is one of Paris's enduring delights. Corneille, Racine, and Mme. de Sévigné lived here. At No. 6 is the *Maison de Victor-Hugo,* once the writer's home and now a museum. Closed Mondays; admission charge (4e; phone: 42-72-10-16).

Musée Carnavalet (Carnavalet Museum) – Also in the Marais, this once was the home of Mme. de Sévigné, a noted 17th-century letter writer, and now its beautifully arranged exhibits cover the history of the city of Paris from the days of Henri IV to the present. Its recent expansion through the *lycée* next door and into the neighboring *Le Peletier* hotel doubled the exhibition space, making it the largest museum in the world devoted to the history of a single capital city. The expansion, done primarily to house a permanent major exhibit on the French Revolution, was part of Paris's celebration of the Revolution's bicentennial. Watch for special exhibitions here. The museum also rents out its concert hall to various music groups. Closed Mondays; no admission charge on Sundays. 23 Rue de Sévigné, 3e (phone: 42-72-21-13).

Musée Picasso (Picasso Museum) – This long-awaited museum, which contains a large part of the artist's private collection, is at the Hôtel du Salé. To tell the truth, the building is at least as interesting as the artwork it houses — too many recent works, too few early ones — but a visit is worthwhile just to see Picasso's collection of works by other artists (the Cézannes are best). Open Mondays and Thursdays through Saturdays from 9:15 AM to 5 PM, Wednesdays from 9:15 AM to 10 PM. 5 Rue de Thorigny, 3e (phone: 42-71-25-21).

Cimetière Père-Lachaise (Père-Lachaise Cemetery) – For those who like cemeteries, this one is a beauty. In a wooded park, it's the final resting place of many illustrious personalities. A map is available at the gate to help you find the tombs of Balzac, Sarah Bernhardt, Chopin, Colette, Corot, Delacroix, Héloise and Abelard, La Fontaine, Modigliani, Musset, Edith Piaf, Rossini, Oscar Wilde, and even Jim Morrison (of the *Doors* rock group), among others. Note, too, the legions of resident cats. Open daily from 8 AM to 5:30 PM. Bd. de Ménilmontant at Rue de la Roquette, 20e (phone: 43-70-70-33).

La Villette – The City of Sciences and Industry, a celebration of technology, stands in its own park on the northeastern edge of the capital and houses a planetarium, the spherical *Géode* cinema, lots of hands-on displays, and a half-dozen exhibitions at any given time. Restaurants and snack bars. Open 10 AM to 6 PM. Closed Mondays. 30 Av. Cotentin Cariou, 20e (phone: 40-05-70-00).

Bois de Boulogne – Originally part of the Forest of Rouvre, on the western edge of Paris, this 2,140-acre park was planned along English lines by Napoleon. Ride a horse or a bike, row a boat, shoot skeet, go bowling, smell roses, picnic on the grass, see horse races at *Auteuil* and *Longchamp,* visit a children's amusement park (*Jardin d'Acclimatation*) and a zoo, see a play, walk to a waterfall — and there's lots more.

Bois de Vincennes – As a counterpart to the Bois de Boulogne, a park, a palace, and a zoological garden were laid out on 2,300 acres during Napoleon III's time. Visit the 14th-century château and its lovely chapel; the large and lovely floral garden; and the zoo, with animals in their natural habitat. It's at the southeast edge of Paris (métro: Château de Vincennes).

Palais de Chaillot – Built just off the Seine, near the Arc de Triomphe, for the *Paris Exposition of 1937* — on the site of the old Palais du Trocadéro left over from the *Exposition of 1878* — its terraces have excellent views across gardens and fountains to the Eiffel Tower on the Left Bank. Two wings house a theater, a *Cinémathèque,* and four museums — *du Cinéma* (phone: 45-53-74-39), *de l'Homme* (anthropology; phone: 45-53-70-60), *de la Marine* (maritime; phone: 45-53-31-70), and *des Monuments Français* (monument reproductions; phone: 47-27-97-27). Closed Tuesdays and major holidays. Pl. du Trocadéro, 16e.

LA RIVE GAUCHE (THE LEFT BANK)

Tour Eiffel (Eiffel Tower) – It is impossible to imagine the Paris skyline without this mighty symbol, yet what has been called Gustave Eiffel's folly was never meant to be permanent. Originally built for the *Universal Exposition of 1889,* it was due to be torn down in 1909, but it was saved because of the development of the wireless — the first transatlantic wireless telephones were operated from the tower in 1916. Its centennial was celebrated with great fanfare in 1989. Extensive renovations have taken place, and a post office, three restaurants (*Jules Verne* is the best), and a few boutiques have opened up on the first-floor landing. On a really clear day, it's possible to see for 50 miles. Open daily from 10 AM to 11 PM; in the summer from 10 AM to midnight. Admission charge. Champ-de-Mars, 7e (phone: 45-55-91-11).

Chaillot to UNESCO – From the Eiffel Tower, it is possible to look out over a group of Paris's 20th-century buildings and gardens on both sides of the Seine, including the Palais de Chaillot, the Trocadéro and Champ-de-Mars gardens, and the UNESCO buildings. Also part of the area (but not of the same century) is the huge Ecole Militaire, an impressive example of 18th-century French architecture on Avenue de la Motte-Picquet. The Y-shaped building just beyond it, facing Place de Fontenoy, is the main UNESCO building, dating from 1958. It has frescoes by Picasso, Henry Moore's

Reclining Silhouette, a mobile by Calder, murals by Miró, and Japanese gardens by Noguchi.

   Les Invalides – Built by Louis XIV as a refuge for disabled soldiers, this vast classical building has more than 10 miles of corridors and a golden dome by Mansart. For yet another splendid Parisian view, approach the building from the Alexandre III bridge. Besides being a masterpiece of the age of Louis XIV (17th century), the royal Church of the Dôme, part of the complex, contains the impressive red-and-green granite Tomb of Napoleon (admission charge). Also at Les Invalides is the *Musée de l'Armée,* one of the world's richest museums, displaying arms and armor together with mementos of French military history. Open daily from 10 AM to 5 PM. Av. de Tourville, Pl. Vauban, 7e (phone: 45-51-92-84).

   Musée d'Orsay (Orsay Museum) – This imposing former railway station has been transformed (by the Milanese architect Gae Aulenti, among others) into one of the shining examples of modern museum curating. Its eclectic collection includes not only the Impressionist paintings decanted from the once-cramped quarters in the *Jeu de Paume,* but also less consecrated academic work and a panorama of the 19th century's achievements in sculpture, photography, and the applied arts. Closed Mondays. Admission charge; reduced on Sundays. 1 Rue de Bellechasse, 7e (phone: 40-49-48-14).

   Musée Rodin (Rodin Museum) – The famous statue *The Thinker* is in the garden of this splendid 18th-century residence. The chapel and the mansion also contain Rodin sculpture. Open daily except Mondays from 10 AM to 4:30 PM. Admission charge. 77 Rue de Varenne, 7e (phone: 47-05-01-34).

   Montparnasse – Just south of the Luxembourg Gardens, in the early 20th century there arose an artists' colony of avant-garde painters, writers, and Russian political exiles. Here Hemingway, Picasso, and Scott and Zelda sipped and supped in places like *La Closerie des Lilas, La Coupole, Le Dôme, Le Select,* and *La Rotonde.* The cafés, small restaurants, and winding streets still exist in the shadow of a new shopping center.

   Tour Montparnasse – This giant complex dominates Montparnasse. The fastest elevator in Europe whisks Parisians and tourists alike (for a fee) up 59 stories for a view *down* at the Eiffel Tower, from 9:30 AM to 9:30 PM daily; Fridays and Saturdays until 10:30 PM. The shopping center here boasts all the famous names, and the surrounding office buildings are the headquarters of some of France's largest companies. 33 Av. du Maine, 15e, and Bd. de Vaugirard, 14e (phone: 45-38-52-56).

   Palais et Jardin du Luxembourg (Luxembourg Palace and Garden) – In what once were the southern suburbs, the Luxembourg Palace and Garden were built for Marie de Médici in 1612. A prison during the Revolution, the Renaissance palace now houses the French Senate. The classic, formal gardens, with lovely statues and the famous Médicis fountain, are popular with students meeting under the chestnut trees and with neighborhood children playing around the artificial lake. 15 Rue de Vaugirard, 6e.

   Mosquée de Paris (Paris Mosque) – One of the most beautiful structures of its kind in the non-Muslim — or even in the Muslim — world, it is dominated by a 130-foot-high minaret in gleaming white marble. Shoes are taken off before entering the pebble-lined gardens full of flowers and dwarf trees. Inside, the Hall of Prayer, with its lush Oriental carpets, may be visited daily except Fridays, from 9:30 AM to noon and 2 to 6 PM. Admission charge. Next door is a restaurant and a patio for sipping Turkish coffee and tasting Oriental sweets. Pl. du Puits-de-l'Ermite, 5e (phone: 45-35-97-33).

   Panthéon – This 18th-century "nonreligious Temple of Fame dedicated to all the gods" has an impressive interior, with murals depicting the life of Ste.-Geneviève, patron saint of Paris. It contains the tombs of Victor Hugo, the Résistance leader Jean Moulin, Rousseau, Voltaire, and Emile Zola. Open daily from 10 AM to 12:30 PM and 2 to 5:30 PM. Admission charge. Pl. du Panthéon, 5e (phone: 43-54-34-51).

Quartier Latin (Latin Quarter) – Extending from the Luxembourg Gardens and the Panthéon to the Seine, this famous neighborhood still maintains its unique atmosphere. A focal point for Sorbonne students since the Middle Ages, it's a mad jumble of narrow streets, old churches, and academic buildings. Boulevard St.-Michel and Boulevard St.-Germain are its main arteries, both lined with cafés, bookstores, and boutiques of every imaginable kind. There are also some charming old side streets, such as the Rue de la Huchette, near Place St.-Michel. And don't miss the famous *bouquinistes* (bookstalls) along the Seine, around the Place St.-Michel on the Quai des Grands-Augustins and the Quai St.-Michel.

Eglise St.-Germain-des-Prés (Church of St.-Germain-des-Prés) – Probably the oldest church in Paris, it once belonged to an abbey of the same name. The original basilica (AD 558) was destroyed and rebuilt many times. The Romanesque steeple and its massive tower date from 1014. Inside, the choir and sanctuary are as they were in the 12th century, and the marble shafts used in the slender columns are 14 centuries old. Pl. St.-Germain-des-Prés, 6e (phone: 43-25-41-71).

Surrounding the church is the *quartier* of Paris's "fashionable" intellectuals and artists, with art galleries, boutiques, and renowned cafés for people watching such as the *Flore* (Sartre's favorite) and *Les Deux Magots* (once a Hemingway haunt).

Musée de Cluny (Cluny Museum) – One of the last remaining examples of medieval domestic architecture in Paris. The 15th-century residence of the abbots of Cluny later became the home of Mary Tudor and now is a museum of medieval arts and crafts, including the celebrated *Lady and the Unicorn* tapestry. Open daily, except Tuesdays, from 9:30 AM to 5:15 PM. Admission charge. 6 Pl. Paul-Painlevé, 5e (phone: 43-25-62-00).

Eglise St.-Séverin (Church of St. Séverin) – This church still retains its beautiful Flamboyant Gothic ambulatory, considered a masterpiece of its kind, and lovely old stained glass windows dating from the 15th and 16th centuries. The small garden and the restored charnel house also are of interest. 3 Rue des Prêtres, 5e (phone: 43-25-96-63).

Eglise St.-Julien-le-Pauvre (Church of St. Julien le Pauvre) – One of the smallest and oldest churches (12th to 13th century) in Paris offers a superb view of Notre-Dame from its charming Place René-Viviani. 1 Rue St.-Julien-le-Pauvre, 5e (no phone).

THE ISLANDS

Ile de la Cité – The birthplace of Paris, settled by Gallic fishermen about 250 BC, this island in the Seine is so rich in historical monuments that an entire day could be spent here and on the neighboring Ile St.-Louis. A walk all around the islands, along the lovely, tree-shaded quays on both banks of the Seine, opens up one breathtaking view of Notre-Dame Cathedral after another.

Cathédrale de Notre-Dame de Paris (Cathedral of Our Lady) – It is said that the Druids once worshiped on this consecrated ground. The Romans built their temple, and many Christian churches followed. In 1163, the foundations were laid for the present cathedral, one of the world's finest examples of Gothic architecture, grand in size and proportion. Henri VI and Napoleon were crowned here. Take a guided tour (offered in English at noon Tuesdays and Wednesdays and in French at noon other weekdays, 2:30 PM Saturdays, and 2 PM Sundays) or quietly explore on your own, but be sure to climb the 225-foot towers for a marvelous view of the city and try to see the splendid stained glass rose windows at sunset. Pl. du Parvis, 4e (phone: 43-26-07-39).

Palais de Justice and Sainte-Chapelle – This complex recalls centuries of history; it was the first seat of the Roman military government, then the headquarters of the early kings, and finally the law courts. In the 13th century, St.-Louis (Louis IX) built a new palace and added Sainte-Chapelle to house the Sacred Crown of Thorns and other holy relics. Built in less than 3 years, the chapel, with its 15 splendid stained glass windows and 247-foot spire, is one of the jewels of Paris. Open daily from 10 AM to 4:30 PM. Admission charge. 4 Bd. du Palais, 1er (phone: 43-54-30-09).

Conciergerie – This remnant of the Old Royal Palace was used as a prison during the Revolution. Here Marie-Antoinette, the Duke of Orléans, Mme. du Barry, and many others of lesser fame awaited the guillotine. It was restored extensively for the celebration of the bicentennial of the French Revolution, and the great arch-filled hall is especially striking. Open daily. Admission charge. 4 Bd. du Palais, 1er (phone: 43-54-30-06).

Ile St.-Louis – Walk across the footbridge at the back of Notre-Dame and you're in a charming, tranquil village. This "enchanted isle" has managed to keep its provincial charm despite its central location. Follow the main street, Rue St.-Louis-en-l'Ile, down the middle of the island, past courtyards, balconies, old doors, curious stairways, the Eglise St.-Louis, and discreet plaques bearing the names of illustrious former residents (Mme. Curie, Voltaire, Baudelaire, Gautier, and Daumier, for example); then take the quay back along the edge.

■**EXTRA SPECIAL:** Versailles, by far the most magnificent of all the French châteaux, is 13 miles (21 km) southwest of Paris, accessible by train or bus. Louis XIV, called the Sun King because of the splendor of his court, took a small château used by Louis III, enlarged it, and really outdid himself. The vast, intricate, formal gardens, designed by the great Lenôtre, cover 250 acres and include 600 fountains, for which a river had to be diverted. At one time, the palace itself housed 6,000 people, and the court numbered 20,000. Louis kept his nobles in constant competition over his favors, hoping to distract them from any opposition to his rule. It's impossible to see all of Versailles in one day, but don't miss the Hall of Mirrors, the Royal Apartments, and the Chapel. Also on the grounds are the Grand Trianon, a smaller palace often visited by Louis XIV, and the Petit Trianon, a favorite of Marie-Antoinette, who also liked Le Hameau (the hamlet), a model farm where she and her companions played at being peasants. More than 20 additional rooms — the apartments of the dauphin and dauphine — are open to visitors Thursdays through Sundays. The gardens are open daily from 9 AM to 5 PM; the château and Trianons are closed Mondays and holidays. Guided tours in English are available from 10 AM to 3:30 PM. Admission charge (phone: 30-84-74-00). A spectacular illumination and display of the great fountains takes place on Sunday afternoons during the summer. For more information, contact the Versailles Tourist Office, 7 Rue des Réservoirs (phone: 39-50-36-22).

LOCAL SOURCES AND RESOURCES

TOURIST INFORMATION: For information in the US, contact the French Government Tourist Office (610 Fifth Ave., New York, NY 10020; phone: 212-757-1125). In Paris, the Office du Tourisme de Paris (127 Champs-Elysées, 8e; phone: 47-23-61-72), open daily from 9 AM to 8 PM, is the place to go for information, brochures, maps, or hotel reservations. If you call the office, be prepared for a 4- to 5-minute wait before someone answers. Other offices are found at major train stations, such as the Gare du Nord (phone: 45-26-94-82) and the Gare de Lyon (phone: 43-43-33-24).

Local Coverage – *Paris Selection* is the official tourist office magazine in French and English. It lists events, sights, "Paris by Night" tours, places to hear jazz, some hotels, restaurants, shopping, and other information. Far more complete are three weekly guides, *L'Officiel des Spectacles, Paris 7,* and *Pariscope.* All are in simple French and are available at newsstands.

For insights on eating out and finding the best of French food and wine, consult *The Food Lover's Guide to Paris* (Workman, $12.95) by American-in-Paris Patricia Wells. She also contributes a weekly column on restaurants to the *International Herald Tribune.*

TELEPHONE: The French telephone system is not too different from our own. The French have direct dialing, operator-assisted calls, collect calls, and so on.

When to Call – As in the US, phone rates in France vary with the time of day. Reductions range from 30% to 65% and the rates tend to change every few hours, so it's best to check the schedule in the brochure *Bienvenue,* issued by the ministry of Postes, Télécommunications, et Télédiffusion (PTT) and available at French post offices.

For long-distance calls *within* France, a 50% reduction in rates is in effect weekdays from 7:30 PM until 8 AM the next day. On Saturdays, the reduced rate goes into effect at 4 PM and continues all day Sunday until 8 AM Monday. (This reduction also is in effect all day on national holidays.) For calls to the US, the reduction in rates, approximately 15%, is not nearly so dramatic, but it is in effect longer. Regular rates prevail daily from 2 PM to 8 PM; reduced rates are in effect the remaining hours and on Sundays. (Don't forget the time difference when placing your call; see *Time Zones, Business Hours, and Public Holidays* in GETTING READY TO GO.)

Making connections in Europe sometimes can be hit or miss — not all exchanges are always in operation on the same day. If the number dialed does not go through, try later or the next day. So be warned: Those who have to make an important call — to make a hotel reservation in another city, for instance — should start to do so a few days ahead.

How to Call – All French telephone numbers have 8 digits. The procedure for calling most areas of France from the US is as follows: dial 011 (the international access code) + 33 (the country code) + the local 8-digit number (which includes the city code). For example, to place a call from anywhere in the US to Lyons, dial 011 + 33 + the local 8-digit number. The only exception to this rule is when calling the Paris/Ile-de-France area: You must add a 1 (the city code) before the local 8-digit number. For instance, to make a call from the US to Paris, dial 011 + 33 (the country code) + 1 (the city code) + the local 8-digit number.

Direct dialing within the country, between nations, and overseas is possible throughout France. The procedure for making a station-to-station call to the US from France is as follows: dial 19 (wait for a dial tone) + 1 (the US country code) + the area code + the local number. For instance, to call directly to New York from anywhere in France, dial 19 + 1 + 212 + the local number. For an operator-assisted call to the US, dial 19, wait for a dial tone, then dial 3311. If you need a French number and can speak a minimum of French, dial 12 for directory assistance.

France is divided into essentially two zones: Paris/Ile-de-France and all the rest, that is, the provinces. The procedure for dialing within France is as follows:

> *To call within Paris and the Ile-de-France area:* Dial the local 8-digit number (beginning with 4, 3, or 6).
> *To call from the Paris/Ile-de-France area to the provinces:* Dial 16 (wait for a dial tone) + the local 8-digit number.
> *To call from the provinces to the Paris/Ile-de-France area:* Dial 16 (wait for a dial tone) + 1 + the local 8-digit number.
> *To call between provinces:* Dial the local 8-digit number.

For emergency assistance throughout France: Dial 17 for the police (who can arrange for other emergency assistance) or dial 18 for the fire department. For further information on what to do in the event of an emergency, see *Medical and Legal Aid and Consular Services,* GETTING READY TO GO.

Where to Call From – Public pay phones are found in post offices, cafés, and in booths on the street. Phone booths from which you can direct-dial long-distance calls within France, as well as international calls to most European countries and the United States, are now found in even the smallest French towns. Instructions on their use usually are in the booth. Simply put, a fistful of coins is dropped into the phone before you begin. When your call is connected, the coins begin to drop automatically and you can continue to feed coins as you talk. Any unused coins are returned after your call is completed.

If you have trouble placing a call from a phone booth or if you cannot gather a sufficient amount of change, remember that long-distance and international calls also can be made at post offices in France. In fact, this may be the simplest way to place such a call. Go to the telephone counter and explain what kind of call you want to make. You may be assigned a *cabine* (booth) from which to direct-dial the call yourself, or the clerk may put the call through for you, telling you which *cabine* to go to when he or she is about to connect the call. In either case, after you have hung up, return to the counter and pay the clerk for the call. There is no extra charge for phone calls made at the post office with or without the assistance of the attendant (surcharges for operator-assisted calls such as collect and person-to-person still apply, naturally); the only drawback to using the post office is that there frequently is a line of people already waiting for an empty booth.

Though many French pay phones still take coins (inserted before dialing), most pay phones in major cities now use plastic phone cards, *télécartes,* which may be purchased at post offices, train stations and other transportation centers, and tobacco shops or newsstands. The *télécarte* may be purchased in three denominations: 40, 50, and 120 units. The units, like message units in US phone parlance, are a combination of time and distance. To use the card, you insert it into a slot in the phone and dial the number you wish to reach. A display gradually will count down the value (in francs) that remains on your card. When you run out of units on your card, you can insert another card.

Although you can use a telephone company credit card number on any phone, pay phones that take major credit cards (*American Express, MasterCard, Visa,* and so on) are increasingly common, particularly in transportation and tourism centers. Also now available is the "affinity card," a combined telephone calling card/bank credit card that can be used for domestic and international calls. Cards of this type include the following:

AT&T/Universal (phone: 800-662-7759). Cardholders can charge calls to the US from overseas.

Executive Telecard International (phone: 800-950-3800). Cardholders can charge calls to the US from overseas, as well as between most European countries.

Sprint Visa (phone: 800-446-7625). Cardholders can charge calls to the US from overseas.

Similarly, *MCI VisaPhone* (phone: 800-866-0099) can add phone card privileges to the services available through your existing *Visa* card. This service allows you to use your *Visa* account number, plus an additional code, to charge calls on any touch-tone phone in the US and Europe.

 GETTING AROUND: Boat – See Paris from the Seine by day and by night for about 30–35 francs (about $5–$6). Modern, glass-enclosed river ramblers provide a constantly changing picture of the city. Contact *Bateaux-Mouches* (Pont d'Alma, 7e; phone: 42-25-96-10), *Les Bateaux Parisiens* (Pont d'Iéna, 7e; phone: 47-05-50-00), or *Vedettes Pont-Neuf* (Square Vert-Galant, 1er; phone: 46-33-98-38). For 90F ($15), *Paris Canal* (phone: 42-40-96-97) offers a 3-hour barge trip starting on the Seine, then navigating through some of the city's old canals, locks, and a subterranean water route under the Bastille. An interesting commmentary is given in both English and French. There are two trips daily between the *Musée d'Orsay* and the Parc de la Villette — one leaves from the *Musée d'Orsay* at 9:30 AM and the other departs from the Parc de la Villette at 2:30 PM. Reservations are required.

Bus – They generally operate from 6:30 AM to 9:30 PM, although some run later. Slow, but good for sightseeing. Métro tickets are valid on all city-run buses. Lines are numbered, and both stops and buses have signs indicating routes. One or two tickets may be required, depending on the distance traveled. The *RATP,* which operates both the métro and bus system, also has designated certain lines as being of particular interest to tourists. A panel on the front of the bus indicates in English and German "This bus is good for sightseeing." *RATP* has a tourist office at Place de la Madeleine, next to the flower market (phone: 43-46-14-14), which organizes bus trips in Paris and the region.

Car Rental – Book when making your plane reservation, or contact *Avis* (phone: 45-50-32-31), *Budget* (phone: 46-86-65-65), *Europcar* (phone: 45-00-08-06), or *Hertz* (phone: 47-88-51-51). For more information on renting a car in Paris, see "Car Rental" in *Traveling by Plane,* GETTING READY TO GO.

Métro – Operating from 5:30 AM to about 1 AM, it is safe, clean, quiet, easy to use, and since the Paris regional rapid transit authority (*RATP*) began to sponsor cultural events and art exhibits in some subway stops in an effort to cut down on crime and make commuting more enjoyable, entertaining as well. The events have been so popular that so far they've been offered in about 200 of Paris's 368 métro stations.

The different lines are identified by the names of their terminals at either end. Every station has clear directional maps, some with push-button devices that light up the proper route after a destination button is pushed. Keep your ticket (you may need to show it to one of the controllers who regularly patrol the métro) and don't cheat; there are spot checks. In August 1991, the Paris Regional Transit Authority abolished the métro's long-standing first and second-class system. There is now only one class of ticket.

A 10-ticket book (*carnet*) is available at a reduced rate. The Paris-Visite card, a tourist ticket that entitles the bearer to 1, 3, or 5 consecutive days of unlimited travel on the métro and on city-run buses, may be purchased in France upon presentation of your passport at 44 subway stations and 4 regional express stations, or at any of the 6 *French National Railroad* stations. In the US, the card is available by money order from *Marketing Challengers International* (10 E. 21st St., New York, NY 10010; phone: 212-529-8484) — $7.50 for a 1-day ticket, $20 for a 3-day ticket, and $30 for a 5-day ticket, plus $3 for postage and handling.

SITU – Handy streetside bus and subway directions are now available in some métro stations from *SITU* (*Système d'Information des Trajets Urbains*), a computer that prints out the fastest routing onto a wallet-size piece of paper, complete with the estimated length of the trip. The *RATP* service is free and augments the lighted wall maps that guide métro riders. High-traffic spots such as the Châtelet métro station, outside the Gare Montparnasse, and on the Boulevard St.-Germain, now sport *SITU* machines.

Taxi – Taxis can be found at stands at main intersections, outside railway stations and official buildings, and in the streets. A taxi is available if the entire "TAXI" sign is illuminated (with a white light); the small light *beside* the roof light signifies availability after dark. But be aware that Parisian cab drivers are notoriously selective about whom they will pick up, and how many passengers they will allow in their cab — a foursome inevitably has trouble. You also can call *Taxi Bleu* (phone: 49-36-10-10) or *Radio Taxi* (phone: 47-39-33-33). The meter starts running from the time the cab is dispatched, and a tip of about 15% is customary. Fares increase at night and on Sundays and holidays.

Train – Paris has six main train stations, each one serving a different area of the country. The general information number is 45-82-50-50; for telephone reservations, 45-65-60-60. North: Gare du Nord (18 Rue de Dunkerque; phone: 42-80-63-63); East: Gare de l'Est (Pl. du 11-Novembre; phone: 42-03-96-31); Southeast: Gare de Lyon (20 Bd. Diderot; phone: 40-19-60-00); Southwest: Gare d'Austerlitz (51 Quai d'Austerlitz; phone: 45-84-14-19); West: Gare Montparnasse (17 Bd. de Vaugirard; phone: 40-48-10-00); West and Northwest: Gare St.-Lazare (20 Rue de Rome; phone: 42-85-88-00). The *TGV* (*train à grande vitesse*), the world's fastest train, has cut 2 hours off the usual 4-hour ride between Paris and Lyons; it similarly shortens traveling time to Marseilles, the Côte d'Azur, the Atlantic Coast, and Switzerland. It leaves from the Gare de Lyon, except for the Atlantic Coast run, which departs from the Gare d'Austerlitz; reservations are necessary. As we went to press, a new *TGV* station was scheduled to open in Massy, 16 miles (25 km) south of Paris. Located right near Orly, a 15-minute ride on the *RER* (suburban train), it is ideal for those who are traveling to other parts of France and want to avoid going into Paris.

LOCAL SERVICES: Dentist (English-Speaking) – Dr. Edward Cohen, 20 Rue de la Paix, 2e (phone: 42-61-65-64 or 42-61-78-71).

Baby-Sitting – Two of the many agencies in Paris are *Baby Sitting* (157 Rue de Bercy, 13e; phone: 43-43-35-55) and *Kid's Service* (17 Rue Molière, 1er; phone: 42-96-04-16). Whether the sitter is hired directly or through an agency, ask for and check references.

Dry Cleaner/Tailor – Dry cleaners are available throughout the city. Note that many have two different price schedules, one for "economic" service, another for faster, more expensive service. The less expensive prices may be posted outside, but unless you specify, your clothes will be given the expensive treatment. *John Baillie, Real Scotch Tailor* (1 Rue Auber at Place de l'Opéra, 2e; phone: 47-42-49-24 or 47-42-49-17) is a reputable firm that does tailoring French-style, despite its name.

Limousine Service – *Compagnie des Limousines* (26 Rue Armand-Silvestre, Courbevoie; phone: 47-89-43-08); *Executive Car/Carey Limousine* (25 Rue d'Astorg, 8e; phone: 42-65-54-20; fax: 42-65-25-93).

Medical Emergency – The *American Hospital* has 24-hour emergency service. The hospital also has a dental service and maintains an extensive network of English-speaking specialists. 63 Bd. Victor-Hugo, Neuilly (phone: 46-41-25-25).

Messenger Service – *Neuilly Courses,* 6 Villa des Sablons, Neuilly (phone: 47-45-54-00).

National/International Courier – *Federal Express* (*Copyshop,* 44 Rue du Colisée, 8e; phone: 40-85-38-88); *DHL International* (59 Av. d'Iéna, 16e; phone: 45-01-91-00 or 48-63-70-00).

Office Equipment Rental – *Chapchool Distribution,* for typewriters with English keyboards (minimum 2-week rental). 11 Rue Etienne-Marcel, Pantin (phone: 48-45-05-25).

Pharmacy – *Pharmacie Derhy* is open 24 hours a day, including holidays. Located in the *Galerie Les Champs,* 84 Av. des Champs-Elysées, 8e (phone: 45-62-02-41).

Photocopies – In addition to the numerous small outlets specializing in photocopies, facilities are available in many stationery stores and post offices.

Post Office – The main post office (52 Rue du Louvre, 1er; phone: 42-33-71-60) is open 24 hours a day; night hours are restricted to simpler operations such as posting a registered letter. Other branches are open from 8 AM to 7 PM on weekdays and until noon on Saturdays.

Secretary/Stenographer (English-Speaking) – *Multiburo* also rents office space. 17 Rue Galilée, 16e (phone: 47-23-47-47).

Teleconference Facilities – *Hôtel Méridien,* 81 Bd. Gouvion-St.-Cyr, 17e (phone: 40-68-34-34).

Telex – *PTT* (Postes et Télécommunications), open daily, including Sundays, from 8 AM to 7:30 PM, at 7 Rue Feydeau, 2e (phone: 42-33-20-12), and from 8 to 10:30 PM at 5 Rue Feydeau, just next door.

Translator – *Bilis Traduction,* 24 Rue Lafitte, 9e (phone: 47-70-50-80).

Tuxedo Rental – *Au Cor de Chasse,* 40 Rue de Buci, 6e (phone: 43-26-51-89).

SPECIAL EVENTS: After the *Christmas* season, Paris prepares for the January fashion shows, when press and buyers come to town to pass judgment on the spring and summer haute couture collections. (The general public can see what the designers have wrought after the professionals leave.) More buyers come to town in February and March for the ready-to-wear shows (fall and winter clothes), open to the trade only. March is the month of the first *Foire Nationale à la Brocante et aux Jambons* of the year. This fair of regional food products held concurrently with an antiques flea market (not items of the best quality, but not junk, either) is repeated in September. The running of the *Prix du Président de la République,* the first big horse race of the year, takes place at *Auteuil* in April. From late April to early May is the *Foire de Paris,* the capital's big international trade fair. In late April or May there's the *Paris Marathon;* in late May (through early June), the *French Open Tennis Championships.* Odd years only, the *Paris International Air Show* is an early June attraction at Le Bourget Airport. Horse races crowd the calendar in June — there's not only the *Prix de Diane* at *Chantilly,* but also the *Grande Semaine* at *Longchamp, Auteuil,* and *St.-Cloud.* And in the middle of June, the *Festival du Marais* begins a month's worth of music and dance performances in the courtyards of the Marais district's old townhouses. *Bastille Day,* July 14, is celebrated with music and fireworks, parades, and dancing till dawn in every neighborhood. Meanwhile, the *Tour de France* is under way; the cyclists arrive in Paris for the finish of the 3-week race later in July. Also in July, press and buyers arrive to view the fall and winter haute couture collections, but the ready-to-wear shows (spring and summer clothes) wait until September and October, because August for Parisians is vacation time. Practically the whole country takes a holiday then, and in the capital the classical concerts of the *Festival Estival* (in July and August) are among the few distractions. When they finish, the *Festival d'Automne,* a celebration of the contemporary in music, dance, and theater, takes over (from mid-September through December). The *Foire Nationale à la Brocante et aux Jambons* returns in September, but in even-numbered years it's eclipsed by the *Biennale des Antiquaires,* a major antiques event from late September to early October. Also in even years, usually in November, is the *Paris Motor Show.* Every year on the first Sunday of October, the last big horse race of the season, the *Prix de l'Arc de Triomphe,* is run at *Longchamp;* and every year in early October, Paris holds the *Fête des Vendanges à Montmartre* to celebrate the harvest of the city's last remaining vineyard. On November 11, ceremonies at the Arc de Triomphe and a parade mark *Armistice Day.* An *International Cat Show* and a *Horse and Pony Show* come in early December; then comes *Christmas,* which is celebrated most movingly with a *Christmas Eve* midnight mass at Notre-Dame. At midnight a week later, the *New Year* bows in to spontaneous street revelry in the Latin Quarter and along the Champs-Elysées.

MUSEUMS: Some Paris museums (*musées*) are free or offer reduced admission fees on Sundays. "La Carte," a pass that can be used at over 60 museums and monuments in the city, is available at métro stations and at major museums (or in the US from *Marketing Challengers International,* 10 E. 21st St., New York, NY 10010; phone: 212-529-8484). Prices are the equivalent of

$15.50 for a 1-day pass, $27.50 for a 3-day pass, and $37.50 for a 5-day pass. Note that "La Carte" is not valid for certain special exhibits. Museums of interest not described in *Special Places* include the following:

Archaeological Crypt of Notre-Dame – Under the square in front of walls and floor plans from later periods. Open daily from 10 AM to 4:30 PM. Parvis de Notre-Dame, 4e (phone: 43-29-83-51).

Catacombs – Dating from the Gallo-Roman era and also containing the remains of Danton, Robespierre, and many others. Bring a flashlight. Closed Mondays. 1 Pl. Denfert-Rochereau, 14e (phone: 43-22-47-63).

Egouts (Sewers of Paris) – Underground city of tunnels, a very popular afternoon tour, daily except Thursdays and Fridays, and on holidays and the days preceding and following them. Pl. de la Résistance, in front of 93 Quai d'Orsay, 7e (phone: 47-05-10-29).

Galerie Nationale de Jeu de Paume – Inaugurated in June 1991, this museum is devoted to contemporary art from 1960 on and includes paintings, sculpture, photographs, and videos, all installed in what was formerly the temple of Impressionism — the *Jeu de Paume,* at one end of the Tuileries. The interior has been redone to provide more and better exhibition space. Open Wednesdays, Thursdays, and Fridays from noon to 7 PM; Tuesdays from noon to 9:30 PM; and Saturdays and Sundays from 10 AM to 7 PM. Corner of the Tuileries gardens at the Place de la Concorde.

Maison de Balzac – The house where the writer lived, with a garden leading to one of the prettiest little alleys in Paris. Closed Mondays. 47 Rue Raynouard, 16e (phone: 42-24-56-38).

Manufacture des Gobelins – The famous tapestry factory, in operation since the 15th century. Guided tours of the workshops take place Tuesdays, Wednesdays, and Thursdays from 2:15 to 3:15 PM. 42 Av. des Gobelins, 13e (phone: 42-74-44-50).

Mémorial de la Déportation – Set in a tranquil garden in the shadow of Notre-Dame at the tip of Ile de la Cité, this monument is dedicated to 200,000 French women and men of all religions and races who died in Nazi concentration camps during World War II. Square de l'Ile-de-France, 4e.

Mémorial du Martyr Juif Inconnu – A moving tribute to Jews killed during the Holocaust, this 35-year-old, newly renovated memorial includes World War II documents and photographs. Open daily, except Friday afternoons and Saturdays, from 10 AM to noon and 2 to 5:30 PM. 17 Rue Geoffroy L'Asniers, 4e (phone: 42-77-44-72). The French Government Tourist Office has published a booklet, *France for the Jewish Traveler,* that describes these two memorials, as well as other places of interest to Jews visiting France. See "Tourist Information" in *Sources and Resources,* GETTING READY TO GO, for a list of the offices in the US.

Musée des Antiquités Nationales – Archaeological specimens from prehistoric through Merovingian times, including an impressive Gallo-Roman collection. Open daily, except Tuesdays, from 9:30 AM to noon and 1:30 to 5:15 PM. Pl. du Château, St.-Germain-en-Laye, 14e (phone: 34-51-53-65).

Musée des Arts Africains et Océaniens – One of the world's finest collections of African and Oceanic art. Closed Tuesdays. 293 Av. Daumesnil, 12e (phone: 43-43-14-54).

Musée des Arts Décoratifs – Furniture and applied arts from the Middle Ages to the present, Oriental carpets, and Dubuffet paintings and drawings. Galerie Art Nouveau–Art Deco features Jeanne Lanvin's bedroom and bath. It also houses 3 centuries of French posters formerly displayed in the now-closed *Musée de l'Affiche et de la Publicité.* Closed Mondays and Tuesdays. 107 Rue de Rivoli, 1er (phone: 42-60-32-14).

Musée Cernuschi – Art of China. Closed Mondays and holidays. 7 Av. Velásquez, 8e (phone: 45-63-50-75).

Musée de la Chasse et de la Nature – Art, weapons, and tapestries relating to the hunt. Of particular interest is the courtyard where horses once were kept — it is decorated with sculpture. Open daily except Tuesdays from 10 AM to 12:30 PM and 1:30 to 5:30 PM. Admission charge. 60 Rue des Archives, 3e (phone: 42-72-86-43).

Musée Cognacq-Jay – Art, snuffboxes, and watches from the 17th and 18th centuries. Closed Mondays. 8 Rue Elzévir, 3e (phone: 40-27-07-21).

Musée des Collections Historiques de la Préfecture de Police – On the second floor of the modern police precinct, in the 5th *arrondissement,* are historic arrest orders (for Charlotte Corday, among others), collections of contemporary engravings, and guillotine blades. Open Mondays through Saturdays from 9 AM to 5 PM. 1 *bis* Rue des Carmes, 5e (phone: 43-29-21-57).

Musée Eugène-Delacroix – Studio and garden of the great painter; exhibits change yearly. Closed Tuesdays. 6 Rue de Furstenberg, 6e (phone: 43-54-04-87).

Musée Grévin – Waxworks of French history from Charlemagne to the present day. 10 Bd. Montmartre, 9e (phone: 47-70-85-05). A branch devoted to La Belle Epoque is in the *Forum des Halles* shopping complex. Open daily. Pl. Carrée, 1er (phone: 40-26-28-50).

Musée Guimet – The *Louvre*'s Far East collection. Closed Tuesdays. 6 Pl. d'Iéna, 16e (phone: 47-23-61-65).

Musée Gustave-Moreau – A collection of the works of the early symbolist. Closed Mondays and Tuesdays. 14 Rue de la Rochefoucauld, 9e (phone: 48-74-38-50).

Musée Jacquemart-André – Eighteenth-century French decorative art and European Renaissance treasures, as well as frequent special exhibitions. Closed Mondays and Tuesdays. 158 Bd. Haussmann, 8e (phone: 42-89-04-91).

Musée Marmottan – Superb Monets, including the nine masterpieces that were stolen in a daring 1985 robbery. Happily, however, all were recovered in a villa in Corsica and have been cleaned — some for the first time — before being rehung. Closed Mondays. 2 Rue Louis-Boilly, 16e (phone: 42-24-07-02).

Musée de la Mode et du Costume – A panorama of French contributions to fashion in the elegant Palais Calliéra. Closed Mondays. 10 Av. Pierre-I de Serbie, 16e (phone: 47-20-85-23).

Musée de la Monnaie – More than 2,000 coins and 450 medallions, plus historic coinage machines. Open daily, except Mondays, from 1 to 6 PM. Admission charge. 11 Quai de Conti, 6e (phone: 40-46-56-66).

Musée Montmartre – A rich collection of paintings, drawings, and documents depicting life in this quarter. Open Mondays through Saturdays from 2:30 to 6 PM, Sundays from 11 AM to 6 PM. 12 Rue Cortot, 18e (phone: 46-06-61-11).

Musée Nissim de Camondo – A former manor house filled with beautiful furnishings and art objects from the 18th century. Closed Mondays, Tuesdays, and holidays. 63 Rue de Monceau, 8e (phone: 45-63-26-32).

Musée de Sèvres – Just outside Paris, next door to the Sèvres factory, is one of the world's finest collections of porcelain. Closed Tuesdays. 4 Grand-Rue, Sèvres (phone: 45-39-99-99).

Musée du Vin – Housed in a 13th-century abbey that was destroyed during the revolution, the museum was restored in 1981. The history and making of wine is traced through displays, artifacts, and a series of wax figure tableaux. Open daily, except Mondays, from noon to 6 PM; Saturdays and Sundays to 5:30 PM. Admission charge includes a glass of wine. 5-7 Sq. Charles-Dickens, 16e (phone: 45-25-63-26).

Parc Océanique Cousteau – Based on the work of the French oceanographer, this museum houses ocean exhibits and interactive displays. Open Mondays, Tuesdays, and Thursdays from noon to 7 PM; Wednesdays, Saturdays, Sundays, and holidays from 10 AM to 7:30 PM. Admission charge. *Forum des Halles,* Pl. Carrée, 1er (phone: 40-28-98-98).

Pavillon des Arts – An exhibition space in the mushroom-shaped buildings overlooking the *Forum des Halles* complex. Presentations range from ancient to modern, paintings to sculpture. Closed Mondays and holidays. 101 Rue Rambuteau, 1er (phone: 42-33-82-50).

GALLERIES: Few artists live in Montparnasse nowadays, as the center of the Paris art scene has shifted from the narrow streets of the Latin Quarter, which set the pace in the 1950s, to the Right Bank around the *Centre Georges-Pompidou*. Here are some galleries of note:

Agathe Gaillard – Contemporary photography, including Cartier-Bresson and the like. 3 Rue du Pont-Louis-Philippe, 4e (phone: 42-77-38-24).

Artcurial – Early moderns, such as Braque and Sonia Delaunay, as well as sculpture and prints, with a fine art bookshop. 9 Av. Matignon, 8e (phone: 42-99-16-16).

Beaubourg – Well-known names in the Paris art scene, including Niki de Saint-Phalle, César, Tinguely, Klossowski. 23 Rue du Renard, 4e (phone: 42-71-20-50).

Caroline Corre – Exhibitions by contemporary artists, specializing in unique artists' books. 14 Rue Guénégaud, 6e (phone: 43-54-57-67).

Claude Bernard – Francis Bacon, David Hockney, and Raymond Mason are among the artists exhibited here. 5 Rue des Beaux-Arts, 6e (phone: 43-26-97-07).

Daniel Malingue – Works by the Impressionists, as well as notable Parisian artists from the 1930s to the 1950s — Foujita, Fautrier, and so forth. 26 Av. Matignon, 8e (phone: 42-66-60-33).

Darthea Speyer – Run by a former American embassy attaché, now an art dealer. Contemporary painting. 6 Rue Jacques-Callot, 6e (phone: 43-54-78-41).

Hervé Odermatt Cazeau – Early moderns — among them Picasso, Léger, Pissarro — and antiques. 85 *bis* Rue du Faubourg-St.-Honoré, 8e (phone: 42-66-92-58).

Isy Brachot – Master surrealists, American hyper-realists, and new realists. 35 Rue Guénégaud, 6e (phone: 43-54-22-40).

Maeght-Lelong – The great moderns on display include Chagall, Tàpies, Bacon, Moore, Miró. 13-14 Rue de Téhéran, 8e (phone: 45-63-13-19).

Nikki Diana Marquardt – Spacious gallery of contemporary work opened by an enterprising dealer from the Bronx. 9 Pl. des Vosges, 4e (phone: 42-78-21-00).

Virginia Zabriskie – Early and contemporary photography by Atget, Brassaï, Diane Arbus. Also painting and, occasionally, sculpture. 37 Rue Quincampoix, 4e (phone: 42-72-35-47).

SHOPPING: From new wave fashions to classic haute couture, Paris starts the trends and sets the styles the world copies. Prices are generally high, but more than a few people are willing to pay for the quality of the products, not to mention the cachet of a Paris label, which enhances the appeal of many things besides clothing. Perfume, cosmetics, jewelry, leather goods and accessories, wine and liqueurs, porcelain, and art are among the many other things for which Paris is famous.

The big department stores are excellent places to get an idea of what's available. They include *Galeries Lafayette* (40 Bd. Haussmann, 9e; phone: 42-82-34-56; and other locations); *Au Printemps* (64 Bd. Haussmann, 9e; phone: 42-85-80-00); *Aux Trois Quartiers-Madelios* (17 Bd. de la Madeleine, 1er; phone: 42-60-39-30); *La Samaritaine* (19 Rue de la Monnaie, 1er; phone: 40-41-20-20); *Le Bazar de l'Hôtel de Ville* (52 Rue de Rivoli, 4e; phone: 42-74-90-00); and *Au Bon Marché* (22 Rue de Sèvres, 7e; phone: 45-49-21-22). Two major shopping centers — *Porte Maillot* (Pl. de la Porte Maillot) and *Maine Montparnasse* (at the intersection of Bd. Montparnasse and Rue de Rennes) — also are worth a visit.

There are several shopping neighborhoods, and they tend to be specialized. Haute couture can be found in the streets around the Champs-Elysées: Av. George-V, Av.

Montaigne, Rue François Ier, and Rue du Faubourg-St.-Honoré; famous designers are also represented in department stores. Boutiques are especially numerous on Av. Victor-Hugo, Rue de Passy, Bd. des Capucines, in the St.-Germain-des-Prés area, in the neighborhood of the *Opéra,* in the *Forum des Halles* shopping center, and around the Place des Victoires. The Rue d'Alésia has several blocks devoted solely to discount fashion shops.

The Rue de Paradis is lined with crystal and china shops, and St.-Germain-des-Prés has more than its share of art galleries. The best and most expensive antiques dealers are along the Faubourg-St.-Honoré on the Right Bank. On the Left Bank there's *Le Carré Rive Gauche,* an association of more than 100 antiques shops in the area bordered by Quai Voltaire, Rue de l'Université, Rue des Sts.-Pères, and Rue du Bac. Antiques and curio collectors should explore Paris's several flea markets, which include the *Montreuil,* near the Porte de Montreuil; *Vanves,* near the Porte de Vanves; and the largest and best known, *Puces de St.-Ouen,* near the Porte de Clignancourt.

A few more tips: Sales take place during the first weeks in January and in late June and July. Any shop labeled *dégriffé* (the word means, literally, "without the label") offers discounts on brand name clothing, often last season's styles. Discount shops also are known as "stock" shops. The French value added tax (VAT; typically 18.6% and as high as 33.33% on luxury articles) can be refunded on most purchases made by foreigners provided a minimum of 1,200F (about $200) is spent in one store. Forms must be filled out and the refund usually is mailed to your home. Large department stores and the so-called duty-free shops have facilitated the procedure, but refunds can be obtained from any store willing to cooperate. If the refund is not exactly equal to the tax — 15% to 25% refunds are common — it's because stores may retain some of it as reimbursement for their extra expense in handling the paperwork.

Here is a sampling of the wealth of shops in Paris, many of which have more than one location in the city:

Agnès B – Supremely wearable, trendy, casual clothes. 3 and 6 Rue du Jour, 1er (phone: 40-26-36-87 or 45-08-56-56); 13 Rue Michelet, 6e (phone: 46-33-70-20); 25 Av. Pierre-I-de-Serbie, 16e (phone: 47-20-22-44); and 81 Rue d'Assas, 6e (phone: 43-54-69-21). The latter store is for children only.

Alfred Dunhill – Menswear, toiletries, and luggage articles from the celebrated English tobacconist. 15 Rue de la Paix, 2e (phone: 42-67-57-58).

Arnys – Conservative and elegant men's clothing. 14 Rue de Sèvres, 6e (phone: 45-48-76-99).

Azzedine Alaïa – The Tunisian designer who brought the body back. 14 Rue de la Verrerie, 4e (phone: 48-04-03-60).

Baccarat – High-quality porcelain and crystal. 30 *bis* Rue du Paradis, 10e (phone: 47-70-64-30); and 11 Pl. de la Madeleine, 8e (phone: 42-65-36-26).

La Bagagerie – Perhaps the best bag and belt boutique in the world. 12 Rue Tronchet, 8e (phone: 42-65-03-40), and other locations.

Au Bain Marie – The most beautiful kitchenware and tabletop accessories, with emphasis on Art Deco designs. 10 Rue Boissy-d'Anglas, 8e (phone: 42-66-59-74).

Balenciaga – Ready-to-wear and designer haute couture. 10 Av. George-V, 8e (phone: 47-20-21-11).

Bazaar de Hôtel de Ville – Perhaps the world's most celebrated hardware store — with everything from nuts and bolts to a French bistro sign or a washing machine. Some people travel to Paris just to visit *BHV*'s grim, cavernous expanse. 52 Rue de Rivoli, 3e (phone: 42-74-90-00).

Beauté Divine – Antique perfume bottles, Art Deco bathroom accessories, glove stretchers, nail buffers, and mustache cups. 40 Rue St.-Sulpice, 6e (phone: 43-26-25-31).

Boucheron – One of several fine jewelers clustered around the elegant Place Vendôme. 26 Pl. Vendôme, 1er (phone: 42-61-58-16).

Brentano's – British and American novels, critiques on the American arts, and a variety of books on technical and business subjects — in English. 37 Av. de l'Opéra, 2e (phone: 42-61-52-50).

Cacharel – Fashionable ready-to-wear in great prints. 34 Rue Tronchet, 8e (phone: 47-42-12-61), and other locations.

Cadolle – Founded in 1889 by the woman credited with inventing the brassiere, it still sells corsets as well as other items of frilly, pretty lingerie. 14 Rue Cambon, 1er (phone: 42-60-94-94).

Carel – Beautiful shoes. 12 Rond-Point des Champs-Elysées, 8e (phone: 45-62-30-62), and other locations.

Carita – Paris's most extensive — and friendliest — beauty/hair salon. 11 Rue du Faubourg-St.-Honoré, 8e (phone: 42-68-13-40).

Cartier – Fabulous jewelry. 11-13 Rue de la Paix, 2e (phone: 42-61-58-56), and other locations.

Castorama – One of 86 stores throughout France, this department store sells 45,000 European-designed housewares — from flowerpots to home security systems. 1-3 Rue Caulaincourt, 18e (phone: 45-22-07-11).

Céline – A popular women's boutique for clothing and accessories. 24 Rue François-1er, 8e (phone: 47-20-22-83); 3 Av. Victor-Hugo, 16e (phone: 45-01-70-48).

Cerruti – For women's clothing, 9 Pl. de la Madeleine, 8e (phone: 40-17-03-16); for men's, 27 Rue Royale, 8e (phone: 42-65-68-72).

Chanel – Classic women's fashions, inspired by the late, legendary Coco Chanel, now under the direction of Karl Lagerfeld. 42 Av. Montaigne, 8e (phone: 47-20-84-45); and 29-31 Rue Cambon, 1er (phone: 42-86-28-00).

Chantal Thomass – Ultra-feminine fashions, 5 Rue du Vieux-Colombier, 6e (phone: 45-44-07-52); sexy lingerie, 12-14 Galerie du Rond-Point, 8e (phone: 43-59-87-34), and other locations.

Charles Jourdan – Sleek, high-fashion shoes. 86 Av. des Champs-Elysées, 8e (phone: 45-62-29-28); 5 Bd. de la Madeleine, 1er (phone: 42-61-50-07); and other locations.

Charley – Excellent selection of lingerie at fairly low prices. 14 Rue du Faubourg-St.-Honoré, 8e (phone: 47-42-17-70).

Charvet – Paris's answer to Savile Row. An all-in-one men's shop, where shirts are the house specialty — they stock more than 4,000. Ties, too. 28 Pl. Vendôme, 1er (phone: 42-60-30-70).

Chaumet – Crownmakers for most of Europe's royalty. Expensive jewels, including antique watches covered with semi-precious stones. 12 Pl. Vendôme, 1er (phone: 42-60-32-82); and 46 Av. George-V (phone: 49-52-08-25).

Chloé – Designs for women. 3 Rue de Gribeauval and 60 Rue du Faubourg-St.-Honoré, 8e (phone: 42-66-01-39).

Christian Dior – One of the most famous couture names in the world. 28-30 Av. Montaigne, 8e; *Miss Dior* and *Baby Dior* for children also are at this location (phone: 40-73-54-44).

Christian Lacroix – The first major new fashion house to open in Paris in 2 decades. Offers the "hautest" of haute couture. 73 Rue du Faubourg-St.-Honoré, 8e (phone: 42-65-79-08).

Christofle – The internationally famous silversmith. 9 Rue Royale, 8e (phone: 49-33-43-00).

Claude Montana – Ready-to-wear and haute couture from this au courant designer. 31 Rue de Grenelle, 7e (phone: 42-22-69-56).

Commes des Garçons – Asymmetrical-style clothing for *des filles* and *des garçons*. 40-42 Rue Etienne-Marcel, 1er (phone: 42-33-05-21).

Courrèges – Another bastion of haute couture, with its own boutique. 40 Rue François Ier, 8e, and 46 Rue du Faubourg-St.-Honoré, 8e (phone: 47-23-00-73).

Daniel Hechter – Sportswear and casual clothing for men and women. 146 Bd. St.-Germain, 6e (phone: 43-26-96-36), and other locations.

Destination Paris – Glittering selection of knickknacks, hand-painted T-shirts, scarves, picture frames, and souvenirs. 9 Rue du 29 Juillet, 1er (phone: 49-27-98-90).

Dorothée Bis – Definitely a trendsetter in women's wear. 33 Rue de Sèvres, 6e (phone: 42-22-02-90).

Les Drugstores Publicis – A uniquely French version of the American drugstore, with an amazing variety of goods — perfume, books, records, foreign newspapers, magazines, film, cigarettes, food, and more, all wildly overpriced. 149 Bd. St.-Germain, 6e (phone: 42-22-92-50); 133 Av. des Champs-Elysées, 8e (phone: 47-23-54-34); and 1 Av. Matignon, 8e (phone: 43-59-38-70).

E. Dehillerin – An enormous selection of professional cookware. 18-20 Rue Coquillière, 1er (phone: 42-36-53-13).

Emanuel Ungaro – Couturier boutique for women. 2 Av. Montaigne, 8e (phone: 47-23-61-94).

Erès – Avant-garde sportswear for men and women. 2 Rue Tronchet, 8e (phone: 47-42-24-55).

Fabrice – Trendy, fine costume jewelry. 33 and 54 Rue Bonaparte, 6e (phone: 43-26-57-95).

Fauchon – *The* place to buy fine food and wine of every variety, from *oeufs en gêlée* to condiments and candy. 26-30 Pl. de la Madeleine, 8e (phone: 47-42-60-11).

Fouquet – Beautiful displays of chocolates, fresh fruit candies, herbs, condiments, and jams. 22 Rue François Ier, 8e (phone: 47-23-30-46), and other locations.

France Faver – Top-quality beautiful and comfortable shoes for women. 79 Rue des Sts.-Pères, 6e (phone: 42-22-04-29).

Fratelli Rossetti – All kinds of shoes, made from buttery-soft leather, for men and women. 54 Rue du Faubourg-St.-Honoré, 8e (phone: 42-65-26-60).

Freddy – A popular shop for gifts, perfume, gloves, ties, scarves, and other items at good prices. 10 Rue Auber, 9e (phone: 47-42-63-41).

Galignani – Recently renovated, this shop sells books in English and French. It has been run by the same family since the beginning of the 19th century. 224 Rue de Rivoli, 1er (phone: 42-60-76-07).

La Gaminerie – Reasonably priced, good sportswear; outstanding window displays. 137 Bd. St.-Germain, 6e (phone: 43-26-27-98).

Gianni Versace – Women's clothing. 11 Rue du Faubourg-St.-Honoré, 8e (phone: 42-65-27-04); and 67 Rue des Sts.-Pères, 7e (phone: 42-84-00-40).

Givenchy – Beautifully tailored clothing by the master couturier. 3 Av. George-V, 8e (phone: 47-23-81-36).

Le Gourmet – The *Galeries Lafayette*'s chic, new grocery featuring exotic and high-priced food, wine, and confections from around the world. 40 Bd. Haussmann, 9e (phone: 48-74-37-13).

Guerlain – For fine perfume and cosmetics. 2 Pl. Vendôme, 1er; 68 Champs-Elysées, 8e (phone: 45-62-52-57); 29 Rue de Sèvres, 6e; and 93 Rue de Passy, 16e.

Guy Laroche – Classic and conservative couture. 30 Rue du Faubourg-St.-Honoré, 8e (phone: 42-65-62-74); and 29 Av. Montaigne, 8e (phone: 40-69-69-50).

Hanae Mori – The grande dame of Japanese designers in Paris. 17 Av. Montaigne, 8e (phone: 47-23-52-03); and 9 Rue du Faubourg-St.-Honoré, 8e.

Hédiard – Pricey but choice food shop, notable for its assortment of coffees and teas. Chic tearoom upstairs. 21 Pl. de la Madeleine, 8e (phone: 42-66-44-36).

Hermès – For very high quality ties, scarves, handbags, shoes, saddles, and accessories, though the prices may send you into cardiac arrest. 24 Rue du Faubourg-St.-Honoré, 8e (phone: 40-17-47-17).

Hôtel Drouot – Paris's huge auction house operates daily except Sundays. Good buys. 9 Rue Drouot, 9e (phone: 48-00-20-20).

***IGN* (French National Geographic Institute)** – All manner of maps — ancient and modern, foreign and domestic, esoteric and mundane — are sold here. 136 *bis* Rue Grenelle, 7e (phone: 42-25-87-90); and 107 Rue La Boétie, 8e.

Issey Miyake – "In" shop, selling women's clothing made by the Japanese artist-designer. Classic, more expensive line at 201 Bd. St.-Germain, 7e (phone: 45-44-60-88); latest collections at 3 Pl. des Vosges, 4e (phone: 48-87-01-86).

Jacadi – Classic designs for children from 3 months to 12 years. Excellent quality for a relatively affordable price. 7 Rue Gustave-Courbet, 16e (phone: 45-53-33-73); 51 Rue de Passy, 15e (phone: 45-27-03-01); and other locations.

Jean-Louis Scherrer – A top designer, whose clothes are favored by the Parisian chic. 51-53 Av. Montaigne, 8e (phone: 45-59-55-39).

Jean-Paul Gaultier – Designer clothes for men and women. 6 Rue Vivienne, 2e (phone: 42-86-05-05).

Karl Lagerfeld – Women's clothing. 17 Rue du Faubourg-St.-Honoré, 8e (phone: 42-66-64-64).

Kenzo – Avant-garde fashions by the Japanese designer. 3 Pl. des Victoires, 1er (phone: 40-39-72-02).

Lachaume – Stem for stem, the most beautiful flower shop in Paris. Buy a bouquet for an *ami(e)* or for *vous-même*. 10 Rue Royale, 8e (phone: 42-60-57-26).

Lalique – The famous crystal. 11 Rue Royale, 8e (phone: 42-65-33-70).

Lancôme – Cosmetics. 29 Rue du Faubourg-St.-Honoré, 8e (phone: 42-65-30-74).

Lanvin – Another fabulous designer, with several spacious, colorful boutiques under one roof. 15 and 22 Rue du Faubourg-St.-Honoré, 8e (phone: 42-65-14-40); and 2 Rue Cambon, 1er (phone: 42-60-38-83).

Laura Ashley – The English designer's familiar Victorian styles. 94 Rue des Rennes, 6e (phone: 42-22-77-80); and 261 Rue St.-Honoré, 1er (phone: 42-86-84-13).

Loewe – Classic leather goods in elegant quarters. One of Spain's oldest and highest-quality names in leather, and owned since 1985 by Louis Vuitton. 57 Av. Montaigne, 8e (phone: 45-63-73-38).

Louis Féraud – Couturier fashions for women at 88 Rue du Faubourg-St.-Honoré, and men at No. 62, 8e (phone: 40-07-01-16); and other locations.

Louis Vuitton – High-quality luggage and handbags. 78 *bis* Av. Marceau, 8e (phone: 47-20-47-00); and 54 Av. Montaigne, 8e (phone: 45-62-47-00).

Maison de la Truffe – The world's largest truffles retailer. (They're fresh, not preserved, from November to March.) 19 Pl. de la Madeleine (phone: 42-65-53-22).

Marché aux Puces – Paris's famous *Flea Market,* with 3,000 dealers in antiques and secondhand items. Open Saturdays, Sundays, and Mondays. Bargaining is a must. Porte de Clignancourt, 18e.

Marie Papier – Handsome marbled stationery and writing accessories. 26 Rue Vavin, 6e (phone: 43-26-46-44).

Marithé & François Girbaud – Not just jeans at this shop for men and women. 33 Rue Etienne-Marcel, 2e (phone: 42-33-54-69).

Maud Frizon – Sophisticated, imaginative shoes and handbags. 83 Rue des Sts.-Pères, 6e (phone: 42-22-06-93 or 42-22-19-86).

Miss Maud – Shoes aimed at a young market, but classy and fashionable enough for all ages. No longer connected with *Maud Frizon,* above. Several locations, including 90 Rue du Faubourg-St.-Honoré, 8e (phone: 42-65-27-96).

Missoni – Innovative, original Italian knitwear. 43 Rue du Bac, 7e (phone: 45-48-38-02).

Monique Germain – Unique hand-painted silk clothing at affordable prices: cocktail dresses, bridal wear, padded patchwork jackets. 59 Bd. Raspail, 6e (phone: 45-48-22-63).

M.O.R.A. – One of Paris's "professional" cookware shops, though it sells to individuals as well. Just about any piece of equipment you can imagine, and an interesting selection of cookbooks — in French. 13 Rue Montmartre, 1er (phone: 45-08-19-24).

Morabito – Magnificent handbags and luggage at steep prices. 1 Pl. Vendôme, 1er (phone: 42-60-30-76).

Le Must de Cartier – Actually two boutiques, on either side of the *Ritz* hotel, offering such Cartier items as lighters and watches at prices that, though not low, are almost bearable when you deduct the 25% VAT tax. 7 23 Pl. Vendôme, 1er (phone: 42-61-55-55).

Au Nain Bleu – The city's greatest toy store. 408 Rue St.-Honoré, 8e (phone: 42-60-30-01).

Nina Ricci – Women's fashions, as well as the famous perfume. 17 Rue François Ier, 8e (phone: 47-23-78-88); and 39 Av. Montaigne, 8e (phone: 47-23-78-88).

Les Olivades – Provençal printed yard goods, a little less pricey than *Souleiado* (see below). Shops throughout France, including 25 Rue de l'Annonciation, 16e (phone: 45-27-07-76).

Paloma Picasso – Perfume, clothing, and jewelry from one of France's preeminent designers and you-know-who's daughter. 5 Rue de la Paix, 2e (phone: 42-86-02-21).

Per Spook – One of Paris's best young designers. 18 Av. George-V, 8e (phone: 47-23-00-19), and elsewhere.

Le Petit Faune – A marvelous place to buy children's things. 33 Rue Jacob, 6e (phone: 42-60-80-72), and other locations.

Au Petit Matelot – Classic sportswear, outdoor togs, and nautical accessories for men, women, and children. Especially terrific are their Tyrolean-style olive or navy loden coats. 27 Av. de la Grande-Armée, 16e (phone: 45-00-15-51).

Pierre Balmain – Couturier boutique for women's fashions. 44 Rue François Ier, 8e (phone: 47-20-35-34), and other locations.

Pierre Cardin – A famous designer's own boutique. 83 Rue du Faubourg-St.-Honoré, 8e (phone: 42-66-62-94); 27 Av. Victor-Hugo, 16e (phone: 45-01-88-13); 14 Pl. François Ier, 8e (phone: 45-63-29-13); and other locations.

Pixi & Cie – Terrific collection of dolls, toy soldiers, and antique windup cars. 95 Rue de Seine, 6e (phone: 43-25-10-12).

Porthault – Terribly expensive, but elegantly exquisite bed and table linen. 18 Av. Montaigne, 8e (phone: 47-20-75-25).

Puiforcat – Art Deco tableware in a beautiful setting. 22 Rue François Ier, 8e (phone: 47-20-74-27).

Raymond – Charming and fairly inexpensive Porcelaine de Paris items. 100 Rue du Faubourg-St.-Honoré, 8e (phone: 42-66-69-49).

Romeo Gigli – Men's and women's arty ready-to-wear and haute couture. 46 Rue de Sévigné, 3e (phone: 42-71-08-40).

Sabbia Rosa – Simple, chic, and sexy lingerie is sold in this tiny shop on the Left Bank. 73 Rue des Sts.-Pères, 6e (phone: 45-48-88-37).

Shakespeare and Company – This legendary English-language bookstore, opposite Notre-Dame, is something of a tourist attraction in itself. 37 Rue de la Bûcherie, 5e (no phone).

Simon – A wide range of professional cookware, and a dazzling, but confusing, array of bistroware, flatware, cheese trays, snail holders, and tiny terrines. 36 Rue Etienne-Marcel, 2e (phone: 42-33-71-65).

Sonia Rykiel – Stunning sportswear and knits. 6 Rue de Grenelle, 15e; and 70 Rue du Faubourg-St.-Honoré, 8e (phone: 42-65-20-81).

Souleiado – Vibrant, traditional Provençal fabrics made into scarves, shawls, totes, and tableware. 78 Rue de Seine, 6e (phone: 43-54-62-25); and 83 Av. Paul-Doumer, 16e (phone: 42-24-99-34).

Stéphane Kélain – High-fashion, high-quality, and high-priced (but not completely unreasonable) men's and women's shoes, in several locations, including 4 Pl. des Victoires, 1er (phone: 42-36-31-84).

Tartine et Chocolat – Clothing for children, from infancy to 12 years old, and dresses for moms-to-be. Their trademark item: striped unisex overalls (about $90). 90 Rue de Rennes, 6e (phone: 42-22-67-34).

Ted Lapidus – A compromise between haute couture and excellent ready-to-wear. 23 Rue du Faubourg-St.-Honoré, 8e (phone: 44-60-89-91); 35 Rue François Ier, 8e (phone: 47-20-56-14); and other locations.

Thierry Mugler – Dramatic ready-to-wear for women. 49 Av. Montaigne, 8e (phone: 47-23-37-62).

Torrente – Women's fashions. 60 Av. Montaigne, 8e (phone: 42-56-14-14).

Trussardi – Italian ready-to-wear from a designer whose leather goods and canvas carryalls are much appreciated by the French and Japanese. 21 Rue du Faubourg-St.-Honoré, 8e (phone: 42-65-11-40).

Upla – Sporty handbags, scarves, and casual clothing. 17 Rue des Halles, 1er (phone: 40-26-49-96).

Valentino – Ready-to-wear and haute couture fashions for men and women from the Italian designer. 17-19 Av. Montaigne, 8e (phone: 47-23-64-61).

Van Cleef & Arpels – One of the world's great jewelers. 22 Pl. Vendôme, 1er (phone: 42-61-58-58).

Vicky Tiel – Strapless evening gowns decorated with beads and bows, as well as contemporary sweaters and baseball-style jackets. 21 Rue Bonaparte, 6e (phone: 46-33-53-58).

Victoire – Ready-to-wear, with attractive accessories. 12 Pl. des Victoires, 2e (phone: 47-04-49-87), and other locations.

Walter Stiger – Some of the capital's most expensive and exclusive footwear for men and women. The flagship shop displays satin slippers like precious jewels — and with prices to match. 83 Rue du Faubourg-St.-Honoré, 8e (phone: 42-66-65-08).

W. H. Smith and Sons – The largest (and best) Parisian bookstore for reading material in English. It sells the Sunday *New York Times,* in addition to many British and American magazines and books. 248 Rue de Rivoli, 1er (phone: 42-60-37-97).

Yves Saint Laurent – The world-renowned designer, considered one of the most famous names in high fashion. 38 Rue du Faubourg-St.-Honoré, 8e (phone: 42-65-74-59); 5 Av. Marceau, 8e (phone: 47-23-72-71); 6 Pl. St.-Sulpice, 6e (phone: 43-29-43-00); and other locations.

BEST DISCOUNT SHOPS

If you're one of those — like us — who believes that the eighth deadly sin is buying retail, you'll treasure these inexpensive outlets.

Anna Lowe – Saint Laurent's styling, among others, at a discount. 35 Av. Matignon, 8e (phone: 45-63-45-57).

Bab's – High fashion at low — or at least reasonable — prices. 29 Av. Marceau, 16e (phone: 47-20-84-74); and 89 *bis* Av. des Ternes, 17e.

Biderman – Menswear from Yves Saint Laurent, Kenzo, and Courrèges, in a warehouse of a store in the Marais. 11r Rue de Turenne, 3e (phone: 44-61-17-14).

Boétie 104 – Good buys on men's and women's shoes. 104 Rue La Boétie, 8e (phone: 43-59-72-38).

Boutique Stock – A vast selection of big-name knits at less than wholesale. 26, 30, and 51 Rue St.-Placide, 6e (phone: 45-48-83-66).

Cacharel Stock – Surprisingly current Cacharel fashions at about a 40% discount. 114 Rue d'Alésia, 14e (phone: 45-42-53-04).

Catherine – One of the most hospitable of the perfume and cosmetics shops. A 40%

discount (including VAT) is given on purchases totaling 1,500F (about $250) or more. 6 Rue Castiglione, 1er (phone: 42-60-81-49).

Catherine Baril – Women's ready-to-wear by designers such as Yves Saint Laurent and Jean-Louis Scherrer. 14-15 Rue de la Tour, 16e (phone: 45-20-95-21).

Dépôt des Grandes Marques – A third-floor shop near the stock market, featuring up to 50% markdowns on Louis Féraud, Cerruti, Renoma, and similar labels. 15 Rue de la Banque, 2e (phone: 42-96-99-04).

Dorothée Bis Stock – Ms. Bis's well-known designs at about 40% off. 74 Rue d'Alésia, 14e (phone: 45-42-17-11).

Drôles des Choses pour Drôles de Gens – Half-price clothes by Marithé and François Girbaud. 33 Rue Etienne-Marcel, 1er (phone: 43-72-15-23).

Emmanuelle Khanh – The designer's clothes at a substantial discount. 6 Rue Pierre-Lescot, 1er (no phone).

Georges Rech – Currently one of the most popular makers of classy, very Parisian styles, and at more affordable prices than other manufacturers of similarly styled goods. 273 Rue St.-Honoré, 1er (phone: 42-61-41-14); and 23 Av. Victor-Hugo, 16e (phone: 45-00-83-19).

Griff 'Mod – Names like Laroche and Lapidus at sale prices. 20 Rue des Petits-Champs, 2e (phone: 42-97-47-45).

Halle Bys – High fashions at discount prices. 60 Rue de Richelieu, 2e (phone: 42-96-65-42).

Jean-Louis Scherrer – Haute couture labels by Scherrer and others at about half their original prices. 29 Av. Ledru-Rollin, 12e (phone: 46-28-39-27).

Lady Soldes – Prime fashion labels at less than normal prices. 221 Rue du Faubourg-St.-Honoré, 8e (phone: 45-61-09-14).

Lanvin Soldes Trois – Lanvin fashions at about half their normal retail cost. 3 Rue de Vienne, 8e (no phone).

Max Mara – Italian ready-to-wear for many different moods. High quality, yet affordable. 37 Rue du Four, 6e (phone: 43-29-91-10); 265 Rue St.-Honoré, 1er (phone: 40-20-04-58); and other locations.

Mendès – Less-than-wholesale prices on haute couture, especially Saint Laurent and Lanvin. 65 Rue Montmartre, 2e (phone: 45-08-52-62 or 42-36-83-32).

Michel Swiss – Huge selection of perfume, cheerful service, and discounts of almost 44% to American visitors who pay with cash or traveler's checks, and who buy more than 1,200F ($200) of scents. 16 Rue de la Paix, 2e (phone: 42-61-71-71).

Miss Griffes – The very best of haute couture in small sizes (up to size 10) at small prices. Alterations. 19 Rue de Penthièvre, 8e (phone: 42-65-10-00).

Mouton à Cinq Pattes – Ready-to-wear clothing for men, women, and children at 50% off original prices. 8, 10, and 14 Rue St.-Placide, 6e (phone: 45-48-86-26).

Pierre Cardin Stock – Terrific buys on the famed designer's men's clothing. 72 Rue St.-Honoré, 1er (phone: 40-26-74-73).

Reciproque – Billed as the largest *"depot-vent"* in Paris, this outlet features names like Chanel, Alaia, Lanvin, and Scherrer. Several hundred square yards of display area are arranged by designer and by size. 95 Rue de la Pompe, 16e (phone: 47-04-82-24); men's clothing and accessories next door at No. 101. New boutiques are at Nos. 89, 91, and 123 Rue de la Pompe.

Stéphane – Men's designer suits by Pierre Balmain, Ted Lapidus, and André Courrèges at 25% to 45% discount. 130 Bd. St.-Germain, 6e (phone: 46-33-94-55).

Stock Coupons – Features discounted Daniel Hechter for men, women, and children. 92 Rue d'Alésia, 14e (phone: 45-42-82-66).

Stock Griffes – Women's ready-to-wear apparel at 40% off their original prices. 17 Rue Vielle du Temple, 4e (phone: 48-04-82-34); and 1 Rue des Trois-Frères, 18e (phone: 42-55-42-49).

Stock System – Prêt-à-porter clothing for men and women at a 30% discount. 112 Rue d'Alésia, 14e (phone: 45-43-80-86).

Also, Rue du Paradis (10e) is the best area to shop for crystal and porcelain — Baccarat, Saint-Louis, Haviland, Bernardaud, and Villeroy & Boch — at amazing prices. Try *Cristalerie de Paris* at No. 10; *Boutique Paradis,* 1 *bis; L'Art et La Table,* 3; *Limoges-Unio,* Nos. 8 and 12; *Porcelain Savary,* 9; *Arts Céramiques,* 15; and *Cristallerie Paradis,* at No. 17.

■ ***Note***: For a modest price ($15 and up), you can also take home a bit of the *Louvre.* The museum's 200-year-old Department of Calcography houses a collection of 16,000 engraved copper plates — renderings of monuments, battles, coronations, Egyptian pyramids, and portraits — dating from the 17th century. Prints made from these engravings come reproduced on thick vellum, embossed with the *Louvre*'s imprint. The Calcography Department (open daily, except Tuesdays, from 2 to 5 PM) is 1 flight up from the Porte Barbet de Jouy entrance on the Seine side of the *Louvre.*

 SPORTS AND FITNESS: Biking – Rentals are available in the Bois de Boulogne and the Bois de Vincennes, or contact the *Fédération Française de Cyclo-tourisme* (8 Rue Jean-Marie-Jégo, 13e; phone: 45-80-30-21); *Bicyclub* (8 Pl. de la Porte Champerret, 17e; phone: 47-66-55-92); or *Paris-Vélo* (2 Rue du Fer à Moulin, 5e; phone: 43-37-59-22). In addition to renting bicycles, *Paris by Cycle* (99 Rue de la Jonquière, 17e; phone: 42-63-36-63) arranges guided group tours of the city, Versailles, and bike trips alternating with horseback rides. The world-famous *Tour de France* bicycle race takes place in July and ends in Paris.

Fitness Centers – The *Garden Gym* (26 Rue de Berri, 8e; phone: 43-59-04-58; and 123 Av. Charles-de-Gaulle, Neuilly; phone: 47-47-62-62) is open daily to non-members for a fee.

Golf – For general information, contact the *Fédération Française de Golf* (69 Av. Victor-Hugo, 16e; phone: 45-02-13-55). It usually is possible to play on any course during the week by simply paying a greens fee. Weekends may be more difficult. *Ozoir-la-Ferrière* (Château des Agneaux, 15 miles/24 km away; closed Tuesdays; phone: 60-28-20-79) welcomes Americans; and *St.-Germain-en-Laye* (12 miles/19 km away; phone: 34-51-75-90) accepts non-members on weekdays only (closed Mondays). The *Racing Club de France* (La Boulie, Versailles; phone: 39-50-59-41) and *St.-Nom-la-Bretèche* (in the suburb of the same name; phone: 34-62-54-00) accept only guests of members. It's best to call at least 2 days in advance to schedule a time. (Also see *Great French Golf,* DIVERSIONS.)

Horse Racing – Of the eight tracks in and around Paris, two major ones are in the Bois de Boulogne: *Longchamp* (phone: 42-24-13-29) for flat races and *Auteuil* (phone: 45-27-12-24) for steeplechase. *St.-Cloud* (phone: 43-59-20-70), a few miles west of Paris, and *Chantilly* (phone: 42-66-92-02), about 25 miles (40 km) north of the city, are both for flat racing. *Vincennes* (Bois de Vincennes; phone: 47-42-07-70) is the trotting track. Important races take place from spring through fall, but the *Grande Semaine* (Big Week) comes in mid-June, when nine major races — beginning with the *Grand Steeplechase de Paris* at *Auteuil* and including the *Grand Prix de Paris* at *Longchamp* — are scheduled.

Jogging – The streets and sidewalks of Paris may be ideal for lovers, but they're not meant for runners. There are, however, a number of places where you can jog happily; one of the most pleasant is the 2,500-acre Bois de Boulogne. Four more central parks are the Jardin du Luxembourg (reachable by métro: Luxembourg), the Champ-de-Mars gardens (just behind the Eiffel Tower; métro: Iéna), Parc Monceau (métro: Monceau), and the Jardin des Tuileries (métro: Tuileries, Louvre, or Concorde).

Soccer – There are matches from early August to mid-June at Parc des Princes (Av. du Parc-des-Princes, 16e; phone: 42-88-02-76).

Swimming – At the heart of Paris, rather unsuitably near the National Assembly, lies the *Piscine Deligny*, notorious in the summer for its acres of topless women bathers and, on the top deck, nude sunbathers of both sexes. The pool is set in a floating barge on the Seine beside the Concorde bridge; it is, says the sign, filled with fresh water. Open May to September. 25 Quai Anatole-France, 7e (phone: 45-51-72-15). Other pools include *Piscine des Halles* (10 Pl. de la Rotonde, 4e; phone: 42-36-98-44), *Piscine du Quartier Latin* (19 Rue de Pontoise, 5e; phone: 43-54-82-45), *Butte-aux-Cailles* (5 Pl. Paul-Verlaine, 13e; phone: 45-89-60-05), *Keller* (14 Rue de l'Ingénieur-Robert-Keller, 15e; phone: 45-77-12-12), *Jean-Taris* (16 Rue Thouin, 5e; phone: 43-25-54-03), *Tour Montparnasse* (beneath the tower at 66 Bd. de Montparnasse, 15e; phone: 45-38-65-19), *Piscine Georges-Vallerey* (148 Av. Gambetta, 20e; phone: 40-31-15-20); *Aquaboulevard* (4-6 Rue Louis-Armand, 15e; phone: 40-60-10-00), *Roger La Gall* (34 Bd. Carnot, 12e; phone: 46-28-77-03), and *Neuilly* (50 Rue Pauline-Borghèse, Neuilly; phone: 47-22-69-59).

Tennis – For general information, call *Ligue Régionale de Paris* (74 Rue de Rome, 17e; phone: 45-22-22-08), or the *Fédération Française de Tennis* (*Roland Garros Stadium,* 16e; phone: 47-43-48-00). Americans who wish to attend the annual *French Open Tennis Tournament* may write in advance to the *Fédération Française de Tennis Billetterie* (Service Reservation, BP 33316, Paris 75767; phone: 47-43-48-00).

 THEATER: The most complete listings of theaters, operas, concerts, and movies are found in *L'Officiel des Spectacles* and *Pariscope* (see *Tourist Information,* above). The season generally is from September to June. Tickets are less expensive than in New York and are obtained at each box office, through brokers (*American Express* and *Thomas Cook* act in that capacity and are good), via your hotel's trusty concierge, or with the high-tech Billetels at the *Galeries Lafayette,* the *Centre Georges-Pompidou,* and other locations. Insert a credit card into a slot in the Billetel and choose from over 100 upcoming theater events and concerts. The device will spew out a display of dates, seats, and prices, from which you can order your tickets — they will be printed on the spot and charged to your account. Half-price, day-of-performance theater tickets are available at the kiosks at the Châtelet-les Halles, 1er (Tuesdays through Saturdays from 12:45 to 7 PM), and at 15 Place de la Madeleine, 8e (Tuesdays through Saturdays from 12:30 to 8 PM, Sundays from 12:30 to 4 PM). The curtain usually goes up at 8:30 PM.

For those who speak French: Performances of classical plays by Molière, Racine, and Corneille take place at the *Comédie-Française* (Pl. du Théâtre, 1er; phone: 40-15-00-15). Two other national theaters are *L'Odéon–Théâtre de l'Europe* (1 Pl. Paul-Claudel, 6e; phone: 43-25-70-32) and *Théâtre National de Chaillot* (Pl. du Trocadéro, 16e; phone: 47-27-81-15). Last, but not least, the *Théâtre du Soleil,* in an old cartridge factory, La Cartoucherie de Vincennes (on the outskirts of Paris in the Bois de Vincennes, 12e; phone: 43-74-24-08 or 43-74-87-63), offers colorful productions ranging from contemporary political works to Shakespeare.

It's not really necessary to speak the language to enjoy the opera, dance, or musical comedy at *L'Opéra* (Pl. de l'Opéra, 9e; phone: 47-42-57-50), the new *Opéra de La Bastille* (120 Rue de Lyon in the Place de la Bastille, 11e; phone: 40-01-17-89 or 40-01-16-16), *Salle Favart–Opéra Comique* (5 Rue Favart, 2e; phone: 42-86-88-83), or *Théâtre Musical de Paris* (1 Pl. du Châtelet, 1er; phone: 40-28-28-40). Theater tickets can be reserved through *SOS-Théâtre* (73 Champs-Elysées, 8e; phone: 42-25-67-07).

For those who consider French their second language, Paris's many café-theaters offer amusing songs, sketches, satires, and takeoffs on topical trends and events. Among them are *Café de la Gare* (41 Rue du Temple, 4e; phone: 42-78-52-51) and *Café d'Edgar* (58 Bd. Edgar-Quinet, 14e; phone: 43-22-11-02).

 CINEMA: With no fewer than 200 movie houses, Paris is a real treat for film buffs. No other metropolis offers such a cinematographic feast — current French chic, recent imports from across the Atlantic, grainy 1930s classics, and the latest and most select of Third World and Eastern European offerings. In any given week, there are up to 200 different movies shown, the foreign films generally in their original versions with French subtitles.

Film distribution is erratic, to say the least, so the French often get their *Silence of the Lambs* and *Robin Hood* flicks up to 6 months late. But the system works both ways: Many of the front-runners at Cannes first hit the screens here, which gives you a jump on friends back home.

Both *Pariscope* and *L'Officiel de Spectacles,* which come out on Wednesday, the day the programs change, contain the full selection each week. *Pariscope* has thought of almost every possible way to classify films, sorting them into new releases and revivals, broad categories (for instance, the *drame psychologique* label means it will be heavier than a *comédie dramatique*), location by *arrondissement,* late-night showings, and so on.

Films shown with their original-language soundtracks are called VO (*version originale*); it's worth watching out for that crucial "VO" tag, or you may find yourself wincing at a French-dubbed version, called VF (*version française*). Broadly speaking, the undubbed variety of film flourishes on the Champs-Elysées and on the Left Bank, and it's also a safe bet to avoid the mostly French-patronized houses of les Grands Boulevards.

The timetables aren't always reliable, so it's worth checking by telephone — if you can decipher the recorded messages that spell out exactly when the five or so showings a day begin. A *séance* (sitting) generally begins with advertisements, and the movie proper begins 15 to 20 minutes later.

There's more room in the big movie houses on the Champs-Elysées, but the cozier Latin Quarter establishments tend to specialize in the unusual and avant-garde — often the only showing such films will ever get. The ultimate in high-tech, the *Géode,* offers a B-Max hemispherical screen, cupped inside a reflecting geodesic dome, at La Villette Sciences and Industry complex. The program is, however, limited to a single scientifically oriented film at any given time, whereas the *Forum Horizon,* in the underground section of the *Forum des Halles,* offers a choice of four first-run movies and claims to have one of the city's best sound systems. Some more out-of-the-way venues like the *Olympique Entrepôt* and the *Lucernaire* in Montparnasse are social centers in themselves, incorporating restaurants and/or other theaters.

Paris's *Cinémathèque* — at the Palais de Chaillot, which also has an interesting *Cinema Museum* — runs a packed schedule of reruns at rates lower than those of the commercial cinemas. Daily afternoon and evening programs from the museum's eclectic archives of over 20,000 films often include several running concurrently, so that a James Cagney gangster epic can share billing with a 1950s British comedy and a Brazilian thriller (phone: 47-04-24-24). (The *Cinémathèque* also operates theaters in the *Centre Georges-Pompidou*'s Salle Garance; phone: 42-78-37-29; and in the *Palais de Tokyo;* 13 Av. President-Wilson; phone: 47-04-24-24). The *Videothèque de Paris,* in the *Forum des Halles,* is the world's first public video library. Visitors can select individual showings or attend regularly scheduled theater screenings of films and television programs chronicling Paris's history (phone: 40-26-34-30).

Then there are two period pieces almost worth a visit in themselves. *Le Ranelagh* (5 Rue des Vignes, 16e; phone: 42-88-64-44) has an exquisite 19th-century interior where films are screened and live theater performed. *La Pagode* (57 *bis* Rue de Baby-lone, 7e; phone: 47-05-12-15), with flying cranes, cherry blossoms, and a tearoom, is built around a Japanese temple that was shipped over to Paris by the proprietor of a department store in the 1920s.

MUSIC: The *Orchestre de Paris,* under the direction of Semyon Bychkov, is based at the *Salle Pleyel* — the *Carnegie Hall* of Paris (252 Rue du Faubourg-St.-Honoré, 8e; phone: 45-61-06-30). Other classical recitals are held at the *Salle Gaveau* (45 Rue La Boëtie, 8e; phone: 49-53-05-07), at the *Théâtre des Champs-Elysées* (15 Av. Montaigne, 8e; phone: 47-20-36-37), and at the *Palais des Congrès* (Porte Maillot; phone: 46-40-22-22). The *Nouvelle Orchestre Phil-harmonic* performs at a variety of places, including the *Grand Auditorium* at *Maison de Radio France* (116 Av. du Président-Kennedy, 16e; phone: 42-30-15-16 or 42-30-18-18). Special concerts frequently are held in Paris's many places of worship, with moving music at high mass on Sundays. The *Palais des Congrès* and the *Olympia* (28 Bd. des Capucines, 9e; phone: 47-42-82-45) are the places to see well-known international pop and rock artists. Innovative contemporary music — much of it created by computer — is the province of the *Institut de Recherche et de Coopération Acoustique Musique* (*IRCAM*), whose musicians can be heard in various auditoriums of the *Centre Georges-Pompidou* (31 Rue St.-Merri, 4e; phone: 42-77-12-33).

NIGHTCLUBS AND NIGHTLIFE: Organized "Paris by Night" group tours (*Cityrama, Paris Vision,* and other operators offer them; see *Special Places*) include at least one "Spectacle" — beautiful girls in minimal, yet elaborate, costumes, with lavish sets and effects and sophisticated striptease. Most music halls offer a package (starting as high as $120 per person), with dinner, dancing, and a half bottle of champagne. It is possible to go to these places on your own, save money by skipping dinner and the champagne (both usually way below par), and take a seat at the bar to see the show. The most famous extravaganzas occur nightly at *Crazy Horse* (12 Av. George-V, 8e; phone: 47-23-32-32), *Folies-Bergère* (32 Rue Richer, 9e; phone: 42-46-77-11), *Lido* (116 *bis* Champs-Elysées, 8e; phone: 40-76-56-10), *Moulin Rouge* (Pl. Blanche, 18e; phone: 46-06-00-19), and *Paradis Latin* (28 Rue du Cardinal-Lemoine, 5e; phone: 43-29-07-07). An amusing evening can also be spent at smaller cabaret shows like *René Cousinier* (*La Branlette;* 4 Impasse Marie-Blanche, 18e; phone: 46-06-49-46), *Au Lapin Agile* (22 Rue des Saules, 18e; phone: 46-06-85-87), and *Michou* (80 Rue des Martyrs, 18e; phone: 46-06-16-04). Reserve all a few days in advance.

There's one big difference between discotheques and private clubs. Fashionable "in" spots like *Le Palace* (8 Rue Faubourg-Montmartre, 9e; phone: 42-46-10-87), *Régine's* (49 Rue de Ponthieu, 8e; phone: 43-59-21-60), *Chez Castel* (15 Rue Princesse, 6e, members only; phone: 43-26-90-22), *Olivia Valère* (40 Rue de Colisée, 8e, members only; phone: 42-25-11-68), *Les Bains* (7 Rue du Bourg-l'Abbé, 3e; phone: 48-87-01-80), and *Elysées Matignon* (48 Av. Gabriel, 8e; phone: 42-25-73-13) superscreen potential guests. No reason is given for accepting some and turning others away; go here with a regular or look as if you'd fit in with the crowd. Go early and on a weeknight — when your chances of getting past the gatekeeper are at least 50-50. Don't despair if you're refused; the following places are just as much fun and usually more hospitable: *La Scala* (188 *bis* Rue de Rivoli, 1er; phone: 42-61-64-00), *L'Aventure* (122 Rue d'Assas, 6e; phone: 46-34-22-60), and *L'Ecume des Nuits* (*Hôtel Méridien,* 81 Bd. Gouvion-St.-Cyr, 17e; phone: 40-68-30-89).

Some pleasant, popular bars for a nightcap include *Bar de la Closerie des Lilas* (171 Bd. Montparnasse, 6e; phone: 43-26-70-50), *Harry's New York Bar* (5 Rue Daunou, 2e; phone: 42-61-71-14), *Fouquet's* (99 Champs-Elysées, 8e; phone: 47-23-70-60), *Ascot*

Bar (66 Rue Pierre-Charron, 8e; phone: 43-59-28-15), *Bar Anglais* (*Plaza-Athénée Hôtel,* 25 Av. Montaigne, 8e; phone: 47-23-78-33), and *Pub Winston Churchill* (5 Rue de Presbourg, 16e; phone: 45-00-75-35).

Jazz buffs have a large choice including *Caveau de la Huchette* (5 Rue de la Huchette, 5e; phone: 43-26-65-05), *Le Bilboquet* (13 Rue St.-Benoît, 6e; phone: 45-48-81-84), *New Morning* (7-9 Rue des Petites Ecuries, 10e; phone: 45-23-51-41), and *Le Petit Journal* (71 Bd. St.-Michel, 6e; phone: 43-26-28-59).

Enghien-les-Bains, 8 miles (13 km) away, is the only casino in the Paris vicinity (3 Av. de Ceinture, Enghien-les-Bains; phone: 34-12-90-00). Open 3 PM to about 4 AM, it easily can be reached by train from the Gare du Nord.

BEST IN TOWN

CHECKING IN: The annual *Guide des Hôtels de France,* issued by the French ministry in charge of tourism, lists tourist hotels that are officially graded according to the government's star system of classification. The highest rating is four stars plus L, indicating, to use the official definition, a luxury hotel. Four stars means a top hotel; three stars, a very comfortable hotel; two stars, a good average hotel; and one star or *HRT* (for *Hôtels Rattachés Tourisme;* literally, hotels linked to tourism), a plain but fairly comfortable hotel. The listing for each hotel includes its address and telephone number, number of rooms, amenities, star category, and minimum and maximum room prices; though the latter inevitably are somewhat out of date by the time of publication, they include service charges and applicable taxes and certainly serve as a valid estimate. The French Government Tourist Office also distributes a list of US representatives handling reservations for French hotels, as well as a special list of selected Paris hotels, with their ratings and the names of the US representatives.

Even without such a guide in hand, it is not difficult for visitors in Paris to figure out where a particular hotel fits in the scheme of things. A dark blue, octagonal "Commissariat Général au Tourisme" sign on the front of any hotel that has been classified clearly reveals the number of stars attained. Inside, a detailed rendering of prices appears by law near the reception desk. A good many hotels, in fact, actually display minimum and maximum prices on the front door, where they are easily legible from the street. The posted prices include service and, except in a few cases, all taxes, so that receiving the bill at the end of a stay is rarely a cause for shock. The prices also usually are for double rooms (since in Paris, as elsewhere, there are more double than single rooms), and the price of a double usually holds whether it's occupied by one or two people. The price of breakfast — which may be obligatory or optional — also must be posted by the reception desk.

Hotels earn their stars according to a variety of criteria, among them the percentage of rooms with private bathrooms. All rooms in a four-star L hotel and 90% of the rooms in a four-star hotel must have them; the required proportion drops to 30% in a two-star; and there is no requirement for one-star hotels. There may be, therefore, a number of room types in any given hotel, especially in two- and three-star establishments, where the most expensive rooms will have private bathrooms containing a tub or a shower (usually slightly less expensive) and the least expensive rooms will have only a *cabinet de toilette* (that is, a washbasin with hot and cold water and a bidet) or, simply, a washbasin. (Guests in rooms with a *cabinet de toilette* or less have access to the public bathroom in the hall.) Central heating is universal in classified tourist hotels (though it may not always be adequate by American standards), and the type of breakfast provided is nearly universal: continental, which consists of coffee, tea, or hot chocolate with bread, rolls, or croissants, butter, and jam. Also nearly universal is the bolster pillow found on a French bed; for those who prefer it, the more familiar kind of pillow usually is stashed in the closet (if not, ask for one).

An attractive alternative for the visitor content to stay in Paris for a week or more is to rent an apartment or a villa. These offer a wide range of luxury and convenience, depending on the price you want to pay. One of the advantages to staying in a house, apartment (usually called a "flat" overseas), or other rented vacation home is that you will feel much more like a visitor than a tourist.

Known to Europeans as a "holiday let" or a "self-catering holiday," a vacation in a furnished rental has both the advantages and disadvantages of living "at home" abroad. It can be less expensive than staying in a first class hotel, although very luxurious and expensive rentals are available, too. It has the comforts of home, including a kitchen, which means potential savings on food. Furthermore, it gives a sense of the country that a large hotel often cannot. On the other hand, a certain amount of housework is involved because if you don't eat out, you have to cook, and though some rentals (especially the luxury ones) include a cleaning person, most don't. (If the rental doesn't include daily cleaning, arrangements often can be made with a maid service.)

For a family, two or more couples, or a group of friends, the per-person cost — even for a luxurious rental — can be quite reasonable. Weekly and monthly rates are available to reduce costs still more. But best of all is the amount of space, which no conventional hotel room can equal. As with hotels, the rates for properties in some areas are seasonal, rising during the peak travel season, while for others they remain the same year-round. To have your pick of the properties available, you should begin to make arrangements for a rental at least 6 months in advance.

There are several ways of finding a suitable rental property. For those who wish to arrange a rental themselves, write or call the French Government Tourist Office (for locations in the US, see *Tourist Information* in GETTING READY TO GO), or contact the *Fédération Nationale des Agents Immobiliers* (129 Rue du Faubourg-St.-Honoré, Paris 75001; phone; 1-44-20-77-00) for a list of real estate agencies handling rentals in Paris.

The companies listed below rent a wide range of properties. They handle the booking and confirmation paperwork and can be expected to provide more information about the properties than that which might ordinarily be gleaned from a short listing in an accommodations guide.

> *At Home Abroad* (405 E. 56th St., Apt. 6H, New York, NY 10022; phone: 212-421-9165). Offers moderate apartments in Paris. Photographs of properties and a newsletter are available for a $50 registration fee.
>
> *B & D De Vogue Travel Services* (PO Box 1998, Visalia, CA 93279; phone: 800-338-0483; or through *Paris Séjour Réservations,* 90 Av. des Champs-Elysées, Paris 75008; phone: 42-56-30-00). Apartment rentals in Paris are the specialty; the minumum rental period is 7 nights, with weekly maid service included.
>
> *British Travel Associates* (PO Box 299, Elkton, VA 22927; phone: 800-327-6097 or 703-298-2232). Arranges apartment and some cottage rentals in Paris.
>
> *Castles, Cottages, and Flats* (7 Faneuil Hall Marketplace, Boston, MA 02109; phone: 617-742-6030). Some apartments in Paris. Small charge ($5) for receipt of main catalogue, refundable upon booking.
>
> *Chez Vous* (220 Redwood Highway, Suite 129E, Mill Valley, CA 94941; phone: 415-331-2535). Offers apartments in Paris.
>
> *Europa-Let* (PO Box 3537, Ashland, OR 97520; phone: 800-462-4486 or 503-482-5806). Offers apartments and some private homes in Paris.
>
> *The French Experience* (370 Lexington Ave., New York, NY 10017; phone: 212-986-1115). Rents apartments in Paris.
>
> *Heart of England Cottages* (PO Box 878, Eufala, AL 36072-0878; phone: 205-687-

9800). Besides cottages in England, it also has some apartments in Paris.

Hideaways International (15 Goldsmith St., PO Box 1270, Littleton, MA 01460; phone: 800-843-4433 or 508-486-8955). Rents apartments in Paris.

Home Tours International (1170 Broadway, New York, 10001; phone: 800-367-4668 or 212-689-0851). Handles apartments in Paris.

Rent a Vacation Everywhere (*RAVE;* 328 Main St. E., Suite 526, Rochester, NY 14604; phone: 716-454-6440). Moderate to luxurious villas and apartments in Paris.

Vacances en Campagne (PO Box 297, Falls Village, CT 06031; phone: 800-533-5405). Represents over 400 properties in France, including Paris. A catalogue is available for $5.

VHR Worldwide (235 Kensington Ave., Norwood, NJ 07648; phone: 201-767-9393, locally; 800-NEED-A-VILLA elsewhere in the US). Rents apartments in Paris.

Villas International (605 Market St., Suite 510, San Francisco, CA 94105; phone: 800-221-2260 or 415-281-0910). Rents some apartments in Paris.

For further information, including a general discussion of all forms of vacation rentals, evaluating costs, and information on rental opportunities in France, see *A Traveler's Guide to Vacation Rentals in Europe.* Available in general bookstores, it also can be ordered from Penguin USA (120 Woodbine St., Bergenfield, NJ 07621; phone: 800-331-4624, and ask for cash sales) for $11.95, plus postage and handling.

In addition, a useful publication, the *Worldwide Home Rental Guide,* lists properties throughout France, as well as the managing agencies. Issued twice annually, single copies may be available at newsstands for $10 an issue. For a year's subscription, send $18 to *Worldwide Home Rental Guide,* PO Box 2842, Sante Fe, NM 87504 (phone: 505-988-5188).

When considering a particular vacation rental property, look for answers to the following questions:

- How do you get from the airport to the property?
- What size and number of beds are provided?
- How far is the property from whatever else is important to you, such as a golf course or nightlife?
- If there is no grocery store on the premises (which may be comparatively expensive, anyway), how far is the nearest market?
- Are baby-sitters, cribs, bicycles, or anything else you may need for your children available?
- Is maid service provided daily?
- Is air conditioning and/or a phone provided?
- Is a car rental part of the package? Is a car necessary?

Before deciding which rental is for you, make sure you have satisfactory answers to all your questions. Ask your travel agent to find out, or call the company involved directly.

HOME EXCHANGES: Still another alternative for travelers who are content to stay in one place during their vacation is a home exchange: The Smith family from Chicago moves into the home of the Chabrol family in Paris, while the Chabrols enjoy a stay in the Smiths' home. The home exchange is an exceptionally inexpensive way to ensure comfortable, reasonable living quarters with amenities that no hotel possibly could offer; often the trade includes a car. Moreover, it allows you to live in a new community in a way that few tourists ever do: For a little while, at least, you will become something of a resident.

Several companies publish directories of individuals and families willing to trade homes with others for a specific period of time. In some cases, you must be willing to list your own home in the directory; in others, you can subscribe without appearing in it. Most listings are for straight exchanges only, but each directory also has a number of listings placed by people interested in either exchanging or renting (for instance, if they own a second home). Other arrangements include exchanges of hospitality while owners are in residence or youth exchanges, where your teenager is put up as a guest in return for your putting up their teenager at a later date. A few house-sitting opportunities also are available. In most cases, arrangements for the actual exchange take place directly between you and the foreign host. There is no guarantee that you will find a listing in the area in which you are interested, but each of the organizations given below includes French homes among its hundreds or even thousands of foreign listings.

> *Home Base Holidays* (7 Park Ave., London N13 5PG England; phone: 44-81-886-8752). For $42 a year, subscribers receive four listings, with an option to list in all four.
>
> *Intervac US/International Home Exchange Service* (Box 190070, San Francisco, CA 94119; phone: 415-435-3497). For $45 (plus postage) subscribers receive copies of the three directories published yearly, and are entitled to list their home in one of them; a black-and-white photo may be included with the listing for an additional $10. A $5 discount is given to travelers over age 62.
>
> *Loan-A-Home* (2 Park Lane, Apt. 6E, Mt. Vernon, NY 10552; phone: 914-664-7640). Specializes in long-term (4 months or more — excluding July and August) housing arrangements worldwide for students, professors, businesspeople, and retirees, although its two annual directories (with supplements) carry a small list of short-term rentals and/or exchanges. $35 for a copy of one directory and one supplement; $45 for two directories and two supplements.
>
> *Vacation Exchange Club* (PO Box 820, Haleiwa, HI 96712; phone: 800-638-3841). Some 10,000 listings. For $50, the subscriber receives two directories — one in late winter, one in the spring — and is listed in one.
>
> *World Wide Exchange* (1344 Pacific Ave., Suite 103, Santa Cruz, CA 95060; phone: 408-476-4206). The $45 annual membership fee includes one listing (for house, yacht, or motorhome) and three guides.
>
> *Worldwide Home Exchange Club* (13 Knightsbridge Green, London SW1X OJZ, England; phone: 71-589-6055; or 806 Brantford Ave., Silver Spring, MD 20904; no phone). Handles over 1,500 listings a year worldwide, including homes throughout France. For $25 a year, you will receive two listings yearly, as well as supplements.

Better Homes and Travel (formerly *Home Exchange International*), with an office in New York, and representatives in Los Angeles, London, Paris, and Milan, functions in a different manner in that it publishes no directory and shepherds the exchange process most of the way. Interested parties supply the firm with photographs of themselves and their homes, information on the type of home they want and where, and a registration fee of $50. The company then works with its other offices to propose a few possibilities, and only when a match is made do the parties exchange names, addresses, and phone numbers. For this service, *Better Homes and Travel* charges a closing fee, which ranges from $150 to $500 for switches from 2 weeks to 3 months in duration, and from $300 to $600 for longer switches. Contact *Better Homes and Travel* at 185 Park Row, PO Box 268, New York, NY 10038-0272 (phone: 212-349-5340).

HOME STAYS: If the idea of actually staying in a private home as the guest of a French family appeals to you, check with the *United States Servas Committee,* which maintains a list of hosts throughout the world (at present, there are over 800 in France) willing to throw open their doors to foreigners, entirely free of charge.

The aim of this nonprofit cultural program is to promote international understanding and peace, and every effort is made to discourage freeloaders. *Servas* will send you an application form and the name of the nearest of some 200 interviewers around the US for you to contact. After the interview, if you're approved, you'll receive documentation certifying you as a *Servas* traveler. There is a membership fee of $45 per person and there also is a deposit of $15 to receive the host list, refunded on its return. The list gives the name, address, age, occupation, and other particulars of each host, including languages spoken. From then on, it is up to you to write to prospective hosts directly, and *Servas* makes no guarantee that you will be accommodated.

Servas stresses that you should choose only people you really want to meet, and that during your stay (which normally lasts between 2 nights and 2 weeks) you should be interested mainly in your hosts, not in sightseeing. It also suggests that one way to show your appreciation once you've returned home is to become a host yourself. The minimum age of a *Servas* traveler is 18 (however, children under 18 may accompany their parents), and though quite a few are young people who have just finished college, there are travelers (and hosts) in all age ranges and occupations. Contact *Servas* at 11 John St., Room 706, New York, NY 10038 (phone: 212-267-0252).

You also might be interested in a publication called *International Meet-the-People Directory,* published by the *International Vistor Information Service.* It lists several agencies in a number of foreign countries (37 worldwide, 18 in Europe) that arrange home visits for Americans, either for dinner or overnight stays. To order a copy, send $5.95 to the *International Visitor Information Service* (733 15th St. NW, Suite 300, Washington, DC 20005; phone: 202-783-6540). For other local organizations and services offering home exchanges, contact the local tourist authority.

■**A warning about telephone surcharges in hotels::** A lot of digits may be involved once a caller starts dialing beyond national borders, but avoiding operator-assisted calls can cut costs considerably and bring rates into a somewhat more reasonable range — except for calls made through hotel switchboards. One of the most unpleasant surprises travelers encounter in many foreign countries is the amount they find tacked onto their hotel bill for telephone calls, because foreign hotels routinely add on astronomical surcharges. (It's not at all uncommon to find 300% or 400% added to the actual telephone charges.)

Until recently, the only recourse against this unconscionable overcharging was to call collect when phoning from abroad or to use a telephone credit card — available through a simple procedure from any local US phone company. (Note, however, that even if you use a telephone credit card, some hotels still may charge a fee for line usage.) Now, *American Telephone and Telegraph (AT&T)* offers USA Direct, a service that connects users, via a toll-free number, with an *AT&T* operator in the US, who will then put the call through at the standard international rate. A new feature of this service is that travelers abroad can reach US toll-free (800) numbers by calling a USA Direct operator, who will connect them. Charges for all calls made through USA Direct appear on the caller's regular US phone bill. To reach USA Direct in France, you dial 19, wait for a dial tone, then dial 0011. For a brochure and wallet card listing the toll-free numbers for other countries, contact International Information Service, *AT&T Communications,* 635 Grant St., Pittsburgh, PA 15219 (phone: 800-874-4000).

AT&T also has put together Teleplan, an agreement among certain hoteliers that sets a limit on surcharges for calls made by guests from their rooms. Teleplan currently is in effect in selected hotels in France. Teleplan agreements stipulate a flat amount for credit card or collect calls (currently between $1 and $10), and a flat percentage (between 20% and 100%) on calls paid for at the hotel. For further information, contact *AT&T*'s International Information Service (address above).

It's wise to ask about surcharges *before* calling from a hotel. If the rate is high, it's best to use a telephone credit card, or the direct-dial service listed above; make a collect call; or place the call and ask the party to call right back. If none of these choices is possible, make international calls from the local post office or special telephone center to avoid surcharges. Another way to keep down the cost of telephoning from France is to leave a copy of your itinerary and telephone numbers with people in the US so that they can call you instead.

Paris offers a broad choice of accommodations, from luxurious palaces with every service to more humble budget hotels. However, they all are strictly controlled by the government and must post their rates, so you can be sure that the price you are being charged is correct. Below is our selection from all categories; in general, expect to spend at least $300 and way up per night for a double room in the "palace" hotels, which we've listed as very expensive; from $200 to $300 in the expensive range; $100 to $200 is considered moderate; $50 to $100 is inexpensive; and $50 or less is very inexpensive (a miracle!).

Except for July, August, and December, the least crowded months, hotel rooms usually are at a premium in Paris. To reserve your first choice, we advise making reservations at least a month in advance, even farther ahead for the smaller, less expensive places listed. Watch for the dates of special events, when hotels are even more crowded than usual. The apartment rentals offered by *Paris Accueil/Paris Séjour* are an alternative to the hotel options listed here.

Street addresses of the hotels below are followed by the number of their *arrondissement* (neighborhood).

Bristol – A palace with a special, almost intimate cachet. Service is impeccable, as are the 188 spacious, quiet rooms and huge, marble baths. The beautiful little restaurant and comfortable lobby cocktail lounge are additional pleasures. There also is another wing with a heated swimming pool on the sixth-floor terrace. Business facilities include 24-hour room service, meeting rooms for up to 100, English-speaking concierge, foreign currency exchange, secretarial services in English, audiovisual equipment, photocopiers, computers, cable television news service, and translation services. Major credit cards accepted. 112 Rue du Faubourg-St.-Honoré, 8e (phone: 42-66-91-45; from the US, 800-223-6800; fax: 42-66-68-68; telex: 280961). Very expensive.

Crillon – No sign out front, just discreet gold "C's" on the doors, it is currently the only "palace" hotel in Paris still owned by a Frenchman. The rooms on the Place de la Concorde side, though rather noisy, have the view of views; rooms facing the courtyards are just as nice and much more tranquil. The popular bar and 2 elegant restaurants, *L'Obélisque* and *Les Ambassadeurs* (which rates two Michelin stars), often are frequented by journalists and US and British embassy personnel. Business facilities include 24-hour room service, meeting rooms for up to 150, English-speaking concierge, foreign currency exchange, secretarial services in English, audiovisual equipment, photocopiers, computers, cable television news, translation services, and express checkout. Major credit cards accepted. 10 Pl. de la Concorde, 8e (phone: 42-65-24-24; fax: 47-42-72-10; telex: 290204). Very expensive.

George V – This nonpareil pick of movie moguls and international tycoons has 288 elegantly traditional or handsome contemporary rooms and 63 suites: some, facing the lovely courtyard, have their own balconies; those on the upper floors, a nice view. And there are 2 recently renovated restaurants, *Les Princes* and a grill, as well as a tearoom. One of the liveliest and chicest bars in the city is here, with a bartender who mixes a mean martini. The patio is a summer delight. Business facilities include 24-hour room service, meeting rooms for up to 20, English-speaking concierge, foreign currency exchange, secretarial services in English, audiovisual equipment, photocopiers, computers, cable television news, translation services, and express checkout. Major credit cards accepted. 31 Av. George-V, 8e (phone: 47-23-54-00; fax: 47-20-40-00; telex: 650082). Very expensive.

Meurice – Refined Louis XV and XVI elegance and a wide range of services are offered at prices slightly below those of the other "palaces." The hotel, a member of the CIGA chain, has 187 rooms and especially nice suites, a popular bar, a restaurant, *Le Meurice* (which was recently renovated and moved to a *grand salon* overlooking the Rue de Rivoli), and the chandeliered *Pompadour* tearoom. The location and hospitality couldn't be better, and the first-floor public room has been restored. Business facilities include 24-hour room service, meeting rooms for up to 150, English-speaking concierge, foreign currency exchange, secretarial services in English, audiovisual equipment, photocopiers, computers, cable television news, and translation services. Major credit cards accepted. 228 Rue de Rivoli, 1er (phone: 42-60-38-60; fax: 49-27-94-91; telex: 220256). Very expensive.

Plaza-Athénée – One of the legendary hotels, this favorite of the sophisticated seeking serene surroundings and superior service has 218 rooms, some now being refurbished. This is an haute bastion that takes its dignity very seriously (a discreet note in each bathroom offers an unobtrusive route in and out of the hotel for those in jogging togs). The *Relais* tables are much in demand at lunch and late supper, and the two-star *Régence*, summer patio, tea tables, and downstairs English bar are places to see and be seen. Business facilities include 24-hour room service, meeting rooms for up to 120, English-speaking concierge, foreign currency exchange, secretarial services in English, audiovisual equipment, photocopiers, computers, translation services, and express checkout. Major credit cards accepted. 25 Av. Montaigne, 8e (phone: 47-23-78-33; fax: 47-20-20-70; telex: 650092). Very expensive.

Relais Carré d'Or – For those visitors who are in Paris for a long stay, this hostelry (with all the amenities of a luxury hotel) provides a variety of accommodations — from studios to multi-room apartments — all with modern kitchens, marble bathrooms, and lovely, understated furnishings. Most have a balcony overlooking the hotel's garden or Avenue George-V. Business facilities include 24-hour room service, meeting rooms for up to 30, English-speaking concierge, foreign currency exchange, secretarial services in English, audiovisual equipment, photocopiers, computers, cable television, translation services, and express checkout. Major credit cards accepted. 46 Av. George-V, 8e (phone: 40-70-05-05; fax: 47-23-30-90; telex: 640561). Very expensive.

Résidence Maxim's – Pierre Cardin's luxurious venture is located near the Elysée Palace. No expense has been spared here to create sybaritic splendor. The 38 suites range in style from sleek modern to Belle Epoque, with original Art Nouveau pieces from Cardin's own collections, and every bathroom has been individually designed. *Atmosphere*, its restaurant, has made a name in the city, and has a pleasant terrace in summer; *La Tonnelle* serves breakfast, and doubles as a tea salon; and the bar, *Le Maximin*, is open late. Business facilities include 24-hour room service, meeting rooms for up to 70, English-speaking concierge, foreign currency exchange, secretarial services in English, audiovisual equipment, photocopiers, cable television news, translation services, and express checkout. Major credit cards accepted. 42 Av. Gabriel, 8e (phone: 45-61-96-33; fax: 42-89-06-07; telex: 642794F). Very expensive.

Ritz – Optimum comfort, privacy, and personal service are offered here, in one of the world's most gracious and distinguished hotels. There is an extraordinary underground health club (with pool, sauna, squash courts, ozone baths, and massages), an extensive business center, and the Ritz Escoffier Ecole de Cuisine. The latest addition is the *Ritz Club*, a nightclub and discotheque on the hotel's lower level that is open to hotel guests and club members only. The 162 redecorated rooms still preserve their antique treasures. This turn-of-the-century monument is *the* place to splurge, and even its sale to Egyptian interests (some say the Sultan of Brunei is the real financial force) has not diminished the glow one iota. The bars are fashionable meeting places, and the two-star *Ritz-Espadon* restaurant carries on the tradition of the legendary Escoffier. Business facilities include 24-hour room service, meeting rooms for up to 150, English-speaking concierge, foreign currency exchange, secretarial services in English, audiovisual equipment, photocopiers, computers, cable television news, translation services, and express checkout. Major credit cards accepted. 15 Pl. Vendôme, 1er (phone: 42-60-38-30; fax: 42-86-00-91; telex: 220262). Very expensive.

Royal Monceau – This elegant, impeccably decorated property, not far from the Arc de Triomphe, has 3 restaurants — including one with an attractive garden setting — as well as 2 bars, a fitness center, pool, Jacuzzi, and beauty salon. Business facilities include 24-hour room service, meeting rooms for up to 250, English-speaking concierge, foreign currency exchange, secretarial services in English, audiovisual equipment, photocopiers, computers, translation services, and express checkout. Major credit cards accepted. 37 Av. Hoche, 8e (phone: 45-61-98-00; fax: 45-63-28-93; telex: 650361). Very expensive.

St. James's Club – Located in a château in a residential section of the city, this hotel is really a private club (there are others in this group: one in London, one in Antigua, another in Los Angeles). For an additional 50F ($8), non-members can stay here for a few nights and feel as if they are living in an elegant home. The penthouse suites have a winter roof garden. There's a health center, a 5,000-volume library, and 2 restaurants. Business facilities include 24-hour room service, meeting rooms for up to 30, English-speaking concierge, foreign currency exchange, secretarial services in English, audiovisual equipment, photocopiers, computers, translation services, and express checkout. Major credit cards accepted. 5 Pl. Chancelier Adenauer, Av. Bugeaud, 16e (phone: 47-04-29-29; in the US, 800-641-0300; fax: 45-53-00-61). Very expensive.

San Régis – This is an elegant place to feel at home in comfortable surroundings. Business facilities include English-speaking concierge, foreign currency exchange, photocopiers, computers, and cable television news. Major credit cards accepted. 12 Rue Jean-Goujon, 8e (phone: 43-59-41-90; fax: 45-61-05-48; telex: 643637). Very expensive to expensive.

Westminster – Between the *Opéra* and the *Ritz,* it was at one time quite prestigious, but declined somewhat before its recent renovation. The paneling, marble fireplaces, and parquet floors of its traditional decor remain; air conditioning has been installed; and a new restaurant, *Le Céladon,* and cocktail lounge replace the old grill and bar. Some of the 101 rooms and apartments overlook the street, some an inner courtyard. Business facilities include 24-hour room service, meeting rooms for up to 70, English-speaking concierge, foreign currency exchange, secretarial services in English, audiovisual equipment, photocopiers, and translation services. Major credit cards accepted. 13 Rue de la Paix, 2e (phone: 42-61-57-46; fax: 42-60-30-66; telex: 680035). Very expensive to expensive.

Balzac – Very private, this luxurious, charming hotel with 70 rooms and suites is ideally located off the Champs-Elysées. Another plus is that the Paris branch of the *Bice* restaurant is right there. Business facilities include 24-hour room service, English-speaking concierge, foreign currency exchange, and photocopiers. Major credit cards accepted. 6 Rue Balzac, 8e (phone: 45-61-97-22; fax: 45-25-24-82; telex: 290298). Expensive.

Colbert – Each of the 40 rooms in this Left Bank hostelry has a glass door leading onto a balcony. Decorated in pastel tones, there is a mini-bar and television set in each one. No restaurant, but breakfast included. Major credit cards accepted. 7 Rue de l'Hôtel Colbert, 5e (phone: 43-25-85-65; in the US, 800-366-1510). Expensive.

Grand – This renovated property, part of the Inter-Continental chain, has long been a favorite of Americans abroad, with its "meeting place of the world," the *Café de la Paix*. It has 530 rooms and 10 luxurious suites, plus cheerful bars and restaurants — and a prime location (next to the *Opéra*). Business facilities include 24-hour room service, meeting rooms for up to 1,200, English-speaking concierge, foreign currency exchange, secretarial services in English, audiovisual equipment, photocopiers, cable television news, and express checkout. Major credit cards accepted. 2 Rue Scribe, 9e (phone: 40-07-32-32; fax: 42-66-12-51; telex: 220875). Expensive.

Holiday Inn Place de la République – In the heart of town, in a 120-year-old edifice that evokes the grandeur of the Second Empire — its façade is unlike any *Holiday Inn* you've seen before. Of the 333 pleasantly decorated rooms, those facing the courtyard are preferable to those facing the square. Restaurant, piano bar, and air conditioning. Major credit cards accepted. 10 Pl. de la République, 11e (phone: 43-55-44-34; fax: 47-00-32-34; telex: 210651). Expensive.

L'Hôtel – Small, but chic, this Left Bank hostelry is favored by experienced international travelers (Oscar Wilde died here). The 27 rooms are tiny, but beautifully appointed (antiques, fresh flowers, marble baths). The attractive restaurant, complete with waterfall, is flanked by a piano bar, and the location can't be beat. Business facilities include 24-hour room service, meeting rooms for up to 50, English-speaking concierge, foreign currency exchange, secretarial services in English, photocopiers, translation services, and express checkout. Major credit cards accepted. 13 Rue des Beaux-Arts, 6e (phone: 43-25-27-22; fax: 43-25-64-81; telex: 270870). Expensive.

Hôtel des Saints-Pères – In a great location in the heart of the Left Bank, its attractively decorated guestrooms, courtyard garden, and a charming bar make this one of Paris's best little hotels. Book far in advance — it's often difficult to get a room. Business facilities include meeting rooms for up to 5, English-speaking concierge, foreign currency exchange, and photocopiers. Major credit cards accepted. 65 Rue des Sts.-Pères, 6e (phone: 45-44-50-00; fax: 45-44-90-83; telex: 205424). Expensive.

Inter-Continental – The 500 rooms and suites have been meticulously restored to re-create turn-of-the-century elegance with modern conveniences. The top-floor Louis XVI "garret" rooms are cozy and look out over the Tuileries. There's an American-style coffee shop, a grill, and a popular bar. Business facilities include 24-hour room service, meeting rooms for up to 1,000, English-speaking concierge, foreign currency exchange, secretarial services in English, audiovisual equipment, photocopiers, translation services, and express checkout. Major credit cards accepted. 3 Rue de Castiglione, 1er (phone: 44-77-11-11; fax: 44-77-14-60; telex: 220114). Expensive.

Lancaster – Small and still smart, this recently renovated 57-room townhouse has quiet, comfortable accommodations. There are flowers everywhere, a cozy bar, a topnotch restaurant with courtyard service in summer, and underground parking. Run by London's Savoy group. Business facilities include 24-hour room service, meeting rooms for up to 20, English-speaking concierge, foreign currency exchange, secretarial services in English, audiovisual equipment, photocopiers, and cable television news. Major credit cards accepted. 7 Rue de Berri, 8e (phone: 43-59-90-43; fax: 42-89-22-71; telex: 640991). Expensive.

Lutétia – This recently renovated Belle Epoque hostelry is centrally located between Montparnasse and Odéon. Its 270 spacious and stylishly decorated rooms all have air conditioning. Its *Le Paris* restaurant has been awarded one Michelin star. Business facilities include 24-hour room service, meeting rooms for up to 450, English-speaking concierge, foreign currency exchange, secretarial services in English, audiovisual equipment, photocopiers, translation services, and express checkout. Major credit cards accepted. 45 Bd. Raspail, 6e (phone: 45-44-38-10; fax: 45-44-50-50; telex: 270424). Expensive.

Méridien – *Air France*'s well-run, 1,027-room, modern American-style property has all the expected French flair. Rooms are on the small side, but tastefully decorated, quiet, and with good views. There are 4 attractive restaurants, a shopping arcade, lively bars, and a chic nightclub, *L'Ecume des Nuits*. Business facilities include 24-hour room service, meeting rooms for up to 2,000, English-speaking concierge, foreign currency exchange, secretarial services in English, audiovisual equipment, photocopiers, translation services, and express checkout. Major credit cards accepted. 81 Bd. Gouvion-St.-Cyr, 17e (phone: 40-68-34-34; fax: 40-68-31-31; Telex 651952). Expensive.

Méridien Montparnasse – With 952 rooms, this ultramodern giant is in the heart of Montparnasse. It has a futuristic lobby, efficient service, a coffee shop, bars, and the *Montparnasse 25* restaurant, with a view, and in summer, a garden restaurant. Business facilities include 24-hour room service, meeting rooms for up to 2,000, English-speaking concierge, foreign currency exchange, secretarial services in English, audiovisual equipment, photocopiers, computers, translation services, and express checkout. Major credit cards accepted. 19 Rue du Commandant-René-Mouchotte, 14e (phone: 43-20-15-51; fax: 43-20-61-03). Expensive.

Montalembert – Recently completely renovated inside (its lovely façade remains), this small and exquisite hotel is known for its privacy. The 51 rooms, suites, and public areas are decorated in Art Deco style. A favorite spot for the literary and artistic crowd. The menu at its restaurant emphasizes simplicity and freshness. Business facilities include 24-hour room service, meeting rooms for up to 30, English-speaking concierge, foreign currency exchange, secretarial services in English, audiovisual equipment, photocopiers, and express checkout. Major credit cards accepted. 3 Rue Montalembert, 7e (phone: 45-48-68-11; in the US, 800-628-8929; fax: 42-22-58-19; telex: 200132). Expensive.

Paris Hilton International – Its 474 modern rooms are only a few steps from the Eiffel Tower. Those facing the river have the best view. The glass-walled rendez-vous *Le Toit de Paris* has dancing and a glittering nighttime view; *Le Western* serves T-bone steaks, apple pie à la mode, and brownies (mostly to French diners). The coffee shop is a magnet for homesick Americans. Business facilities include 24-hour room service, meeting rooms for up to 1,000, English-speaking concierge, foreign currency exchange, secretarial services in English, audiovisual equipment, photocopiers, translation services, and express checkout. Major credit cards accepted. 18 Av. de Suffren, 15e (phone: 42-73-92-00; fax: 47-83-62-66; telex: 200955). Expensive.

Pavillon de la Reine – Supreme location for the Marais's only luxury hotel, owned by the management of the *Relais Christine* (see below) and similarly appointed. Its 49 spacious rooms look out on a garden or courtyard. The setting on the Place des Vosges is regal, and the *Picasso Museum* is only a couple of minutes away on foot. Business facilities include 24-hour room service, foreign currency exchange, and photocopiers. Major credit cards accepted. 28 Pl. des Vosges, 3e (phone: 42-77-96-40; fax: 42-77-63-06; telex: 216160). Expensive.

Prince de Galles – An excellent location (a next-door neighbor of the pricier *George V*) and impeccable style make this hostelry a good choice. All 160 rooms and suites are individually decorated. This Marriott member offers a restaurant and an oak-paneled bar; parking is available. Business facilities include 24-hour room service, meeting rooms for up to 150, English-speaking concierge, foreign currency exchange, secretarial services in English, audiovisual equipment, photocopiers, computers, translation services, and express checkout. Major credit cards accepted. 33 Av. George-V, 8e (phone: 47-23-55-11; fax: 47-20-96-92; telex: 800627). Expensive.

Pullman St.-Jacques – This four-star hotel has 797 up-to-date rooms, a nice shopping arcade, a cinema, 4 restaurants (one Japanese, one Chinese, one French, and an informal coffee shop), and the lively *Bar Tahonga*. A bit out of the way, but the métro is close by. Business facilities include 24-hour room service, meeting rooms for up to 3,000, English-speaking concierge, foreign currency exchange, secretarial services in English, audiovisual equipment, photocopiers, computers, translation services, and express checkout. Major credit cards accepted. 17 Bd. St.-Jacques, 14e (phone: 40-78-79-80; fax: 45-88-43-93; telex: 270740). Expensive.

Raphaël – A very spacious, stately place, with a Turner in the lobby downstairs and paneling painted with sphinxes in the generous rooms. Less well known among the top Paris hotels, but favored by film folk and the like. Business facilities include 24-hour room service, meeting rooms for up to 150, English-speaking concierge, foreign currency exchange, secretarial services in English, audiovisual equipment, photocopiers, computers, translation services, and express checkout. Major credit cards accepted. 17 Av. Kléber, 16e (phone: 45-02-16-00; fax: 45-01-21-50; telex: 610356). Expensive.

Relais Christine – This lovely small hotel, with modern fixtures and lots of old-fashioned charm, formerly was a 16th-century cloister. Ask for a room with a courtyard or garden view (we especially like No. 31; other rooms tend to be small and noisy). Business facilities include meeting rooms for up to 20, foreign currency exchange, and photocopiers. Major credit cards accepted. 3 Rue Christine, 6e (phone: 43-26-71-80; fax: 43-26-89-38; telex: 202606). Expensive.

Le Relais Saint-Germain – In a 17th-century building, this 10-room hostelry is ideally situated on the Left Bank just steps from Boulevard St.-Germain and the area's best shops, eateries, and galleries. It is attractively decorated, and charming down to its massive ceiling beams and huge flower bouquets. A rare find. Major credit cards accepted. 9 Carrefour de l'Odéon, 6e (phone: 43-29-12-05; fax: 46-33-45-30; telex: 201889). Expensive.

Résidence du Roy – Within easy reach of the Champs-Elysées, this establishment offers self-contained studios, suites, and duplexes, complete with kitchen facilities. No restaurant. Business facilities include meeting rooms for up to 20, English-speaking concierge, audiovisual equipment, photocopiers, and express checkout. Major credit cards accepted. 8 Rue François Ier, 8e (phone: 42-89-59-59; fax: 40-74-07-92; telex: 648452). Expensive.

Le Vernet – Recently totally renovated, this sister hotel to the elegant *Royal Monceau* has 36 modern rooms and suites and is located just a few steps from the Arc de Triomphe. Business facilities include 24-hour room service, meeting rooms for up to 15, English-speaking concierge, foreign currency exchange, audiovisual equipment, photocopiers, computers, translation services, and express checkout. Major credit cards accepted. 25 Rue Vernet, 8e (phone: 47-23-43-10; fax: 40-70-10-14; telex: 290347). Expensive.

Abbaye St.-Germain – On a quiet street, this small, delightful place once was a convent. The lobby has exposed stone arches, and the elegant public and private rooms are furnished with antiques, tastefully selected fabrics, and marble baths. There's a lovely garden and a bar, but there continue to be some complaints about the service. Business facilities include English-speaking concierge, foreign currency exchange, and photocopiers. No credit cards accepted. 10 Rue Cassette, 6e (phone: 45-44-38-11; fax: 45-48-07-86). Expensive to moderate.

Angleterre – Its 29 classic, clean, unpretentious rooms are in what once was the British Embassy, now a national monument. Business facilities include English-speaking concierge, foreign currency exchange, and photocopiers. Major credit cards accepted. 44 Rue Jacob, 6e (phone: 42-60-34-72; fax: 42-60-16-93). Moderate.

Britannique – Within minutes of the *Louvre* and Notre Dame, this hotel was a Quaker mission house during World War I. All 40 rooms have been renovated and are equipped with mini-bars, hair dryers, and satellite television. Major credit cards accepted. 20 Av. Victoria, 1er (phone: 42-33-74-59; in the US, 800-366-1510). Moderate.

Danube St.-Germain – The rooms, with their four-poster bamboo beds, are comfortable, and some of them overlook an attractive courtyard typical of the Left Bank. American Express accepted. Business facilities include foreign currency exchange and photocopiers. 58 Rue Jacob, 6e (phone: 42-60-34-70; fax: 42-60-81-18; telex: 211062). Moderate.

Deux Continents – A cozy red sitting room looks invitingly onto the street here, in this 40-room establishment on the Left Bank. Major credit cards accepted. 25 Rue Jacob, 6e (phone: 43-26-72-46). Moderate.

Deux Iles – This beautifully redecorated 17th-century house is on the historic Ile St.-Louis. It has a tropical garden and the decor is in bamboo, rattan, and braided rope. The rooms have French provincial fabrics and Louis XIV ceramic tiles in the bathrooms. But there's one drawback: The rooms aren't very large. Business facilities include foreign currency exchange. No credit cards accepted. 59 Rue St.-Louis-en-l'Ile, 4e (phone: 43-26-13-35; fax: 43-29-60-25). Moderate.

Duc de St.-Simon – If you're in search of things past, this may be one of the best places in town, despite the rather small rooms. In 2 big townhouses in a beautiful, quiet backwater off the Boulevard St.-Germain, this elegant little spot veritably reeks of Proust. Just a 5-minute walk from the spectacular *Musée d'Orsay*. Business facilities include a foreign currency exchange and photocopiers. No credit cards accepted. 14 Rue de St.-Simon, 7e (phone: 45-48-35-66; fax: 45-48-68-25; telex: 203277). Moderate.

Grand Hôtel Taranne – Anybody anxious to get into the Left Bank scene should love it here, for the 35 rooms are literally on top of the *Brasserie Lipp*. Each room is unique: No. 4 has exposed beams, a TV set, and a mini-bar; No. 3 has a Louis XIII–style bed; No. 17, the oddest, has lights and a disco ball. Business facilities include foreign currency exchange and photocopiers. Major credit cards accepted. 153 Bd. St.-Germain, 6e (phone: 42-22-21-65; fax: 45-48-22-25; telex: 205340). Moderate.

Grand Hôtel de l'Univers – Modern and tucked away on a quiet street, it's also only 2 steps away from St.-Germain-des-Prés and the Latin Quarter. No restaurant. Major credit cards accepted. 6 Rue Grégoire-de-Tours, 6e (phone: 43-29-37-00; fax: 40-51-06-45; telex: 204150). Moderate.

Jeu de Paume – The architect-owner of this former *jeu de paume* (tennis court) has artfully married old and new in this newest addition to the exclusive Ile St.-Louis hotels. High-tech lighting, modern artwork, and a sleek glass elevator are set against ancient ceiling beams and limestone brick hearths. There's a country feeling here. Rooms are comfortable and reasonably priced. Business facilities include 24-hour room service, meeting rooms for up to 30, foreign currency exchange, secretarial services in English, and photocopiers. Major credit cards accepted. 54 Rue St.-Louis-en-l'Ile, 4e (phone: 43-26-14-18; telex: 205160). Moderate.

Lord Byron – On a quiet street off the Champs-Elysées, it has a pleasant courtyard and 30 comfortable, homey rooms. The staff is friendly and speaks good English, and a family atmosphere prevails. Major credit cards accepted. 5 Rue de Chateaubriand, 8e (phone: 43-59-89-98; fax: 42-89-46-04; telex: 649662). Moderate.

Lutèce – Here are 23 luxurious rooms (one split-level) on the charming Ile St.-Louis. Positively ravishing, with exquisite toile fabric and wallpaper and raw wood beams. 65 Rue St.-Louis-en-l'Ile, 4e (phone: 43-26-23-52; fax: 43-29-60-25). Moderate.

Madison – Offers 55 large, bright rooms, some with balconies and all with air conditioning. Major credit cards accepted. 143 Bd. St.-Germain, 6e (phone: 43-29-72-50; fax: 43-29-72-50; telex: 201628). Moderate.

Odéon – Small, modernized, and charming, it's in the heart of the St.-Germain area on the Left Bank. No restaurant. Major credit cards accepted. 3 Rue de l'Odéon, 6e (phone: 43-25-90-67; fax: 43-25-55-98; telex: 202943). Moderate.

Parc St.-Séverin – An interesting property in the heart of the 5th *arrondissement* on the Left Bank, it has a total of 27 rooms, including a top-floor penthouse with a wraparound balcony. The decor is modern but understated, and the overall ambience is appealing even though the neighborhood is less than the quietest in Paris. Major credit cards accepted. 22 Rue de la Parcheminerie, 5e (phone: 43-54-32-17; fax: 43-54-70-71). Moderate.

Regent's Garden – On a quiet street near l'Etoile, it has 40 spacious rooms, some with large marble fireplaces. The property is run by young hoteliers who make you feel as if you are in your own home. A country atmosphere pervades. There's also a garden and parking. Major credit cards accepted. 6 Rue Pierre-Demours, 17e (phone: 45-74-07-30; fax: 40-55-01-42; telex: 640127). Moderate.

Résidence Charles-Dullin – In a sleepy corner of Montmartre, near the leafy square of the *Théâtre de l'Atelier*, this residential hotel charges nightly, weekly, and monthly rates. The apartments have kitchens, and some overlook a peaceful garden. Major credit cards accepted. 10 Pl. Charles-Dullin, 18e (phone: 42-57-14-55; fax: 42-54-48-87). Moderate.

Ste.-Beuve – A stylish place in Montparnasse with rooms and lobby designed by David Hicks. Major credit cards accepted. 9 Rue Ste.-Beuve, 6e (phone: 45-48-20-07; fax: 45-48-67-52). Moderate.

Le St.-Grégoire – A small 18th-century mansion on the Left Bank, this recently renovated hostelry has an intimate cozy atmosphere, a warm fire in the hearth, and 20 tastefully furnished rooms, some with terraces overlooking a garden. Major credit cards accepted. 43 Rue de l'Abbé Grégoire, 6e (phone: 45-48-23-23; fax: 45-48-33-95). Moderate.

St.-Louis – On magical Ile St.-Louis, practically in the shadow of Notre-Dame, this small hotel will make the first-time visitor fall in love with the city forever. The 21 rooms aren't large, but they're pretty, and the 3 fifth-floor rooms under the eaves are enchanting, with tiny balconies overlooking Parisian rooftops. No TV sets, but baths are clean and modern, and there's a charming breakfast room and a warm welcome. No credit cards accepted. 75 Rue St.-Louis-en-l'Ile, 4e (phone: 46-34-04-80; fax: 46-34-02-13). Moderate.

St.-Louis Marais – On a quiet residential street on the edge of the newly chic Marais (Paris's oldest neighborhood), this tiny hotel is a short walk from the Place des Vosges, the *Louvre,* the quays along the Seine, and the Bastille nightclubs. Dating from the 18th century, when it belonged to the Celestin Convent, it has 14 small rooms, which were being remodeled as we went to press. Historical status has barred installation of an elevator, however. No credit cards. 1 Rue Charles-V, 4e (phone: 48-87-87-04; fax: 46-34-02-13). Moderate.

St.-Merry – A stone's throw from the *Centre Georges-Pompidou* arts complex, this mock-medieval establishment may be the most bizarre hotel in Paris. It not only backs onto the Eglise St.-Merry, but it has a communion rail as a banister and ancient oaken confessionals as broom closets. The rooms, hung with dark, demonic oil portraits, have church pews for benches, and some rooms are even spliced by a flying buttress. In dubious taste, perhaps, but there's nothing else like it. No credit cards accepted. 78 Rue de la Verrerie, 4e (phone: 42-78-14-15; fax: 40-29-06-82). Moderate.

Tuileries – With a good location in a "real" neighborhood in the heart of the city, it has a well-tended look and attractive carved wood bedsteads. Major credit cards accepted. 10 Rue St.-Hyacinthe, 1er (phone: 42-61-04-17 or 42-61-06-94; fax: 49-27-91-56). Moderate.

L'Université – Its 28 charming rooms of all shapes and sizes are in a former 18th-century mansion. No credit cards accepted. 22 Rue de l'Université, 7e (phone: 42-61-09-39). Moderate.

Vendôme – This older "house" has 36 immaculate high-ceilinged rooms with brass beds, and the location couldn't be better. There is a small restaurant with a limited menu, and a bar. Major credit cards accepted. 1 Pl. Vendôme, 1er (phone: 42-60-32-84; fax: 49-27-97-89). Moderate.

La Villa – Popular with American fashion writers, this 35-room hostelry in the St.-Germain area was completely renovated in post-modern decor. Although the rooms are incredibly small, the luxurious bathrooms alone are worth a stay here. Major credit cards accepted. Business facilities include an English-speaking concierge and foreign currency exchange. 29 Rue Jacob, 6e (phone: 43-26-60-00; telex: 202437). Moderate.

West End – Friendly, with 60 rooms, it's on the Right Bank. The front desk keeps a close, concerned watch on comings and goings, which some may find reassuring. Major credit cards accepted. 7 Rue Clément-Marot, 8e (phone: 47-20-30-78; fax: 47-20-34-42). Moderate.

Chomel – Sprucely decorated, this establishment is near the *Au Bon Marché* department store. Major credit cards accepted. 15 Rue Chomel, 7e (phone: 45-48-55-52; fax: 45-48-89-76). Moderate to inexpensive.

Ferrandi – Popular with international businessmen, this no-frills hostelry is done up in browns and blues, with a winding wood staircase and a quiet lounge. Major credit cards accepted. 92 Rue du Cherche-Midi, 6e (phone: 42-22-97-40). Moderate to inexpensive.

Des Marroniers – Good rates and an excellent location, in the heart of the Left Bank, makes this 37-room hotel a real bargain. It has a courtyard and pretty breakfast room. No credit cards accepted. 21 Rue Jacob, 6e (phone: 43-25-30-60). Moderate to inexpensive.

St.-Thomas-d'Aquin – Built in the 1880s, this unpretentious hotel is a simple, functional base from which to explore a shopper's paradise of new wave designer boutiques and tiny restaurants. The 21 rooms are clean and neat, and baths are modern (though tubs are half-size). Breakfast is included. Major credit cards accepted. 3 Rue d'Pré-aux-Clercs, 7e (phone: 42-61-01-22; fax: 42-61-41-43). Moderate to inexpensive.

Amélie – Centrally located, this comfortable spot has 15 rooms, each with color TV set, direct-dial telephone, and mini-bar. Breakfast is included in the rate, which makes this one of Paris's better bargains. Major credit cards accepted. 5 Rue Amélie, 7e (phone: 45-51-74-75; fax: 45-56-93-55). Inexpensive.

D'Argenson – The upper middle class residential district in which this hotel is located is off the typical tourist track but convenient to major department stores on the Boulevard Haussmann and a 15-minute walk from the *Opéra*. The show-place rooms — Nos. 23, 33, 43, and 53 — feature fireplaces and up-to-date bathrooms. Room rate includes breakfast. Major credit cards accepted. 15 Rue d'Argenson, 8e (phone: 42-65-16-87). Inexpensive.

Bretonnerie – This restored 17th-century townhouse takes itself seriously, with petit point, dark wood furnishings, and several attic rooms with beams that overlook the narrow streets of the newly fashionable Marais area. Major credit cards accepted. 22 Rue Ste.-Croix-de-la-Bretonnerie, 4e (phone: 48-87-77-63; fax: 42-77-26-78). Inexpensive.

Ceramic – Close to the Champs-Elysées, the Faubourg St.-Honoré, and the métro, this 53-room establishment with an Art Nouveau façade has been designated a national historic treasure. Request a room facing the street, particularly No. 412 — enormous, with a crystal chandelier and wide bay windows. Room rates include breakfast. Major credit cards accepted. 34 Av. de Wagram, 8e (phone: 42-27-20-30; fax: 46-22-95-83). Inexpensive.

Delavigne – Good value and location (just down the street from the *Odéon* theater), it has an enlightened manager who says he isn't interested in simply handing out keys, but enjoys introducing foreigners to Paris. Major credit cards accepted. 1 Rue Casimir-Delavigne, 6e (phone: 43-29-31-50; fax: 43-29-78-56). Inexpensive.

Esmeralda – Some of the rooms look directly at Notre-Dame over the gardens of St.-Julien-le-Pauvre, one of Paris's most ancient churches. The oak beams and furniture round out the medieval atmosphere. Small and friendly, especially popular with the theatrical crowd. No credit cards accepted. 4 Rue St.-Julien-le-Pauvre, 5e (phone: 43-54-19-20). Inexpensive.

Family – A longtime favorite with Americans — you're treated just like part of the family. There are 25 small but comfortable rooms. Major credit cards accepted. 35 Rue Cambon, 1er (phone: 42-61-54-84). Inexpensive.

Grandes Ecoles – Just the sort of place that shouldn't appear in a guidebook (even the proprietress says so) and that people recommend only to the right friends. Insulated from the street by a delightful courtyard and its garden, it is a simple 19th-century private house with plain comforts, but it's long on atmosphere. There aren't many like it in Paris. Major credit cards accepted. 75 Rue Cardinal-Lemoine, 5e (phone: 43-26-79-23; fax: 43-25-28-15). Inexpensive.

Hôtel de Bellevue et du Chariot d'Or – Slightly eccentric, but friendly, this is the best of more than a score of tiny hotels in the wholesale garment district. Although the hallway carpets and wallpaper are in dire need of replacement, the rooms are clean and comfortable, and most of the baths have been redone. Room No. 110 is on the courtyard (which means it's quiet) and has twin beds, a pink bathroom, and a marble fireplace. Some rooms are large enough to sleep four. Breakfast included. Major credit cards accepted. 39 Rue de Turbigo, 3e (phone: 48-87-45-60; fax: 48-87-95-04). Inexpensive.

Le Jardin des Plantes – In addition to a magnificent setting across from the Parisian Botanical Gardens, near the Sorbonne, there are 33 airy, spotless rooms and baths, each with its own floral motif. The owner, a psychologist, has anticipated the traveler's every need: All rooms have mini-bars, TV sets, and hair dryers; some have alcoves large enough for extra beds for children; a sauna is available in the basement. Breakfast can be enjoyed in the sunny ground-floor coffee bar or on the fifth-floor terrace and rose garden. Art exhibits and classical music concerts are held on Sundays in the vaulted cellar. Major credit cards accepted. 5 Rue Linné, 5e (phone: 47-07-06-20). Inexpensive.

Jeanne d'Arc – This little place on a quiet street in the Marais doesn't get top marks for decor and its facilities are simple, but somehow its appeal has spread from Minnesota to Melbourne. It's well placed at the colorful end of the Rue de Rivoli, and the management is friendly and speaks English. Major credit cards accepted. 3 Rue Jarente, 4e (phone: 48-87-62-11). Inexpensive.

Lenox – Between the busy St.-Germain area and the boutiques nearby, it's small and very tastefully done, with a small bar. Popular with the fashion crowd. Major credit cards accepted. 9 Rue de l'Université, 7e (phone: 42-96-10-95; fax: 42-61-52-82). Inexpensive.

London – In the heart of the business district, this comfortable hotel has 50 rooms, each with color TV set and direct-dial telephone. Major credit cards accepted. 32 Bd. des Italiens, 9e (phone: 48-24-54-64; fax: 48-00-08-83). Inexpensive.

Prima Lepic – A 38-room hotel in Montmartre, a busy neighborhood of winding little streets that evoke the romance of *la vie bohème,* Utrillo, Picasso, Toulouse-Lautrec and the *Moulin Rouge.* Decorated by cheerful young owners, rooms sport pretty floral wallpapers and one-of-a-kind furnishings — a wicker chair, a mirrored armoire, a 1930s lamp. No. 56, on the top floor, looks out over Paris, and travelers with a child should make special note of room No. 2, which connects to another room. There's an elevator, and the public spaces are charming. Major credit cards accepted. 29 Rue Lepic, 18e (phone: 46-06-44-64). Inexpensive.

Prince Albert – Despite its unprepossessing aura of faded glory, this has its site to recommend it: just off the quiet and unspoiled Marché St.-Honoré and a hop, skip, and jump from the Tuileries. Major credit cards accepted. 5 Rue St.-Hyacinthe, 1er (phone: 42-61-58-36; fax: 42-60-04-06). Inexpensive.

St.-André-des-Arts – A rambling old favorite among the chic and hip whose purses are slim but whose tastes are discerning. No credit cards accepted. 66 Rue St.-André-des-Arts, 6e (phone: 43-26-96-16). Inexpensive.

Sévigné – If it's a little noisy (right on the Rue de Rivoli), the warm welcome and handy location make up for it. Major credit cards accepted. 2 Rue Malher, 4e (phone: 42-72-76-17). Inexpensive.

Solférino – A cozy place with Oriental rugs scattered about. The 34 tiny rooms have floral wallpaper, and there's a plant-filled breakfast and sitting room. Major credit cards accepted. 91 Rue de Lille, 7e (phone: 47-05-85-54). Inexpensive.

Le Vieux Marais – Near the *Centre Georges-Pompidou,* this is one of the few agreeable hostelries in the Marais area, with brightly sprigged walls in the cheerful, if not very large, rooms. The breakfast room has an impressive wall-size engraving of the Place des Vosges, not far away. Major credit cards accepted. 8 Rue du Plâtre, 4e (phone: 42-78-47-22; fax: 42-78-34-32). Inexpensive.

Welcome – Recently renovated and overlooking the Bd. St.-Germain, it's simple but comfortable. No credit cards accepted. 66 Rue de Seine, 6e (phone: 46-34-24-80; fax: 40-46-81-59). Inexpensive.

Boucherat – A plain, friendly establishment with no airs and with a clientele that returns. Near the Place de la République. Major credit cards accepted. 110 Rue de Turenne, 3e (phone: 42-72-86-83). Very inexpensive.

Du Globe – Tiny and charming, it's on a quiet street in the heart of the St.-Germain area. No credit cards accepted. 15 Rue des Quatre-Vents, 6e (phone: 43-26-35-50). Very inexpensive.

Henri IV – No one could call this modern — the fittings obviously haven't been changed for decades, and there's only a bidet and basin in the room, since the bathrooms are down the hall. But it has a reputation and a history, not least because it is the only hotel on the Place Dauphine on the Ile de la Cité — the real core of Paris. Prices are breathtakingly low. No credit cards accepted. 25 Pl. Dauphine, 1er (phone: 43-54-44-53). Very inexpensive.

EATING OUT: Paris considers itself the culinary capital of the world, and you will never forget food for long here. Whether you grab just a freshly baked croissant and café au lait for breakfast or splurge on an epicurean fantasy for dinner, this is the city in which to indulge all your gastronomic dreams. Remember, too, that there is no such thing as "French" food; rather, Paris provides the perfect mosaic in which to try regional delights from Provence, Alsace, Normandy, Brittany, and many other delicious places.

Restaurants classed as very expensive charge $250 and way up for two; expensive is $150 to $200; moderate, $100 to $150; inexpensive, less than $100; and very inexpensive, $50 or less. A service charge of 15% is added to the bill, but most people leave a small additional tip for good service; wine is not included in the price. Street addresses of the restaurants below are followed by their *arrondissement* number.

Note: To save frustration and embarrassment, always *reconfirm* dinner reservations before noon on the appointed day. Also remember that some of the better restaurants do not accept credit cards; it's a good idea to check when making your reservations. It may come as a surprise to discover that many of the elite Paris restaurants close over the weekend; also note that many Paris restaurants are closed for part or all of July or August. It's best to check ahead in order to avoid disappointment at the restaurant of your choice, and it's also worth remembering that many offer special lunch menus at considerably lower prices. Here is a sampling of the best restaurants that Paris has to offer:

L'Ambroisie – Quietly elegant, beneath the arcade of historic Place des Vosges, this is the showcase for chef Bernard Pacaud's equally elegant cuisine. The menu is limited to only a few entrées, such as duck with foie gras, skate and sliced green cabbage in sherry vinegar sauce, veal sweetbreads with shallots and parsley on ultra-fresh pasta, delicately battered chicken thighs in a piquant sauce, and oxtail in a savory sauce, but the quality has earned the place three Michelin stars. Closed Sundays, Monday lunch, August, and holidays. Reservations necessary. Major credit cards accepted. 9 Pl. des Vosges, 4e (phone: 42-78-51-45). Very expensive.

Beauvilliers – Deliciously flirtatious and festive, this restaurant on the northern slope of the Butte of Montmartre is one of the most romantic spots in Paris. Proust or Balzac might have felt at home in its intimate dining rooms or on hydrangea-rimmed summer terraces in the shadow of a white-stone cathedral. The food — a rich, generous cuisine prepared in the best bourgeois tradition — complements the surroundings. Try the sweetbreads with foie gras, guinea hen with spices and mussels, or the *turbot au jus de jarret.* Closed the first 2 weeks in September, Monday lunch, and Sundays. Reservations necessary. Major credit cards accepted. 52 Rue Lamarck, 18e (phone: 42-54-54-42). Very expensive.

Le Grand Vefour – Founded in 1760, this sedately elegant Empire-style establishment — with paintings on the mirrors — is known for refined menus (two Michelin stars) and perfect service. It's famous for toast Rothschild (shrimp in crayfish sauce set in a brioche) and pigeon Aristide Briand (boned roast pigeon stuffed with foie gras and truffles). Closed Saturdays at lunch, Sundays, and August. Reservations necessary. Major credit cards accepted. 17 Rue Beaujolais, 1er (phone: 42-96-56-27). Very expensive.

Jamin – Due to the culinary talents of owner-chef Joël Robuchon, this is one of the city's finest restaurants — with a three-star ranking by Michelin — and one of the most difficult to get into. Robuchon calls his cuisine "moderne," similar to but not always as light as nouvelle. The dining room is *very* small, so reserve far in advance. Waiting time is almost 8 weeks. Closed weekends and July. Reservations necessary. Major credit cards accepted. 32 Rue de Longchamp, 16e (phone: 47-27-12-27). Very expensive.

Lasserre – The ultimate in luxury, with a magical ceiling that opens periodically during dinner to reveal the nighttime sky. Equally sublime is the food, served in the *style Lasserre* — that is, vermeil dessert settings, plates rimmed in gold, and extravagant garnishes with each dish. The classic menu is heavy on foie gras, caviar, truffles, and rich sauces. Michelin downgraded the food to two stars a few years ago, but we think it's still topnotch. Closed Sundays, Monday lunch, and August. Reservations necessary. Major credit cards accepted. 17 Av. Franklin-D.-Roosevelt, 8e (phone: 43-59-53-43). Very expensive.

Lucas-Carton – Once proprietor of the Michelin three-star restaurant called *L'Archestrate,* chef Alain Senderens dropped that name (but not his triple-star rating) in 1985 when he moved to larger, more elegant quarters in a historic building that boasts a gorgeous Belle Epoque interior. Senderens enjoys the reputation of being one of France's most innovative culinary talents, combining many tenets of nouvelle cuisine with Oriental and African influences. Closed Saturdays, Sundays, and most of August. Reservations necessary. Major credit cards accepted. 9 Pl. de la Madeleine, 8e (phone: 42-65-22-90). Very expensive.

Maxim's – A legend for its Belle Epoque decor and atmosphere. It's good for celebrations, but though the service is impeccable, it's hard to feel comfortable if you aren't known here. Owned by fashion designer Pierre Cardin, this is one of the few places in Paris where you are expected to dress formally — on Friday evenings. There's an orchestra for dancing from 9:30 PM until 2 AM. Closed Sundays in July and August. Reservations necessary. Major credit cards accepted. 3 Rue Royale, 8e (phone: 42-65-27-94). Very expensive.

Le Taillevent – Full of tradition, Louis XVI furnishings, 18th-century porcelain dinner service — all in a 19th-century mansion — this epicurean haven offers no-nonsense *cuisine classique,* which currently is the best in Paris. Try terrine of truffled sweetbreads, seafood sausage, duck in cider, and especially chef Claude Deligne's soufflés in original flavors like Alsatian pear and cinnamon chocolate. Three stars in the *Guide Michelin.* Closed weekends, part of February, and most of August. Reservations necessary. Americans often have difficulty reserving here (although it's a bit easier if there are four in your party), and it's best to try at least 60 days ahead. No credit cards accepted. 15 Rue Lamennais, 8e (phone: 45-61-12-90). Very expensive.

La Tour d'Argent – Another of the five Parisian restaurants to be awarded three stars by the *Guide Michelin* and probably the best known — though recent visits have not been up to the standards of years past. The spectacular view of Notre-Dame and the Ile St.-Louis competes with the food for the attention of a very touristy clientele. Pressed duck — prepared before you — is the specialty, but the 15 other varieties of duck are equally interesting. A single main dish here can cost $100, and to be quite frank, it just ain't worth it. Closed Mondays. Reservations necessary. Major credit cards accepted. 15 Quai de la Tournelle, 5e (phone: 43-54-23-31). Very expensive.

L'Ami Louis – This is the archetypal Parisian bistro, unattractive physically but with huge portions of food that we rate as marvelous. Though the original Louis is gone, his heirs have maintained the rough welcome and informal ambience. Specialties include foie gras, roast chicken, spring lamb, ham, and burgundy wines. A favorite among Americans, this is the place to sample authentic French fries. Closed Mondays, Tuesdays, and most of July and August. Reservations necessary. Major credit cards accepted. 32 Rue de Vertbois, 3e (phone: 48-87-77-48). Expensive.

Amphyclés – Since it opened in May 1989, Philippe Groult's tiny restaurant near the Arc de Triomphe has won praise and in 1991, a second Michelin star. A former student of star-chef Joël Robuchon of *Jamin,* Groult prepares wonderful dishes, including *crême de morilles au chou nouveau* (cream of mushroom soup flavored with new cabbage). Reservations necessary. Major credit cards accepted. 78 Av. des Ternes, 17e (phone: 40-68-01-01). Expensive.

Apicius – Jean-Pierre Vigato's highly original recipes have won him a reputation as one of Paris's finest chefs (and earned him two Michelin stars). Favorites include such delicacies as sweet-and-sour foie gras, *rougets* (a Mediterranean fish) with olive oil and potato purée, and a *panaché* of five mouth-watering chocolate desserts. Closed weekends and August. Reservations necessary. Major credit cards accepted. 122 Av. de Villiers, 17e (phone: 43-80-19-66). Expensive.

L'Arpège – Paris's current rage is two-star chef Alain Passard, who prepares specialties such as *ris de veau a la truffes* (sweetbreads with truffles and chestnuts) and *lotte aux épices* (spicy monkfish). The prix fixe lunch at this eatery near the *Musée Rodin* is easily the best bargain around. Closed Saturdays and Sunday lunch and August. Reservations necessary. Major credit cards accepted. 84 Rue de Varenne, 7e (phone: 45-51-20-02). Expensive.

Le Carré des Feuillants – Alain Dutournier of *Le Trou Gascon* has set up shop right in midtown. The cuisine is still Gascon-inspired, but Dutournier is allowing his imagination more license with, for example, such creations as frogs' legs with watercress sauce and salmon served with braised cabbage and bacon. Michelin has awarded him two stars. Closed Saturdays for lunch and Sundays. Reservations necessary. Major credit cards accepted. 14 Rue de Castiglione, 1er (phone: 42-86-82-82). Expensive.

Castel – You might be able to get a reservation at this, one of the few private clubs in Paris, if you ask for help from the concierge at one of the town's grand hotels. The Belle Epoque interior is breathtaking, the cooking fine, and there's a disco in the basement. Specialties include lobster and chicken with cucumbers. Closed Sundays. Reservations necessary. Major credit cards accepted. 15 Rue Princesse, 6e (phone: 43-26-90-22). Expensive.

Chiberta – Elegant and modern, and boasting the acclaimed (two Michelin stars) nouvelle cuisine of Jean-Michel Bédier. Try *bavarois de saumon au coulis de tomates frais* (salmon mousse with fresh tomato sauce) and *marbré de rouget au fenouil* (red mullet with fennel). Closed weekends and August. Reservations necessary. Major credit cards accepted. 3 Rue Arsène-Houssaye, 8e (phone: 45-63-77-90). Expensive.

Le Divellec – This bright and airy place serves some exquisitely fresh seafood. Try the sea bass, the *rouget,* and the sautéed turbot. The latter is served with "black pasta" — thick strips of pasta flavored with squid ink — an unusual and delicious concoction. Closed Sundays, Mondays, and August. Reservations necessary. Major credit cards accepted. 107 Rue de l'Université, 7e (phone: 45-51-91-96). Expensive.

Dodin-Bouffant – Popular because it was set up by the gifted, imaginative, and long-gone Jacques Manière, it still offers excellent seafood and inventive dishes (it has been awarded one Michelin star). Open late. Closed Sundays, 2 weeks at *Christmastime,* and August. Reservations necessary. Major credit cards accepted. 25 Rue Frédéric-Sauton, 5e (phone: 43-25-25-14). Expensive.

Drouant – Founded in 1880, this classic favorite reopened after an extensive face-lift, with an ambitious chef and menu. Michelin has awarded it one star. Open daily. Reservations necessary. Major credit cards accepted. 18 Rue Gaillon, 2e (phone: 42-65-15-16). Expensive.

Duquesnoy – Jean-Paul Duquesnoy, one of Paris's most promising young chefs, is in his element in nifty quarters. Warm carved woods and tasteful decor set the stage for specialties that include a new potato and caviar salad, terrine of leeks and langoustine, and a chocolate mousse and pistachio-filled *mille-feuille.*

Two Michelin stars. Closed Saturday lunch and Sundays. Reservations necessary. Major credit cards accepted. 6 Av. Bosquet, 7e (phone: 47-05-96-78). Expensive.

Faugeron – Among the finest nouvelle restaurants, awarded two stars by Michelin, it rates even higher with us. Superb food, lovely service, and one of Paris's prettiest table settings in what once was an old school. Closed weekends and August. Reservations necessary. Major credit cards accepted. 52 Rue de Longchamp, 16e (phone: 47-04-24-53). Expensive.

Fouquet's Bastille – Sister restaurant to the Champs-Elysées institution (see *Wine Bars and Cafés*), this post-modern location next to Paris's new *Opéra Bastille* offers traditional fare with a modern touch. Closed Saturday lunch and Sundays. Reservations advised. Major credit cards accepted. 130 Rue de Lyon, 12e (phone: 43-42-18-18). Expensive.

Gérard Besson – Michelin has given this small and formal eatery two stars. The service is impeccable and the classic menu includes specialties such as fricassee of lobster. Closed Saturdays and Sundays July 13 to 30, and from December 22 to January 7. Reservations necessary. Major credit cards accepted. 5 Rue Coq-Héron, 1er (phone: 42-33-14-74). Expensive.

Jacques Cagna – The talented eponymous chef always provides an interesting menu at these charming premises on the Left Bank, very near the Seine. *Guide Michelin* has awarded it two stars. Closed August, *Christmas* week, Saturdays, and Sundays. Reservations necessary. Major credit cards accepted. 14 Rue des Grands-Augustins, 6e (phone: 43-26-49-39). Expensive.

Lamazère – Truffle heaven. The menu is a triumph of rich products from the southwest of France. The owner is a magician in the real sense of the word, as well as with food. The elegant bar and salons are open late. Closed Sundays and August. Reservations necessary. Major credit cards accepted. 23 Rue de Ponthieu, 8e (phone: 43-59-66-66). Expensive.

Ledoyen – This grand dowager of Paris dining places received a major face-lift in 1988 when Régine, the capital's nightlife queen, took it over. Its look, and menus ordained by consulting chef Jacques Maximin, have received generally favorable reviews (one star from Michelin), particularly from high-powered businesspeople. Closed Sundays. Reservations necessary. Major credit cards accepted. Carré des Champs-Elysées, 8e (phone: 47-42-23-23). Expensive.

Miravile – Gilles Epié, one of Paris's promising young chefs, recently moved across the river into larger quarters. He brought with him his customers, his Michelin star, and memorable dishes such as a lobster and potato cake. Closed Saturday lunch and Sundays. Reservations necessary. Major credit cards accepted. 72 Quai de l'Hôtel de Ville, 4e (phone: 42-74-72-22). Expensive.

Olympe – Owner and chef Dominique Nahmias is the first female chef to be awarded three toques — very high honors — by Gault Millau. Her nouvelle cuisine is painstakingly prepared and simply glorious; an excellent wine list adds to the meal's enjoyment. Closed Saturday and Sunday lunch, Mondays, and August. Reservations necessary. Major credit cards accepted. 8 Rue Nicolas-Charlet, 15e (phone: 47-34-86-08). Expensive.

Le Petit Montmorency – In his location near the Champs-Elysées, chef Daniel Bouché presents one of the most exciting and unusual menus in Paris. Very, very popular. Closed weekends and August. Reservations necessary. Major credit cards accepted. 5 Rue Rabelais, 8e (phone: 42-25-11-19). Expensive.

Pré Catelan – It's the large restaurant right in the middle of the Bois de Boulogne, and believe it or not, the food here is very good. Ingredients are fresh and sauces are light. Specialties include four or five new dishes daily. Michelin has awarded it one star. Closed Sunday evenings, Mondays, and 2 weeks in February. Reservations necessary. Major credit cards accepted. Rte. de Suresnes, Bois de Boulogne, 16e (phone: 45-24-55-58). Expensive.

Régine's – The food actually is good in this beautifully decorated nightclub, which is frequented by Parisians as well as the chic international set. Ask your hotel manager to get you in, because it's nominally a private club. Try the foie gras (made on the premises) and the goose. Closed Sundays. Reservations advised. Major credit cards accepted. 49 Rue de Ponthieu, 8e (phone: 43-59-21-60). Expensive.

Relais Louis XIII – Old-style decor and new cuisine in one of Paris's prettiest houses. The *Guide Michelin* has given it two stars. Closed Sundays, Monday lunch, and August. Reservations advised. Major credit cards accepted. 1 Rue Pont de Lodi, 6e (phone: 43-26-75-96) Expensive.

Tan-Dinh – The perfect pause from a constant diet of French specialties. Despite the loss of its Michelin star, its Vietnamese specialties are simply superb. Shrimp rolls, Vietnamese ravioli, and minced filet of beef are only three examples of the marvelous menu (ask for the version in English). Remarkable wine list. Closed Sundays and August. Reservations advised. Major credit cards accepted. 60 Rue de Verneuil, 7e (phone: 45-44-04-84). Expensive.

Le Toit de Passy – Not only is the food here good (Michelin has awarded chef Yann Jacquot one star), but the rooftop view in one of Paris's more exclusive districts is spectacular. Try specialties such as *pigeonneau en croûte de sel* (squab in a salt crust) while dining outdoors. Closed Saturdays (except for September through mid-December), Sundays, and holidays, 1 week in May, 1 week in September and *Christmas* week. Reservations necessary. Major credit cards accepted. 94 Av. Paul-Doumer, 16e (phone: 45-24-55-37). Expensive.

Vivarois – Claude Peyrot is one of France's finest chefs. Specialties in his small, elegant eating place include curried oysters au gratin, turbot, and assortments of desserts. Michelin has awarded it two stars. Closed weekends and August. Reservations necessary. Major credit cards accepted. 192 Av. Victor-Hugo, 16e (phone: 45-04-04-31). Expensive.

Auberge des Deux Signes – This place was once the cellars of the priory of St.-Julien-le-Pauvre; try to get an upstairs table overlooking the gardens. Auvergnat cooking à la nouvelle cuisine. Closed Sundays. Reservations necessary. Major credit cards accepted. 46 Rue Galande, 5e (phone: 43-25-46-56). Expensive to moderate.

Le Bistrot d'à Côté Flaubert – Michelin two-star chef Michel Rostang offers *cuisine de terroir* (uncomplicated, back-to-basics regional fare) in a turn-of-the-century bistro. Closed Saturday lunch, Sundays, and holidays. Reservations advised. Major credit cards accepted. 10 Rue Gustave-Flaubert, 17e (phone: 42-67-05-81). Expensive to moderate.

Brasserie Lorraine – Bustling and convivial until late at night, this place pulls in the neighborhood's bourgeoisie for animated evenings over the foie gras salads. Open daily from noon to 2 AM. Reservations unnecessary. Major credit cards accepted. Pl. des Ternes, 8e (phone: 42-27-80-04). Expensive to moderate.

La Cantine des Gourmets – This restaurant specializes in light, inventive creations of high quality (one Michelin star). Closed Sundays. Reservations advised. Major credit cards accepted. 113 Av. Bourdonnais, 7e (phone: 47-05-47-96). Expensive to moderate.

La Coquille – A classic bistro, where the service is unpretentious and warm, and the food consistently good. From October to May, the house specialty is *coquilles St.-Jacques,* a version that consists of scallops roasted with butter, shallots, and parsley. Closed Sundays, Mondays, holidays, and August. Reservations advised.

Major credit cards accepted. 6 Rue du Débarcadère, 17e (phone: 45-74-25-95). Expensive to moderate.

Le Duc – The atmosphere is warm and comfortable, and Paul Minchelli is incomparably inventive with fish and shellfish (cooked and raw). Quality and variety are the rule here, with such specialties as curried oysters, tuna tartar, *coquilles St.-Jacques cru*, and an extraordinary seafood platter. Closed Saturdays, Sundays, and Mondays. Reservations necessary. No credit cards accepted. 243 Bd. Raspail, 14e (phone: 43-22-59-59 or 43-20-96-30). Expensive to moderate.

Faucher – Rising star Gerard Faucher opened this elegant restaurant 2 years ago and has drawn praise for his light touch with fish dishes and desserts ever since. Michelin awarded him a star this year. Closed Saturday lunch and Sundays. Reservations necessary. Major credit cards accepted. 123 Av. Wagram, 17e (phone: 42-27-61-50). Expensive to moderate.

Morot-Gaudry – On the top floor of a 1920s building with a great view of the Eiffel Tower, especially from the flowered terrace. Among the inventive dishes are calf's liver with raspberry vinegar, compote of chicken with leeks, and rice cake with ginger. One Michelin star. Closed weekends. Reservations necessary. Major credit cards accepted. 6 Rue de la Cavalerie, 15e (phone: 45-67-06-85). Expensive to moderate.

Pavillon des Princes – Under the direction of Pascal Bonichon, it serves produces delicious duck sausage salad with avocado, *coquilles St.-Jacques* with fresh pasta, and lamb nuggets with cabbage and tomatoes. On the edge of the Bois de Boulogne. Open daily. Reservations advised. Major credit cards accepted. 69 Av. de la Porte d'Auteuil, 16e (phone: 47-43-15-15). Expensive to moderate.

Au Quai d'Orsay – Fashionable, sophisticated, very French, and very intimate. Traditional copious bourgeois cooking and good beaujolais. Closed Sundays. Reservations advised. Major credit cards accepted. 49 Quai d'Orsay, 7e (phone: 45-51-58-58). Expensive to moderate.

Timonerie – Be sure to reserve 3 or 4 days in advance in order to dine at this one-Michelin-star restaurant. Specialties include *sandre rôti au chou et pommes de terre* (perched pike with cabbage and potatoes) and the chocolate tart. Especially recommended is the very affordable prix fixe lunch. Closed Mondays from March to August, Saturdays from September to February, Sundays, and mid-February to mid-March. Visa and MasterCard accepted. 35 Quai de la Tournelle, 5e (phone: 43-25-44-42). Expensive to moderate.

Le Trou Gascon – Alain Dutournier created the inspired and unusual cooking that features southwestern French specialties and a vast choice of regional wines and armagnacs. He has moved on to a more elegant neighborhood, but his wife holds down the fort at this one-Michelin-star restaurant. Closed weekends. Reservations advised. Major credit cards accepted. 40 Rue Taine, 12e (phone: 43-44-34-26). Expensive to moderate.

Allard – A very popular bistro with hearty country cooking and excellent burgundy wines. Snails, turbot, and beef bourguignon are the prime lures. Spring, when white asparagus and the new turnips arrive, is a special time here. Don't miss the chocolate charlotte for dessert. Closed weekends and August and for 10 days at *Christmas.* Reservations advised. Major credit cards accepted. 41 Rue St.-André-des-Arts, 6e (phone: 43-26-48-23). Moderate.

L'Amanguier – This series of garden restaurants serves an appetizing brand of nouvelle cuisine. Stick to a main course, which comes with a choice of appetizers, and the price is surprisingly low. The desserts are tempting. Open daily for lunch and dinner. Reservations advised. Major credit cards accepted. 51 Rue du Théâtre, 15e (phone: 45-77-04-01); 110 Rue de Richelieu, 2e (phone: 42-96-37-79); 43 Av.

des Ternes, 17e (phone: 43-80-19-28); and 12 Av. de Madrid, Neuilly (phone: 47-45-79-73). Moderate.

Ambassade d'Auvergne – Its young chef creates delicious, unusual, classic Auvergnat dishes with a modern touch (try the lentil salad and the sliced ham). Also known for seasonal specialties and wonderful cakes. Open daily for lunch and dinner. Reservations advised. Major credit cards accepted. 22 Rue du Grenier-St.-Lazare, 3e (phone: 42-72-31-22). Moderate.

Astier – An honest-to-goodness neighborhood hangout that always is packed, because the clientele knows they can rely on it for the staples of bourgeois cooking, lovingly prepared. Closed Saturdays, Sundays, and August. Reservations advised. Major credit cards accepted. 44 Rue Jean-Pierre-Timbaud, 11e (phone: 43-57-16-35). Moderate.

Balzar – Perhaps because of its location right next to the Sorbonne, this mirrored brasserie has always attracted intellectuals. The steaks and *pommes frites* also are worth a visit. Open daily for lunch and dinner; closed *Christmas* week and August. Reservations necessary. Major credit cards accepted. 49 Rue des Ecoles, 5e (phone: 43-54-13-67). Moderate.

La Barrière Poquelin – The excellent cooking à la nouvelle cuisine includes a splendid foie gras salad. Closed Saturdays for lunch, Sundays, and 3 weeks in August. Reservations advised. Major credit cards accepted. 17 Rue Molière, 1er (phone: 42-96-22-19). Moderate.

Bistro 121 – A hearty menu and excellent wines are offered in a modern setting that's always chic and crowded. Try *poisson cru mariné au citron vert* (seafood marinated in lime juice) and chocolate charlotte for dessert. One Michelin star. Closed Sundays, Mondays, and mid-July to mid-August. Reservations advised. Major credit cards accepted. 121 Rue de la Convention, 15e (phone: 45-57-52-90). Moderate.

Le Bistrot de Paris – Michel Oliver offers informality, original and classic bistro fare, and a good wine list, which attract a crowd. Closed Saturdays for lunch and Sundays. Reservations advised. Major credit cards accepted. 33 Rue de Lille, 7e (phone: 42-61-16-83). Moderate.

Le Boeuf sur le Toit – In the building that once housed a restaurant of the same name, a haunt of Jean Cocteau and other Paris artists in the 1940s, this eatery off the Champs-Elysées is managed by the Flo group, well known for good value in atmospheric surroundings. Piano bar until 2 AM. Reservations advised. Major credit cards accepted. 34 Rue du Colisée, 8e (phone: 43-59-83-80). Moderate.

Bofinger – For magnificent Belle Epoque decor, this is the place; it's one of Paris's oldest brasseries and it is beautiful, even if the food is occasionally disappointing. Order onion soup and *choucroute* and you won't be unhappy. Open daily. Reservations advised. Major credit cards accepted. 3 Rue de la Bastille, 4e (phone: 42-72-87-82). Moderate.

Café de la Jatte – Only those in the know venture this far down the Seine for dinner. This leafy island, l'Ile de la Jatte, was ripe for a smart renovation, and this huge, high-ceilinged dining room, with half-moon-shaped windows and a pink floor, is now full of the chicest local clientele. The fare is healthy and simple: generous salads and roast chicken along with more nouvelle items. Open daily for lunch and dinner. Reservations advised. Major credit cards accepted. 60 Av. Vital Bouhot, Neuilly, 15 minutes by car from central Paris (phone: 47-45-04-20). Moderate.

Chez André – A classic, bustling bistro near the chic shopping of Avenue Montaigne. Although a bit too noisy and crowded, it is quite popular with the well-heeled crowd, perhaps because it offers impeccably prepared sole meunière, *blanquette de veau, gigôt d'agneau,* and other traditional dishes. Reservations advised. Major credit cards accepted. 12 Rue Marbeuf, 8e (phone: 47-20-59-57). Moderate.

Chez Benoît – A pretty but unpretentious bistro with wonderful old-fashioned Lyonnaise cooking and exquisite wines. Just about at the top of the bistro list, it's rated one Michelin star. Closed weekends and August. Reservations necessary. No credit cards accepted. 20 Rue St.-Martin, 4e (phone: 42-72-25-76). Moderate.

Chez Georges – This narrow, old-fashioned bistro — with a whole platoon of matronly waitresses in starched aprons — is a bastion of traditional French cooking. Closed Sundays and holidays. Reservations advised. Major credit cards accepted. 1 Rue du Mail, 2e (phone: 42-60-07-11). Moderate.

Chez Josephine and ***La Rôtisserie Chez Dumonet*** – Two restaurants share the same building and the same management. *Josephine* is an old-time bistro with traditional cuisine and an excellent wine cellar; the *Rôtisserie* is lively and more modern, with steaks and grills over an open fire. *Josephine* is closed weekends and July; the *Rôtisserie,* Mondays, Tuesdays, and August. Reservations advised. Major credit cards accepted. 117 Rue du Cherche-Midi, 6e (phone: 45-48-52-40). Moderate.

Chez Maître Paul – The cooking of the Franche-Comté region is the specialty of this recently expanded restaurant with an *auberge* ambience. Try the *saucisse Montbéliard* (smoked garlic sausage), the *poulet au vin jaune* (chicken cooked in Jura wine), and the *gâteau aux noix* (nut cake). Closed Saturday lunch and Sunday. Reservations advised. Major credit cards accepted. The prix fixe menu is a good value. 12 Rue Monsieur-le-Prince, 6e (phone: 43-54-74-59). Moderate.

Chez Pauline – The perfect bistro. The tiny, wood-paneled downstairs room (ask to be seated there) is brightened by large mirrors and fresh flowers; the place settings look like Florentine marbling. Try the oysters in a watercress sauce or the assortment of seafood with a saffron sauce, and save room for dessert — *mille-feuille* of orange with raspberry sauce is sublime. Closed Saturdays, Sundays, July, and from December 24 to January 2. Reservations advised. Major credit cards accepted. 5 Rue Villedo, 1er (phone: 42-96-20-70). Moderate.

Chez Pierre Vedel – Truly original cuisine. Closed weekends, from mid-July to mid-August, and at *Christmastime.* Reservations advised. Major credit cards accepted. 19 Rue Duranton, 15e (phone: 45-58-43-17). Moderate.

Chez René – This neighborhood bistro in the heart of the Left Bank offers hearty helpings of regional fare. Closed Saturdays, Sundays, August, and *Christmas* week. Reservations advised. Major credit cards accepted. 14 Blvd. St.-Germain, 5e (phone: 43-54-30-23). Moderate.

Chez Toutoune – This modest place specializing in Provençal dishes has become very popular for two good reasons: The food is tasty and the prices are fairly reasonable. The five-course, prix fixe menu features a rather short but very interesting selection of appetizers, entrées, and desserts. Closed Sundays, Monday lunch, and mid-August to mid-September. Reservations advised. Major credit cards accepted. 5 Rue de Pontoise, 5e (phone: 43-26-56-81). Moderate.

La Coupole – A big, brassy brasserie, once the haunt of Hemingway, Josephine Baker, and Picasso, it is owned by the Flo group. The atmosphere is still great, the food still mediocre. Open daily until 2 AM. Closed August. Reservations advised. Major credit cards accepted. 102 Bd. du Montparnasse, 14e (phone: 43-20-14-20). Moderate.

Le Dômarais – This used to be the Crédit Municipal, or state pawnshop, and its elegant cupola now houses a restaurant serving such inventions as camembert fondue, grilled Bayonne ham, and a *petit salé* of duck. Closed Saturdays for lunch and Mondays. Reservations advised. Major credit cards accepted. 53 *bis* Rue des Francs-Bourgeois, 4e (phone: 42-74-54-17). Moderate.

L'Escargot Montorgueil – The polished wood paneling, the brass fittings, and the spiral staircase at this beautiful place, which dates from 1830, only add to the pleasure of a meal that might include snails in any of half a dozen styles or duck with orange sauce. Closed Monday lunch. Reservations advised. Major credit cards accepted. 38 Rue Montorgueil, 1er (phone: 42-36-83-51). Moderate.

La Ferme St.-Simon – Among our favorites for wholesome *cuisine d'autrefois* (old-fashioned cooking). Nothing very chichi here, just well-prepared, authentic dishes — the kinds you'd expect from a traditional Left Bank restaurant. Leave room for dessert; the owner once was a top assistant to Gaston Lenôtre. A perfect place for lunch. Michelin has awarded it one star. Closed Saturday lunch, Sundays, and August. Reservations advised. Major credit cards accepted. 6 Rue de St.-Simon, 7e (phone: 45-48-35-74). Moderate.

Au Gamin de Paris – Combines the coziness of a classic bistro with the chic of a historic Marais building and serves well-prepared, imaginative food. Open daily. No reservations after 8 PM. Major credit cards accepted. 51 Rue Vieille-du-Temple, 4e (phone: 42-78-97-24). Moderate.

Le Grand Colbert – Bright and brassy, with delightful polychrome, Belle Epoque motifs, and traditional offerings such as *boeuf gros sel* (boiled beef with coarse salt) and *merlan Colbert* (lightly breaded, pan-fried whiting), this renovated 19th-century brasserie is next to the Bibliothèque Nationale. Open daily. Reservations advised. Major credit cards accepted. In the *Galerie Colbert,* 2 Rue Vivienne, 2e (phone: 42-86-87-88). Moderate.

Jo Goldenberg – The best-known eating house in the Marais's quaint Jewish quarter, with good chopped liver and cheesecake and a range of Eastern European Jewish specialties. It's also a fine place to sip mint tea at the counter in the middle of a busy day. Open daily. Reservations unnecessary. Major credit cards accepted. 7 Rue des Rosiers, 4e (phone: 48-87-20-16 or 48-87-70-39). Moderate.

Julien – Belle Epoque decor with all the flourishes. Reliable, if uninspired, meals are served in a bustling atmosphere until 1:30 AM. Open daily. Reservations advised. Major credit cards accepted. 16 Rue du Faubourg-St.-Denis, 10e (phone: 47-70-12-06). Moderate.

La Manufacture – The second eatery of two-star chef Jean-Pierre Vigato (of *Apicius*), this starkly modern place in an old cigar factory at the southern edge of Paris offers an excellent quality/price ratio. Closed Saturday afternoons and Sundays. Reservations advised. Visa accepted. 30 Rue Ernest-Renan, Issy-les-Moulineaux, 15e (phone: 40-93-08-98). Moderate.

La Marée – Unobtrusive on the outside, there is great comfort within — also the freshest of fish, the best restaurant wine values in Paris, and fabulous desserts. Michelin has awarded it one star. Closed weekends, holidays, and August. Reservations advised. Major credit cards accepted. 1 Rue Daru, 8e (phone: 47-63-52-42). Moderate.

Le Moulin du Village – Light and airy, especially in summer, when tables are put out on the cobbles of Cité Berryer, a tiny pedestrian alley very near the Madeleine, just off the Rue Royale. Cuisine is nouvelle and wines good. Closed Sundays. Reservations advised. Visa accepted. 25 Rue Royale, 8e (phone: 42-65-08-47). Moderate.

Le Muniche – St.-Germain's best brasserie is a bustling place with a rather extensive menu, and it's popular until 3 AM. Open daily. Reservations advised. Major credit cards accepted. 27 Rue de Buci, 6e (phone: 46-33-62-09). Moderate.

La Petite Chaise – Founded in 1680, it occupies 2 stories of a 17th-century stone house on the Left Bank. The intimate (and slightly run-down) atmosphere of the home of an ancient aunt characterizes this place, with brocaded walls, brass chandeliers, and antique oils contributing to the period decor. The trout you see swimming in a tank also are on the menu, as are specialties like shellfish crêpes and veal Pojarsky, in which the meat is combined with minced chicken. Always open. Reservations advised. Major credit cards accepted. 36 Rue de Grenelle, 7e (phone: 42-22-13-35). Moderate.

Au Pied de Cochon – No more *choucroute* on the menu (sob!). Crowded and colorful 24 hours a day, and its customers enjoy shellfish, pigs' feet, and great crocks of onion soup, all in the old *Les Halles* area. Unfortunately, the food and service aren't what they used to be, and a garish redecoration has mangled most of the old atmosphere. But it still has atmosphere. Reservations advised. Major credit cards accepted. 6 Rue Coquillière, 1er (phone: 42-36-11-75). Moderate.

Pierre au Palais Royal – A delightful place with admirable bourgeois cooking (one Michelin star) and lovely chinon and saumur wines. Closed weekends and August. Reservations necessary. Major credit cards accepted. 10 Rue de Richelieu, 1er (phone: 42-96-27-17). Moderate.

Le Récamier – The so-called garden is actually a courtyard between a couple of high-rise buildings, but as the sun goes down, it's a very congenial place to dine in good weather. Martin Cantegrit is a perfect host, and the menu features first-rate (and one-Michelin-star) fish dishes (try the turbot, if possible). The apple tart for dessert is special (order it warm), and the wine list is one of the most fairly priced on the Left Bank. Closed Sundays. Reservations necessary. Major credit cards accepted. 4 Rue Récamier, 7e (phone: 45-48-86-58). Moderate.

Restaurant du Marché – Cuisine Landaise, which means solid, country-style cooking — foie gras, *confits d'oie,* and fine wines from the Landes region in the southwest of France, near Bordeaux. An amazing choice of herb teas, and a pretty terrace for summer dining. Open daily for lunch and dinner. Reservations advised. Major credit cards accepted. 59 Rue de Dantzig, 15e (phone: 45-32-26-88 or 45-33-23-72). Moderate.

La Rôtisserie du Beaujolais – A de rigueur spot for Paris's "in set" is Claude Terrail's recently opened casual canteen on the quay in the shadow of his three-star gastronomic temple, *La Tour d'Argent*. Most of the meat, produce, and cheese served come from Lyons. Closed Monday and Tuesday afternoons. No reservations. Major credit cards accepted. 19 Quai de la Tournelle, 5e (phone: 43-54-17-47). Moderate.

Le Soufflé – On the street just behind the Rue Rivoli, not far from Place Vendôme, this is the place to enjoy an orgy of soufflés. We suggest crayfish soufflé for an appetizer, cheese soufflé as a main course, and chocolate soufflé for dessert — then head directly to your cardiologist! Closed Sundays. Reservations advised. Major credit cards accepted. 36 Rue du Mont-Thabor, 1er (phone: 42-60-27-19). Moderate.

Le Télégraphe – This former dormitory for female employees of the French post office attracts a trendy crowd, including Princess Stephanie of Monaco. The food is simple — *saumon unilatéral* (salmon filet cooked on one side with olive oil and herbs), and a good *crème brûlée*. Open daily. Reservations advised. Major credit cards accepted. 41 Rue de Lille, 7e (phone: 40-15-06-65). Moderate.

Le Train Bleu – Fine food, good wine, and baroque decor so gorgeous it's been made a national monument. And it's in a train station. Open daily for lunch and dinner. Reservations usually unnecessary. Major credit cards accepted. Gare de Lyon, 20 Bd. Diderot, 12e (phone: 43-43-09-06). Moderate.

Ty-Coz – Breton cuisine features fish, cider, and crêpes; no meat, no cheese. Closed Sundays and Mondays. Reservations advised. Major credit cards accepted. 35 Rue St.-Georges, 9e (phone: 48-78-34-61). Moderate.

Le Zeyer – After a hard morning discount shopping on the nearby Rue d'Alesia, here's a good neighborhood place for mussels *marinière,* grilled *lotte* with sorrel, or platters of shellfish. Open daily. Reservations unnecessary. Major credit cards accepted. 234 Av. du Maine, 14e (phone: 45-40-43-88). Moderate.

Androuët – There's a great cheese emporium on the main floor and, upstairs, a unique restaurant where cheese is the base of every dish. In recent years the quality has slipped somewhat, but it still is a unique experience. Closed Sundays. Reservations advised. Major credit cards accepted. 41 Rue Amsterdam, 8e (phone: 48-74-26-90). Moderate to inexpensive.

Brasserie Lipp – This famous café is fashionable for a late supper of *choucroute* and Alsatian beer and for people watching inside and out. The food's just as good there, however. Closed 15 days at *Christmas*. Reservations advised. Major credit cards accepted. 151 Bd. St.-Germain, 6e (phone: 45-48-53-91). Moderate to inexpensive.

Chez La Vieille – Adrienne's cooking is simple, savory, and very popular. For lunch only. Closed weekends. Reservations necessary. No credit cards accepted. 28 Rue de l'Arbre-Sec, 1er (phone: 42-60-15-78). Moderate to inexpensive.

Clos de la Tour – This popular restaurant has "bistro moderne" decor. Closed Saturdays at lunch, Sundays, and August. Reservations advised. Major credit cards accepted. 22 Rue Falguière, 15e (phone: 43-22-34-73). Moderate to inexpensive.

Coup de Coeur – With a 2-level design reminiscent of Manhattan's stark Upper West Side eating establishments, this place features inventive cooking, eager waiters, and an interesting wine list. Closed Saturday lunch and Sundays. Reservations advised. Major credit cards accepted. 19 Rue St.-Augustin, 2e (phone: 47-03-45-70). Moderate to inexpensive.

Les Grandes Marches – Formerly the *Tour d'Argent Bastille,* though never related to Claude Terrail's 3-star temple overlooking the Seine, it is a bustling, turn-of-the-century-style brasserie serving oysters and shellfish platters, fish, and grilled meats. Located next to the new *Opéra de La Bastille.* Reservations advised. Major credit cards accepted. 6 Pl. de la Bastille, 11e (phone: 43-42-90-32). Moderate to inexpensive.

Joe Allen's – Just like the original on West 46th Street in New York City, it has good T-bone steaks, hamburgers, chili, and apple pie. Open till 1 AM. Open daily. Reservations advised after 8 PM. Major credit cards accepted. 30 Rue Pierre-Lescot, 1er (phone: 42-36-70-13). Moderate to inexpensive.

Les Noces de Jeannette – Under new management, this place now offers inventive cuisine at reasonable prices. Closed Sunday evenings. Reservations advised. Major credit cards accepted. 14 Rue Favart, 2e (phone: 42-96-36-89). Moderate to inexpensive.

Le Petit Niçois – This tiny bistro, serving delicious bouillabaisse, is a favorite of French TV news crews who broadcast from a nearby building. A few good specials vary from night to night. Closed Sundays and Monday lunch. Reservations advised. Major credit cards accepted. 10 Rue Amélie, 7e (phone: 45-51-83-65). Moderate to inexpensive.

Au Petit Riche – Genuine 1900s decor, subtle Touraine cooking, and inexpensive vouvray, chinon, and bourgueil wines. Closed Sundays and August. Reservations advised. Major credit cards accepted. 25 Rue Le Peletier, 9e (phone: 47-70-68-68). Moderate to inexpensive.

Le Pharamond – Serves only the best Norman food in a beautiful Belle Epoque, timbered townhouse that has been declared a historic monument by the French government. Famous for *tripes à la mode de Caen* and *pommes soufflés* since 1862. Closed Sundays, Monday lunch, and July. Reservations advised. Major credit cards accepted. 24 Rue de la Grande-Truanderie, 1er (phone: 42-33-06-72). Moderate to inexpensive.

Atelier Maître Albert – Unlike most other eateries on the Left Bank, this one is pleasantly roomy, with a log fire in winter and an honest prix fixe menu year-round. Notre-Dame looms up in front of you as you walk out the door and onto the quay. Open daily except Sundays for dinner. Reservations advised. Major credit cards accepted. 1 Rue Maître-Albert, 5e (phone: 46-33-13-78). Inexpensive.

Aux Bigorneaux – A souvenir of the old *Les Halles,* this place is frequented by arty types and journalists. Especially recommended are the *foie gras frais maison,* the chicory salad, the steak au poivre, the Réserve Maison wine, and the sumptuous desserts. Closed Sundays, Mondays, and for dinner in winter. Reservations advised. Major credit cards accepted. 12 Rue Mondétour, 1er (phone: 45-08-49-33). Inexpensive.

Brasserie Flo – One of the last of the brasseries of the 1900s, owned by the enterprising Flo group. Hidden in a hard-to-find courtyard, it's excellent for oysters, foie gras, wild boar, and Alsatian specialties. Open daily and late. Reservations advised. Major credit cards accepted. 7 Cour des Petites-Ecuries, 10e (phone: 47-70-13-59). Inexpensive.

Brissemoret – Popular with Parisians, this eatery serves basic quality food at bargain prices. The tasteful ambience is a perfect setting for excellent foie gras, raw salmon marinated in fresh herbs, and great sauces (try the breast of duck in wine sauce). Closed Saturdays and Sundays. Reservations necessary. Major credit cards accepted. 5 Rue St.-Marc, 2e (phone: 42-36-91-72). Inexpensive.

Chez Fernand – A nondescript hole in the wall that produces surprisingly tasty dishes. *Pot-au-feu,* steaks with shallots, and fish pâté all are first-rate, but the real lure is the huge tub of chocolate mousse served for dessert — a chocoholic's fantasy come true. Open evenings only. Reservations advised. Visa accepted. 13 Rue Guirsade, 6e (phone: 43-54-61-47). Inexpensive.

Chez Jenny – A roisterous Alsatian brasserie, where the waitresses still wear white lace collars and dirndls. There are oysters year-round, though perhaps more in keeping with the place's character are the huge platters of *choucroute* (sauerkraut and assorted pork meats) accompanied by good riesling wine. Open daily. No reservations. Major credit cards accepted. 39 Bd. du Temple, 3e (phone: 42-74-75-75). Inexpensive.

Chez Marianne – A friendly Jewish delicatessen and restaurant; the falafels make nourishing fuel for any exploration of the Marais. Closed Fridays. Reservations unnecessary. Major credit cards accepted. 2 Rue des Hospitalières-St.-Gervais, 4e (phone: 42-72-18-86). Inexpensive.

Chez Yvette – This excellent, small, bourgeois restaurant has good home cooking, lots of choices, and great desserts. Closed weekends and August. Reservations advised. Major credit cards accepted. 46 *bis* Bd. Montparnasse, 6e (phone: 42-22-45-54). Inexpensive.

Chicago Meatpackers – If homesickness strikes, head here for hamburgers or chili; finish your American food fix with apple pie or chocolate chip cheesecake. Open daily. Reservations unnecessary. Major credit cards accepted. 8 Rue Coquillière, 1er (phone: 40-28-02-33). Inexpensive.

Gérard – A hearty *pot-au-feu* and other country favorites are served at this bistro. Closed Saturday lunch and Sundays. Reservations unnecessary. No credit cards accepted. 4 Rue du Mail, 2e (phone: 42-96-24-36). Inexpensive.

Le Jardin de la Mouffe – A choice of hors d'oeuvres, entrées, and desserts, plus a cheese course, half a carafe of wine, and a pretty garden view. Closed Mondays. Reservations unnecessary. Visa accepted. 75 Rue Mouffetard, 5e (phone: 47-07-19-29). Inexpensive.

Lunchtime – One of the few eateries in Paris that satisfies the desire for a light lunch, serving crispy mixed salads made with the freshest greens and a wide range of sandwiches, including blue cheese with cream, curried chicken with currants, and American standbys such as roast beef. The desserts are homemade and delicious. Lunch only. Closed Saturdays, Sundays, holidays, and August. Reservations unnecessary. No credit cards accepted. Two locations: 156 *bis* Av. Charles-de-Gaulle, Neuilly (phone: 46-24-08-99), and 255 Rue St.-Honoré, 1er (phone: 42-60-80-40). Inexpensive.

Moulin à Vent (Chez Henri) – Located across the street from what was once Paris's wine market, this bistro's decor has remained intact for over 40 years. The bar is adorned with half barrels and small lights that are inscribed with the names of different wines and growers. The menu of meats (especially sausages from the Ardèche) and salads also has stayed the same. Try the frogs' legs and the steaks with shallots. Closed Sundays, Mondays, and August. Reservations necessary. Major credit cards accepted. 20 Rue des Fossés St.-Bernard, 5e (phone: 43-54-99-37). Inexpensive.

Paul – Once a secret bistro, it is now known by the whole world. There's good solid fare here, and the premises always are packed. Closed Mondays, Tuesdays, and August. Reservations advised. No credit cards accepted. 15 Pl. Dauphine, 1er (phone: 43-54-21-48). Inexpensive.

Petit Zinc – A popular late (3 AM) spot for fish, oysters, foie gras, and an ample, reasonably priced wine list. Open daily. Reservations advised. Major credit cards accepted. 25 Rue de Buci, 6e (phone: 46-33-51-66). Inexpensive.

Polidor – Regulars here keep their napkins in numbered pigeonholes, and the place's history includes frequent patronage by such starving artists as Paul Verlaine, James Joyce, Ernest Hemingway, and, more recently, Jean-Paul Belmondo. The *College de Pataphysique,* founded by Raymond Queneau and Ionesco, still meets here regularly for the good family-style food. Ask to see the house scrapbook. Closed in August. Reservations unnecessary. No credit cards accepted. 41 Rue Monsieur-le-Prince, 6e (phone: 43-26-95-34). Inexpensive.

Le Procope – One of Paris's oldest restaurants, where the food is reasonably good and the atmosphere couldn't be more Parisian; the service, however, leaves a lot to be desired. Open daily. Reservations advised. Major credit cards accepted. 13 Rue de l'Ancienne-Comédie, 6e (phone: 43-26-99-20). Inexpensive.

Relais de Venise – There's always a crowd waiting outside this place near the Porte Maillot, better known as "L'Entrecôte." The prix fixe menu includes free second helpings of steaks with pepper sauce and French fries. Fancy strawberry desserts cost extra. Open daily. No reservations. Major credit cards accepted. 271 Bd. Pereire, 17e (phone: 45-74-27-97). Inexpensive.

Robert et Louise – Family bistro, with warm paneled decor and a very high standard for ingredients and cooking. Try the *boeuf bourguignon* or the open-fire–grilled *côte de boeuf.* Also good are the *fromage blanc* and the *vin en pichet.* Closed Sundays, holidays, and August. Reservations unnecessary. No credit cards accepted. 64 Rue Vieille-du-Temple, 3e (phone: 42-78-55-89). Inexpensive.

Le Roi du Pot-au-Feu – A very good place to sample this delicious peasant dish. Closed Sundays. Reservations advised. Major credit cards accepted. 34 Rue Vignon, 9e (phone: 47-42-37-10). Inexpensive.

La Route du Beaujolais – It's a barn-like workers' bistro on the Left Bank, serving Lyonnaise specialties and beaujolais wines. Don't miss the charcuterie and the fresh bread here, and try the *tarte tatin* (caramelized apple tart) for dessert. Closed Saturday lunch and Sundays. Reservations unnecessary. Visa accepted. 17 Rue de Lourmel, 15e (phone: 45-79-31-63). Inexpensive.

Le Trumilou – The formidable proprietress sets the tone of this robust establishment, which serves huge, steaming portions of boar, pheasant, and venison in season under a frieze of some excruciatingly bad rustic oils. Closed Mondays. Reservations unnecessary. Major credit cards accepted. 84 Quai de l'Hôtel-de-Ville, 5e (phone: 42-77-63-98). Inexpensive.

Vagenende – An Art Nouveau spot with fantasy decor that has changed little since it opened in 1898. It features adequate, filling meals at low prices. Open daily until 1 AM. Reservations unnecessary. Major credit cards accepted. 142 Bd. St.-Germain, 6e (phone: 43-26-68-18). Inexpensive.

Assiette au Boeuf – Steaks, salad, and *pommes frites,* with music in the evening. Open daily until 1 AM. No reservations. Major credit cards accepted. 123 Champs-Elysées, 8e (phone: 47-20-01-13). Very inexpensive.

Bistro de la Gare – Michel Oliver offers a choice of three appetizers and three main courses with *pommes frites.* Excellent for a quick lunch. Open daily. No reservations. Major credit cards accepted. Ten locations, including 73 Champs-Elysées, 8e (phone: 43-59-67-83); 59 Bd. Montparnasse, 6e (phone: 45-48-38-01); 38 Bd. des Italiens, 9e (phone: 48-24-49-61). Very inexpensive.

Chartier – Huge, turn-of-the-century place with lots of down-to-earth food for the money. No reservations. No credit cards accepted. 7 Rue du Faubourg-Montmartre, 9e (phone: 47-70-86-29). Very inexpensive.

Drouot – The younger member of the Chartier family, but less known, and with more berets and fewer tourists. The waiters and waitresses, clad in black and white, look as if they emerged from a Renoir painting, although the decor is 1920s, with brass hat stands. The simple food is a bargain. To avoid a long wait for a table, arrive before 9 PM. No reservations. No credit cards accepted. 103 Rue de Richelieu, 2e (phone: 42-96-68-23). Very inexpensive.

L'Etoile Verte – Not much to look at, but always full, it serves fresh and generous helpings of standard French classics — quenelles, seafood timbales, and so forth — at rock-bottom prices. Open daily. Reservations unnecessary. Major credit cards accepted. 13 Rue Brey, 17e (phone: 43-80-69-34). Very inexpensive.

L'Olympic Bar – Crowded at all hours, this popular hangout is open for meals at lunch only. Blue-collar workers, students, executives, fashionable women, and others eat and drink with pinball noise as a background. The decor is nothing to speak of, but the food is good, the portions are huge, and the price is right. Closed Sundays and sometimes for Saturday lunch. Reservations unnecessary. No credit cards accepted. 77 Rue St.-Dominique, 7e (phone: 45-51-75-87). Very inexpensive.

Le Petit Gavroche – A hole-in-the-wall bistro-cum-restaurant with a lively clientele, an inexpensive and classic menu, and the feeling that nothing has changed in years. Closed Sundays. Reservations unnecessary. No credit cards accepted. 15 Rue Ste.-Croix-de-la-Bretonnerie, 4e (phone: 48-87-74-26). Very inexpensive.

Le Petit St.-Benoît – French cooking at its simplest, in a plain little place with tiled floors and curlicued hat stands. Open weekdays. Reservations unnecessary. No credit cards accepted. 4 Rue St.-Benoît, 6e (phone: 42-60-27-92). Very inexpensive.

Au Pied de Fouet – This former coach house has had its habitués, including celebrities as diverse as Graham Greene, Le Corbusier, and Georges Pompidou. Service is fast and friendly, and it's a place to order the daily special. Desserts, such as *charlotte au chocolat,* are marvelous. Arrive early; it closes at 9 PM. Closed Saturday evenings, Sundays, 2 weeks at *Christmas* and *Easter,* and August. No reservations. No credit cards accepted. 45 Rue de Babylone, 7e (phone: 47-05-12-27). Very inexpensive.

■**EXTRA SPECIAL:** Although we've noted the existence of *Fauchon* in *Shopping,* we would be remiss in omitting it from the restaurant listings. Actually three spectacular stores stocking elegant edibles (at 26, 28, and 30 Pl. de la Madeleine, 8e), *Fauchon* is considered so much a bastion of the privileged that one of its stores was bombed by radicals back in 1978. But the shops thankfully have long been back in full working order, which is a blessing for every abdomen in town.

One *Fauchon* shop specializes in the most beautiful fruits and vegetables available anywhere, plus pâtés, terrines, and as many other incomparable carryout items as even the most jaded gourmet's palate could conceive. If you're planning any sort of picnic, and are looking for something out of the ordinary, this is the place to pack your hamper. There also is a new grocery and sweetshop on the street level.

But it's across the narrow street in the far corner of the Place de la Madeleine that all of Paris congregates for nonpareil pastries, coffee, and an occasional snack or drink. Chocolate *opéra* cakes and macaroons in many hues, as well as *mille-feuilles* and other custardy concoctions, are sold by the slice and can be sampled downstairs. Two years ago, the two original shops were joined by a *Fauchon* cafeteria/bar in the basement of the building located at 30 Place de la Madeleine and by a first class restaurant on the second floor. Breakfasts, lunches, snacks, and coffee are served downstairs throughout the day, while the restaurant upstairs is open for lunch and dinner. If you need a sugar surge during the course of your Paris meanderings, these are the places to take your high-caloric breaks.

For chocoholics: The very best hot chocolate in Paris (if not the universe) is served at *Angelina's* on the Rue de Rivoli, 1er, and at its other location in the Palais de Congrès, near the Porte Maillot métro. The best chocolate ice cream in the City of Light is at *Berthillon* on the Ile St.-Louis (31 Rue St.-Louis-en-l'Ile, 4e). The best (and most generous) servings of chocolate mousse are offered at *Chez Fernand* (13 Rue Guirsade, 6e, on the Left Bank).

The name for the crusty sourdough loaf — *pain Poilâne* — so beloved by the French comes from the tiny bakery *Poilâne* (8 Rue du Cherche-Midi, 6e; phone: 45-48-42-59). Also be sure not to miss their flaky apple tarts or the hearty walnut bread, and take a peek at the chandelier made of bread dough that lights up Monsieur Lionel Poilâne's office. Open daily, except Sundays, from 7:15 AM to 8:15 PM.

 WINE BARS AND CAFÉS: Choosing a place to drink is not a pressing problem in Paris. Following is a selection of watering holes to suit a variety of tastes and thirsts. Prices tend to be higher than in the United States, with a *café crème* or a glass of red wine costing $3 or more in the more expensive establishments. The moderate ones charge $2 to $3 for the same, and you pay less than $2 in the inexpensive spots.

Café Costes – Paris's post-post-modernism and something of a pioneer on the scene. It has an impressive marble stairway, a clock inspired by Fritz Lang's film *Metropolis,* some wild high-tech restrooms, and a fashionable complement of lounge lizards. Open daily. Reservations unnecessary. Major credit cards accepted. 4 Rue Berger, 1er (phone: 45-08-54-38 or 45-08-54-39). Expensive.

Fouquet's – All the cafés on the Champs-Elysées are overpriced and most are nasty, so it may be worth paying the inflated tab for a coffee at this one (also a full-blown and overblown restaurant), which at least has more style than all the rest — as well as a large corner for outdoor tables in summer. Always open. Reservations advised for dinner; unnecessary for the café. Major credit cards accepted. 99 Champs-Elysées, 8e (phone: 47-23-70-60). Expensive.

Harry's Bar – The son of the original Harry, who opened this celebrated establishment in 1911, is still at the helm here. And the memories of past patrons like Ernest Hemingway, Gertrude Stein, and George Gershwin are almost as tangible as the university flags and banners that hang from the paneled walls. Open 10:30 AM to 4 AM every day but *Christmas*. Reservations unnecessary. Major credit cards accepted. 5 Rue Daunou, 2e (phone: 42-61-71-14). Expensive.

Willi's – An enterprising Englishman set up this smart little wine bar, a pleasant walk through the Palais Royal gardens and only minutes from the *Louvre.* The wine selection — a list of 150 — is one of the best in Paris, with an emphasis on Côtes du Rhône. The chef creates some appetizing salads as well as a *plat du jour.* Closed

Sundays. Reservations unnecessary. Major credit cards accepted. 13 Rue des Petits-Champs, 1er (phone: 42-61-05-09). Expensive to moderate.

Blue Fox – On a cobbled market street behind the Madeleine, this wine bar has a list of about 20 reasonably priced wines by the glass that changes every 2 weeks. And there's good charcuterie to go with them. Closed Saturday evenings and Sundays. Reservations unnecessary. Major credit cards accepted. Cité Berryer, 25 Rue Royale, 8e (phone: 42-65-08-47 or 42-65-10-72). Moderate.

L'Ecluse – This unassuming wine bar looking onto the Seine has fathered five others, more sophisticated, in the Rue François Ier, at the Madeleine, at the *Opéra*, in *Le Forum des Halles*, and in Neuilly. Its red velvet benches and wooden tables — not to mention its bordeaux and its fresh, homemade foie gras — remain unchanged. Open daily. Reservations unnecessary. Major credit cards accepted. 15 Quai des Grands-Augustins, 6e (phone: 46-33-58-74), and several other locations in Paris. Moderate.

Le Pain et Le Vin – An imaginative wine bar with daily hot luncheon specials. It's operated by four Parisian chefs, including Alain Dutournier of *Le Carré des Feuilliants* and *Le Trou Gascon*. Closed Wednesday evenings. Reservations unnecessary. Major credit cards accepted. Several locations, including 1 Rue d'Armaille, 17e (phone: 47-63-88-29). Moderate.

Le Petit Bacchus – A wine bar specializing in unusual regional wines, displayed in crowded rows. You can buy wine by the bottle to take home or on a picnic, or sample them at the counter with cheese and charcuterie. Closed Sundays and Mondays. Reservations unnecessary. Major credit cards accepted. 13 Rue du Cherche-Midi, 6e (phone: 45-44-01-07). Moderate.

Taverne Henri IV – A selection of nearly 20 wines are offered by the glass, along with generous servings of simple food such as open sandwiches of ham, cheese, sausage, or a terrine of wild boar. You also can order cold food combinations by the platter. Closed weekends. Reservations unnecessary. No credit cards accepted. 13 Pl. du Pont-Neuf, 1er (phone: 43-54-27-90). Moderate.

Zimmer – Centrally located and with new moldings and chandeliers, this is the place to stop off for a drink before or after a show at one of the nearby theaters. Reservations unnecessary. Major credit cards accepted. 1 Pl. du Châtelet, 4e (phone: 42-36-74-04). Moderate.

Au Duc de Richelieu – Specializes in the wines of Beaujolais, Chiroubles, Juliénas, St.-Amour, and so on. A cozy atmosphere and lots of wine tasting certificates on the walls. Closed Sundays and August. Reservations unnecessary. No credit cards accepted. 110 Rue de Richelieu, 2e (phone: 42-96-38-38). Inexpensive.

Jacques Melac – An old-fashioned wine bar run by a young, extravagantly mustachioed man from the Auvergne, who bottles and sells his own rustic wines. Closed Sundays and Mondays. Open until 6:30 PM except Tuesdays and Thursdays when a set dinner is served. No reservations. No credit cards accepted. 42 Rue Léon-Frot, 11e (phone: 43-70-59-27). Inexpensive.

La Palette – This Left Bank hideaway on a quiet square, with outdoor tables during the summer, stays lively with a young crowd until 2 AM every day except in August. Perhaps the monocled gentlemen on the 1930s tiles and the oils hung on the walls paid the bills of never-to-be-successful painters. Closed Sundays, holidays, and August. Reservations unnecessary. No credit cards accepted. 43 Rue de Seine, 6e (phone: 43-26-68-15). Inexpensive.

Le Rubis – A tiny corner bar with an old-fashioned atmosphere and a big selection of wines — about 30 in all. With your glass of wine try the pork *rillettes*, a savory meat paste made on the premises. Closed on weekends and 2 weeks in August. No reservations. No credit cards accepted. 10 Rue du Marché-St.-Honoré, 1er (phone: 42-61-03-34). Inexpensive.

Au Sauvignon – The no-nonsense couple in blue overalls who run this tiny corner bar look as if they just stepped in from the country. They seem to be in perpetual motion, pouring the white sauvignon and carving up chunky sandwiches from the famous *Poilâne* bakery not far away. Closed Sundays, 2 weeks in January, *Easter,* and August. Reservations unnecessary. No credit cards accepted. 80 Rue des Sts.-Pères, 7e (phone: 45-48-49-02). Inexpensive.

La Tartine – One of the old, authentic bistros, with a colorful local clientele and a good selection of wine by the glass. Closed Tuesdays and Wednesday mornings. Reservations unnecessary. No credit cards accepted. 24 Rue de Rivoli, 4e (phone: 42-72-76-85). Inexpensive.

La Tour de Monthlery – Hidden away on a small street near *Le Forum des Halles,* this animated bistro with sawdust on the floor and hams hanging from the rafters serves hearty, simple fare at bargain prices. Reservations unnecessary. Major credit cards accepted. 5 Rue de Prouvaires, 1er (phone: 42-36-21-82). Inexpensive.

DIVERSIONS

For the Experience

Quintessential Paris

We hear a lot of complaints about Paris these days. Traffic. Pollution. The once harmonious, elegant sweep of Haussmann's boulevards are, say critics, increasingly disregarded, marred by such modern intrusions as La Defense, the futuristic-looking business center that obstructs the skyline to the west, or the Big Mac invasion that is threatening the sanctity of the corner café.

A century ago, the Eiffel Tower had its critics, too, and while it may be necessary to look a little harder these days to find the Paris of Proust and Hemingway, happily it still exists. We still encounter with reassuring regularity the Frenchman and his dog on a morning stroll to the *pâtisserie*. An organ grinder still plays for Sunday crowds at Place des Vosges. Piaf sing-alongs occur nightly in Montmartre bistros. And just when we begin to despair that this century has erased the best of the old, and wonder what the next will possibly retain, we happen upon the quintessential Paris bistro, a perfect little red-awninged gem, hidden away on a tiny, sun-dappled square.

Paris is, after all, still Paris, the quintessential City of Light, and life. Yes, it is more crowded than when Gershwin immortalized it in song. Yes, it becomes more expensive with each passing season. But when the lights rise along the Seine or the Bois de Boulogne is filled with the fresh, crisp scent of chestnuts, you really wouldn't want to be anywhere else.

ILE ST.-LOUIS: Where the city began, and where, for many, it frequently ends in the evenings, this island floats like a medieval oasis between the Left and Right banks in the middle of the Seine. Once home to the likes of Voltaire, Rousseau, and Baudelaire, the narrow cobblestone lanes that radiate from the island's single lengthwise street (Rue St.-Louis-en-l'Ile) are among the most coveted and expensive of Paris real estate. The center street, a narrow one-way lane, is lined with shops (mostly tourist traps) and charming restaurants, some with stone walls and vaulted ceilings. Try the *Montecristo,* a superb, yet inexpensive, Italian trattoria, or the outrageous (and loud) *Brasserie de l'Ile St.-Louis* for the best views of Notre-Dame across the Pont St.-Louis footbridge. No trip here would be complete without generous samplings of the island's own Berthillon ice cream. Served in two company-owned parlors on the island and several other local *glaciers,* Berthillon has become a legend in its own time — handmade, rich mixtures with inspired combinations of ingredients (try the crunchy chocolate nougat — and die!). So confident are they of their reputation that Berthillon not only steadfastly refuses to expand off the island, they insist on closing altogether during the prime ice cream–consuming month of August.

LUXEMBOURG GARDENS: Every day is Sunday in Hemingway's favorite park, where Parisians stroll with babies in prams, children "race" miniature sailboats in the fountains, and young lovers sit on benches beneath the trees. George Moore may have captured the mood best when he wrote in his *Memories of My Dead Life,* "I loitered in the Luxembourg Gardens to watch the birds and the sunlight . . . and began to wonder if there was anything better in the world worth doing than to sit in an alley of clipped limes smoking, thinking of Paris and myself." Enchanting as is the idea of doing absolutely nothing here, there is in fact plenty to do in this 46-acre garden. Requisitioned in 1615 by Marie de Médici and designed, in part, by Salomon de Brosse, today it's a popular jogging spot; there are six tennis courts (available on first-come, first-served basis); and for children, there's a puppet theater near the orchards, pony rides, a small carousel, a playground, and toy sailboats for cruising around the Médicis fountain. Honey is still produced by the garden's hives, where a beekeeping course is taught in summer by a priest. Enjoy the serenity. The 20th century hasn't made its mark here — yet.

CAFÉ SOCIETY: If you've ever read a novel, or ever thought of writing one, you shouldn't leave Paris without visiting one of its thousands of cafés. Those along the Boulevard St.-Germain are as well known for the inspiration and comfort they have afforded generations of novelists and intellectuals as for the thick *serré* coffees they serve.

Among the city's most celebrated hangouts are the *Café Les Deux Magots*, reputed by some to have the world's best hot chocolate (we give the nod to *Angelina's*, on the Rue de Rivoli, opposite the Tuileries, and at its other location in the Palais de Congrès, near the Porte Maillot métro), and the place where Sartre drank whiskey while de Beauvoir nursed a Coke. Down the street is the revived *Café de Flore*, an exceptional breakfast stop for brioche and *oeufs brouilles* (scrambled eggs) before wandering through the bookstores and chic clothing boutiques that line the boulevard. Across the street, the old *Brasserie Lipp* has been a popular *choucroute*-and-conversation spot for actors and politicians for over a century. And the neighborhood continues to attract a lively arts and tourist crowd. Be warned, though: The price of "membership" in café society is high (as we went to press, the price of a cup of coffee was $2), and service can be excrutiatingly slow and indifferent. But then, you never know — the same muse who inspired Sartre may be seated at the table next to yours.

FAUCHON AND PLACE DE LA MADELEINE: *Fauchon* is one of the good things about Paris that only keeps getting better. Started in 1886 as a simple pushcart, the legendary food shop stocks some 20,000 items, from Cambodian peppers and African mangoes to New England clam chowder. Here, food is art, and the window displays are the stuff of which dreams (and picnics) are made. At *Christmas*, the glittering still-life tableau slows traffic to a crawl on this corner and draws nearly as many gawkers as New York City's *Lord & Taylor* department store's holiday windows. The city's most celebrated *épicerie* (grocery) has recently made some major changes, transferring several of its operations to a new store next door that includes an Italian bar, a cafeteria, and an elegant restaurant, all arranged around a sleek skylighted atrium. Mornings begin at 8 AM downstairs with an American- or French-style breakfast (offering over 40 different types of coffee) in *Fauchon*'s new cafeteria. Lunchtime (in the same space) features reasonably priced daily specials (to attract shoppers from nearby department stores). In the afternoons (until about 5 PM), the room serves as a tearoom, offering the house's celebrated pastries. Lunch and dinner are also available upstairs in the chic *Le 30* restaurant, with its splendid view of La Madeleine.

In Paris, the tradition of window shopping is called *léché-vitrine*, literally, "window licking." You'll understand why after a walk around the shops fringing the Madeleine. Across from *Fauchon*, you'll find the *épicerie Hédiard*, specialist in exotic fruits; *Maison de la Truffe*, the world's largest truffle retailer; and *Caviar Kaspia*, a retail caviar vendor with a small restaurant upstairs. And Alain Senderens's *Lucas-Carton*, one of Paris's Michelin three-star restaurants, is just a few steps away across from the Madeleine.

LE FORUM DES HALLES: They'll always call it "the belly of Paris," but frankly, these days it's hard to digest. The city's central market has long since moved to the suburbs, and the fabled bistros and cafés favored by early morning greengrocers and butchers are gone or have been brutally gentrified. On weekdays, it's impossibly crowded with young urban mall-ites carrying records purchased from France's largest record/book/video store (*FNAC*) or acquisitions from the hundreds of clothing boutiques that are housed in this above-and-below ground shopping area. On weekends, it's equally crowded, as thousands descend on *Le Forum des Halles'* multiplex movies, swimming pool, *Videothèque,* American and French fast-food outlets, wax museum, and hundreds of sex shops. But at night, when the cafés and restaurants spring to life and the neon lights filter across the expanse of green park that replaced the market, visitors have an opportunity to see Paris from yet another perspective. Replete with fountains, the lovely park still boasts enough authentic bistros at its far end (near the circular, turn-of-the-century Bourse du Commerce) to let lovers rediscover the romance of Paris dining. Try the Belle Epoque *Au Pied de Cochon* for its massive seafood platters arranged on tiered halo trays, or Le *Pharamond* for its *tripe à la mode de Caen,* or visit *Le Chien Qui Fume* (The Smoking Dog) for authentic bistro fare.

PLACE DES VOSGES: In the heart of the Marais, Paris's most beautiful and oldest (1605) square remains a most privileged and prestigious address. Among the 39 houses that grace the red-brick quadrangle are the *Maison de Victor-Hugo* (No. 6) and *L'Ambroisie,* Paris's newest three-star restaurant (No. 9). With its vaulted arches and arcades, Place des Vosges was also the model for the Places Dauphine, Vendôme, and later, de la Concorde. This location was the site of *l'Hôtel des Tournelles,* where Henri II was killed in a jousting tournament. In 1612, it became known as Place Royale; in 1800 the square was baptized Vosges in honor of the first French *département* to pay all its taxes to the new French Republic.

Today, the square is a garden spot for area residents and tourists alike. Marais (the name means "marsh," which it was when the city was founded) is to Paris what Greenwich Village is to New York City, with its sense of history, its jumble of interesting shops, restaurants, and museums, and its historical architecture. Directly behind the Place des Vosges are synagogues designed by Alexandre-Gustave Eiffel and Art Nouveau architect Hector Guimard. The Marais bristles with art galleries and museums: *Musée Carnavalet* (devoted entirely to the history of the city of Paris, the largest municipal museum in the world), *Musée Picasso,* and *Musée de la Chasse et de la Nature.* The area is also home to Paris's largest Jewish population; the colorful Rue des Rosiers is chockablock with restaurants and shops that remind one of a street in central or Eastern Europe.

RUE DE SEINE/RUE DE BUCI MARKET: Paris's markets provide some of its great sensory pleasures, and the lively little sixth-*arrondissement* morning market that begins at the eastern end of Rue de Buci and winds around the corner onto Rue de Seine is a typically tantalizing example. From early morning, the scents of freshly baked bread and creamy camembert waft above neatly arranged spears of white asparagus, seas of super-slim green beans, carts filled with nothing but wild mushrooms, and an array of fruits worthy of a still-life by Gauguin. A fishmonger shouts out prices of the day's catch, glistening and fresh *comme l'oeil.* At 81 Rue de Seine is an old-fashioned charcuterie, pleasingly cluttered with hams hanging from ceiling beams, prepared dishes, and pâtés — the makings of divine picnics. Next door (also No. 81) is an excellent cheese shop; try their *fromage frais* and goat cheeses. Around the corner on Rue de Buci (No. 8), foie gras terrines of all sizes glitter like jewels in the windows of *J. Papin,* a sleek, modern *traiteur* (caterer). For cakes, homemade candies, and *fruits glacé* (glazed fruit), try *La Vieille France* (No. 14), one of Paris's oldest *pâtisseries* (pastry shops), founded in 1834. If you happen to visit around lunchtime, stop at *Le Petit Zinc,* a frosted glass–windowed, turn-of-the-century bistro with a raw bar — and charm to spare — or gather up an armful of market goodies and head south to the Luxembourg Gardens for a *déjeuner sur l'herbe.*

BOULEVARD ST.-MICHEL: In the glitter of streetlamps, and the evening glow from floodlit Notre-Dame, there is a simmering mix of arguing students, drumming youths, and strumming guitars, roasting chestnuts, and sizzling street-corner crêpes — a feast that hasn't moved since Hemingway's day. Latin no longer is the lingua franca of this quarter, but you'll hear plenty of Greek, Arabic, Farsi, and Wolof, and sharing billboard space in front of the multilingual movie theaters are posters for the latest films from India — and Indiana Jones. The bookstalls along the Seine hold anything from a first edition of Proust to a paperback mystery from 1962 — or a single, illuminated page from a medieval manuscript.

RUE DU FAUBOURG-ST.-HONORÉ AND RUE ST.-HONORÉ: Like the *Grand Bazaar* of Istanbul, the souk of Marrakesh, and the agora of ancient Athens, the mile-long stretch of designer sidewalks between the president's palace and the Palais-Royal is one of the world's great shopping experiences. It has the finest names in everything, and an unsurpassed array of specialized retailers of chocolate, leather, and lingerie. Try *Au Nain Bleu* for a miniature tea set in Limoges porcelain, *Hermès* for an equestrian-print umbrella, or *Raymond* for gold-plated faucets. Nearby, on Place de la Madeleine, visit *Fauchon* for plum mustard or a salmon mousse sprinkled with caviar, and if you can't live without something nobody else could have, tour the galleries and antiques dealers, and stop in at that ultimate purveyor of the unique — *Louvre des Antiquaires* on the Place du Palais-Royal.

Romantic Parisian Hostelries

In an increasingly homogeneous and anonymous world, the fine Parisian hotel remains one of the last bastions of charm and luxury. From the first warm, flaky croissant to the last turned-down eiderdown, a stay in one of them is a study in perpetual pampering which makes for an experience that is not to be missed on any account. Such a hotel may have a sleek, urbane lobby throbbing with the pulse of Paris. Or it may be a small, exclusive, little-known retreat on a cobbled Left Bank street whose stone walls have welcomed weary travelers for centuries. Or a fairy-tale château just outside Paris, with a swan-filled moat and acres of gardens and woodlands. These hostelries exist in a certain harmony with their settings; they seem to be a part of local life rather than something aside from it. They also have a special warmth. And the staff has an ability to make you feel that you count and that they care. Excellent cuisine often is a feature, though not always.

The descriptive list of hotels that follows, a selection of some of the best rather than a comprehensive report, suggests the range of such accommodations that the adventurous traveler in Paris can discover.

BRISTOL: Headquarters to dignitaries visiting the Elysées Palace (the French White House), located just a few steps down the street, this Art Deco establishment boasts 188 beautifully decorated rooms and 2 restaurants — one for summer and another for winter; the first is a light and airy glassed-in room overlooking the garden; the second is a richly wood-paneled room, a reassuring reminder of Old World craftsmanship. A comfortable lobby and cocktail lounge add to the charm. A wing built in 1985 includes a heated swimming pool on the sixth-floor terrace, an amenity seldom found in Paris hotels. Information: *Hôtel le Bristol,* 112 Rue du Faubourg-St.-Honoré, Paris 75008 (phone: 42-66-91-45).

CRILLON: An apparent proving ground for the entire French automotive industry, the Place de la Concorde has a frenetic atmosphere today far at odds with its spirit in the 18th century. But within its Sienese marble foyers, guests here are insulated from the world outside. Diplomats from nearby Embassy Row buy and sell countries in the bar, and journalists seem always on hand trying to overhear the parameters of the deals. The view from the suites facing the *place* are *sans pareil.* This is perhaps Paris's most expertly managed hotel; it is a member of the Relais & Châteaux group. Information: *Hôtel Crillon,* 10 Pl. de la Concorde, Paris 75008 (phone: 42-65-24-24; fax: 47-42-72-10).

GEORGE V: The lobby is a League of Nations of private enterprise, where wheelers and dealers of every nationality seem to be settling matters of planetary importance. It also seems to be where the *Cannes Film Festival* crowd spends the other 11 months of the year, so numerous are the stars and starlets, directors, producers, and other movie folk who congregate here. The Eiffel Tower is just across the river, the Champs-Elysées just down the block, and the Arc de Triomphe around the corner; most of the rest of Paris can be seen from the panoramic windows of rooms higher up in the hotel. Even those who can't afford one of them — or the tranquil chambers facing the gracious courtyard — should be sure to stop for one of the establishment's utterly lyrical croissants. Information: *Hôtel George V,* 31 Av. George-V, Paris 75008 (phone: 47-23-54-00; fax: 47-20-40-00).

PLAZA-ATHÉNÉE: Careful renovations are ongoing here in order to preserve the charm of this most charming of European hotels, much to the relief of those who love it — from the guest quarters done in Louis XV and XVI to the *Relais* grill, where *tout Paris* seems to be eternally lunching, and the idyllic *Régence* restaurant, which is like a set for some Parisian *Mikado,* with its cheeping birds, pools, and a bridge. On the elegant Avenue Montaigne, this hotel is a little more sedate and a little more French than the *George V* (above). Information: *Hôtel Plaza-Athénée,* 25 Av. Montaigne, Paris 75008 (phone: 47-23-78-33; fax: 47-20-20-70).

RITZ: The Right Bank establishment that César Ritz created and made synonymous with all the finer things in life is so much a part of French tradition and literature that every year an occasional perambulator, coming upon it suddenly, is startled to find that it still exists, much less reigns as majestically as ever over the Place Vendôme. Marcel Proust wrote most of *Remembrance of Things Past* in a cork-lined room here; Georges-Auguste Escoffier put France at the top of the culinary Olympus from its kitchen. The latest addition is the *Ritz Club,* a nightclub and discotheque built about the same time as its new super spa, and open to guests and club members only. Like bagging a tiger under Kilimanjaro or owning a palazzo on the Grand Canal, this is one of those experiences that the truly discriminating owe themselves. Information: *Hôtel Ritz,* 15 Pl. Vendôme, Paris 75001 (phone: 42-60-38-30; fax: 42-86-00-91).

RÉSIDENCE MAXIM'S: A few steps from the Champs-Elysées and the Elysées Palace, this distinguished favorite of the rich and famous (it was Bette Davis's Paris hideaway) caters to those who can afford the best. (The Presidential Suite rents for $4,000 a night!) From its classic lobby, secluded bar, and *L'Atmosphere,* its world class restaurant, to its 38 suites, it cleverly combines modern statuary in 19th-century Belle Epoque surroundings. Returning guests often request suites according to the statuary and paintings. Information: *Résidence Maxim's,* 42 Av. Gabriel, Paris 75008 (phone: 45-61-96-33).

ST. JAMES'S CLUB: Like an English club or a private mansion, it's something out of an Evelyn Waugh novel. Located within a stroll of the Bois de Boulogne, this secluded 19th-century château — with its own walled courtyard and regal fountain, library bar, health club, and elegant restaurant overlooking a rose garden, plus a more relaxed grill (the *Club Room*) — gives one a sense of a weekend in the English country-side. The 48 rooms (including 4 penthouse suites with a winter garden) are modern, decorated by star Parisian designer André Putnam. Though billed as a private club, non-members are welcome to stay after paying a temporary membership fee of about

$8. (Non-members not staying at the hotel, however, cannot dine or sip cocktails here.) Information: *St. James's Club*, 5 Pl. Chancelier Adenauer, Av. Bugeaud, Paris 75116 (phone: 47-04-29-29; 800-641-0300 in the US).

LUTÉTIA: The only real palace hotel on the Left Bank, this aristocratic place of elegantly ornamented quarry stone has reigned at the corner of Rue de Sèvres and Boulevard Raspail since 1910. Lovers of the Belle Epoque and Art Deco find their element here. From outrageous gray-striped balloon awnings and bowers of sculptured stone flowers framing its graceful arched windows to regal red lobby appointed with crystal chandeliers, Art Deco skylights, and intricately carved wrought iron, this is a quintessentially Parisian place (owned by the Taillevent family, it's one of the city's few grand hotels not now in the hands of foreigners); it also offers some of the most fantastic views in Paris from its upper floors. Best perspective in the house is from Room 71, a seventh-floor corner room from whose balcony nearly all of Paris's most famous monuments can be seen. Information: *Lutétia*, 45 Bd. Raspail, Paris 75006 (phone: 45-44-38-10; fax: 45-44-50-50).

MONTALEMBERT: Also on the Left Bank, this intimate little place, renovated by designer Christian Liaigre, reopened recently with its original Art Deco features shined up and mixed with touches of Oriental whimsy. Rooms are now available in two styles — traditional yellow- and mustard-stripe schemes with restored period armoires and sleigh beds, or in contemporary style with straight geometric lines and fireplaces. Bathrooms are small, but high-tech. (If you're over 6 feet tall, ask for one of the modern rooms — the beds are longer.) *L'Arpège*, the hotel's restaurant, bears the signature of Michelin two-star chef Alain Passard, and is remarkably popular with locals who come for artichoke salad and *côté de boeuf* with onion confits. Information: *Hôtel Montalembert*, 3 Rue Montalembert, Paris 75007 (phone: 45-48-68-11; 800-628-8929 in the US; fax: 42-22-58-19).

Romantic Hostelries an Hour or Less from Paris

BAS-BRÉAU, Barbizon: Fashionable, well-heeled Parisians have been coming to this mid-19th-century inn since shortly after Robert Louis Stevenson lived and wrote here. Located in the village that gave its name to a school of 19th-century painters including Théodore Rousseau, Corot, and Millet, this is a perfect place to idle away a fall weekend, or at least a Sunday afternoon. There are 12 rooms, 8 suites, and a villa for families, all decorated *à l'ancienne* with modern bathrooms. And the dining room, warmed by a flickering fire during fall and winter, serves first-rate food — worth the half-hour drive from Paris even if you don't plan to spend the night. Try the *langouste rôtie au sel de Guérande* (rock lobster roasted in salt) or, in the fall, game dishes such as *noisettes de chevreuil* (medallions of venison) or *pâté chaud de grouse* (warm pâté of grouse). Closed in January. Information: *Hôtellerie du Bas-Bréau*, 22 Rue Grande, Barbizon 77630 (phone: 60-66-40-05; fax: 60-69-22-89).

LA CLÉ D'OR, Barbizon: Barbizon's oldest establishment, this former postal *relais* at the forest's edge has quiet and well-appointed rooms overlooking an expanse of well-groomed lawn. Though modest by comparison to the neighboring *Bas-Bréau*, it has enough charm and quiet elegance to compensate for its lack of pretension. The restaurant here is excellent. There's always a roaring fire in winter and a garden terrace for outdoor dining in summer. Open year-round. Information: *Hostellerie de la Clé d'Or*, Barbizon 77630 (phone: 60-66-40-96; fax: 60-66-42-71).

FORESTIÈRE/CAZAUDEHORE, St.-Germain-en-Laye: A superb garden setting just 20 minutes from Paris, it's one of the Ile-de-France's best-kept secrets — an agreeable inn with 6 affordable apartments and 24 rooms, and a refined restaurant featuring classic and Basque cuisine. Restaurant closed Mondays. Information: *Forestière/ Cazaudehore,* 1 Av. du Président-Kennedy, St.-Germain-en-Laye 78100 (phone: 39-73-36-60; fax: 39-73-73-88).

L'ESCLIMONT: Set on 150 acres of private woodlands and landscaped French gardens near Chartres, this 16th-century fairy-tale castle has 54 rooms, including romantic circular suites in the turrets. There are tennis courts and a pool; though the restaurant is a bit pricey, the food is good, if not always memorable — but the gardens are worth the visit (Parisians arrive here by helicopter for Sunday lunch, touching down neatly on the expansive lawn). 45 minutes from Orly airport. Information: *L'Esclimont,* St-Symphorien-le Château, Auneau 28700 (phone: 37-31-15-15; fax: 37-31-57-91).

TRIANON PALACE: Attached by private gardens to Versailles, this renovated palace is one of France's most historic hotels. Its vaulted marble dining room, resembling a great mirrored ballroom, was the site of the signing of the Treaty of Versailles. It has also played host to the likes of Wilson, Proust, Colette, and Marlene Dietrich. Romantic legends abound here. Sarah Bernhardt used to arrive in a horse-drawn carriage, wrapped from head to wooden leg in tulle and feathers. And when King Edward VIII abdicated the throne of England for the woman he loved, he and the former Wallis Simpson honeymooned here. Michelin-starred chef Gérard Vié (formerly of *Les Trois Marches*) presides over the kitchens; the beauty salon and spa (described as "a beauty kingdom") are an exclusive Givenchy operation; and construction of a hotel conference center, shops, a tennis park, and underground parking are well under way. Information: *Trianon Palace,* 1 Bd. de la Reine, Versailles 78000 (phone: 39-50-34-12; fax: 39-49-00-77).

Haute Gastronomie

Inspiring the same fierce passions and loyalties that soccer does in Brazil, eating is the French national sport. The French talk about food instead of the weather, reminisce about one meal while downing another, and select restaurants as if they were putting together an investment portfolio. The light, sauce-free fashion of the nouvelle cuisine brought a few mouthfuls of moderation to the nationwide gourmandizing — until the country's super-chefs began to recant, labeling it "big plates with small ingredients and nothing in between."

So we're happy to report that Paris is once again awash in béchamel and ablaze with cognac, and the turbot once again reigns *suprême.*

Before you take to the field, a few morsels of advice. Once you're seated, don't be intimidated by the ritual or its priesthood. Remember that you are quite literally the consumer. While it is customary to conceive of the meal as a whole, insist on ordering one course at a time if you can't think about *moules* and mousse at once. In addition, consider that many restaurants are happy and even proud to present their guests with small portions of dishes they'd simply like to sample. And some restaurants also offer *dégustation* menus, which include a sampling of the chef's noblest creations. Ask the wine waiter for advice, but unless you're a true oenophile, don't spend unnecessarily for sought-after châteaux or venerable vintages. And if a dish is unsatisfactory, by all means send it back to the kitchen. Restaurateurs hold their reputations in deadly earnest (to such an extent that one eminent chef did away with himself on learning he'd been stripped of one of his three Michelin stars). And, above all, be sure to make reservations — if only a few days in advance. Far better, write for reservations months in advance of your anticipated arrival at one of Paris's authentic temples of gastronomy, then call to confirm after you arrive. There is very little impulse dining in Paris, and tables at restaurants that are among the most favored are sometimes booked months ahead. This also ensures that you won't show up hungry — only to find that the chef has gone off on his annual holiday. In the list of some of the best restaurants in Paris that follows, we note the *fermetures annuelles* (yearly closings), but do bear in mind that last-minute changes can (and frequently do) occur. What's more, don't forget to *reconfirm* reservations once you arrive in Paris — even if no request for reconfirmation has been made formally. Reservations at the top restaurants are routinely (and automatically) canceled without timely reconfirmation. When making your reservations, check to determine if credit cards are accepted.

Finally, *bon appétit!*

L'AMBROISIE: Promoted to three-star status by Michelin in 1988, this tiny, quietly elegant establishment on the Place des Vosges is the showcase for chef Bernard Pacaud's equally elegant cuisine. Matched in scale, the menu is limited to only a few entrées, such as duck with foie gras, skate and sliced green cabbage in sherry vinegar sauce, veal sweetbreads with shallots and parsley on ultra-fresh pasta, lightly battered chicken thighs in a piquant sauce, and oxtail in a savory sauce. But the quality more than compensates for the limited number of choices. Closed Sundays, Monday lunch, August, and holidays. Information: *L'Ambroisie,* 9 Pl. des Vosges, Paris 75004 (phone: 42-78-51-45).

AMPHYCLÉS: Paris's latest wunderkind, chef Philippe Groult, received two Michelin stars two years ago, just a few months after opening his own restaurant near the Place des Ternes. Protégé and former sous chef of Paris's super-chef Joël Robuchon (see *Jamin*), Groult turns out a fine, well-tempered, and contemporary cuisine. If the brightly lit modern decor of his small establishment is forgettably neutral and pastel, the food is certainly memorable. There are splendid creamy soups, duck seasoned with coriander and orange, and lobster risotto. Closed most of July, Saturday lunch, and Sundays. Information: *Amphyclés,* 78 Av. des Ternes, Paris 75016 (phone: 40-68-01-01; fax: 40-68-91-88).

BEAUVILLIERS: Deliciously flirtatious and festive, this restaurant on the northern slope of the Butte of Montmartre is one of the most romantic spots in Paris. Proust or Balzac might have felt at home in its intimate dining rooms or on hydrangea-rimmed summer terraces in the shadow of a white-stone cathedral. The food — a rich, generous cuisine prepared in the best bourgeois tradition — complements the surroundings. Try the sweetbreads with foie gras, guinea hen with spices and mussels, or the *turbot au jus de jarret.* Closed the first 2 weeks in September, Monday lunch, and Sundays. Information: *Beauvilliers,* 52 Rue Lamarck, Paris 75018 (phone: 42-54-54-42; fax: 42-62-70-30).

L'ESCARGOT MONTORGUEIL: The polished wood paneling, the brass fittings, and the stunning spiral staircase at this beautiful restaurant dating from 1830 — the Second Empire period — only add to the pleasure of a meal, which might include snails in any of half a dozen styles or duck with orange sauce. Perhaps less *haute* than some, it has that intangible *je ne sais quoi.* Closed Mondays. Information: *L'Escargot Montorgueil,* 38 Rue Montorgueil, Paris 75002 (phone: 42-36-83-51).

LE GRAND VEFOUR: In the stately courtyard of the Palais-Royal, this 232-year-old corner of Paris at its most patrician is a place of thick carpets and frescoed mirrors, where the choice dishes (two Michelin stars) have been named for dignitaries who have discussed affairs of state here since the time of Robespierre. The house specialties are every bit as enthralling as the history. In honor of both, gentlemen still are required to wear jacket and tie. Closed Saturday lunch, Sundays, and all of August. Information: *Le Grand Vefour,* 17 Rue de Beaujolais, Paris 75001 (phone: 42-96-56-27).

JAMIN: Due to the culinary talents of owner-chef Joël Robuchon, this is one of Paris's finest restaurants, meriting a three-star ranking by Michelin. Robuchon calls his cuisine "moderne," similar to but not always as light as nouvelle. Specialties include *gelée de caviar à la crème de chou-fleur* (caviar aspic with cream of cauliflower) and *ravioli de langoustine au chou* (lobster ravioli on a bed of cabbage). The dining room is very small, so reserve well in advance. Closed Saturdays, Sundays, and the month of July. Information: *Jamin,* 32 Rue de Longchamp, Paris 75016 (phone: 47-27-12-27).

LASSERRE: The waiters are in tails, the ceiling glides open to reveal the stars, the decanted burgundy is poured over the flame of a candle to detect sediment, and the impeccable service makes diners feel that somehow they deserve all this. The cuisine is traditional French at its most heavenly (two Michelin stars), and the wine cellar is a virtual museum of French oenology. Not surprisingly, making dinner reservations is akin to booking seats for a sold-out Broadway musical, so think ahead. Way ahead. Closed Sundays, Monday lunch, and August. Information: *Lasserre,* 17 Av. Franklin-D.-Roosevelt, Paris 75008 (phone: 43-59-53-43; fax: 45-63-72-23).

LEDOYEN: When French nightclub queen Regine took over and renovated this historic restaurant in 1988, she set out to re-create its former grande dame ambience and reputation. And she has partially succeeded, restoring the grandeur of its salons and converting upstairs rooms into business quarters and suites. One of five grand restaurants along the parkland between the Concorde and the Champs-Elysées, it has become a major Paris power-lunch place, and the club-like banquettes of its *Carré Champs-Elysées* are popular with local glitterati: actors, writers, and lots of foreign businessmen. In the evenings, dining moves into *Le Guépard,* an elegant dining room with a garden retreat designed to compete with its 3-star rivals. Our advice, however, is to stick with the more relaxed *Carré Champs-Elysées,* where the food is brasserie style and terrace dining is also possible on soft summer evenings. Open daily from 7 AM to 1 AM; closed Sundays. Information: *Ledoyen,* Champs-Elysées and Av. Edward-Tuck, Paris 75008 (phone: 47-42-23-23; fax: 47-42-55-01).

LUCAS-CARTON: The splendid Belle Epoque premises were taken over several years back by the near-legend Alain Senderens, who made his reputation as owner-chef of *L'Archestrate,* once the capital's three-star temple of nouvelle cuisine. The change of surroundings took the chill off the old hauteur somewhat, and the lush, plush premises are the perfect place to sample a few bites of truffle salad, lobster with vanilla, or the *carpaccio de canard Eventhia.* This is innovative cuisine at its quirkiest best, and Michelin lost no time in awarding it three stars. The utensils and serving pieces are almost as alluring as the food. Be sure to reconfirm all reservations. Closed Saturdays and Sundays, most of August, and the last 10 days of December. Information: *Lucas-Carton,* 9 Pl. de la Madeleine, Paris 75008 (phone: 42-65-22-90; fax: 42-65-06-23).

MAXIM'S: Paris's most celebrated Belle Epoque restaurant was a century old last year; happily, more than just a memory of its glory endures. There are Parisians who say it's too crowded with Japanese high school girls pretending they're Gigi; many feel it's highly overrated. (In fact, at owner Pierre Cardin's request, it is completely unrated by Michelin.) And yet, for the experience, the gentle rustle of silk, the sparkle of silver, and the soft strains of a string quartet, there's none like it. The service is impeccable; you'll find twice as many waiters at your table as at any comparable restaurant (and trying to keep track of them can be as dizzying as champagne). The food is surprisingly good; try the *Challans canard aux cerise* (Challans duck with cherries). The wine list is extensive and intelligent; sommeliers, delightfully helpful; and the scenes at tables around its elegant salons are tableaux strictly from Colette. Careful, though: Fridays remain a strictly black-tie-only tradition, and they don't always mention this on the phone. Closed Sundays in July and August. Information: *Maxim's,* 3 Rue Royale, Paris 75008 (phone: 42-65-27-94).

PRÉ CATELAN: Gaston Lenôtre's dreamy dinner palace in the Bois de Boulogne is another one of those wonderfully festive special occasion spots — particularly in summer. Dining on the terrace here is a memorable experience in itself and the food, if not as spectacular as that of *Jamin* or *Taillevent,* is still very good. The *pigeon de Bresse farci aux choux verts et truffes noires* (Bresse pigeon stuffed with cabbage and truffles) and the *tartare de Saint-Jacques au coulis de caviar* (tartar of scallops with a caviar sauce) are both excellent. Desserts here are to die for, not surprising since owner Lenôtre is, above all, a pastry chef, his main claim to fame being the string of glittering pastry shops around the capital bearing his name. Closed Sunday evenings, Mondays, and 2 weeks in February. Information: *Pré Catelan,* Rte. de Suresnes, Bois de Boulogne, Paris 75016 (phone: 45-24-55-58; fax: 45-24-43-25).

LE TAILLEVENT: The culinary classic that continues to rise to ever greater heights is currently the very best in the City of Light. This three-star dining room occupies a distinguished 19th-century mansion complete with fine paintings, porcelain dinnerware, and aristocratic decor that make it look as if the French Revolution was really just a bad dream. The salad of warm sweetbreads, the salmon with fresh mint, the tarragon-perfumed lobster casserole, and the rainbow assortment of soufflés are among the pillars of the Parisian gastronomic community. One of the most difficult restaurant reservations in France. A tip: Booking a table for three or more usually is easier than trying to book a table for two. Closed Saturdays, Sundays, holidays, part of February, and most of August. Information: *Le Taillevent,* 15 Rue Lamennais, Paris 75016 (phone: 45-61-12-90).

LA TOUR D'ARGENT: It's fashionable these days to dismiss this place as too trendy, too touristy, overrated, and overpriced, but Paris's senior three-star restaurant continues to amaze and entertain with its cuisine and the most romantic view of any restaurant in the city. The gold-toned room brings to mind Cole Porter's "elegant, swellegant party." In fact, Porter occasionally dined here, as did a host of other luminaries, from Franklin Roosevelt to Paul McCartney, Greta Garbo to the Aga Khan. The specialty here is a Charente duck pressed at tableside just as it was a century ago (each duck is assigned a number); also not to be missed are the classic quenelles in mornay sauce with fresh black truffles. Because it has a reservations book thicker than the Manhattan telephone directory, it's often impossible to book for evenings at certain times of the year. Best tip: Book a windowside table for lunch when there's a fixed price menu. The view of Notre Dame and the Seine is just as splendid by sunlight. Ask to see the spectacular wine cellar, one of France's best. Closed Mondays. Information: *La Tour d'Argent,* 15 Quai de la Tournelle, Paris 75005 (phone: 43-54-23-31).

Paris's Best Cafés

Paris without cafés would be like Rome without churches, Dublin without pubs, or New York without Broadway. One simply cannot imagine the city without them. The corner café is the glue that holds the French neighborhood together; it's a place for coffee and gossip, or just a spot to sit and watch the world go by.

There are over 5,000 cafés in Paris (approximately 1 for every 400 residents and their dogs), and each is a microcosm of Paris society. Mornings begin with street sweepers and locals arriving for the first *coup de rouge* and office workers taking *petites crèmes* and croissants over the lingering scent of a Gauloises. The French café is a multipurpose, multi-service marvel, a place for buying everything from cigarettes to batteries, telephone cards, stamps — even for placing a bet on a horse race or buying a lottery ticket.

The traditional café is strictly a family affair: *maman* cooks the plat du jour, *papa* tends bar, the younger generation wait tables, and the family dog chases bottle caps, nuzzles your leg, and in some cases even opens the door! Since the opening of *Le Procope* more than 3 centuries ago (where it's said Voltaire drank 40 cups of coffee a day), cafés have spawned a literary tradition. Mystery writer Gaston Leroux wrote *Phantom of the Opera* in installments from a café beside the *Opéra*, while Hemingway and Fitzgerald would begin arguments at *La Coupole* and carry them on to *Le Dôme, La Closerie des Lilas,* and the *Dingo* bar. Happily, the tradition continues.

CAFÉ DE LA PAIX: Designed by architect Charles Garnier to complement his baroque *Opéra,* this grande dame has undergone a recent restoration and emerged the better for it. Best for an afternoon tea; keep your eye out for the illusive pastry cart. Open daily. Information: *Café de la Paix,* 12 Bd. des Capucines and 2 Rue Scribe (2 entrances), Paris 75009 (phone: 40-07-32-32).

CAFÉ COSTES: A post-modernist design (inspired by Fritz Lang's *Metropolis*) located in the Beaubourg district near the *Centre Georges-Pompidou,* this café was the trendiest of trendsetters. A decade ago no one could be too thin or too rich to enter. Nowadays, its fame is such that it rates mention in *Time* magazine. Open daily. Information: *Café Costes,* 4 Rue Berger, Paris 75001 (phone: 45-08-54-38 or 45-08-54-39).

LA COUPOLE: Like an ocean liner moored amid the office buildings and multiplex cinemas of Montparnasse, this largest and most celebrated of the Left Bank cafés (now under new ownership) has been happily resurrected, and the fate of its historic pillars (painted in exchange for meals by artists like Fernand Léger and Othon Friesz), assured. Everyone who is anyone — including Picasso, Fitzgerald, Josephine Baker and her lion cub — has been here. Open daily until 2 AM year-round. Information: *La Coupole,* 102 Bd. du Montparnasse, Paris 75014 (phone: 43-20-14-20).

FOUQUET'S: Arguably, Paris's best-located café and now declared an official historic monument, this institution is far from perfect. (The drinks are too expensive; the sidewalk is often too crowded; the bar carries a sign offensive to women; and the downstairs dining is forgettable some nights and simply mediocre the next.) But if there is still magic in the world, it comes from sitting here at dusk and watching the lights come up on the Arc de Triomphe. Open daily 9 PM to midnight. Information: *Fouquet's,* 99 Av. des Champs-Elysées, Paris 75008 (phone: 47-23-70-60).

MA BOURGOGNE: Set beneath the vaulted arcades of the Place des Vosges, this was a frequent haunt for mystery writer George Simenon, whose Inspector Maigret solved crimes over the café's wines. A great spot for an afternoon stop, not for food, but for the view of Paris's most beautiful square. Closed Mondays. Information: *Ma Bourgogne,* 19 Pl. des Vosges, Paris, 75004 (phone: 42-78-44-64).

LA PALETTE: Since the 1920s, when evening falls, it fills with students from the nearby Ecole Nationale des Beaux-Arts. Artists, sculptors, and models crowd its bar and tables (in spring and fall, there's a terrace scene spilling into the street). Always lively, it's a good meeting point and particularly well placed for a rendezvous after a browse through the district's trendy art galleries. Closed Sundays, holidays, and August. Information: *La Palette,* 43 Rue du Seine, Paris 75006 (phone: 43-26-68-15).

LE PIANO ZINC: Tiny and authentic, this 1900s-era hole-in-the-wall (with a zinc-top, horseshoe-shape bar) has a regular — though eclectic — clientele of artists and workers. Central to Marais shopping, museums, designer boutiques, and the Hôtel de Ville, it's well worth the detour. Closed August. Information: *Le Piano Zinc,* 49 Rue des Blancs-Manteaux, Paris 75003 (phone: 42-74-32-42).

LE PROCOPE: Opened by a Sicilian named Procope in 1686, Paris's oldest café is more active now as a restaurant. Sadly tarted up during a recent renovation, the restaurant's previous habitués — Rousseau, Benjamin Franklin, Robespierre, and Napoleon — would be hard-pressed to recognize it. Best to stop in for a late-afternoon coffee and a glance at the newspapers after shopping the specialty boutiques of Boulevard St.-Germain. Open daily, year-round. Information: *Le Procope,* 13 Rue de l'Ancienne-Comédie, Paris 75006 (phone: 43-26-99-20).

LE SELECT: Opened in 1925 during the height of Paris's Jazz Age, this was the first Montparnasse café to stay open all night. Edna St. Vincent Millay adored it. So did Erik Satie and Leonard Foujita, and in 1927 Isadora Duncan got into a fistfight here with an American newspaperman (history records the dancer won by a decision). The café hasn't changed much since, and has one of the liveliest early-morning-coffee and midnight scenes imaginable, reminiscent of the photos of Robert Doisneau, whose camera often captured its steamy atmosphere. Open daily until 2 AM year-round. Information: *Le Select,* 99 Bd. du Montparnasse, Paris 75006 (phone: 42-22-65-27).

LE VOLTAIRE: Opposite the *Louvre* and close to the *Musée d'Orsay,* this tiny café along the Seine is an often-overlooked gem. Located in the hotel where Voltaire died, it's one of the oldest and most enjoyable cafés in Paris. Constructed at the end of the Pont du Carrousel, it was the site of Voltaire's legendary encounter with Benjamin Franklin. It also has its own very rich literary history as the place where Baudelaire wrote *Fleurs de Mal* (he lived at No. 29), Wagner wrote *Der Meistersinger* (his home was at No. 22), and Willa Cather wrote her *Pulitzer Prize*–winning novel, *One of Ours* (she resided at No. 19). Closed Sundays, Mondays, and the month of August. Information: *Le Voltaire,* 27 Quai Voltaire, Paris 75007 (phone: 47-61-17-49).

Best Bistros

In Paris, the bistro boom continues, with celebrated chefs opening casual, marble-table eateries serving earthy, satisfying fare next to their more elegant dining counterparts. And don't overlook the humble wine bar where the plat du jour and a glass of wine can be surprisingly good and affordable.

ALLARD: The zinc bar is still there, as are the smoky windows and the terra cotta floor sprinkled with the sawdust of the traditional Paris bistro of old. It also has some of the finest Burgundian country cooking this side of the Côte d'Or — including garlicky escargots, buttery scallops, turbot in *beurre blanc,* coq au vin, guinea hen, cassoulet, leg of lamb, and a chocolate charlotte that is one of the legends of the Left Bank. Closed Saturdays, Sundays, holidays, August, and 10 days at *Christmas.* Information: *Allard,* 41 Rue St.-André-des-Arts, Paris 75006 (phone: 43-26-48-23).

BENOÎT: A Michelin star and an exquisite Belle Epoque decor distinguish this bistro at the edge of the *Forum des Halles* area from all others in town. Small, usually packed, and so quintessentially turn-of-the-century that you might expect Jean Gabin to stroll in at any moment. But the best part is the food — bistro fare with generous, elaborate bourgeois touches. Monsieur Petite, a gentle giant of a man, is in charge, and his kitchen produces such marvels as *pigeon de Bresse en croute de sel* (a Bresse pigeon baked in a salt crust), *boeuf mode braisé à l'ancienne* (old-fashioned wine braised beef with carrots), and an exquisite foie gras and calf's tongue terrine. If you have the time to visit only one bistro in Paris, choose this one. Closed Saturdays, Sundays, and August. Information: *Benoît,* 20 Rue St.-Martin, Paris 75004 (phone: 42-72-25-76).

L'AMI LOUIS: This is the archetypal Parisian bistro: unattractive physically but with huge portions of marvelous food. Specialties include foie gras, spectacular roast chicken, spring lamb, ham, and burgundy wines. It's a particular favorite among Americans, and *the* place to sample authentic French fries. Though its fabled owner has died, the current regime carries on gallantly. Hardly inexpensive, but worth the cost. Closed Mondays, Tuesdays, and most of July and August. Information: *L'Ami Louis,* 32 Rue du Vertbois, Paris 75003 (phone: 48-87-77-48).

Shopping Spree

 For centuries, France has been producing some of the world's most fashionable clothing, its most delicious food and wine, and its most bewitching perfumes. And all of these items benefit from that same pinch of Gallic flair and good taste that characterize just about everything else to which the French put their hearts and hands. So it's no wonder that shopping in this country — and especially in its capital — is such a delight.

Long considered the international capital of fashion, Paris excels in the area of stylish, high-quality clothing and accessories. Prices range from the wildly extravagant to the fairly reasonable; but in any case they are lower than for the same merchandise sold outside France. Perfume, first-rate leather goods, food, wine, and cooking equipment and related items are good buys here.

PARIS SHOPPING STREETS: Stores selling similar merchandise tend to cluster along a certain one of the capital's celebrated boulevards and avenues, and for visitors who want to browse rather than go out of their way to find a specific shop, these are prime destinations:

Boulevard Haussmann – The *Galeries Lafayette* and *Au Printemps,* the city's two leading department stores, and the Paris branch of London's *Marks & Spencer* are here.

Place de la Madeleine – Several emporia purveying fine foods and wine — including *Hédiard,* specializing in exotic fruit and spices at No. 21, and the famous, fabulous *Fauchon* at Nos. 26, 28, and 30 — can be found here.

Rue d'Alésia – Several blocks of discount shops in Montparnasse.

Rue de Rivoli – This not only is the best place to find souvenir scarves decorated with Eiffel Towers and handkerchiefs imprinted with maps of the Paris métro system, but also it abounds in shops selling perfume and other gifts. Two of the city's more famous bookstores with an English-language stock are *W. H. Smith* at No. 248 and *Galignani* at No. 224.

Les Halles – Trendy and often inexpensive clothing boutiques are concentrated in this area.

St.-Germain – Sprinkled among the boulevard's famous cafés are not-so-inexpensive shops selling au courant clothing.

Rue du Faubourg-St.-Honoré – *The* shopping street for elegant fashions, chic shoes, and leather goods, including *Courrèges, Guy Laroche, Hermès, Lanvin, Yves Saint Laurent,* and others.

Rue des Sts.-Pères – Terrific shoes, off Boulevard St.-Germain.

Place Vendôme – The *haute joaillerie* of France — the jewelry with the most splendid designs and the highest prices — is sold on this square adjoining the Rue de la Paix at shops such as *Boucheron, Cartier,* and *Van Cleef & Arpels.*

Place des Victoires – Stylish boutiques for women are the specialty, but there are some for men as well.

PARIS DEPARTMENT STORES: The *grands magasins,* as these emporiums are called, stock at least a little bit of everything, so it's hardly necessary to go from shop to shop for many types of items. In addition, these stores offer the opportunity to purchase several small gifts under one roof and thereby qualify to receive a refund of France's value added tax (VAT).

Galeries Lafayette and *Au Printemps* – Of the nation's large stores, these two are deservedly the most popular with visitors. In addition to carrying an extensive and fashionable stock of men's, women's, and children's clothing, housewares, perfume, shoes, gifts, and all the miscellaneous merchandise ordinarily sold by such emporiums, they also provide tourists with special shopping information, translations, and instructions on how to obtain tax refunds on goods purchased here. In Paris, their main stores are next to each other near the *Opéra*.

Note: Both stores hold excellent fashion shows that are open to the public at no charge. *Galeries Lafayette* has shows on Wednesdays at 11 AM from April through October; there also are shows on Fridays. Reservations are necessary, and you should make them as early as possible by contacting the store (40 Bd. Haussmann, 9e; phone: 48-74-02-30 or 42-82-30-25; fax: 40-16-09-15). *Au Printemps* (64 Bd. Haussmann, 9e) holds shows every Tuesday at 10 AM. They also take place on Fridays from March through October, and on Mondays from May through September. Admittance to these shows can be arranged through the store's US representative, *Printemps* (10 E. 21st St., Suite 600, New York, NY 10010; phone: 529-8484). In addition to receiving an invitation card that will get you into fashion shows for a full calendar year, you will receive a discount card that's good for 10% off any *Printemps* purchase over $20.

Galeries Lafayette's main store in Paris is at 40 Bd. Haussmann (phone: 42-82-34-56); it has a branch in the *Maine Montparnasse Shopping Center* (22 Rue du Départ, 14e; phone: 45-38-52-87).

Au Printemps stores include the main one (64 Bd. Haussmann, 9e; phone: 42-85-80-00), as well as three others around the city.

Au Bon Marché – A Left Bank department store, it carries everything from household items to antique furniture. Rue de Sèvres, 7e (phone: 45-49-21-22).

Monoprix and *Prisunic* – These low-priced stores are good to remember for attractive, inexpensive children's clothing and toys. The fashion accessories, housewares, and stationery departments also can yield treasures.

CRYSTAL AND CHINA: Paris has crystal and china to make the humblest table gleam like a royal banquet hall, and one of the best ways to get an overview of the nation's best is to take a stroll along the length of the Rue de Paradis. The entire street is lined with stores specializing in objects related to what merchants here call "the arts of the table." Near the Gare de l'Est and the Gare du Nord, this area is less than chic. Nevertheless, it yields some sparkling treasures.

Baccarat, a dazzling museum as much as a store at No. 30 *bis,* is worth a visit even for those with no intention of purchasing an elegantly proportioned champagne flute or a multifaceted crystal champagne bucket (phone: 47-70-64-30). *Limoges-Unic* has a branch at No. 58, which carries many different types of Limoges china as well as a good supply of typically French Porcelaine de Paris patterns (phone: 47-70-61-49), and another at No. 12, which offers more expensive items, including china decorated with 18-karat gold (phone: 47-70-54-49). *Lumicrystal,* located in a landmark building where Corot lived and died, carries such names as Baccarat, Daum, Limoges, and items from the prestigious Puiforcat company (No. 22; phone: 47-70-27-97).

Other Paris Locations – A couple of other places in Paris are worth a detour for those seeking French expertise in matters breakable:

Au Bain Marie features a fine line of glassware and elaborate majolica plates (12 Rue Boissy d'Alglais, 8e; phone: 42-66-59-74).

Cristalleries de Saint Louis offers handmade lead crystal at good prices. They will also pack and ship purchases (13 Rue Royale, 83; phone: 40-17-01-74).

Lalique, famed for its large pieces of sculptured, decorative crystal, has a shop at 11 Rue Royale, 8e (phone: 42-65-33-70).

Raymond (100 Rue du Faubourg-St.-Honoré, 8e; phone: 42-66-69-49) is noteworthy for its charming and relatively inexpensive Porcelaine de Paris items, including coffee and tea sets, plates, soufflé dishes, mustard pots, and jam jars, all bedecked with wild strawberries, herbs, and garlands of French flowers.

WOMEN'S CLOTHING: The haute couture designers who put Paris on the map as the center of the fashion world still are flourishing in the French capital, and still welcoming those able to afford their distinctive and luxurious made-to-order clothing. However, they often sell much less expensive clothing of very high quality in couturier boutiques, usually at the same address:

Balenciaga, 10 Av. George-V, 8e (phone: 47-20-21-11)

Chanel, 29-31 Rue Cambon, 1er (phone: 42-86-28-00), and 42 Av. Montaigne, 8e (phone: 47-20-84-45)

Christian Dior, 28-30 Av. Montaigne, 8e (phone: 40-73-54-44)

Christian Lacroix, 73 Rue du Faubourg-St.-Honoré, 8e (phone: 42-65-79-08)

Claude Montana, 31 Rue de Grenelle, 7e (phone: 42-22-69-56)

Courrèges, 46 Rue du Faubourg-St.-Honoré, 8e (phone: 47-23-00-73)

Emanuel Ungaro, 2 Av. Montaigne, 8e (phone: 47-23-61-94)

Gianni Versace, 11 Rue du Faubourg-St.-Honoré, 8e (phone: 42-65-27-04); 67 Rue des Sts.-Pères, 7e (phone: 42-84-00-40)

Givenchy, 3 Av. George-V, 8e (phone: 47-23-81-36)

Guy Laroche, 29 Av. Montaigne, 8e (phone: 40-69-69-50)

Hanae Mori, 17 Av. Montaigne, 8e (phone: 47-23-52-03)

Jean-Louis Scherrer, 51-53 Av. Montaigne, 8e (phone: 43-59-55-39). This is the bigger outlet (see below).

Karl Lagerfeld, 17 Rue du Faubourg-St.-Honoré, 8e (phone: 42-66-64-64)

Lanvin, 15 and 22 Rue du Faubourg-St.-Honoré, 8e (phone: 42-65-14-40); 2 Rue Cambon, 1er (phone: 42-60-38-83)

Louis Féraud, 88 Rue du Faubourg-St.-Honoré, 8e (phone: 40-07-01-16)

Nina Ricci, 39 Av. Montaigne, 8e (phone: 47-23-78-88)

Per Spook, 18 Av. George-V, 8e (phone: 47-23-00-19)

Pierre Balmain, 44 Rue François Ier, 8e (phone: 47-20-35-34)

Pierre Cardin, 14 Pl. François Ier, 8e (phone: 45-63-29-13)

Romeo Gigli, 46 Rue de Sévigné, 3e (phone: 42-71-08-40)

Ted Lapidus, 35 Rue François Ier, 8e (phone: 47-20-56-14)

Torrente, 60 Av. Montaigne, 8e (phone: 42-56-14-14)

Yves Saint Laurent, 5 Av. Marceau, 8e (phone: 47-23-72-71)

For those interested in attending Paris's haute-couture fashion shows (usually limited to buyers and very good customers), the *Anne-Marie Victory Organization* (136 E. 64th St., New York, NY 10021; phone: 212-486-0353) sponsors trips that include viewing collections from fashion designers such as Chanel, Givenchy, Nina Ricci, Ungaro, and Vicky Tiel.

High-Fashion Bargains – The concept of selling at a discount is gradually catching on in France, and new designs from the top couturiers are available a season (sometimes only a few months) later at many outlets.

Anne Lowe carries Chanel, Ungaro, Valentino and others at savings of up to 50%. 35 Av.-Matignon, 8e (phone: 43-59-96-61).

Bab's is one of a trio with an especially devoted following. Most couturiers are represented, and the selection of evening gowns at reasonable prices is exceptional. Several locations include one at 29 Av. Marceau, 16e (phone: 47-20-84-74).

Georges Rech, with at least three Paris locations, is currently one of the most popular makers of classy, very Parisian styles, and at more affordable prices than other manufacturers of similarly styled goods. 273 Rue St.-Honoré, 1er (phone: 42-61-41-14), and 23 Av. Victor-Hugo, 16e (phone: 45-00-83-19).

Jean-Louis Scherrer is a bit out of the way, but it's possible to make its very inconvenience part of the pleasure of shopping and exploring. Prices for very fancy couturier labels run about 50% less than original retail. 29 Av. Ledru-Rollin, 12e (phone: 46-28-39-27).

Max Mara carries a line of Italian ready-to-wear that expresses many different moods (in six distinct collections) — from classic chic to trendy. The quality of fabrics and workmanship is high and the prices surprisingly affordable. Among several locations: 37 Rue du Four, 6e (phone: 43-29-91-10), and 265 Rue St.-Honoré, 1er (phone: 40-20-04-58).

Mendès, another shop particularly well loved by knowledgeable French women, specializes in the creations of Yves Saint Laurent; the winter season's designs are available beginning in mid-January and his summer collection from July 1 — all at substantial markdowns. There are mirrors everywhere, but no dressing rooms; it's the kind of place that inspires a lady to wear her best underwear. 65 Rue Montmartre, 2e (phone: 45-08-52-62 or 42-36-83-32).

Réciproque carries second-hand couturier and top designer ready-to-wear in good condition at a string of shops on Rue de la Pompe. 95, 101, and 123 Rue de la Pompe, 16e (phone: 47-04-30-28).

Other shops selling high-fashion clothing at discounted prices include the following: *Boutique Stock* (26, 30, and 51 Rue St.-Placide, 6e); *Cacharel Stock* (114 Rue d'Alésia, 14e); *Catherine Baril* (14-15 Rue de la Tour, 16e); *Dorothée Bis Stock* (74 Rue d'Alésia, 14e); *Drôles de Choses pour Drôles de Gens* (33 Rue Etienne-Marcel, 1er); *Halle Bys* (60 Rue de Richelieu, 2e); *Miss Griffes* (19 Rue de Penthièvre, 8e); *Le Mouton à Cinq Pattes* (8, 10, and 14 Rue St.-Placide, 6e); *Pierre Cardin Stock* (72 Rue St.-Honoré, 1er); *Stock Griffes* (17 Rue Vielle-du-Temple, 4e); and *Stock System* (112 Rue d'Alésia, 14e).

Boutiques – The attractive and innovative clothing that the French so nicely call *votre bonheur,* "your happiness," is stocked at thousands of small boutiques all over the country. But nowhere are these so abundant as they are in Paris, most notably at the following shops:

Agnès B offers colorful and chic yet wearable fashions from its namesake designer, who has committed herself publicly to holding her prices down. 3 and 6 Rue du Jour, 1er (phone: 40-26-36-87 or 45-08-56-56), and other locations.

Dorothée Bis, long established though still avant-garde, specializes in sportswear with a young look. 33 Rue de Sèvres, 6e (phone: 42-22-02-90).

Kenzo, with its flashy colors and whimsical shapes, is especially fun for young shoppers. 3 Pl. des Victoires, 1er (phone: 40-39-72-02).

Victoire is slightly crowded, but congenial, and packed with all types of attractive clothing from top ready-to-wear designers — and coordinated accessories to add extra dash. 12 Pl. des Victoires, 2e (phone: 47-04-49-87).

Lingerie – It's true that many Americans living in France buy their own lingerie in the US, swearing that American products are not only better made and better fitting but even less expensive and prettier than their French counterparts. But the lacy, frilly, silk undergarments sold in France, often covered with polka dots or dripping with ribbons, are the stuff of which fantasies are made, and lingerie makes a delightful souvenir.

Department stores carry a wide selection of brands, styles, and sizes and display their wares clearly, making choices simpler than in small shops, where much of the stock may be tucked in boxes behind the counter.

Cadolle was founded in 1889 by the woman widely credited with inventing the brassiere, and it is still run by her great-great- and great-great-great-granddaughters.

They sell charming, ribbon-bedecked garters and lacy bras, as well as sturdy, made-to-measure corsets. 14 Rue Cambon, 1er (phone: 42-60-94-94).

Chantal Thomass is known for her romantic lingerie, her currently de rigueur shiny black opaque stockings, as well as her ready-to-wear, including evening clothes. If you're a fan of bustiers, a visit to one of Thomass's boutiques is essential. 5 Rue du Vieux-Colombier, 6e (phone: 45-44-07-52) and 12-14 Galerie du Rond-Point, 8e (phone: 43-59-87-34).

Charley, just a few doors away from *Hermès,* offers an excellent selection, personal attention, and relatively low prices. 14 Rue du Faubourg-St.-Honoré,8e (phone: 47-42-17-70).

Christian Dior, while sold all over the world and in many stores in France, makes a few exceptionally lovely articles, including ensembles of gowns and robes, which are sold only in the exclusive collection one flight up from the main Dior salesroom. 28-30 Av. Montaigne, 8e (phone: 40-73-54-44).

Sabbia Rosa specializes in luxurious, chic, and sexy lingerie; there's plenty from which to choose in the pret-à-porter line, but you can also specially order custom-made items for a price. 73 Rue des Sts.-Pères, 6e (phone: 45-48-88-37).

MEN'S CLOTHING: Men's clothing is not generally considered to be a good buy, and many a male has gone into shock after looking at a price tag. But for some, the blend of classic styling and French flair is irresistible.

Arnys offers Anglo-French conservatism and elegance in suits, jackets, and the other components of a gentleman's wardrobe. 14 Rue de Sèvres, 6e (phone: 45-48-76-99).

Charvet specializes in shirts, ties, and everything else for the complete *gentilhomme.* 28 Pl. Vendôme, 1er (phone: 42-60-30-70).

Daniel Hechter has clothing for a sporty lifestyle; it all has a touch of class. 146 Bd. St.-Germain, 6e (phone: 43-26-96-36).

Saint Laurent Rive Gauche is well known for its classic designs in suits, shoes, socks, and accessories. 38 Rue du Faubourg-St.-Honoré, 8e (phone: 42-65-43-76).

Designer discounts for men can be found at the following two shops:

Biderman offers menswear from Yves Saint Laurent, Kenzo, and Courrèges in this warehouse of a store in the Marais. Saint Laurent suits can be had for about $350. 114 Rue de Turenne, 3e (phone: 44-61-17-14).

Dépôt des Grandes Marques is a third-floor shop near the stock market featuring such labels as Louis Féraud, Cerruti, and Renoma, marked down as much as 50%. 15 Rue de la Banque, 2e (phone: 42-96-99-04).

CHILDREN'S CLOTHING: Gorgeous hand-smocked and hand-decorated clothing for babies and older children can still be found in Paris, but at prices that are painfully high. For all but the most indulgent grandparents, the best idea is to head for department stores, which generally display a wide selection of charming clothing for youngsters, often decorated with motifs that make them look very French.

Jacadi carries classic designs for children from 3 months to 12 years; their pale blue and white boutiques scattered around Paris offer excellent quality for a relatively affordable price. Two addresses, among many others, are 7 Rue Gustave-Courbet, 16e (phone: 45-53-33-73), and 51 Rue de Passy, 15e (phone: 45-27-03-01).

Tartine et Chocolat opened about a decade ago on the Left Bank's super shopping street (Rue de Rennes). Clothing for newborns to 12-year-olds is sold here. Their trademark item: striped unisex overalls for about $90. They also sell dresses for moms-to-be. 90 Rue de Rennes, 6e (phone: 42-22-67-34).

FABRIC: The colorful and distinctive cotton fabrics of the south of France make a delightful souvenir, and can be purchased in Paris at the following shops:

Souleiado is the most famous and expensive trademark for Provence's bright peasant prints. The quality is good, and the choice of yard goods and finished products including skirts, shirts, bags, placemats, and other table linen is usually wide and varied.

Prices in Paris are no more expensive than in the south, so you might as well buy here. 78 Rue de Seine, 6e (phone: 43-54-62-25), and 83 Av. Paul-Doumer, 16e (phone: 42-24-99-34). Souleiado products are also sold in most of the capital's major department stores.

Les Olivades, another brand of Provençal printed yard goods with shops throughout France, these a little less pricey than the more prestigous *Souleiado.* There are also wallpapers to match many of the prints. 25 Rue de l'Annonciation, 16e (phone: 45-27-07-76).

Good bargains on fabrics can also be found at the *Marché St.-Pierre* (at the foot of the Basilique du Sacré-Coeur), which also houses dozens of small shops, as well as two multi-story fabric emporiums. The best of these is *Aux Tissus Reine,* 5 Pl. St.-Pierre, 18e (phone: 46-06-02-31).

FOOD AND WINE: At any given point in Paris, it's possible to put together a sumptuous picnic by making exactly four stops: the closest charcuterie, or butcher shop, often much like a deli; the *fromagerie,* or cheese store; the *marchand de vin,* or wine merchant; and the *boulangerie,* or bakery. Usually, these shops will be within a block or two of one another, sometimes right next door.

Androuët is devoted to cheese, and many varieties are available either to eat in the restaurant upstairs or to take out. 41 Rue d'Amsterdam, 8e (phone: 48-74-26-90).

Berthillon sells such delicious ice cream that Parisians often line up outside for a small carton for a special party. Flavors, which change with the season, include wild strawberry, calvados crunch, and candied chestnut. 31 Rue St.-Louis-en-l'Ile, 4e (phone: 43-54-31-61). Several cafés on the Ile St.-Louis also serve scoops of Berthillon.

Fauchon is one of the world's great purveyors of food, and every day there's a new exhibition of fresh and packaged food from all corners of France and around the world, lavishly laid out with taste and style found nowhere else. Fine wine also is available, along with delicacies prepared in the shop's own charcuterie. Lotus tea (*tchando*) makes a special souvenir. The store is very experienced in shipping gift packages. The two original shops are at 26 and 28 Pl. de la Madeleine, 8e (phone: 47-42-60-11); a grocery and sweetshop have been added to *Fauchon*'s new premises a few doors away at 30 Pl. de la Madeleine, 8e.

Le Gourmet is *Galeries Lafayette*'s chic new grocery, featuring exotic and often quite reasonably priced foods, wines, and confections from around the world. 40 Bd. Haussmann, 9e (phone: 48-74-37-13).

Hédiard, in business since 1854, sells an array of products similar to *Fauchon*'s, but specializes in exotic fruit and spices. 21 Pl. de la Madeleine, 8e (phone: 42-66-44-36).

Legrand Fille et Fils offers an excellent selection of wine, including bottles that are both good and inexpensive, in a charming old wine shop near the city's stock market. 1 Rue de la Banque, 2e (phone: 42-60-07-12).

Lenôtre specializes in pastries and other desserts, and everything is exquisite, from the simplest éclair to the fruit mousses, charlottes, and chocolates. 44 Rue d'Auteuil, 16e (phone: 45-24-52-52), and several other locations.

La Maison de l'Escargot prepares and sells more than 10 tons of snails annually, following a secret recipe that is 75 years old. 79 Rue Fondary, 15e (phone: 45-75-31-09).

La Maison du Chocolat is the place where Robert Linxe, perhaps the most talented chocolate maker in the French capital, produces delicate, meltingly delicious chocolate creations such as his raspberry chocolate truffles. He also offers a selection of champagnes and an excellent array of armagnacs. 225 Rue de Faubourg-St.-Honoré, 8e (phone: 42-27-39-44), and 52 Rue François 1er, 8e (phone: 47-23-38-25).

Poilâne is considered by many French to sell the best bread in the country, and the large and crusty round country-style loaves dubbed *pain Poilâne,* baked in wood-burning ovens, taste delicious with soup, pâté, cheese, or cassoulet. 8 Rue du Cherche-Midi, 6e (phone: 45-48-42-59).

HOUSEWARES: *Castorama,* a chain with 86 branches throughout the country, carries 45,000 different European-designed basics for the home — from a simple flowerpot to a sophisticated security system. Although you may not want to cart home a bidet or a set of wrought-iron andirons (*Castorama* does not arrange shipping), you will find dozens of moderately priced and stylish smaller items — doorknobs, soap dishes, coat hooks, decorative door plaques — that will travel well and add European panache to your home. Forget about electrical wall switches and anything else you have to connect to existing wiring; the two systems are not compatible. At Place Clichy, near the St.-Lazare railway station, in the basement of a shopping complex. 1-3 Rue Caulaincourt, 18e (phone: 45-22-07-11).

Can you think of any hardware center that is known to take calls from Hong Kong and has been written up in *The New York Times?* The basement of *BHV* (the *Bazaar de Hôtel de Ville*) is probably Paris's (if not the world's) most celebrated hardware center — and deservedly so. Its counters are chockablock with everything from nuts and bolts to plugs and wires; this is a place where you can buy anything from a French bistro sign to a washing machine. A grim, cavernous expanse beneath a somewhat dreary department store, it resembles scenes from *Raiders of the Lost Ark*. We have friends whose only reason for a trip to Paris is a visit to *BHV* to pick up one of their distinctive blue-enamel numbers or Louis XIV door handles. 52 Rue de Rivoli, 3e (phone: 42-74-90-00).

JEWELRY: Several of the world's greatest jewelers are clustered around the elegant Place Vendôme in Paris — a dazzling place to window shop, if not to pick up an heirloom or two.

>   *Boucheron,* 26 Pl. Vendôme, 1er (phone: 42-61-58-16)
>   *Cartier,* 11-13 Rue de la Paix, 2e (phone: 42-61-58-56)
>   *Van Cleef & Arpels,* 22 Pl. Vendôme, 1er (phone: 42-61-58-58)

KITCHENWARE: In a country that reveres cooking among the highest of the arts, it is not surprising to find an abundance of kitchen items at nearly every turn. Pots and pans that are almost sculptural in their classic beauty are everywhere, as are odd-looking gadgets that perform tasks that most cooks never even imagined. Department stores provide an overview of both the most traditional and the latest utensils in the world of French cookery. But for real fun, a cook simply cannot beat a store devoted solely to kitchen supplies:

E. Dehillerin is where some of the finest chefs in France have gone to supply their kitchens for the last 150 years. The 2 stories are stacked from nearly floor to ceiling with pots and pans in copper, cast iron, and tin plate in an array that ranges from tiny saucepans to enormous stockpots; with fine carbon steel knives; and with all kinds of casseroles. A number of fascinating little bins contain just about every kind of kitchen accessory conceivable. 18 Rue Coquillière, 1er (phone: 42-36-53-13).

Simon carries a wide range of professional cookware, and a dazzling, though confusing, array of bistroware, restaurant flatware, cheese trays, menu slates, snail holders, and tiny terrines. You'll feel like a kid in a candy store here if your interests run to culinary paraphernalia. 36 Rue Etienne-Marcel, 2e (phone: 42-33-71-65).

M.O.R.A. is another of Paris's "professional" cookware shops, though it sells to individiuals (there is a $10 minimum purchase) and stocks just about any piece of equipment you can imagine. They also have an interesting selection of professional cookbooks for those who can read recipes written in French. 13 Rue Montmartre, 1er (phone: 45-08-19-24).

LEATHER GOODS: It is a pleasure to shop for leather goods in Paris, especially in the best establishments, where every piece of merchandise from key cases to steamer trunks is impeccably designed and perfectly crafted. Bear in mind, however, that lower-quality leather goods are probably more expensive and not as well made as comparable items in the US.

Americans should be aware that some exotic skins that are sold legally in France —

including certain species of alligator, crocodile, ostrich, and lizard — could be seized on arrival back home, since these animals are on the endangered-species list in the United States. The best Parisian stores will steer American shoppers to merchandise that meets US import laws, but it's still wise to check the latest regulations with the US Fish and Wildlife Service before leaving home.

Céline, whose subdued setting is as classy as its merchandise, offers especially nice small shoulder bags in a great variety of colors and skins. 24 Rue François Ier, 8e (phone: 47-20-22-83).

Hermès, generally considered *the* place to find leather objects of quality and beauty (at extremely high prices), stocks classics such as the popular Constance and Kelly bags in a wealth of sizes, skins, and colors. And there are attaché cases, suitcases, saddles, and small address books and coin purses that make useful and eminently packable gifts of great cachet. 24 Rue du Faubourg-St.-Honoré, 8e (phone: 40-17-47-17).

Loewe sells classic leather goods including handbags, belts, gloves, and shoes in elegant quarters. One of Spain's oldest and highest-quality names in leather, this company has been owned by Louis Vuitton since 1985. 57 Av. Montaigne, 8e (phone: 45-63-73-38).

Louis Vuitton is the first stop in Paris for many affluent shoppers after matched sets of the status LV luggage and leather goods — from billfolds to dog carriers. *Vuitton* has sparkling new quarters on Avenue Montaigne, as well as many other points of sale in the capital. 54 Av. Montaigne, 8e (phone: 45-62-47-00), and 78 *bis* Av. Marceau, 8e (phone: 47-20-47-00).

Trussardi is an Italian ready-to-wear designer whose leather goods and canvas carryalls are well appreciated by the French and Japanese. The quality is good, the designs fairly classic, but with enough variety to appeal to many. 21 Rue du Faubourg-St.-Honoré, 8e (phone: 42-65-11-40).

PERFUME: For centuries, the French have been making enticing scents that are synonymous with luxury and romance, and around the world, in all languages, the adjective that springs most quickly to mind to modify the word "perfume" is "French." Consequently, it's not surprising that perfume heads the shopping lists of more visitors to Paris than any other item.

But today, with virtually all names and sizes of French perfume available in US stores, is there any reason beyond this mystique to buy French perfume in France?

The answer is yes. By shopping in the right places and following the rules for getting tax refunds as described below, it's possible to save significant money — and to pay as much as 40% less than the price of some of France's most expensive and sought-after perfumes. Even without the additional reduction afforded by the tax refund, in fact, the cost of French perfume in a department store is roughly 90% of what you would pay stateside.

Do not be taken in by the flashy Tax Free signs sported by perfume stores all over the country. Most shops, the major department stores included, sell basically the same brands and sizes at rates set by the manufacturers. Regardless of where you shop, the perfume becomes tax-free only after you have purchased enough of it at a single store to qualify for the tax refund set up by the government. The exception is airport duty-free shops, which sell without tax even on small bottles of inexpensive perfumes; the selection is more limited than in Paris stores, however.

There are two good addresses for buying perfume in the capital. *Michel Swiss* (16 Rue de la Paix, 2e; phone: 42-61-71-71) offers a voluminous selection, cheerful service, discounts of 25% for payment with cash or traveler's checks (20% for credit cards), and, in addition, a 25% tax refund on the balance to American visitors who spend more than 1,200F (about $200). That brings the total discount to almost 44%. *Catherine* gives a 40% discount — including VAT — on purchases totaling 1,500F (about $250) or more (6 Rue Castiglione, 1er; phone: 42-60-81-49).

SHOES: France is a country for shoe fiends, and it is full of places to buy footwear that is not only stylish but also — probably because the French walk a good deal themselves and refuse to clump around in ugly shoes — comfortable. Paris offers exceptional shoe stores:

Carel sells classy shoes in the latest shapes and colors — sometimes, but not always, suited to the American foot. At several locations, including 12 Rond-Point des Champs-Elysées, 8e (phone: 45-62-30-62).

Charles Jourdan sells high-fashion shoes of good quality. 86 Av. des Champs-Elysées, 8e, and other locations (phone: 45-62-29-28).

France Faver offers stylish beauty and welcome comfort in its shoes. They are moderately expensive, but the quality makes them worth the price. 79 Rue des Sts.-Pères, 6e (phone: 42-22-04-29).

Maud Frizon offers some of the most sophisticated shoes in Paris. The designs are often lovely and usually costly, especially the boots. 83 Rue des Sts.-Pères, 6e (phone: 42-22-06-93).

Stéphane Kélain has several points of sale in the capital for their high-fashion men's and women's shoes. Quality is high, as are prices, but the latter are not completely unreasonable. 4 Pl. des Victoires, 1er (phone: 42-36-31-84).

Miss Maud is aimed at a young market, but classy and fashionable enough for all ages. Sold at several locations, including 90 Rue du Faubourg-St.-Honoré, 8e (phone: 42-65-27-96).

Walter Stiger carries some of the capital's most expensive and exclusive footwear for men and women in his flagship shop on Faubourg-St.-Honoré, which displays satin slippers like precious jewels — and with prices to match. 83 Rue du Faubourg-St.-Honoré, 8e (phone: 42-66-65-08).

MARKETS AND MOVABLE FEASTS

Going to market is so much a part of Parisian life and culture that it should probably be on every tourist's itinerary. Aside from the rich feast for the eyes — perfectly piled pyramids of oranges, sunbursts of yellow-white endive, and stands of steaming-hot *choucroute* — Paris markets offer enlightening glimpses of the Gallic manner and mentality. Note the brassy produce vendor crooning, "Deal of the century — 4 avocados for 10 francs," or the rosy-cheeked cheese man serving up a wink with the camembert. There'll be a buxom matron, basket in hand and dog in tow, huffing indignantly at a skinny chicken. Paris's markets are not only the most brilliantly stocked and colorful in the world, they are ubiquitous. No matter where in the city you are, you're only a short stroll from one of them.

Paris's first market appeared during the 5th century on the Ile de la Cité; it was followed by small markets at the old gates of the city, many specializing in a single food item. Today, there are 70 open-air and covered food markets in Paris, plus about 10 market streets, and the central wholesale market — *Les Halles de Rungis,* 13e, successor to *Les Halles,* and now the world's largest wholesale market. Most numerous are the open-air roving markets that set up early in the morning 2 or 3 days a week on sidewalks or islands of major boulevards, only to tear down again at 1:30 PM, when they close for the day.

A tour of Paris markets can be a pleasing respite from sightseeing, museums, and three-star restaurants. At the same time, it can rekindle the appetite and provide the fixings for an alfresco lunch on the lawn of one of the city's many parks.

A few tips to the novice: Take along a string bag or basket, since most merchants don't provide bags. Go in the morning, when the produce is freshest and the scene is the liveliest. The general rule is don't touch the merchandise. Vendors take pride in doing the choosing for you. Most markets and market streets are closed Mondays. Below is a small sampling of markets worth visiting.

MARCHÉ BATIGNOLLES: An open-air market existed here, in the 17th *arrondissement* near Place Clichy, for decades before the area was annexed by the city of Paris in 1860. The old covered market built in 1867 came down 8 years ago to make way for the current modern structure. *Batignolles* is noteworthy for its reasonable prices — due, no doubt, to its somewhat out-of-the-way location (a bit west of the Montmartre Cemetery) — and for having more stands (68 in all) than any other covered market. There's a fine selection, including a cluttered stand with Italian specialties (No. 46), one featuring exotic fruit (*Godreau*), an Alsatian selling *choucroute* and sausages, and a small stand with prepared Oriental items. More food shops line the streets surrounding the market. There's a good charcuterie, *Le Cheneau* (44 Rue des Moines), and *Le Terroir,* an inviting wine shop, a few shops away. From here, follow Rue Lemercier to Rue Brochant, turn left at the bakery (which makes a wonderful rye bread ficelle), and walk to the Square des Batignolles, one of the 20 small garden parks built by a protégé of Haussmann named Alphand; a perfect picnic site, it comes complete with duck pond, tiny waterfall and bridge, and stone sculptures.

MARCHÉ DES ENFANTS ROUGES: Built in 1618 and still full of 17th-century character, this is Paris's oldest covered market. Though smaller than many others, it has a good mix of merchants, including cheese stalls, fishmongers, charcuteries, and exquisite produce stalls, as well as a coffee seller who roasts his own beans, a flower stall, and a quaint little antiques shop. Set back in a small covered courtyard off Rue de Bretagne, a bustling market street in its own right, the *Enfants Rouges* is easy to miss if you're not looking for it. Shop the charcuteries and cheese stalls for picnic fixings. There's also a particularly good and friendly charcuterie at 38 Rue de Bretagne, and a well-stocked wine shop at No. 40. A little farther east, at the corner of Rue de Saintonge, is *Onfroy,* an excellent *boulangerie.* A few blocks west, in front of the elaborate Mairie (Town Hall) of the 3rd *arrondissement,* is the Square du Temple park. Though occasionally crowded, there's usually an empty bench, perfect for a picnic. Before leaving the area, take a look at the old *Carreau du Temple,* once a covered market, now a discount clothing center. Then wander south on the quaint crooked streets of the Marais, the heart of Paris (see *Walk 7: The Marais,* DIRECTIONS).

RUE MONTORGUEIL: This busy market street not far west of the *Centre Georges-Pompidou* is all that remains of "the belly of Paris," the old *Les Halles* wholesale food market, which was relocated south of the city to Rungis almost 20 years ago. Some of Paris's chefs still do their marketing here. And even if *Montorgueil* lacks some of the character and intrigue of the erstwhile *Les Halles,* there's still a lot of value to be found here. Most worth a visit is the recently spruced-up *Pâtisserie Stohrer* (No. 51), allegedly Paris's oldest pastry shop, founded in 1730. The decor is magnificent, particularly the ethereal murals painted on glass in 1865 by Paul Baudry, an artist responsible for decorating parts of the Paris *Opéra.* The pastries and prepared foods — including pâtés and individual quiches — of new owner François Duthu are admirable. There are plenty of fruit and vegetable sellers nearby, and farther on is *Ballotin,* a tiny, pristine chocolate shop. Near the start of the street (toward *Le Forum des Halles*) there's an Oriental fruit stand where litchi, cherimoya, and other exotics can be found. You can picnic at the park at the end of the street, where a maze of green trellises and stone animals occupy ground on which the old wholesale market once stood. If the landscape is not to your liking, the surrounding view should be: With the magnificent 16th-century Eglise St.-Eustache on one side and the futuristic shapes and mirrored surfaces of *Le Forum des Halles* on the other, this is one of the most arresting views of old and new Paris.

RUE MOUFFETARD: Most popular of all Paris market streets, *Mouffetard* is criticized by locals for its high prices, dubious quality, and circus atmosphere. But this steep, winding street — about halfway between the Jardin du Luxembourg and the Jardin des Plantes, and invaded in recent decades by ethnic restaurants and tacky clothing shops — retains an old-time flavor and appeal, as well as some very good purveyors. Best known here is *Fachetti* (No. 134), the Italian charcuterie at the bottom of the street, with its appetizing array of hams, pasta, and prepared foods. Farther up the hill, on a small side street, is the African market where fascinating exotic fruits and vegetables, dried fish, and other curiosities can be found. Off another side street are two shops specializing in hams and sausages of the Auvergne region. There's also a fancy food shop, *l'Epicerie* (46 Rue Daubenton), selling a good foie gras for considerably less than you'll pay in the shops at La Madeleine. Back on Rue Mouffetard, there's a small charcuterie worth a visit (No. 120), and there's no lack of good bread and cheese along the street. A cheese shop at the top of the street, *l'Assiette aux Fromages* (No. 27), has a small garden café in the back where cheese and other items are served. From Place de la Contrescarpe at the top of Rue Mouffetard, follow Rue Lacépède east to the Jardin des Plantes (see *Walk 1: Gardens, Bridges, and Islands,* DIRECTIONS).

GRENELLE: From the merchant's point of view, this open-air roving market is the best in Paris, due in part to its affluent clientele and its sheltered location under the elevated métro in the center of Boulevard de Grenelle. Before strolling through this market, stop in the *Poilâne* bakery (at the corner of Grenelle and Rue Clodion) to sample this bread maker's famous sourdough loaf. Once in the market, you'll find 141 generously stocked stands, among them a stall with huge rustic baskets of loose farm eggs, and one with tables filled with nothing but mushrooms, wild and cultivated. Another offers eight varieties of oysters. Plenty of fresh fruit and cheese is sold here; there also are a handful of stalls with pâtés and other prepared picnic-worthy fare. The market extends to La Motte–Picquet métro stop, only a 3-block walk from the Champ-de-Mars park in the shadow of the Tour Eiffel. If your menu lacks a sweet or pastry (items frequently not found at the roving markets), stop at *La Petite Marquise* (50 Av. de La Motte–Picquet) for one of its butter-rich cakes. They're expensive, but worth it.

The best and most enjoyable market here is probably the one set up on Wednesday and Saturday mornings on the Avenue du Président-Wilson between Place d'Iéna and Place de l'Alma, both of which have métro stops. Butchers, bakers, and cheese and flower sellers abound here, along with all types of fresh fish, lettuce and herbs just pulled from the ground and trucked in from farms outside the city, and wonderful fruits and other vegetables. Other good roving markets appear in the Place Monge on Wednesdays, Fridays, and Sundays; on the Boulevard Raspail on Tuesdays and Fridays; and on the Boulevard Edgar-Quinet on Wednesdays and Saturdays. Every neighborhood has one, and everyone has his or her favorite.

HOW TO GET A TAX REFUND

The values available to visitors in Paris on certain merchandise become even more compelling when the refund offered by the French government of its special value added tax (VAT) is added to existing bargains.

To qualify, visitors must be at least 15 years of age, must reside outside France, and must have visited in the country for less than 6 months. No refunds are offered for purchases of food, wine, or tobacco.

To receive a refund, a visitor must spend at least 1,200F (about $200) in a single shop, and must show a passport to prove eligibility. The clerk will then give the buyer an export sales document in triplicate, which must be signed and saved, and an envelope addressed to the store. When leaving France, both the forms and the purchased goods must be taken to the French Customs *détaxe* (tax refund) booth. Note that tax formalities must be taken care of *before* checking baggage and *before* going through passport control at an airport or *before* boarding a train at a station.

The same person who signed the refund forms in the store must present the envelope and the three sheets to the customs officials (who will return one, countersigned, to the buyer in case of later difficulties). The traveler will receive a check for the tax refund mailed from the store. Sometimes, if the buyer pays by credit card, the store makes out a credit slip for the amount of the tax and processes the credit after receiving the validated refund forms from French customs.

Casinos Royal

 Forbidden by Napoleonic decree within 60 miles of Paris, there are only two "legitimate" gaming houses within easy reach of the city. These establishments draw a crowd that is a heady mixture of Parisian chic and Arab sheik. The scenario is pure Hollywood. In fact, behind all the glitter is a system of tight surveillance by the Brigade des Jeux, France's special branch of gaming police, and a gambling code that regulates everything from the odds on the slot machines to the dinner jacket on the croupier — which has (by law) no pockets. The result is an almost totally aboveboard industry, though internecine squabbles among operators have occasionally evoked memories of Chicago in the 1920s. Players are nonetheless fairly certain to lose their money according to the inexorable laws of mathematics.

Passports are required for admission. Though marathon games of chemin de fer are allowed to continue until the players drop, most French casinos open in mid-afternoon and close at 3 or 4 AM, day in and day out. Dress has become far more casual in recent years, but there still are many casinos where jacket and tie are de rigueur for gentlemen; in any case, it's always better to err on the side of decorum. A number of the larger casinos have glamorous, first-rate restaurants right on the gaming-room floor; their waiters discreetly reheat the food of those kept away from their meal by a winning streak.

The staples of the French casino diet are roulette, baccarat, and *boule;* craps and blackjack increasingly are in evidence, the result of creeping Americanization. If you're not familiar with the rules or the vocabulary, many casinos will provide an explanatory booklet. And still others have roving *chefs de partie* (game chiefs), who will be more than happy to help a player who doesn't mind looking like a greenhorn in the midst of all that savoir faire.

ENGHIEN-LES-BAINS: Though inside Napoleon's 60-mile zone, this establishment does have roulette as well as all the other requisites of a world class casino. Part of Lucien Barrière's glittering gaming empire, this lakeside casino's faded Art Deco elegance received a face-lift recently. Gaming begins daily at 3 PM and continues well into the night. A rather steep entry fee and hefty minimum betting requirements discourage dilettantes; the gambling here is serious and the crowd is relatively chic. The small café in the gaming room offers light meals and afternoon tea. Arrive from Paris by taxi (a 20-minute to 1-hour ride north, depending on traffic) and the management will exchange your cab receipt for its equivalent in chips. If you hit it big, invite the house to sup with you at the neighboring *Duc d'Enghien,* one of the best restaurants in the area surrounding Paris. There are three meeting and conference rooms (for 35 to 600 guests) and a theater seating 700. A chip's throw away is the *Grand* hotel and the Thermal Bath, somewhat dated monuments to the turn-of-the-century elegance of this resort. Information: *Enghien-les-Bains,* 3 Av. de Ceinture, Enghien-les-Bains 95880 (phone: 34-12-90-00; fax: 34-23-42-70).

FORGES-LES-EAUX, Seine-Maritime: Just outside the 60-mile roulette-free zone that Napoleon decreed must surround Paris, Forges attracts all the capital's players who don't want to risk the wheels at the city's various *clandés,* as its clandestine gaming dives are called. Those who can't face the predawn drive back to Paris can stay at the *Continental* hotel, right in the casino complex — and those who lose enough in the course of the evening are guests of the management. Information: *Casino de Forges,* Av. des Sources, Forges-les-Eaux 76440 (phone: 35-09-80-12).

Learning the Culinary Arts: Cooking Schools

The cooking schools of France are as varied as the nation's landscape and regional cuisine. In Paris, visitors can study with famous chefs such as Gaston Lenôtre. They can gain hands-on experience at the most classic of all cooking schools — Paris's Le Cordon Bleu (recently installed in new quarters). Travelers who want to look behind the scenes at restaurant kitchens or to visit the wholesale markets where the chefs themselves shop can go on tour with Robert Noah (see *Paris en Cuisine,* below). Some schools — such as Paris's newest and Ritziest offering — L'Ecole de Gastronomie Française Ritz-Escoffier — will tailor special courses for groups. And for those who have only an afternoon or two to devote to the pursuit of better cooking skills, afternoon demonstrations are offered by some schools, particularly the Ritz and Cordon Bleu. The course is limited only by one's vision and by one's command of French, a knowledge of which goes a long way toward making the experience meaningful, even though translators are usually available. Programs tend to be casual and are geared to novices and experts alike. The point is to go with an open mind and a willing spirit, ready to acquire a few additional culinary skills and authentic French experiences — and have a good time besides.

A few words of advice on planning a trip. Don't be afraid to go alone. Many lifelong international friendships have been struck over magnificent soufflés. Most schools operate year-round. Be sure to send away for brochures and read them carefully before booking so that you know exactly what to expect.

LE CORDON BLEU: This famous school has been instructing an international group of students in French cooking and pastry making since 1895. During the summer, special 5-week courses are offered in cooking and pastry, while 11-week sessions that give credits toward certificates and diplomas are available during the year. Visitors may reserve a few days ahead for single afternoon demonstrations, with menus available about 30 days in advance for each month's program. There also are intensive 4- or 5-day sessions during holiday periods — *Christmas, Easter,* and throughout the summer. Both the demonstration and intensive courses often are translated into English. Students are responsible for their own lodging. Information: *Le Cordon Bleu,* 8 bis Rue Léon-Delhomme, Paris 75015 (phone: 48-56-06-06; in the US, 800-457-2433).

ECOLE FERRANDI: The only Paris cooking school to offer professionally motivated foreigners preparatory courses for a C.A.P., the French government's culinary certification. Though its basic course runs for 9 months (5 days a week) and is recommended only for the most serious students, shorter programs have recently been introduced. They include twice-annual week-long pastry and cuisine courses. Though it is a private school (owned by the Paris Chamber of Commerce), *Ferrandi* courses have been endorsed by such famous French chefs as Joël Robuchon and Pierre Troisgros. Information: *Ecole Ferrandi,* 49 Rue de Richelieu, Paris 75001 (phone: 42-61-35-23; fax: 42-60-39-96).

ECOLE DE GASTRONOMIE FRANÇAISE RITZ-ESCOFFIER: Escoffier was to food what Daimler was to automobiles. Today, the *Ritz* hotel, where the legendary chef Escoffier made his debut in the last century, houses the ultimate cooking school. Courses last 1 to 6 weeks and involve 25 hours of instruction weekly. There also is a course in *pâtisserie* — the art of cake, ice cream, chocolate, and candy making — and a 12-week program for professionals. Instruction is in French and English. Information: *Ecole de Gastronomie Française Ritz-Escoffier,* 38 Rue Cambon, Paris 75001 (phone: 42-60-38-30).

ECOLE LENÔTRE: Working in groups of up to a dozen under France's best-known and most respected pastry chef, Gaston Lenôtre, professionals and serious amateurs study French pastry, chocolate, bread, ice cream, charcuterie, and catering in the huge, modern, spotless Lenôtre laboratory in the suburb of Plaisir, about 17 miles (28 km) outside Paris. Courses, which are conducted in French, generally last 5 days and include breakfast and lunch (though students are responsible for their own lodging and transportation). Reserve several months in advance. Information: *Ecole Lenôtre,* Rue Pierre-Curie, Plaisir 78370 (phone: 30-55-81-12).

PRINCESS ERE 2001: A well-appointed apartment in Paris and a château in Normandy are the sites for the programs offered by the outgoing, enthusiastic Princess Marie-Blanche de Broglie. In the capital, these include demonstration courses that deal with cooking professionally, the harmony of wines and foods, pastry, the art of entertaining, and French regional cooking. Courses may be arranged in English, French, and Spanish, with translations supplied as necessary. Paris programs run year-round, and students are responsible for their own lodging. Reserve several months in advance. Information: *Marie-Blanche de Broglie, Princess Ere 2001,* 18 Av. de La Motte-Picquet, Paris 75007 (phone: 45-51-36-34).

PARIS EN CUISINE: Travelers who want to visit the wholesale market in the outskirts at Rungis, tour the kitchens of such well-known Paris restaurants as *Taillevent* or *Chiberta,* attend cooking classes with top chefs like Michel and Pierre Troisgros or Michel Guérard, or get an inside view of a chocolate shop, a charcuterie, a *boulangerie,* or a *pâtisserie* can arrange individual or group visits led by Robert Noah, an American based in Paris with excellent contacts in the French food world. The tours are excellent for those who do not speak French, for Noah is a careful translator and groups are small (usually about ten students, depending on the program). Reserve several months in advance. Students are responsible for their own lodging. Information: *Paris en Cuisine,* 49 Rue de Richelieu, Paris 75001 (phone: 42-61-35-23). Noah also publishes a lively, informative newsletter about food and wine in France. Information: *Paris en Cuisine,* PO Box 50099, St. Louis, MO 63105.

Horse Racing: The Sport of Kings

 If Paris has a sporting passion, it's horses. The French invented the parimutuel betting system (based on equally distributed winnings) and there are eight tracks in and around the city, a half-dozen racing sheets, and several hundred places to bet during a season that runs year-round.

Easily reached by métro, either the *Longchamp* or the *Hippodrome d'Auteuil* in the Bois de Bologne or the trotters at *Vincennes* supply a supremely Parisian day at the races.

LONGCHAMP: The temple of racing since 1855, *Longchamp* is the center of the country's thoroughbred racing, the most prestigious site and the one for which hopeful entries train at nearby Maisons-Laffitte, Enghien, Chantilly, Evry, and St.-Cloud. The track's two highlight events are the *Grand Prix de Paris* in late June and the *Prix de* *l'Arc de Triomphe* in early October. Each carries a purse of 1 million francs (what the Parisians call a "brick purse") to its winner. Bois de Boulogne (phone: 42-24-13-29).

AUTEUIL: Opened in 1870 for steeplechase only, *Auteuil* is not like any other park. Over 40 permanent obstacles spread across 30 acres, and its 2.50F (40¢) admission makes it one of the least expensive and chicest shows. Over 60,000 Parisians turn out for the fashion stroll on the third Sunday in June, the *Grand Steeplechase de Paris* (this is where Hemingway took Ezra Pound to the races!). Best tip for *Auteuil* is a reservation at the track's *Panoramique de l'Hippodrome* restaurant (phone: 42-88-91-38), or take your winnings over to the neighboring *Pré Catelan* (phone: 45-24-55-58), a singular, if pricey, dining experience. Bois de Boulogne (phone: 45-27-12-24).

VINCENNES: A taxi ride into the woods, the *Champs de Courses de Vincennes* is the scene of Paris night racing. Popular with diehard bettors, the track has a rough reputation and is, in fact, a center of blue-collar values: red wine at the bar, corn yellow cigarettes, and spicy *merguez* (sausage) sandwiches. The major highlight of the Vincennes season is the *Grand Prix d'Amérique,* in the dead cold of January. Reservations are advised for the track restaurant, *Le Paddock* (phone: 43-68-64-94). Bois de Vincennes (phone: 47-42-07-70).

From late April until early September, a number of historic tracks around Paris open for selected racing dates. In late spring, races are scheduled in Fountainebleu, and the French equivalent of *Ascot,* the *Prix de Diane,* is held at *Chantilly* (phone: 42-66-92-O2), about 25 miles (40 km) north of Paris, as part of the *Grande Semaine.* Chantilly, which many consider the most beautiful racetrack in the world, has recently inaugurated a magnificent horse racing museum. Legend has it that a duke of the 17th century was reincarnated as a horse and had stables fit for a king — or, at least, a duke — built for him. Though never used, the stables have now been converted into the *Musée Vivant du Cheval* (phone: 44-57-40-40). After these events, the Parisian racing crowd moves on to summer racing at Deauville (about 2 hours from Paris). The best way to find out times, dates, and racing tips is by reading *Paris-Turf, Tierce, Le Bilto, France-Soir,* or *L'Equipe,* all available at newsstands.

BEST BETS (OFF-TRACK BETTING): The words win, place, and show are as dear to a Frenchman's heart as liberty, fraternity, and equality. Identifiable by their bright green and red logos, there are over 7,000 PMU (Pari-Mutuel Urbaine) outlets in French cafés and tobacco shops for off-track betting. The overall system is the third-largest public service industry in France, producing over $6 billion in revenues annually, and is easier to play than the lottery. First, the traditional system involves marking an entry card for the next day's feature race. A minimum bet is 6F ($1). Inaugurated last year, a more modern — and costlier — system involves course cafés. Carrying a stiff admission charge, these neighborhood betting parlors offer satellite broadcasts of a full slate of day or night racing direct from trackside; payouts are immediate. The food is often good, and the ambience convivial. There are presently about 2 dozen of these cafés in Paris, and growing rapidly. Try the *Boule Mich* (Pl. St.-Andre-des-Arts; métro: St.-Michel), where the barman usually has a winning tip.

Underground Paris

The City of Light has its darker side as well, including underground malls and the world's largest métro station (Châtelet–Les Halles). What's more, Parisians take a subterranean pride in leading tourists through catacombs and an impossibly popular sewer, not to mention several notable cemeteries (if not exactly underground, their residents are.) Take note: The French celebrate a variation of *Halloween* on November 1 (*Day of the Dead*) and visit cemeteries in numbers you'd never imagine.

PÈRE-LACHAISE CEMETERY: With over 100,000 tombs, sepulchers, and monuments, this is the champion of French cemeteries. Rich and infamous alike are buried here, and it's a common weekend pastime of the French to visit its flowered walks and seek out the plots of famous writers, musicians, and politicians. Stop inside the entry and purchase a map before trying to find Jim Morrison's grave (Section 27), where there's always a profoundly bizarre parade going on. Other tombs of note include Oscar Wilde's morbid-Sphinx statuary, Edith Piaf, Proust, Chopin, Balzac, Modigliani, and Sarah Bernhardt. Also see the Hindu-like tomb of Allen Kardec, the father of Spiritualism. Open daily from 10 AM to 5 PM except holidays. Bd. de Menilmontant, 20e. Métro: Père-Lachaise.

MONTPARNASSE CEMETERY: Smaller and much more centrally located than Père-Lachaise, Montparnasse is no less interesting if your taste runs to cold stone walks. Baudelaire and both Jean-Paul Sartre and Simone de Beauvoir are here, among other notables. Open daily year-round from 10 AM to 5 PM except holidays. 3 Bd. Edgar-Quinet, 14e. Métro: Edgar-Quinet.

DOG CEMETERY: Actually classified a "Historic Monument, Second Class," the 100-year-old pet cemetery across the Seine from Paris in Asnières is a unique collection of somewhat touching, poetical, amusing statues and sculpture. Rin Tin Tin and Barry, a St. Bernard who saved 22 children in an avalanche, are among those canines celebrated here. Set in a hillside glade, many feel it is the most beautiful of French cemeteries. Open Tuesdays through Sundays; call for hours. Quai du Dr.-Dervaux, Asnières (phone: 40-86-21-11). Métro: Gabriel Péri.

CATACOMBS: Opened during the French Revolution, the Catacombs are a macabre and bone-chilling belowground tour of thousands of skeletons and skulls. But this is Paris, and workers were allowed artistic license. There are grottoes, castles, and underground springs among caverns of the unliving — "The Kingdom of the Dead," one sign declares. Fascinating, spectacular, and certainly not for the claustrophobic. Bring your own flashlight. Open Tuesdays through Fridays from 2 to 4 PM; weekends from 9 to 11 AM and 2 to 4 PM; admission charge. 1 Pl. Denfert-Rochereau, 14e (phone: 47-42-57-50). Métro: Denfert-Rochereau.

PARIS OPÉRA: Inspiration for Gaston Leroux's *Phantom of the Opera,* the Garnier-designed opera house conducts guided tours of its backstage, velvet boxes, and underground levels. (Yes, there is an underground lake below it.) The opera stage, which has seen stars from Lola Montez to Rudolf Nureyev, is actually 8 stories aboveground and rises an additional 16 above the street. Dark and narrow, the underground is much spookier than that in the Andrew Lloyd Webber show — and much, much less expensive. Admission charge. Place de l'Opéra, 9e (phone: 47-42-57-50). Métro: Opéra.

LES EGOUTS DE PARIS: The spirit of *Les Misérables* and Jean Valjean lives on in Paris's sewers. Now a city museum with a slide show, souvenirs, and a live on-the-canal walking tour, the dank and rank tour has become an incredibly popular attraction, particularly in summer when it's much cooler than Paris aboveground. Lines can sometimes stretch for an hour. Open Saturdays through Wednesdays from 11 AM to 5 PM. Pl. de la Résistance, on the Left Bank by the Pont de l'Alma, 7e (phone: 47-05-10-29). Métro: Pont de l'Alma.

For the Body

Great French Golf

Food, wine, castles, and cathedrals are what first come to mind when thinking about France — not golf. But golf has been a tradition in Gaul since 1856, when the first course was laid out in Pau (in the Pyrénées). Since that time, the game has grown enormously in popularity. By the end of 1990, there were 370 courses around the country, and 60 more are expected to be completed by the end of this year. In fact, except for England and Scotland, France has more courses than any other country in Europe (and by 1995, there will be *more* here than in Scotland!).

Until recently, Gallic golf was considered a sport for the rich and the old. But with the construction of 77 municipal courses since 1980, golf has become accessible to a far broader group of people — including foreign visitors. The *Fédération Française de Golf* and the French Ministry of Tourism set up a system whereby travelers and others who are not members of a local golf club can play. Greens fees vary according to the day and season, but average about $40, except during weekends, when prices rise. Call ahead to reserve. Information: *France Golf International,* c/o Maison de la France, 8 Av. de l'Opéra, Paris 75001 (phone: 42-96-10-23) or *Fédération Française de Golf,* 69 Av. Victor-Hugo, Paris 75783 (phone: 45-02-13-55).

Not only is the countryside around Paris enticing for an afternoon excursion, but also for a round of golf. The three courses listed below are open to visitors.

Golf Club de Chantilly – Known for food and lace, Chantilly is also famous for the Château de Chantilly, the home of French kings, and this elegant club, only 5 minutes from the historic castle. With its Old World charm and aristocratic ambience, this British-designed course winds through an impressive forest just 25 miles (40 km) north of Paris. Non-members may play for a fee on Mondays, Tuesdays, and Wednesdays. Closed Thursdays. Information: *Golf Club de Chantilly,* Vineuil–St.-Firmin, Chantilly 60500 (phone: 44-57-04-43).

Golf National – Owned and operated by the *Fédération Française de Golf,* this huge public golf complex is in St.-Quentin-en-Yvelines, southwest of Paris. The first of its three courses, the 18-hole, 7,400-yard *Albatros* (designed by Hubert Chesneau and Bob Von Hagge), opened in October 1990. This stadium course is host to the *French Open* this year. Water hazards abound. Greens fees range from $35 to $55. Information: *Golf National,* 2 Av. du Golf, Guyancourt 78280 (phone: 30-43-36-00).

Golf des Yvelines – Set in a protected park, this 18-holer is a par 72 forest course, 28 miles (45 km) southwest of Paris. Its clubhouse is in a château. Greens fees are $35 during the week, $50 on weekends. Information: *Golf des Yvelines,* La Queue-en-Yvelines 78940 (phone: 34-86-48-89).

Scheduled to open this year is the 18-hole competition level *Euro Disneyland* golf course in Marne-la-Vallée, just east of Paris. As part of its "megaresort" project (which will be nearly one-fifth the size of Paris), the Disney people will have two golf courses, one of them an 18-hole Ron Fream design laid out around a lush landscape including manmade lakes with stepped tees and characteristic mouse-ear–shape sand bunkers.

The second course, a 9-holer (which one Disney executive refers to as "our Minnie putt course") is scheduled to open next year. Information: *Euro Disneyland,* Marne-la-Vallée, (phone: 44-57-04-43).

Other golf courses in the Ile-de-France region include *Ozoir-la-Ferrière* (Château des Agneaux; phone: 60-28-20-79; welcomes visitors; closed Tuesdays), 15 miles (24 km) from Paris; *St. Germain-en-Laye* (phone: 34-51-75-90; accepts non-members on weekdays only; closed Mondays), 12 miles (19 km) from Paris; and the *Racing Club de France* (La Boulie, Versailles; phone: 39-50-59-41) and *St.-Nom-la-Bretèche* (La Bretèche; phone: 34-62-54-00), both of which accept only guests of members. It is best to call at least 2 days in advance to schedule a tee-off time.

Game, Set, and Match:
Tennis Around Paris

Like the United States, France has seen an enormous increase in the interest in tennis over the past 20 years — as a sport for spectators and participants alike. The number of tennis courts and camps in France continues to increase, and there are hundreds of tennis clubs — both private and public. The prime surface of choice is red clay, although there are a fair number of all-weather and hard courts in the countryside around Paris. Though it can be hard to get court time in the city itself, conditions are far less crowded outside the capital. Attendance at the country's leading international tournament, the *French Open,* has soared to the point where a major expansion of Paris's *Roland Garros Stadium* was necessary.

TENNIS CLUBS: The many tennis clubs in France — of which by far the most famous is Paris's *Racing Club,* unquestionably one of the greats among the world's athletic clubs — are organized by *département* or league. Most require annual membership, and virtually all are closed to outsiders who aren't personally acquainted with a member. However, some are less exclusive than others, and occasionally it's possible for business associates to provide an entrée.

TENNIS CLUBS NEAR PARIS: The following clubs are located close to the capital:

Aubervilliers, Seine-St.-Denis – Open year-round (except August), the *Tennis Forest Hill* offers lessons for an hour and a half each day in blocks of 4 days on 18 indoor courts. Information: *Tennis Forest Hill,* 111 Av. Victor-Hugo, Aubervilliers 93300 (phone: 48-34-75-10).

Bois-le-Roi, Seine-et-Marne – With 9 hard courts outdoors and 2 indoors, the *UCPA* offers a 7-hour weekend instruction program year-round. Information: *UCPA,* Rue de Tournezy, Bois-le-Roi 77590 (phone: 64-87-83-00).

Boulogne, Hauts-de-Seine – At the *Tennis Club de Longchamp,* just down the road from *Roland Garros Stadium,* in the Bois de Boulogne on the outskirts of Paris, it is possible to enroll for weekly instruction sessions on the 3 hard courts. There is a golf course nearby. Information: *Tennis Club de Longchamp,* 19 Bd. Anatole-France, Boulogne 92100 (phone: 46-03-84-49).

Nanterre, Hauts-de-Seine – Weekend lessons are possible here year-round at the *Tennis Club Défense.* Various periods of instruction and weekend lessons are available on the 8 hard courts. Information: *Tennis Club Défense,* 45 Bd. des Bouvets, Nanterre 92000 (phone: 47-73-04-40).

Villepinte, Seine-St.-Denis – The *Villepinte Tennis Club* has 7 clay and 6 hard courts, with possibilities for indoor and outdoor play year-round. Weekend and extended courses are offered. Information: *Tennis de Villepinte,* Rue du Manège, Ville-pinte 93420 (phone: 43-83-23-31).

Courts in Paris proper include those in the Luxembourg Gardens (rented on a first-come, first-served basis; no phone), as well as a number of municipal courts scattered around the city. For the address of the court nearest your hotel, contact the Hôtel de Ville de Paris and ask for the Service de Sports (phone: 42-76-40-40).

TOURNAMENT TENNIS: The *French Open,* which takes place during the last week of May and the first week in June in Paris, is the world's premier red-clay-court tournament and one of the four *Grand Slam* events (the other three being *Wimbledon,* the *US Open,* and the *Australian Open*), attracting most of the top international men and women players. Tickets for the early matches generally are easy to obtain at the box office or by mail through the *Fédération Française de Tennis Billetterie* (Service Reservation, BP 33316, Paris 75767; phone: 47-43-48-00).

Paris's Best Swimming Pools

One of the few things Paris lacks in the way of tourist attractions is a seashore with sandy beaches for sunning and swimming. Happily, the city does have a network of municipal pools where tourists can enjoy a refreshing dip between monument viewing on sticky summer days. The following are some of our favorite wet spots.

Piscine Deligny – Probably the most famous pool in Paris, it's known for its nude sunbathers and its prime location on a barge moored on the Seine. The 50-meter pool floats inappropriately near the staid Assemblée Nationale. Open from 8:30 AM to 5:30 PM during the summer; admission charge. 25 Quai Anatole-France, 7e (phone: 45-51-72-15).

Piscine des Halles – More centrally located in the vast underground *Forum des Halles* shopping complex, this 50-meter indoor pool is extremely popular with Parisians. Open Mondays, Tuesdays, Thursdays, and Fridays from 11:30 AM to 10 PM; Wednesdays from 10 AM to 7 PM; weekends from 9 AM to 5 PM; admission charge. 10 Pl. de la Rotonde (*Le Forum des Halles*), 1er (phone: 42-36-98-44).

Piscine du Quartier Latin – Recently renovated, this pool (formerly the *Piscine Pontoise*) is centrally located near the Left Bank monuments and universities. Though indoors, its roof lets in plenty of sunlight. It also has a sauna, whirlpool bath, workout facilities, and a restaurant. Call for hours; admission charge. 19 Rue de Pontoise, 5e (phone: 43-54-82-45).

Piscine Georges-Vallerey – Originally built for the *1924 Olympic Games,* this pool was refurbished and reopened in 1989. Though not centrally located, it's well worth the short trip to the Porte des Lilas (not far from the Père-Lachaise Cemetery). Its roof opens to permit tanning on sunny days. Open Mondays through Fridays from 11 AM to 8 PM; weekends from 10 AM to 7 PM; admission charge. 148 Av. Gambetta, 20e (phone: 40-31-15-20).

Aquaboulevard – At the southern end of one of Paris's main métro lines (Balard), this indoor-outdoor amusement park near the Seine has slides, waves, beaches, toboggans, islands, and lagoons. Especially good when traveling with children. Open Mondays through Thursdays from 9 AM to 11 PM; Fridays from 9 AM to midnight; Saturdays from 8 AM to midnight; Sundays from 8 AM to 11 PM; admission charge. 4-6 Rue Louis-Armand, 15e (phone: 40-60-10-00).

Roger La Gall – Another 50-meter pool whose canvas roof folds back in sunny weather, this is the home of a prestigious Paris swim club, *Club des Nageurs de Paris.* Near the Bois de Vincennes. Open from 9:30 AM to 9 PM in summer; admission charge. 34 Bd. Carnot, 12e (phone: 46-28-77-03).

Freewheeling by Two-Wheeler

To understand just how seriously the French have always taken the sport of bicycling, a visitor has only to consider the annual *Tour de France* (won by an American three times in the last 5 years), which takes places in July and ends in Paris. The world's premier bicycle competition, it has the French people cheering from the valleys of the Loire to the mountain passes of the Alps. But though this competition is reserved for professional cyclists, the passion that spawned it is felt by many, and there are all kinds of other activities and competitions for less serious cyclists at every level. Among them, there is a distance program, with merit certificates to recognize accomplishment in a variety of categories; those who cover a stipulated territory, and pass through certain checkpoints in the various *départements,* complete certain short but difficult itineraries, or make certain long-distance trips, and the like, may earn special certificates.

Those who plan on two-wheeling around Paris (it's the best way to explore the area around the Seine and its islands, the Marais, and the Latin Quarter) will find right-hand lanes specifically designated for use on some major streets and plenty of bike racks throughout the city — although it's perfectly legal to lock up next to a lamppost.

Common outings include the Bois de Boulogne (bicycles can be rented on Wednesdays, weekends, and holidays at the Relais du Rois; phone: 47-66-55-92) and the zoo at Vincennes. For the Bois de Vincennes, bicycles can be rented on weekends and holidays at the Esplanade du Château, near the entrance to the Parc Floral. In smaller parks and gardens such as the Tuileries and Luxembourg Gardens, you'll have to walk your bike.

For visitors who just want to pedal through Paris's many parks or out into the countryside in a leisurely fashion, merely take advantage of the itineraries provided through the various regional societies of the *Fédération Française de Cyclo-tourisme* (*FFCT;* 8 Rue Jean-Marie-Jégo, Paris 75013; phone: 45-80-30-21). These (easy to hard) *Randonnées Permanentes,* which can be taken by individuals or by groups at any time of year and normally cover several hundred miles over country roads, are designed to be completed over a period of days or weeks, with stops specified at intervals of a dozen or so miles. While written in French, the place-names, route numbers, and distances are comprehensible even to those who do not speak the language.

Two organizations that also arrange group rides for different levels in and around Paris during spring and fall are *CIMH* (a government-sponsored clearinghouse for sports activities; 15 Rue Gay-Lussac, 5e; phone: 43-25-70-90) and the *Movement for Defense of the Bicycle* (32 Rue Raymond-Losserand; phone: 45-82-84-76 or 43-20-26-02).

River Cruising:
Sailing up the Seine

The Seine cuts through the heart of the French capital, dividing the right and left banks and harboring the two islands where the city began. Among our favorite ways to pass a soft summer afternoon or evening is cruising on one of its many glass-domed tourist boats or canal cruisers.

Everyone knows about the *bateaux-mouches* that parade from morning to evening along the Seine between the Pont de l'Alma and the Pont de Sully at the eastern end of Ile St.-Louis. Less well known, but perhaps even more charming, are the morning and afternoon cruises along the Canal St.-Martin, between the métro stops at Jean-Jaurès and Bastille, and the full-day excursions on the Canal de l'Ourcq, which take in some lovely green areas starting at the Paris-Bassin de la Villette near the métro stop at Jean-Jaurès. Information: Office du Tourisme, 127 Champs-Elysées, Paris 75008 (phone: 47-23-61-72).

There are also two companies offering longer cruises starting on the Seine, traveling to and through Paris's old canal networks, routes by which basic provisions were once delivered to the capital from the provinces. Starting mornings at the quay near the *Musée d'Orsay,* the 3-hour trips pass from the Seine to the Bastille and navigate an underground tunnel below the Place Bastille, resurfacing on the Canal St.-Martin and finally docking at La Villette, the sciences and industries complex. In the afternoons, the route is reversed. Information: *Paris Canal* (phone: 42-40-96-97) or *Canauxrama* (phone: 46-07-13-13).

For the Mind

Memorable Museums
and Monuments

The stunning achievements of French art are an exhilarating hymn to human possibility, from the halls of Mont-St.-Michel to the shores of Cap d'Antibes, from the prehistoric cave paintings of Les Eyzies to the science fiction Tinkertoy that is Paris's *Centre Georges-Pompidou*. There is a breathtaking elegance to French artistic endeavors, whatever the century. It can be seen in the intricate weave of an Aubusson tapestry, in the airy geometry of the Eiffel Tower, in the angular grace of a Lautrec chanteuse; everywhere, the cool complexity of the Gallic mind is in evidence.

Sip these pleasures — don't gulp them. Mix monuments with merriments. Try a few casual nibbles at a museum rather than a single marathon banquet. As soon as you feel a sense of duty creeping over you, it's time to look for the nearest glass of beaujolais. And always remember that in Paris, a rainy Monday in February is far better for quiet contemplation than tourist-mad midsummer. But if you must travel in August, at least present yourself at the gates for their early morning opening — or visit at lunch hour, when the hordes usually forsake Leonardo da Vinci for pâté.

CENTRE GEORGES-POMPIDOU: Known to Parisians as "the Beaubourg," this potpourri of multicolored geometry was a source of great controversy when it first splashed onto the sober Gothic cityscape in 1977. Since then, its annual admissions have been more than double that of the staid *Louvre*, as the French and foreigners alike come to savor its quixotic feast of exhibitions with the basic theme of "the art and culture of the 20th century" — anything from Einstein memorials and the development of the pinball machine to solar heating and disco dancing. The complex also has a vast library and a regular program of films, concerts, poetry readings, and dance recitals. But it would be worth a visit if only for the sci-fi architecture, the fishbowl escalators, and the plaza outside, where swords are swallowed, fire is eaten, and *commedia dell'arte* is enacted by roving mimes. Open weekdays, except Tuesdays, from noon to 10 PM; weekends from 10 AM to 10 PM. Information: *Centre National d'Art et de Culture Georges-Pompidou*, 120 Rue St.-Martin, Paris 75191 (phone: 42-77-12-33).

LA TOUR EIFFEL: Measuring 1,056 feet in height (including a transmitter), 412 feet in breadth, and 8,500 tons in weight, this famous pre-fab — the world's first, whose 18,000 pieces are joined by 2,500,000 rivets — was built to commemorate the centenary of the French Revolution. At the time of its March 1889 inauguration, it was the world's tallest structure; early critics predicted it would keel over in the first high wind, reviling it as a grotesque edifice that marred the city's skyline. From the very start, it was destined to be dismantled, and when its lease expired in 1909, it escaped destruction only by a narrow margin. Since then, it has been scaled by alpine climbers, a plane has flown under it, and an elephant was hoisted up into it. To celebrate its centennial, the lights that illuminate it at night were reworked — a dazzling success. Hundreds upon thousands of visitors have braved the 1,789-step climb to its summit (although most take the elevator), and it is safe to say that visiting Paris and missing the E.T. is like visiting France and skipping Paris. There are three snack shops, as well as three restaurants in the tower. Open daily from 10 AM to 11 PM; in the summer from 10 AM to midnight. Information: *La Tour Eiffel,* Champ-de-Mars, Paris 75007 (phone: 45-55-91-11).

MUSÉE D'ORSAY: The Impressionist paintings that once crowded intimately into the joyfully informal *Jeu de Paume* museum have found a more spacious and sober home. The brilliant transformation of a vast turn-of-the-century glass and cast-iron train station into a museum has brought the best artistic production of France from 1848 to 1914 under one vaulted, translucent roof. Now Degas, Monet, and Renoir are displayed in specially designed spaces within this former railroad-cathedral, along with the works of 600 other painters and 500 sculptors. No detail of light, humidity, or acoustics has been left to chance, making this voyage around the art world a very comfortable one. Don't miss the museum's pièce de résistance — the Van Goghs on the top floor, glowing under the northern Parisian skylight. Open 10 AM to 6 PM daily, except Mondays; Sunday mornings and in summer the museum opens at 9 AM, and Thursday evenings it stays open until 9:45 PM. Information: *Musée d'Orsay,* 1 Rue de Bellechasse, Paris 75007 (phone: 40-49-48-14).

MUSÉE DU LOUVRE: This colossus on the Seine, born in 1200 as a fortress and transformed over the centuries from Gothic mass to Renaissance palace, served as the royal residence in the 16th and 17th centuries until it was supplanted by suburban Versailles, becoming a museum when François I donated a dozen masterpieces from his private collection. Napoleon later turned it into a glittering warehouse of artistic booty from the nations he conquered. Today, its 200 galleries cover some 40 acres; to view all 297,000 items in the collections in no more than the most cursory fashion, it would be necessary to walk some 8 miles. In addition to the *Mona Lisa, Venus de Milo,* and the *Winged Victory of Samothrace,* it has many delights that are easily overlooked — Vermeer's *Lace Maker* and Holbein's portrait of Erasmus, for instance; not to mention Van der Weyden's *Braque Triptych,* Ingres's *Turkish Bath,* Dürer's *Self-Portrait,* Cranach's naked and red-hatted *Venus,* and the exquisite 4,000-year-old Egyptian woodcarving known as the *Handmaiden of the Dead.* More of our favorites include Michelangelo's *The Slaves,* Goya's *Marquesa de la Solana,* Watteau's clown *Gilles* and his *Embarkation to Cythera,* Raphael's great portrait *Baldassare,* Veronese's *Marriage at Cana,* Titian's masterpiece *Man with a Glove,* both *Mary Magdalen* and *The Card Sharps* by Georges de la Tour, Rembrandt's *Bathsheba,* and Frans Hals's *Bohemian Girl.* Try to save time for any one of David's glories: *Madame Récamier, The Oath of the Horatii, The Lictors Bringing Back to Brutus the Body of His Son,* or *The Coronation of Napoleon and Josephine.* And don't miss *Liberty Leading the People* and *The Barque of Dante,* both by Delacroix, and Courbet's *The Artist's Studio, Burial at Ornans,* and *Stags Fighting* — just for openers! There's also ancient statuary (from the Middle East, Egypt, Greece, and Rome), classical sculpture, the French crown jewels, objets d'art, and fine furniture. I. M. Pei's controversial glass pyramid, which was unveiled in time for the celebrations of the bicentennial of the French Revolution in 1989, constituted a step toward expanding gallery space by about 80%. Open Mondays and Wednesdays from 9 AM to 9:45 PM; Thursdays through Sundays from 9 AM to 6 PM. Information: *Musée du Louvre, Palais du Louvre,* Paris 75058 (phone: 40-20-51-51 for a recording in both French and English or 40-20-50-50 for more detailed information).

MUSÉE RODIN: This is one of France's most complete and satisfying museum experiences. Ambling in a leisurely way through one of the great 18th-century aristocratic homes and its grounds, it's possible to follow the evolution of the career of

Auguste Rodin, that genius of modern sculpture. Among the broad terraces and in the serene and elegant gardens are scattered fabled statues like *The Thinker,* the *Bourgeois de Calais,* the superb statues of Honoré de Balzac and Victor Hugo, the stunning *Gate of Hell,* on which the master labored a lifetime, and much, much more. The celebrated *Ugolin* group is placed dramatically in the middle of a pond. Open daily except Mondays from 10 AM to 4:30 PM. Information: *Musée National Auguste Rodin,* 77 Rue de Varenne, Paris 75007 (phone: 47-05-01-34).

LA STE.-CHAPELLE: Tucked away in the monumental complex of the Palais de Justice, the 13th-century Ste.-Chapelle was built by the monarch Louis IX (St.-Louis), on the site of the former palace of the early kings of the Capetian dynasty, as a reliquary for the recently obtained Sacred Crown of Thorns. The 15 soaring stained glass windows (plus a later rose window), with more than 1,100 brilliantly colored and exquisitely detailed miniature scenes of biblical life, are one of the unquestioned masterpieces of medieval French art, and the graceful, gleaming spire is one of the city's most beautiful and understated landmarks. Open daily from 10 AM to 4:30 PM. Information: *La Ste.-Chapelle,* 4 Bd. du Palais, Paris 75004 (phone: 43-54-30-09).

MUSÉE PICASSO: Showing works still amazingly modern, this museum is in a 17th-century mansion in Paris's oldest neighborhood. It houses a part of the collection with which Picasso could never bring himself to part, and gives a panoramic view of the versatile doyen of this century's art. His varied career went from the contemplative self-portrait painted in shades of blue in 1921, through the cubist newspapers and guitars, to the 1961 iron-sheet sculpture of a soccer player looking like an ice cream on a stick. Especially interesting is the master's collection of works by other artists. Open Mondays and Thursdays through Sundays from 9:15 AM to 5 PM; Wednesdays from 9:15 AM to 10 PM. Information: *Musée Picasso,* 5 Rue de Thorigny, Paris 75003 (phone: 42-71-25-21).

JEU DE PAUME: Renovated and reopened as a gallery for contemporary art last year, this is the latest expansion in the Grand Louvre project that began with the opening of the I.M. Pei pyramid. One of the most historic buildings in Paris, the *Jeu de Paume* was originally an indoor tennis court for royalty; it gained a place in history when, in 1789, delegates met here to declare their independence, marking the beginning of the French Revolution. Extensively modernized, the museum now houses exhibitions of contemporary works from the last 20 to 30 years, including those of Takis, Broodthears, and Dubuffet. Previously home to the *Louvre*'s overcrowded Impressionist collection (now in the *Musée D'Orsay*), it has video and conference areas available. Open Tuesdays through Fridays from noon to 7 PM (Tuesdays until 9:30 PM); weekends from 10 AM to 7 PM. Information: *Jeu de Paume,* Place de la Concorde, Paris 75001 (phone: 42-60-69-69; fax: 42-60-39-05).

The Liveliest Arts:
Theater, Opera, and Music

 The theatrical-musical map of France has undergone some startling changes in the past decade, and the country literally bristles with first-rate repertory companies and orchestras. The lively arts are, in fact, livelier than ever, particularly in Paris.

Don't bypass an evening in the theater just because your French is a high school relic; it's a fine way to become a part of local life. In your favor is the current style of splashy, highly visual productions where spectacle trumps text. Where classics are concerned,

English copies generally can be found — and at any rate, Paris's most-performed playwright is the *formidable* Guillaume Shakespeare.

THÉÂTRE DES AMANDIERS, Nanterre (near Paris), Hauts de Seine: Known for its continually evolving and inventive style, the theater is now under the hands of impresario Jean-Pierre Vincent, whose career has taken him all the way from actor with the theatrical school at the Lycée Louis-le-Grand, in 1959, to administrator of the *Comédie Française* in 1983. Recent presentations have included such time-honored classics as the Oedipus trilogy by Sophocles, but a trip to the box office can turn up any number of theatrical surprises. About 20 minutes by the *RER* city-rail from downtown Paris. Information: *Théâtre des Amandiers,* 7 Av. Pablo-Picasso, Nanterre 92022 (phone: 46-14-70-70).

LA COMÉDIE-FRANÇAISE: The undisputed dowager queen of French theater, as much a national monument as the Eiffel Tower, this dramatic doyenne presents a steady diet of lavish productions of great classics by Corneille, Racine, Molière, Rostand, and the happy few 20th-century playwrights like Anouilh, Giraudoux, and Sartre who have been received into the inner circle of French culture. The *CF* is streamlining its fin-de-siècle image, but even at its stodgiest, it's well worth seeing. Information: *La Comédie-Française,* 2 Rue de Richelieu, Paris 75001 (phone: 40-15-00-15).

IRCAM: The versatile musicians of this *Institut de Recherche et de Coopération Acoustique Musique,* France's current center of contemporary music activity, perform in the various auditoriums of the *Centre Georges-Pompidou* — including the *Salle Polivalente,* whose rotating walls, rising floor, and lowering ceiling make it the last word in acoustical acrobatics. Computers are as common as clarinets, and the whole enterprise is under the aegis of Pierre Boulez, who conducts some of the major *IRCAM* concerts. Information: *IRCAM, Centre Georges-Pompidou,* 31 Rue St.-Merri, Paris 75004 (phone: 42-77-12-33).

MAISON DE RADIO FRANCE: This round white fortress on the banks of the Seine is mission control for French radio and television. It also is the principal residence of two of the country's finest orchestras, the *Orchestre National de France* and the *Nouvelle Orchestre Philharmonique,* which subdivides into a number of smaller ensembles specializing in various instrumental combinations or musical periods. Consequently, there is some vintage music making at this *maison* virtually every day of the week. Watch kiosk posters for appearances of the two orchestras in the capital's other major concert halls. Information: *Maison de Radio France,* 116 Av. du Président-Kennedy, Paris 75016 (phone: 42-30-10-86).

OPÉRA DE PARIS: In a futuristic opera house on the Place de la Bastille, the *Opéra de La Bastille* began regular performances in 1990 under the baton of Myung-Whun Chung, and the grand *Palais Garnier* (former home of grand opera) at the melodramatic end of Av. de l'Opéra is the site of the best in ballet. The other mainstays of Paris opera are the *Théâtre Musical de Paris,* in the old *Châtelet* theater, and the *Opéra Comique,* at the *Salle Favart.* The latter isn't especially comic. The theater is smaller, the performers, as a rule, less well known; but the administration is the same, and the repertory is comparably vast. The *Théâtre Musical de Paris,* once the stronghold of the frothy operetta, now does everything from early Offenbach to late Verdi, importing productions from other European operas as well. The touch is light and stylish, the accent utterly French. Information: *Opéra de La Bastille,* 120 Rue de Lyon, Paris 75012 (phone: 40-01-17-89); *Théâtre National de l'Opéra,* 8 Rue Scribe, Paris 75009 (phone: 47-42-57-50); *Théâtre National de l'Opéra Comique,* 5 Rue Favart, Paris 75002 (phone: 42-86-88-83); *Théâtre Musical de Paris,* 1 Pl. du Châtelet, Paris 75004 (phone: 40-28-28-40).

SALLE PLEYEL: Often called the *Carnegie Hall* of Paris, the renovated *Pleyel* is so admirably suited to all types of music that it has even been the site of jazz concerts.

The greatest names in European music visit here, and the superb *Orchestre de Paris* lives at this elegant address on the Faubourg-St.-Honoré. Other temples of Parisian music include the smaller, charming *Salle Gaveau* on nearby Rue La Boëtie; the *Théâtre des Champs-Elysées* on Avenue Montaigne; and the massive *Palais des Congrès* at Porte Maillot. Any of the city's major orchestras may perform at the latter two, but if you turn up at the *Palais* on the wrong night, you may trade sacred Bach for punk rock. Information: *Salle Pleyel,* 252 Rue du Faubourg-St.-Honoré, Paris 75008 (phone: 45-61-06-30; for the *Orchestre de Paris,* 45-61-96-07).

L'ODÉON–THÉÂTRE DE L'EUROPE: The chameleon-like *Odéon* has, for years, been the joker in the French theatrical pack. After the turbulent period when it housed the fabled company under Jean-Louis Barrault and Madeleine Renaud and ranked among the most popular houses in the city, it became an annex of the *Comédie-Française.* Now it can be seen in yet another incarnation, as the *Théâtre de l'Europe.* Under the direction of one of Europe's foremost men of the theater, Giorgio Strehler of Milan's *Piccolo Teatro,* it became a kind of theatrical Common Market, with original-language productions from all over Europe. It presently is under the direction of a Spaniard, Luis Pasqual. But there's no telling whether, by the time we go to press, the *Odéon* will be transformed once again — perhaps into a circus arena or a House of Parliament. Information: *L'Odéon–Théâtre de l'Europe,* Pl. Paul-Claudel, Paris 75006 (phone: 43-25-70-32).

THÉÂTRE NATIONAL DE CHAILLOT: The rightful heir to the great *Théâtre National Populaire* created by the legendary Jean Vilar in the same building, this three-ring theatrical circus consists of a large room, a small room, and Grand Central Station–size corridors that themselves can be transformed into performance spaces. Everything happens here, from *Hamlet* and *The Three Sisters* to *Faust* for children — performed by marionettes — to new texts by Algerian workers, and contemporary musical happenings. New formats, odd curtain times, and a constant redefining of theater and its audience are the watchwords. Information: *Théâtre National de Chaillot,* Pl. du Trocadéro et du 11-Novembre, Paris 75116 (phone: 47-27-81-15).

THÉÂTRE DU SOLEIL: In La Cartoucherie de Vincennes, an old cartridge factory on the outskirts of Paris, this theater always has had a colorful, sweeping style with a popular mood and political overtones. That was true in the dazzling *1789,* which made the troupe's international reputation during that other year of French upheaval, 1968, and in the more recent Shakespeare series as well. Information: *Théâtre du Soleil,* La Cartoucherie de Vincennes, Bois de Vincennes, Paris 75012 (phone: 43-74-24-08 or 43-74-87-63).

CINÉMATHÈQUE/VIDEOTHÈQUE: Going to the movies is considered a cultural event in France, worthy nearly of museum status. The *Cinémathèque* in the *Palais de Chaillot,* the premier film museum since the early 1960s, shows films in their original language. Daily afternoon and evening programs from the museum's eclectic archives of thousands of films often include several running concurrently, so that a James Cagney gangster epic can share billing with a 1950s British comedy and a Brazilian thriller. Since programs change daily, pick up a copy of *L'Official des Spectacles* or *Pariscope,* available at most newsstands. Ticket prices here are the lowest in the city, and substantial discounts are available to students and frequent viewers. (The *Cinémathèque* also operates theaters in the *Centre Georges-Pompidou*'s Salle Garance; phone: 42-78-37-29; and in the *Palais de Tokyo;* 13 Av. President-Wilson; phone: 47-04-24-24). The *Videothèque* offers an overview of French film and video history with newsreels, films, and television programs. There also is a library with a catalogue and retrieval system that allows for private screenings; prices are on an hourly basis. Information: *Cinémathèque,* Av. President-Wilson, Paris 75016; phone: 47-04-24-24). *Videothèque,* 2 Grande Galerie, *Le Forum des Halles,* Paris 75001; phone: 40-26-34-30).

Festivals à la Française

 Festivals, direct descendants of the Greek drama marathons and the first *Olympic* games, are annual celebrations of the pleasures of creating, competing, or just plain existing. They let a visitor cram the best and most of any given experience into the shortest possible time. In Paris, during summer and fall, festival translates into a musical orgy — from classical to pop rock — it's all here for the listening.

FESTIVAL ESTIVAL AND FESTIVAL D'AUTOMNE: The former, in July and August, brings a musical kaleidoscope of Gregorian chants, Bartók string quartets, Rameau opera, and more to the city's most picturesque and acoustically delightful churches. The *Festival d'Automne* takes up where the *Estival* leaves off and concentrates on the musically contemporary, generally focusing on one or two main themes or composers and including a certain number of brand-new works. Its moving spirit is Pierre Boulez, France's top musical talent. Information: *Festival Estival de Paris,* 20 Rue Geoffroy l'Asnier, Paris 75004 (phone: 48-04-98-01); and *Festival d'Automne,* 156 Rue de Rivoli, Paris 75001 (phone: 42-96-12-27).

An Odyssey of the Old: Antiques Hunting in Paris

 The history of France may best be seen in fortresses and châteaux and the Bastille, but it is best felt by holding a fragment of a sculptured choir stall or an Art Deco soup ladle, by touching the satiny surface of a marquetry wedding chest or by slipping on the signet ring that once belonged to a scheming marquise. Such morsels of the nation's past can be savored at some 100-plus Parisian antiques shops and auction houses or at fairs and markets held throughout the city.

SOURCES FOR ANTIQUES IN PARIS

SHOPS: In every neighborhood of Paris you'll stumble across small, often slightly dusty shops where the best of the old is the offering. Some are true *antiquaires,* antiques dealers who handle pieces of established value and pedigrees. Others are *brocanteurs,* secondhand dealers, whose stock may run the gamut from Second Empire snuffboxes to broken 78-rpm Edith Piaf records. Many dealers belong to either the *Syndicat National des Antiquaires* (National Antiques Dealers' Association) or the *Syndicat National du Commerce de l'Antiquité* (National Association of Antiques Businesses), two highly reputable guilds whose members have pledged to tell the truth about all items they are selling.

For an important purchase, the wise buyer will request a certificate of authenticity. With furniture, in particular, the dealer should be precise about just which parts have been restored and how; a number of "antiques" are really superbly carpentered composites of partly salvaged pieces, and there is a thriving industry in the recycling of genuinely ancient wood into pieces of "antique" furniture that were actually born yesterday.

A trend of the past decade has been the clustering of individual shops into *villages d'antiquaires,* which are something like shopping centers for antiques, with dozens of dealers housed under a single roof. The prototype is the giant *Louvre des Antiquaires* (2 Pl. du Palais-Royal, 1er; phone: 42-97-27-00; open daily except Mondays, and Sundays in the summer), whose 250 different shops are in an old Paris department store. Others in Paris include *La Cour aux Antiquaires* (54 Rue du Faubourg-St.-Honoré, 8e; phone: 42-66-38-60; open daily except Sundays and Monday mornings); *Village Suisse* (54 Av. de La Motte-Picquet, 15e; phone: 43-06-69-90; open Thursdays through Mondays); *Village St.-Honoré* (91 Rue St.-Honoré, 1er); and *Village St.-Paul* (entrance on Rue St.-Paul just off Rue St.-Antoine, 4e). *Le Carré Rive Gauche,* an association of more than 100 antiques shops, is located in the square of streets formed by Quai Voltaire, Rue de l'Université, Rue des Sts.-Pères, and Rue du Bac, 7e.

Other good hunting grounds include Bd. St.-Germain, Rue Bonaparte, and Rue Jacob on the Left Bank; and Rue du Faubourg-St.-Antoine, Rue St.-Honoré, Rue du Faubourg-St.-Honoré, Av. Victor-Hugo, Rue La Boëtie, and Rue de Miromesnil on the Right Bank.

The richness and tradition of the French antiques trade have spawned a high degree of specialization, both by genre and by period. Some shops deal exclusively in dolls, maritime instruments, chimneys and mantelpieces, locks and keys, or postcards. Several antiquarians in Paris stock only items from the 1950s. Passionate collectors with a one-track mind should consult the *Guide Emer* (50 Rue/Quai de l'Hôtel-de-Ville, Paris 75004; phone: 42-77-83-44) for information about where in the whole of France to indulge their most exotic whims.

EXPOSITIONS, FAIRS, AND SALONS: Paris's most prestigious antiques salon, the *Biennale International des Antiquaires,* is held astride September and early October in even-numbered years in the *Grand Palais.* With its stock of the finest pieces available in Europe and a range of exhibitors that includes all the top dealers from France and abroad, the *Biennale* may set the tone of the market for the following 2 years.

The *Foire Nationale à la Brocante et aux Jambons* is a curious event that takes place in March and September every year and mixes antiques, handicrafts, and regional foods from all over France; fairgoers do lots of wine tasting, cheese nibbling, and bric-a-brac browsing. This party is held at Ile-de-Chateau, and is organized by *SNCAO,* 18 Rue de Provence, Paris 75009 (phone: 47-70-88-78).

In Ivry-sur-Seine, the new *FIBA (Foire Internationale Brocante Antiquité)* attracts over 1,000 exhibitors every March, June, and September. Organized by *SODAF,* 2 Placette Fauconnières, Ivry-sur-Seine 94200 (phone: 46-71-66-14).

Less impressive, but nonetheless worth a visit if you happen to be here in late November or early December, is the *Salon des Antiquaires,* held in various locations annually (phone: 45-85-01-85).

FLEA MARKETS: Paris's best-known and largest of its *marchés aux puces* — literally, "markets with fleas" — is the *Marché aux Puces de St.-Ouen* (better known as *Puces de Clignancourt*), located at the Porte de Clignancourt, 18e. This incredible collection of some 3,000 stalls is actually a maze of different submarkets, including *Biron, Paul Bert, Vernaison,* and *Serpette,* all sprawled over a vast area and encompassing everything from rather elegant little shops to ramshackle lean-tos and rickety tables or blankets spread on the curbstone. It's easy to get lost here, so stay close to your companions or give each other a precise time and place at which to rendezvous. There are several cafés and even a little restaurant (*Chez Louisette,* in *Marché Vernaison*) where a Piaf sing-alike croons on Sunday afternoons. The Paris tourist office sells an official guide to this market (*Guide Officiel & Practique des Puces*) for 50 francs. The market is open Saturdays, Sundays, and Mondays from 9 or 10 AM (some stands open as early as 8 AM) to around sundown (in summer, this can be as late as 8 PM).

Lesser known and lower brow are *Les Puces de Montreuil* (literally "the fleas of Montreuil"), held on Saturdays, Sundays, and Mondays at the Porte de Montreuil, 11e;

and *Les Puces de Vanves,* held on Saturdays and Sundays at the Porte de Vanves, 14e. Both run from early morning to sunset, or later. Both also consist mostly of *brocanteurs,* people dealing in secondhand items. *Vanves* sprawls along the sidewalk and around a corner for several blocks; you have to venture well along the street before you begin to see items that are more than other people's old junk. But there are some treasures to be found here, including a lot of Art Deco items and old French linen. The *Montreuil* is even more lowbrow than *Vanves,* crowded with peddlers selling everything from an old espresso machine and African beads (in the same stall) to spare automobile parts. Though there are not many great antiques to be found here, the occasional bargain does turn up.

AUCTIONS: Once something of a professional club for dealers only, auctions — known in French as *ventes aux enchères* — have become the favorite indoor sport of the *haute bourgeoisie* in the last few years, and in the *salles des ventes* (salesrooms) of France, there are fewer bargains around than there used to be. However, those who know their market may still save as much as a third of the retail price; and even for those who don't, auctions are hard to beat for pure theater.

But the auction situation in France is a bit different than those in the US, Great Britain, and Ireland, for all sales take place under the aegis of a government-authorized auctioneer known as the *commissaire-priseur.* And Paris's venerable auction house, *Hôtel Drouot,* is basically a cooperative managed by a guild of *commissaires-priseurs,* and it is they who are known for their probity and expertise, rather than salesrooms or specific companies. By law, French auctioneers are responsible for the authenticity of any item they sell for 30 years after the sale.

The *Hôtel Drouot,* on the Right Bank not far from Boulevard Montmartre, is the center of the auction world in Paris. Some 600,000 lots go through its 16 salesrooms every year, and the activity is frantic. If you find yourself in a room full of plumbers' fittings or vintage cognacs when what you really wanted were antiques, just go up to the next floor. Information: *Drouot-Richelieu,* 9 Rue Drouot, Paris 75009 (phone: 48-00-20-20). Sales also are held at the *Drouot-Montaigne,* 15 Av. Montaigne, Paris 75008 (phone: 48-00-20-80 or 48-00-20-20).

The weekly *Gazette de l'Hôtel Drouot* (on sale on newsstands everywhere) prints a calendar of auction sales all over France, as well a running tally of the results (10 Rue du Faubourg-Montmartre, Paris 75009; phone: 47-70-93-00).

A new bidding-free variation on the auction theme is the *dépot-vente,* a salesroom where private sellers leave lots on consignment with a dealer who sets the price and takes a 15% commission. These generally are well patronized by bargain-hunting professionals. The largest is the immense *Dépot-Vente de Paris,* 81 Rue de Lagny, Paris, 20e (phone: 43-72-13-91).

RULES OF THE ROAD FOR AN ODYSSEY OF THE OLD

Buy for sheer pleasure, not for investment. Forget about the carrot of supposed resale values that French dealers habitually dangle in front of amateur clients. If you love something, it probably will ornament your home until the next Revolution.

Don't be afraid to haggle. This is true even in the most awesomely elegant boutique on the Rue du Faubourg-St.-Honoré. Everything is negotiable, and the higher the price, the harder (and farther) it falls.

Buy the finest example you can afford of any item, in as close to mint condition as possible. Chipped or broken "bargains" will haunt you later with their shabbiness.

Train your eye in museums. These probably are the best schools for the acquisitive senses, particularly as you begin to develop special passions. Collections like the Gobelins tapestries or the furniture in the *Louvre* will set the standards against which to measure purchases.

Peruse French art and antiques magazines. French newsstands abound in them. The best include *Connaissance des Arts, L'Estampille, Beaux-Arts,* and *L'Oeuil. Trouvailles* deals with bric-a-brac and flea markets. The weekly *Gazette de l'Hôtel Drouot* details auction action.

Get advice from a specialist when contemplating a major acquisition. Members of the national guild of antiques experts will be able to assist you. For more information, contact the *Syndicat Français des Experts Professionnels en Oeuvres d'Art* (81 Rue St.-Dominique, Paris 75007; phone: 47-05-50-26).

Celebrated Châteaux and Cathedrals

For half a millennium, the Gothic cathedral and the Renaissance château reigned as the most sublime reflections of the French spirit. As their massive stone shadows colored the life of the whole town and the surrounding countryside, these structures were the peaceful statements of the power, both religious and secular, that was France.

The Gothic mode took shape during the middle of the 12th century and then spread throughout Western Europe. With its vaults and spires straining heavenward and its pointed arch, which the sculptor Rodin called "a pair of hands in prayer," the cathedral was a celebration of both God and engineering. Searching for ever greater elevation and ever more light, its architects replaced the massive walls of earlier styles with airy windows and raised the vaulting higher and higher like stakes in some Olympian poker game. The result was a whole new system of stress and support, characterized most obviously by the famous *arc boutant,* flying buttress.

The onset of the Hundred Years War in 1337 put an end to the golden age of Gothic cathedral building. But the end of the conflict in the middle of the 15th century marked the beginning of the château building years, when new generations of royalty subjected Paris and its surrounding countryside to an orgy of regal real estate development. And as decoration replaced defense as a prime architectural motivation, the once stolid and brooding medieval fortress gave way to the fanciful wonder that became the Renaissance château.

CATHÉDRALE DE NOTRE-DAME: Along with the Eiffel Tower, Paris's other great perpendicular, this noble structure rising above the Ile de la Cité in the middle of the Seine rules the skyline with all the accumulated authority of Church and State — which, in fact, split its original cost. Built on the site of a Gallo-Roman temple that dated back to the earliest pre-Christian days of Paris, it took more than 200 years to erect, from the middle of the 12th century until the middle of the 14th, and was built from the plans of a single anonymous architect. Napoleon was crowned emperor here in 1804 by Pope Pius VII. The distances from the rest of France to Paris are measured from the Place du Parvis in front. Among its myriad wonders are the main portals, the portal to the cloister, the portal of St. Stephen, the 13th-century rose windows, and the heart-stopping view from the tower. Information: *Cathédrale de Notre-Dame,* Pl. du Parvis de Notre-Dame, Paris 75004 (phone: 43-26-07-39).

BASILIQUE DU SACRÉ-COEUR: Perched like a white giant atop Paris's highest point, the Butte (or hill) of Montmartre, this basilica was conceived as a symbol of contrition and hope after the nation's defeat in the Franco-Prussian War of 1870–71. Architect Paul Abadie's Roman-Byzantine design was chosen from among 78 entries;

the first stone was laid in 1875. Though the basilica was completed by 1910, it was not consecrated until 1919, after the First World War.

A steep, wide flight of steps leads to a great portico flanked by equestrian statues of St. Louis and Joan of Arc. The basilica's exterior of gleaming white Château-Landon stone — a material that hardens and whitens with age — provoked and continues to provoke criticism. Locals derisively refer to its three beehive-like domes as *les trois biberons* (the three baby bottles). And though the architecture may not be to everyone's liking, the impact and power of its sparkling image, glimpsed for the first time through a maze of tiny Montmartre streets, are unforgettable. The Byzantine interior is rich and ornate, though light and well proportioned. Note the huge mosaics, one depicting Christ and the Sacred Heart over the high altar; another, the Archangel Michael and the Maid of Orleans; and a third, of Louis XVI and his family. One of the largest and heaviest bells (19 tons) in Christendom is housed in the tall bell tower to the north. A small stairway, reached from the western aisle to the left of the entry, leads down to a crypt containing various chapels and the church treasury. The same stairway leads up to the main dome of the structure, from which there's an exceptional panoramic view of the city. Information: *Basilique du Sacré-Coeur,* 37 Rue de Chevalier de la Barre, Paris 75018 (phone: 42-51-17-02).

BASILIQUE DE ST.-DENIS: Located at the northern gate of Paris (off the A1 highway, less than 2 miles north of Porte de la Chapelle), this is perhaps one of the greatest, albeit one of the least visited, of the city's ecclesiastical monuments.

A church has stood on this ground since before the 5th century. In 638, King Dagobert sponsored the construction of the abbey church, but it wasn't until nearly 600 years later that the Abbot Suger, Louis VII, and architect Pierre de Montreuil conspired to promote a new style that included the first rose windows, ogival arches, and buttresses (concealed at this early stage), marking the earliest manifestations of Gothic architecture. Note the restored central portal representing the Last Judgment. The one on the right depicts the last communion of St. Denis, while the portal to the left shows the torture of the saint and his fellow missionaries, Rustique and Eleuthere.

Considered the cradle of French Gothic style, the basilica is noteworthy not only as an architectural milestone, but also for its magnificent tombs. The tombs grouped around the transept are a sketchbook in stone of France's monarchs and their families. Among those who were buried here are Clovis, the first King of France, Dagobert, Charles Martel, and Pepin the Short. Elaborate Renaissance structures, many of them created by the sculptor Germain Pilon, represent Catherine de Médici and Henri II, Louis XII and Anne de Bretagne, and most moving of all, Louis XVI and Marie-Antoinette. Most of the tombs now are empty — the royal remains were exhumed during the Revolution and heaped into a nearby communal grave. There are other tombs in the crypt, including the remains housed in the churches that preceded the present one on this site. Regular guided tours of the transept are available (there is a charge). Visitors may also rent headphones with commentary in one of several languages. Information: *St. Denis Tourist Office,* 2 Rue Légion d'Honneur, Paris 93200 (phone: 42-43-33-55).

CONCIERGERIE: This remnant of the Old Royal Palace sits like a fairy-tale castle on an island in the middle of the Seine. Used as a prison during the Revolution, it was here that Marie-Antoinette, the Duke of Orléans, Mme. du Barry, and others of lesser fame awaited the guillotine. For the bicentennial of the French Revolution in 1989, its prisons were restored and "peopled" with mannequins representing former prisoners. Upstairs are the cells — straw in the cells for those who slept on the floor and the *pistole* cells for those of enough influence and power to merit a bed — and sometimes even a desk, chair, and lantern. There are documents and engravings dating from the time of Ravaillac, the 17th-century royal assassin, illustrating the past of this sinister palace. Don't miss Marie-Antoinette's cell, and the Girondins' chapel where the moderate

Girondin deputies shared their last meal. Open daily from 10 AM to 4:30 PM. Admission charge. Information: *Conciergerie,* 1 Quai de l'Horloge, Paris 75001 (phone: 48-87-24-14).

Châteaux Worth Visiting Within an Hour of Paris

CHÂTEAU DE FONTAINEBLEAU, Fontainebleau, Seine-et-Marne: Set in the midst of a verdant forest 39 miles (63 km) south of Paris, Fontainebleau was built, expanded, redecorated, or otherwise touched by all the greats of French royalty. François I transformed it from hunting lodge to palace, Henri IV created its lakes and carp-filled pond, Louis XIII was born here, Louis XV was married here. And Napoleon turned Louis XIV's bedroom into his own throne room, signed his abdication here, and bade farewell to his Old Guard from the great Horseshoe Staircase. The most beautiful sections of the interior are the Gallery of François I and the Ballroom — but Josephine's bedroom and Marie-Antoinette's boudoir are worth a look as well. Open daily except Tuesdays from 9:30 AM to 12:30 PM and from 2 to 5 PM. Information: *Syndicat d'Initiative,* 31 Pl. Napoléon-Bonaparte, Fontainebleau 77300 (phone: 64-22-25-68), or the *Château* (phone: 64-22-27-40).

DOMAINE DE VAUX-LE-VICOMTE, Melun, Seine-et-Marne: On the evening of August 17, 1661, Louis XIV's superintendent of finance, Nicolas Fouquet, proudly welcomed his 23-year-old king to see the new castle on whose construction he had just spent his entire personal fortune. Serenades especially composed by the renowned Lully, a new stage production by Molière, a fabulous five-course banquet, and a fireworks display all heralded the occasion. Three weeks later, the jealous and fearful Louis XIV had Fouquet clapped into jail for life on trumped-up charges and hired his former superintendent's architect, painter, and landscapist to whip him up a pied-à-terre called Versailles. Vaux-le-Vicomte, Fouquet's castle, is today the largest private property in France; its magical, stylized gardens alone cover more than 125 acres. And it is full of lovely fountains, placid pools, sculptured lawns, and fields of flowers that look like giant illuminated medieval manuscripts. The Vaux-aux-Chandelles (Vaux-by-Candlelight) tours show off all of the château's splendors at their most dramatic. The tours take place on Saturdays at 9:30 PM from June through September. Information: *Service Touristique,* Domaine de Vaux-le-Vicomte, Maincy 77950 (phone: 60-66-97-09).

CHÂTEAU DE VERSAILLES, Versailles, Yvelines: In 1682, 2 decades after its founding, the town and castle of Versailles became the French court's new suburban home. Besides a nucleus of a thousand nobles, Louis XIV's retinue consisted of some 9,000 men-at-arms and an equal number of servants. At any given moment between 5,000 and 6,000 people were living here, which only begins to suggest the scale of this royal commune, and seeing it all in one visit is about as relaxing as running the *Boston Marathon.* But before you drop, be sure to squeeze in the cream-and-gold Chapel where the kings said mass, the State Apartments, the fabled Hall of Mirrors, the Royal Suites, and, on the grand green grounds, the Petit Trianon, Marie-Antoinette's rustic small castle. Between May and September, on specified afternoons, the 600 jets of water in the 50-odd fountains and pools in the park outside the palace are all turned on; it's a spectacular sight. Versailles is accessible by public transportation from downtown Paris. Information: *Office du Tourisme,* 7 Rue des Réservoirs, Versailles 78000 (phone: 39-50-36-22).

DIRECTIONS

Introduction

Paris is a city for walkers. With 20 distinct *quartiers,* or *arrondissements,* each revealing a different aspect of Parisian life, the most often described city on earth still manages to defy the clichés it has engendered. Even for those who think they have seen it all, there will always be an unexpected discovery, whether it is one of the less celebrated of the nearly 150 museums that grace the city, a surprising side street off a major thoroughfare, or perhaps one of the hundreds of unassuming — but wonderful — neighborhood cafés.

The mood of the city changes with the seasons. Paris under the slate gray skies of winter, with bare chestnut trees gracing an elegant boulevard is quite different from Paris in the full bloom of spring, when its numerous parks and well-tended gardens burst into glorious color. (Be aware, however, that this riot of blossoms normally comes far later in the season than the creator of "April in Paris" would have you believe.)

From the circuit of famous monuments that loom like stage sets, the grace notes of France's aristocratic past, to the continual joie de vivre of its fluid street life, to the quiet enclaves of an unassuming little café on the Left Bank, one is constantly reminded that beauty is treasured here. Paris is the spectacle of l'Etoile, with its 12 lanes of traffic defying each other in a daily test of wits and will. It is children sailing their miniature boats in the Luxembourg Gardens. On a busy afternoon in the Tuileries, if you squint your eyes, it appears more like an Impressionist painting by Renoir. Paris also is the silent eloquence of its cemeteries, where homage is regularly paid to painters, poets, musicians (including American rock stars), and philosophers.

To explore this grande dame of European capitals, here are eight walks that encompass some of the most interesting and accessible *arrondissements,* each offering a different perspective on the city.

Paris is arranged in a kind of spiral, which was part of Baron Haussmann's brilliant master plan. The visionary architect/city planner was appointed in 1853 by Napoleon III to transform the layout of the city. The result, a uniform classical elegance surrounded by graceful parks and promenades, has gained it the almost uncontested title as the most beautiful city in the world.

These walks visit the 1st *arrondissement,* with the *Louvre* and the Tuileries providing a contrast to the former market district of *Les Halles;* the gentrified Marais district, the former Jewish quarter of the city, in the 3rd *arrondissement;* and the elegant Place des Vosges, *Le Centre Georges-Pompidou,* and the historic Hôtel de Ville in the 4th *arrondissement.* These walks also go through the student center, the botanical gardens, and the 6th *arrondissement* on the Left Bank, as well as Notre-Dame and the city islands, Ile de la Cité and Ile St.-Louis. Visit the historic square at St.-Germain-des-Prés, once the domain of the existentialists, and the beautiful Luxembourg Gardens. Also on the Left Bank, tour the Eiffel Tower area and the adjacent Invalides, where

Napoleon is buried; and nearby on the Right Bank, wander through the elegant 8th *quartier* with its gastronomic palaces like *Maxim's* and well-known monuments such as the Arc de Triomphe and the majestic Place de la Concorde. We go from the diverse Montparnasse area in the south, with its movie houses, cafés, and theater district, to the Pigalle district, long reputed to be Paris's "sin street," and the nearby 18th *arrondissement* in the north, to stand above the city at Sacré-Coeur, in the heart of Montmartre.

Though some of the terrrain will no doubt be familiar to repeat visitors, the point of these walks is to wander and discover detours off the beaten track. The joy and challenge is to use these suggestions as a guide, and to make them a variation on your own theme. Just think of yourself as a painter, with Paris as your palette of inspiration. And enjoy.

Walk 1: Gardens, Bridges, and Islands

At the turn of the century, the most pleasant way to arrive at the Jardin des Plantes (Botanical Gardens) was by steamboat, gliding up the Seine past the *Louvre* and Notre-Dame; these days one must settle for a local bus or the métro to the Gare d'Austerlitz station. The magnificent 46-acre gardens are in the 5th *arrondissement* on Paris's Left Bank, and they border the Latin Quarter and the Seine. Originally founded by Louis XIII in 1626 as a Royal Garden of Medicinal Herbs, they met with such hostility from the medical community that for years the land lay fallow. Later, the gardens were revived and enlarged to include — in addition to medicinal herbs — live animals, minerals, research laboratories, and a library. During the 19th century, the complex grew to include a museum of natural history; today, the vast range of facilities here enjoys a worldwide reputation for teaching and research.

The gardens boast a varied collection of plants and trees from all over the world. There is an alpine garden, an ecological park, and a tropical plant complex, as well as examples of French and English garden landscape design. Some of the oldest trees in Paris can be found here, including a 200-year-old American sequoia, a ginkgo from China, an iron tree from Persia, and a cedar of Lebanon, 40 feet in circumference, that was supposedly brought from Syria as a seedling in 1735. After wandering up the main promenade and the winding paths, visit the *Museum of Natural History,* which includes, among other exhibitions in several buildings around the garden's perimeter, an interesting fossil collection, extensive displays of rare and exotic insects, and a zoo that is open daily (the museum is closed on Tuesdays).

Outside the gardens, near the southwestern corner, is the Mosquée de Paris (Pl. du Puits-de-l'Ermite; phone: 45-35-97-33). The beautiful mosque is dominated by a 130-foot-high minaret in gleaming white marble. Shoes are removed before entering the pebble-lined gardens. The Hall of Prayer has lush Oriental carpets. Next door is a restaurant and patio where you can sit and sip Turkish coffee while tasting Oriental sweets. Open daily except Fridays, from 9:30 AM to noon and 2 to 6 PM..

Walk up Rue de Quatrefages, turn left on Rue de Lacépède, and then right into Rue de Navarre to take a look at one of the city's oldest monuments. The Arènes de Lutèce is the ruins of a Gallo-Roman arena, destroyed in AD 280, and excavated and restored during the 20th century.

Walk back along Rue Lacépède to the Jardin des Plantes. Keeping the gardens to the right, follow Rue Cuvier to the Seine. Cross over to the Quai St.-Bernard. To the left are the Tino Rossi Gardens, with an open-air sculpture museum boasting several impressive works, including Zadkine's *Develop-*

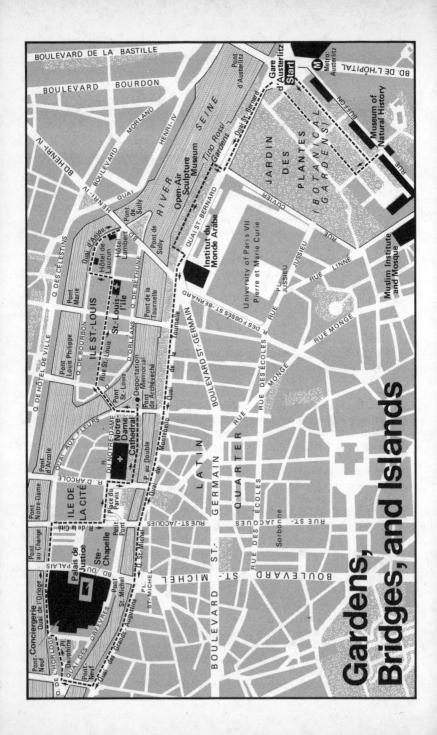

Gardens, Bridges, and Islands

BOULEVARD DE LA BASTILLE

BOULEVARD BOURDON

BD. HENRI-IV

BOULEVARD MORLAND

HENRI-IV

SEINE RIVER

Pont d'Austerlitz

Gare d'Austerlitz

Start

Metro: Austerlitz

BD. DE L'HÔPITAL

BUFFON

Museum of Natural History

Quai St-Bernard

JARDIN DES PLANTES (BOTANICAL GARDENS)

Tino Rossi Gardens

Open-Air Sculpture Museum

CUVIER

RUE

Q. DES CÉLESTINS

Pont de Sully

Pont Marie

Quai d'Anjou

Hôtel de Lauzun

Hôtel Lambert

Q. DE BÉTHUNE

Pont de Sully

QUAI ST-BERNARD

Institut du Monde Arabe

University of Paris VII
Pierre et Marie Curie

RUE LINNÉ

RUE JUSSIEU

JUSSIEU

PL. JUSSIEU

Muslim Institute and Mosque

QUAI HENRI-IV

Q. DE BOURBON

ÎLE ST.-LOUIS

St.-Louis-l'île

Rue St-Louis

D'ORLÉANS

Pont de la Tournelle

Quai de la Tournelle

DES FOSSÉS ST.-BERNARD

RUE MONGE

RUE LINNÉ

Q. DE L'HÔTEL DE VILLE

Pont Louis Philippe

Pont St.-Louis

ÎLE DE LA CITÉ

Rue de la Cité

Deportation Memorial

Pont de l'Archevêché

Notre-Dame Cathedral

Quai de Montebello

Quai de la Tournelle

BOULEVARD ST-GERMAIN

RUE DES ÉCOLES

RUE MONGE

Pont d'Arcole

QUAI AUX FLEURS

R. D'ARCOLE

R. DU NOTRE-DAME

Place du Parvis

P. au Double

P. de Montebello

LATIN

RUE DES ÉCOLES

RUE MONGE

Pont Notre-Dame

ÎLE DE LA CITÉ

Petit Pont

Pont au Change

Pont St.-Michel

Ste.-Chapelle

Palais de Justice

Bd. DU PALAIS

BD. ST-MICHEL

PL. ST-MICHEL

RUE ST-JACQUES

RUE ST-JACQUES

GERMAIN

QUARTER

Sorbonne

RUE DES ÉCOLES

Conciergerie

Quai de l'Horloge

Pont Neuf

Pont au Change

Q. DE L'HORLOGE

PL. DAUPHINE

Quai des Grands-Augustins

Quai des Orfèvres

Q. DES ORFÈVRES

BOULEVARD ST.-MICHEL

BOULEVARD ST.-GERMAIN

RUE ST-JACQUES

Gardens, Bridges, and Islands

ment of Form. Parisians come here to stroll and to walk their dogs; students from the university (across the boulevard) come to relax between lectures. From here one can also enjoy a spectacular view of the Ile St.-Louis, one of two important islands in the middle of Paris (see below). For now, just take a seat on one of the benches and watch the barges floating by and the light shifting over the bridges.

Continue along the path bordering the quay and walk toward Notre-Dame; then go up the ramp and turn right to the Quai de la Tournelle. The tall, modern glass-and-aluminum building on the left is the *Institut du Monde Arabe* (Institute of the Arab World), which houses a museum, a library, a cultural center, and a rooftop café (offering excellent cappuccino) — and splendid city views. The institute was created by France and 20 Arab countries as a cultural exchange, and a means of providing more cooperation with and a better understanding of Arab culture. The building itself is a good example of Paris's modern architecture. Designed by architect Jean Nouvel, it has a spectacular façade of 240 light-sensitive geometric panels that automatically filter the light of the sun. Across the street is *La Tour d'Argent* (15 Quai de la Tournelle; phone: 43-54-23-31), definitely Paris's second-best-known restaurant (after *Maxim's*). Duckling is still a specialty here, and the quality of the food has improved once again after a period of inconsistency. Lunch may be a better idea than dinner, since it is less crowded — and less expensive. There is a vaulted underground wine cellar, and a small museum (where one can buy the restaurant's famous blue and white plates), open to restaurant patrons (see *Eating Out* in THE CITY).

Continue along the riverside quays, whose names change at practically every intersection. (for example, Quai de Montebello becomes Quai St.-Michel, and so on). In all, there are more than 40 quays that run for several miles alongside the Seine. Many date from the Middle Ages, when boats were the quickest, safest, and most efficient way to bring goods into the city. The quays were divided into separate docking areas for wine, coal, grain, and other items. Nowadays, some 30 bridges cross the Seine, while numerous métro tunnels go under the river.

While walking along the Seine, with Notre-Dame on the right, take a look at some of the green, boxlike bookstalls that line both sides of the river. These *bouquinistes* (booksellers) are a Paris institution, but while there were probably some real bargains here a few decades ago, these days be happy to find new postcards that sell for only 1 franc each, or some vintage versions in pastel tints for a bit more. The books are rather pricey, but this is still an interesting stop. The stalls have no fixed hours, so you may find shops that seem closed or look deserted; probably the owner has just walked next door to have a coffee with a colleague.

Walk farther along the Left Bank past the hubbub of the Place St.-Michel intersection, with its raucous mix of milling students from the nearby Sorbonne, bustling bookstores, sidewalk cafés, and Middle Eastern snack bars that constitute Paris's Latin Quarter. A stop into 5 Place St. Michel, a branch of a *Gibert Jeune* bookshop, may yield, among other things, some interesting cookbooks. Continuing along the Seine on the Quai des Grands-Augustins, turn right at the next bridge, the Pont-Neuf, said to be the oldest span in Paris.

Dating from 1578, its construction began during the reign of Henri III, was completed by Henri IV, and was further immortalized several years ago when the artist Christo had it wrapped up in a saffron-colored cloth for a few weeks. Before the Revolution, the Pont-Neuf was the greatest thoroughfare in Paris, attracting beggars, vaudeville acts, medicine shows, and other assorted entertainments. Here one could do almost anything — from having a tooth extracted to getting a poodle trimmed. It was almost certain that if you were looking for somebody, native or foreign, you would surely run across him or her here.

The Pont-Neuf intersects the Ile de la Cité on the right. This island in the middle of Paris is a major historic site, with the Palais de Justice (law courts), Sainte-Chapelle, the Conciergerie (the former prison, today the police headquarters), and the magnificent Notre-Dame cathedral located here. Stroll through the Place Dauphine, just ahead as you turn right off Pont-Neuf. Dating from 1607, this charming square was named after Louis XIII when he was the dauphin. It was one of Henri IV's three urbanization projects; there is a splendid statue of the very popular king on the Pont-Neuf, overlooking the Seine. The original statue was erected by his widow, Marie de Médici, but was melted down during the Revolution and converted into cannon. By way of retaliation, Louis XVIII ordered a statue of Napoleon and one of General Desaix to be melted down in order to provide material for the new statue of the king. But the sculptor commissioned by Louis XVIII, an ardent follower of Bonaparte, had the last laugh: He stashed a small statuette of Napoleon and various written articles favoring the emperor inside his finished sculpture.

Make a note to have a meal at *Paul* (15 Pl. Dauphine; phone: 43-54-21-48), on the far end of the Place Dauphine, an unassuming restaurant with family-style seating and service by friendly and efficient waitresses. Start with a dozen escargots in garlic and oil, which come with a basket of fresh bread, and try the roast duck with cherries and roasted apples. Reservations are advised. Just across the way is *Fanny Tea* (20 Pl. Dauphine; phone: 43-25-83-67), as intimate and cozy as your grandmother's parlor, but with definite Gallic touches. It is the perfect place to have a pot of tea and one (or several) of their warm apple tarts. An ideal escape on a rainy day or a spot to recharge one's batteries.

Henri IV (25 Pl. Dauphine; phone: 43-54-44-53) is still one of Paris's most popular inexpensive and no-frills hotels, more for the student or the eternal bohemian. To give you some idea of how many students and/or eternal bohemians there are in the world today, it is necessary to book a room here at least 3 months in advance!

Head east from the Place Dauphine and walk around the Conciergerie, the former prison (now police headquarters) that housed Marie-Antoinette and many others before they were taken to the guillotine.

The entrance to the Palais de Justice is around the corner, on the Boulevard du Palais. Now the law courts, it was the first seat of the Roman military government, then the headquarters of the early French kings. Inside one of its courtyards, to the left after entering, is one of the jewels of Paris, the 13th-century Sainte-Chapelle of King Louis IX (St.-Louis). The chapel, built to house the Sacred Crown of Thorns and other holy relics (many of which now are in Notre-Dame), has 15 splendid stained glass windows — with practically no walls in between — and a rose window, all under a 247-foot spire. Sainte-Chapelle is especially impressive in sunny weather.

Farther east on the island, cross the Rue de la Cité to reach Notre-Dame, the magnificent cathedral (begun in 1163) that has become (to the world's imagination), the quintessence of Gothic architecture. Its steeple rises 285 feet above the ground, and the entire structure is supported by a series of flying buttresses that were, at the time of their construction, considered an architectural marvel. Note the exquisite stained glass windows, the 37 chapels, the archaeological crypt, and the organ, which dates from 1730. It was here that Napoleon was crowned, and where Victor Hugo's famous hunchback lived.

The views from the church's tower, reached by climbing 397 steps, are still the finest in the city; a popular tourist spot, they rarely offer any solitude. Its great bell, the 16-ton Bourdon of Notre-Dame, is one of the largest in existence — though not quite as large as the one at Sacré-Coeur. After viewing the church, walk through the park on the riverfront to the easternmost tip of the island. Cross the street to the Square de l'Ile de France to the Mémorial de la Déportation. The entrance to this unusual installation is below street level and is easy to miss because of the dozens of Notre-Dame tour buses parked outside. Worth seeking out, the memorial is a moving tribute to the 200,000 French citizens who were exterminated in concentration camps during World War II. Sometimes there is a survivor of one of the camps who unofficially acts as a volunteer guide, giving a short tour in several languages. Though he does not demand a fee, it is customary to give him a few francs.

Retrace your steps toward Notre-Dame and cross Pont St.-Louis to the neighboring Ile St.-Louis. Until the beginning of Louis XIII's reign, this island was still uninhabited pastureland and was composed of two islets: a small one called Ile aux Vaches (Isle of Cows) and a larger one, known as Ile de Notre-Dame. In an ambitious engineering project — begun in 1614 and completed in 1664 — the isles were joined, equipped with streets, and surrounded with stone quays. Described by Anatole France almost a century ago as "a pleasantly quiet and elegant backwater of Paris life," these days it is considered a desirable (albeit exclusive) place to dwell, accessible to the heart of the city, yet apart from it. Still quaint and serene, it is a fine place to ramble. In addition to its classic 17th-century architecture, it offers several refreshing views of Paris. A special bonus is an ice cream at *Berthillon* (31 Rue St.-Louis-en-l'Ile), pricey but worthy of its reputation as the best in the city, if not the world. Flavors change with the season, but the plum armagnac and espresso, chocolate and orange, and cassis sorbet are highly recommended. During the summer, there always is a line stretching around the corner. Since it is closed during August, as well as on Mondays, Tuesdays, and school holidays, a more dependable place to get your Berthillon fix might be *Le Flore en l'Ile,* a tea house/café at the foot of the Pont St.-Louis (42 Quai d'Orleans). Enjoy the cozy ambience inside, or buy a cone from the outdoor vendor and enjoy it while taking a leisurely stroll around the island.

The island is small enough to walk in its entirety from quay to quay, and offers a relaxing place to sit by the riverside, write a postcard alongside a fisherman hauling in his catch, or sip a coffee with businesspeople reading *Le Figaro* during their lunch hour. Rue St.-Louis-en-l'Ile is the main street, which runs down the middle of the island and is the site of several small hotels, restaurants, and quaint shops. Seasoned travelers will enjoy the *Ulysse* bookstore (No. 26), which specializes in travel books, with an extensive inventory of both new and used books. Owner Catherine Domain speaks English and is very helpful in providing information. At No. 21 is the Eglise St.-Louis-en-l'Ile, built between 1664 and 1726, and distinguished by its unusual iron clock. The ornate interior is in the 17th-century Grand Siècle style, adorned with wood, gilt, and marble (closed Sunday afternoons and Mondays). The political caricaturist Honoré Daumier lived at No. 9 for a time. Along the Quai d'Anjou on the north side of the island are several old mansions of note: No. 17, for example, is home to the Hôtel de Lauzun, built in 1657. Its typical, austere 17th-century façade belies the excessiveness of its interior, with its cut-velvet walls, golden nymphs, and elaborate ceilings. Its original owner was an army caterer, but during the 1800s, many poets and writers lived here, among them Baudelaire, Rilke, and Théophile Gautier. Today, it is used by the city of Paris for official receptions. No. 7 is still the site of the Pastry and Bakery Syndicate, founded in 1801.

The walk concludes outside the Hôtel Lambert (2 Rue St.-Louis-en-l'Ile) at the corner, near the Pont de Sully. It was built in 1640 by Le Vau, principal architect to Louis XIV, who also did the early work on the Eglise St.-Louis and many of the other buildings on the island. No expense was spared in creating this magnificent home for Nicholas Lambert de Thorigny, who was known as Lambert the Rich. In 1742, Voltaire completed his *Henriade* while visiting here; during the next couple of centuries it became a girls' school, and later a depot for military stores, before returning again to private ownership.

Walk 2: Montmartre

Until it officially became part of the city of Paris at the turn of the century, Montmartre, in the 18th *arrondissement,* was a secluded, picturesque village, with no more than 1,000 inhabitants living on the tree-lined Butte, amidst a charming landscape of windmills, vineyards, and pleasant country houses. Construction of the Basilique du Sacré-Coeur — which began in 1875 — heralded a brighter future after the devastating defeat in the Franco-Prussian War of 1870–71, and gave the remote village new prominence. Ironically, the church wasn't completed until 1910 and wasn't consecrated until 1919, following World War I.

Located on the site of the ancient abbey of Montmartre, the enormous, grandiose structure is visible for many miles around Paris. While some marvel at its beauty, there are many who think its Roman-Byzantine–influenced design is definitely mediocre from an architectural point of view; some critics have gone so far as to describe it as a giant salt or pepper shaker.

It was built at a cost of about 36 million francs (not at the value of today's franc!), pretty expensive considering the relatively lower 6-million-franc price tag for the Eiffel Tower; monies were raised mostly by subscriptions and government subsidy. The foundations for Sacré-Coeur alone cost 3½ million francs, since the 83 masonry columns that support the structure had to be sunk over 100 feet into the soft soil of the Butte to bear their weight. The foundations are so strong that it has been said that even if the hill were taken away, the church would remain intact. The 19-ton Sacré-Coeur bells, said to be the heaviest in the world, can be heard at least 20 miles away.

During the 19th century, Parisians came to Montmartre to wander at leisure through the steep footpaths along the Butte. These days, crowds of tourists from all over the world make that same trek, trying to recapture a glimpse of "Gay Paree." For those who can't manage the climb, there is a funicular railway at the bottom of the hill. Or take the "tourist train" that weaves up through the surrounding streets, passing other points of interest as well.

It has been said that the name Montmartre is derived from "Mon Mars," the name of the temple dedicated to the god of war. Other historians argue that it was named for another temple dedicated to Mercury. Just as battles rage over Montmartre's history, it seems fitting that this naturally fortified area has been a refuge for armies battling Paris's attackers over the centuries.

During the mid-1800s, Montmartre was home to many aspiring artists; they chose the area partly because of its good light and, more importantly, its inexpensive lodgings. Braque, Van Gogh, Renoir, Toulouse-Lautrec, and Utrillo all made their homes here at one time; in fact, many of their paintings of street scenes were inspired by this neighborhood. Following World War II, the erection of many taller, modern buildings caused Montmartre to lose

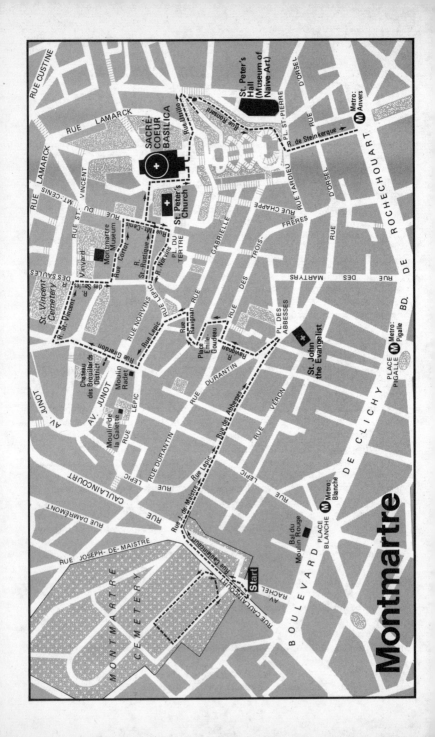

Montmartre

RUE CUSTINE

RUE LAMARCK

RUE LAMARCK

SACRÉ COEUR BASILICA

Rue Utrillo

Rue Ronsard

St. Peter's Hall (Museum of Naive Art)

PL. ST-PIERRE

RUE D'ORSEL

RUE D'ORSEL

R. de Steinkerque

Ⓜ Metro: Anvers

BD. DE ROCHECHOUART

RUE MT-CENIS

RUE ST-VINCENT

RUE ST-VINCENT

DES SAULES

St. Vincent Cemetery

Vinyard

Montmartre Museum

Rue Cortot

R. St-Rustique

RUE DU Mont-Cenis

RUE Norvins

St. Peter's Church

PL. DU TERTRE

RUE GABRIELLE

RUE CHAPPE

RUE TARDIEU

RUE DES TROIS-FRERES

RUE DES MARTYRS

RUE des Saules

Rue Girardin

Château des Brouillards District

Moulin Radet

AV. JUNOT

AV. JUNOT

RUE NORVINS

RUE LEPIC

Rue Ravignan

Place Emile Goudeau

Rue Ravignan

RUE DES

RUE

PL. DES ABBESSES

St. John the Evangelist

Ⓜ Metro: Pigalle

PLACE PIGALLE

PLACE PIGALLE

Moulin de la Galette

RUE LEPIC

RUE LEPIC

RUE DURANTIN

RUE DURANTIN

RUE VÉRON

RUE DES Abbesses

RUE LEPIC

Ⓜ Metro: Blanche

BOULEVARD DE CLICHY

AV. JUNOT

RUE CAULAINCOURT

RUE

RUE LEPIC

Rue t. de Maistre

Rue Caulaincourt

Bal du Moulin Rouge

PLACE BLANCHE

RUE JOSEPH- DE- MAISTRE

RUE DAMREMONT

MONTMARTRE CEMETERY

RUE CAULAINCOURT

AV. RACHEL

Start

BOULEVARD

its sleepy village quality. Once known for its charming windmills, sadly, only two or three of the original ones remain. And although the area's famous nightclub, *Le Moulin Rouge,* is designed as a windmill, it never actually was one.

The "real" surviving windmills have their own unique historical anecdotes. In 1833, the Moulin de la Galette was the place villagers came to get fresh cow's milk and tasty rolls. Père Debray, the proprietor, was also fond of dancing and began selling dance lessons to his customers in addition to bread and milk. Supposedly, this is how the dance hall of the Moulin de la Galette came into being. Over the next 20 years it became quite the nightspot, doubling in size; and since its popularity inspired the opening of other dance halls and clubs, many agree that the toe-tapping M. Galette should be credited with making Montmartre the center of nightlife in Paris.

This walk begins in the southwest corner of the *arrondissement* at the Cimetière Montmartre (Montmartre Cemetery), which dates from the 17th century, when it served as the parish cemetery. Although smaller than the Père Lachaise and Montparnasse cemeteries, it is the final resting place for many illustrious people, and is equally rich in monuments and statuary. Among those who were buried here are Emile Zola (whose remains were later transferred to the Panthéon in 1908), Edgar Degas, Vaslav Nijinsky, François Truffaut, Heinrich Heine, and Hector Berlioz. (The composer has the distinct advantage of being buried between his first and second wives. He arranged this by having one wife exhumed from a prior burial place and taken to Montmartre to wait for him.)

One enters the grounds by passing under a busy, low-hanging overpass. Until 1888, the cemetery blocked direct access into Paris, necessitating the construction of a bridge that would link the Boulevard de Clichy with Rue Caulaincourt. Unfortunately, the span was built directly over some of the older monuments, barely grazing their tops.

Up a few steps at the Carrefour du Croix, a tall column marks the burial spot of the victims of the coup d'état of 1851. There are several tombs of interest: The red granite tomb of Zola has a bust by Solari; nearby, the tomb of Castagnary features a fine bust by Rodin. Turn around and walk under the bridge and up the stairs; turn left to find the grave of Dalida, the popular French singer of the 1960s, who shocked her fans by taking poison. Fresh bouquets are still left here year-round, and on the right, just before reaching her grave, there is an unusual statue. The property of Dr. Guy Pitchal, Dalida's psychiatrist, it is a headless bust holding a pipe, with a lifelike death mask behind it that appears to follow you as you pass it.

Walk out the main entrance again, up the steps to the right and cross the bridge. Look for the *Terrasse* hotel and turn right on Rue Joseph-de-Maistre. Walk down this street toward the busy Rue Lepic, a good venue for observing typical Parisian lifestyle. Continue on the first street until it leads into the Rue des Abbesses and the Place des Abbesses. On the right is St. John the Evangelist, a distinctive brick church built in 1904. It is the first church in Paris to be built with reinforced concrete, a forerunner of the modern style of architecture now represented in many of the city's newer buildings. En route, take a break at one of the *pâtisserie*/tearooms, or buy a slice of quiche to eat along the the way. From the Place des Abbesses, walk up the steep Rue Ravignan, an ancient street that was once part of the only road that led from Paris to the abbey above. A few steps from here is the Place Emile-Goudeau, site of the Bateau-Lavoir, the famous artists colony where Picasso, Braque, and other "modern" artists painted in adjoining studios. These simple, wooden dwellings later earned the moniker "Villa Medici of Modern Art." After Picasso and his group moved on, the equally impressive Ruche ("beehive") took root, with such fledgling artists as Léger, Modigliani, and Soutine seeking inexpensive studios in which to live and work. Unfortunately, these famous shanties burned down in 1970, but many were rebuilt (at No. 13) as artists' studios and apartments. Even for those not artistically inclined, this is a good place to pause and watch the Parisian street scene. The *Tim* hotel (on the square at 11 Rue Ravignan; phone: 42-55-74-79) is a good local base if one wants to stay in Montmartre. When leaving the square, turn right at Rue Garreau, and turn right again into the upper end of Rue Lepic. At the top of a small incline is a view of one of the area's surviving windmills, the Moulin de la Galette, which has topped the Butte for more than 6 centuries (it is no longer accessible to the public). Walk to the corner of Rue Girardon to the *Moulin Radet,* another survivor, now an Italian restaurant. Turn left, following Rue Girardon to a descending stairway; do not take the steps, but turn right to Rue St.-Vincent, where, enclosed by high walls, is the cemetery of the same name. At the crossing of Rue des Saules and Rue St.-Vincent is *Au Lapin Agile* (phone: 46-06-85-87; closed Mondays). Formerly an inn where crowds assembled at the turn of the century to hear local poets read their own works, and later frequented by Picasso and other painters of the time, it remains a popular cabaret attracting an international crowd who love a good French sing-along. Originally called the *Cabaret des Assassins,* it takes its present name from the artist A. Gill, who painted a rabbit on a signboard advertising "poemes et chansons." The name stuck.

Across the street is a modest vineyard, owned by the community and still in use today. It is here that a festive grape harvest takes place on the first Saturday in October. About 500 bottles of a red wine (Clos Montmartre) that makes no pretense of being exceptional are produced here. During the festival, the wine is sold at a special fund-raising auction at the Town Hall (1 Pl. Jules-Joffrin) for about 150 francs per bottle.

Turn south on Rue des Saules to Rue Cortot and turn left to find the *Musée Montmartre* (12 Rue Cortot; phone: 46-06-61-11). This simple, rustic-looking building, dating from the 17th century, houses a rich collection of paintings, drawings, and documents, depicting life in the quarter (open Mondays through Saturdays from 2:30 to 6 PM; Sundays from 11 AM to 6 PM). At No. 6 is the house where the composer Erik Satie lived. An enjoyable detour with some interesting examples of architecture is the Château des Brouillards neighborhood around to the left off Rue Girardon, home to many French celebrities. At the end of Rue Cortot, look to the left down the descending walkway for a magnificent view of the northern suburbs of Paris. Turn right at the steps and go to Place du Tertre, which unfortunately has become a tourist trap; crowded with souvenir market stalls, it is all but impossible to really appreciate the charming 18th-century houses surrounding the square.

While art is a tradition in this area, the plethora of portrait artists who hawk their wares here have become a matter of controversy, as the government is now deciding whether to regulate the number of licenses issued.

And speaking of tourist traps, be sure to check the prices at the local cafés carefully; many of them take advantage of visitors. Off to the left of Place du Tertre is the narrow and often deserted Rue St.-Rustique, a good place for a leisurely stroll before encountering the crowds at Sacré-Coeur. Note l'Eglise St.-Pierre (St. Peter's Church) on the left. One of the oldest churches in Paris, it was founded by Louis VI in 1134, and completed during that century. It has been added to, rebuilt, and revived so many times since then that there is a real contrast in architectural styles — though a few sections of its original Gothic roots remain. It is interesting to note the sharp contrast of this simple church with the massive scale of Sacré-Coeur. Just to the back of St.-Pierre, on the site of the ancient cemetery, is the Jardin du Calvaire (Calvary Garden), which is no longer open to the public. For a magnificent view of the city (especially on a clear day), bear left and walk a short distance toward the Sacré-Coeur terrace. Unfortunately, the vendors who clog the steps of Sacré-Coeur often obstruct the view of Paris.

At Sacré-Coeur, it is still possible to make the very steep ascent into the dome for a view that is about equal to that from the top level of the Eiffel Tower. A stroll through the vast interior of this famous church, with its capacity of 8,000, is a must experience.

When leaving Sacré-Coeur's grounds, avoid the busy stairs directly in front and go instead via the scenic Rue Maurice-Utrillo to the left. (If a break from the crowds is in order at this point of the tour, turn right for a stroll through the church's terraced gardens.) At the bottom of the steps, turn right and head for the Rue de Steinkerque area, the heart of Paris's fabric district, recognizable by the abundance of yard goods and trimmings supply stores, and the crowds of needle-and-thread aficionados. While walking south along Rue de Steinkerque, to the right notice St.-Pierre Halle (St. Peter's Hall), a fine 19th-century iron structure that houses a children's museum (*Musée en Herbe*) on the ground floor and the *Museum of Naïve Art* on the first floor. Turn right to the Montmartre carousel; then proceed farther down Rue de Steinkerque to Boulevard de Rochechouart, a wide shopping street with a large métro station to the left, where it seems all of the immigrant population of Paris comes to buy clothes at bargain prices, mostly at the stretch of *Tati* shops (a chain of clothing boutiques).

It is important to realize that there is an upper Montmartre and a lower Montmartre, and nothing depicts lower Montmartre better than Place Pigalle, with its dubious strip of entertainment spots lining the edge of Boulevard de Clichy, the western continuation of Boulevard de Rochechouart. If planning a visit here, remember that Place Pigalle comes to life only at night. The American author Henry Miller immortalized it in several of his books during the late 1930s and early 1940s. But it first earned its image as "sin street" with the first burlesque cabaret, *Chat Noir,* founded in 1884. These days, Boulevard de Clichy and its tacky neon surroundings have become more of a cliché.

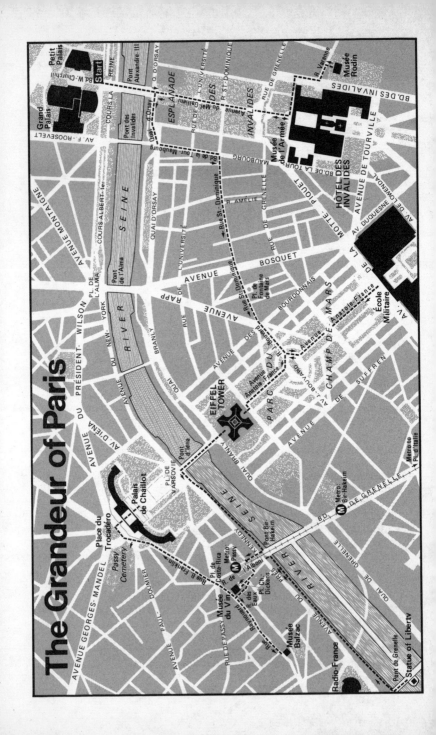

Walk 3: The Grandeur of Paris

This walk begins just off the Avenue des Champs-Elysées, on Avenue Winston-Churchill, site of the *Petit Palais* and the *Grand Palais*. The *Grand Palais*, a magnificent building with an Ionic colonnade, mosaic frieze, and three porches conceived and built from the designs of three different architects, has long been used for a variety of annual industrial exhibitions and shows, and is now a cultural center where such temporary exhibitions as the *Paris Book Fair* are held. The back of the *Grand Palais* is the science museum and planetarium, called the *Palais de la Découverte* (Av. Franklin-D.-Roosevelt).

The *Musée du Petit Palais*, now a museum of fine arts, is architecturally distinguished by an ornamental flat glass dome. The Grand and Petit palaces were built for the *1900 Paris International Exposition*, replacing the former Palais de l'Industrie.

Walk to the Seine and across the Pont Alexandre-III, which was built at the same time as the palaces. This single-span bridge, with its numerous gilded statues, is a fine example of popular 19th-century steel architecture and ornate style. Walk down the busy Avenue du Maréchal-Galliéni along the vast tree-lined Esplanade toward the Hôtel des Invalides. The Hôtel des Invalides was founded by Louis XIV in the 1670s as an asylum for wounded and aged soldiers; initially intended to house 4,000, it more often was a refuge for twice that number. The classically balanced buildings were designed by Libéral Bruant. The royal church (Eglise du Dôme), constructed from 1675 to 1706, is topped by an elaborate golden dome designed by Mansart and built between 1843 and 1861. This houses the tomb of Emperor Napoleon I. The monument is surrounded by 12 huge white marble statues, interspersed with 54 flags, each symbolizing another of Napoleon's victories. The church has an impressive courtyard, and frescoes that are worthy of note. If time allows, stop at the *Musée de l'Armée* (Army Museum), which houses one of the world's richest collections of military artifacts and memorabilia. If your interests are more aesthetic, visit the *Musée Rodin* (see *Special Places* in THE CITY), just east of it, across the Boulevard des Invalides. Then retrace your steps, proceeding ahead along the rather noisy Esplanade, past the Quai d'Orsay, heading west to the quieter environs of Boulevard de La Tour–Maubourg (named for the original Governor of the Invalides). For a typical Parisian Sunday lunch, make a note to return to *Chez les Anges* (54 Bd. de La Tour–Maubourg; phone: 70-58-98-86). The food served in this large convivial room is simple, typical French fare. Try a thick slice of grilled calf's liver or the filet of turbot with fennel.

Continue along the boulevard, walking back away from the Seine, and turn right at Rue St.-Dominique, with its lineup of cafés, greengrocers, wine shops, *patisseries, boucheries,* and *boulangeries.* Neighborhood folk casually go about their business, more often than not ignoring the fact that the magnificent Eiffel Tower is right in their own backyard. If you're ready to rest and sample some Parisian sweets, stop at *La Cour du Sable* (111 Rue St.-Dominique). It is an exceptional *pâtisserie,* where one should indulge in a tart of fresh orange slices (*tarte à la orange*) or the simple cheese tart (*tarte du fromage*). Continue on Rue St.-Dominique — the neighborhood shifts from a French ambience to an Italian one, as you pass the heavy-arched Place des Fontaine de Mars with its adjacent fountain. There is a choice of two restaurants at which to lunch, depending on your mood — and the availability of a table. The small (only four tables) *L'Auverge Normande* (No. 127) specializes in *produits du terroir,* or rural cuisine. Next door, *La Fontaine de Mars* (No. 129) is a family bistro that serves Provençal cooking in a friendly atmosphere. The simple and tasty dishes include grilled sardines, fresh foie gras, a changing plat du jour, and a delicious ice cream dessert with chocolate sauce and meringue.

Cross the busy intersection of Avenue de la Bourdonnais and Place du Général-Gouraud and walk ahead to Avenue Joseph-Bouvard, which leads directly to the extensive grounds of the Champ-de-Mars. In 1793 a guillotine was erected at its northeast corner. A good way to soak up some of the history of this area is to visit l'Ecole Militaire (the French Military Academy), the impressive complex to the left. Originally built to accommodate 500 soldiers-to-be, it has been through many transitions over the centuries — alternatively used as a barracks, then headquarters of the Imperial Guard, and back to a training school once again. It is one of the best examples of 18th-century French architecture, with its distinct 2-story Corinthian columns and handsome gilded dome. Not long after it opened in 1752, Napoleon I was among its many students.

The Champ-de-Mars was the scene of a battle in 888 between the Parisians and the Normans, who were ultimately defeated. From 1770 to 1900, the area was the place for both military reviews and the great *Paris International Expositions* of 1867, 1878, 1889, and 1900. In 1908, it was transformed into a park in order to be more in keeping with the high class residences that were built in the surrounding neighborhood.

Although all of those international exhibitions were significant, it was perhaps the 1889 exhibition that was most memorable, as it commemorated the centenary of the 1789 French Revolution. The newly erected Eiffel Tower was unveiled as a monument to that event. During the exhibition period, more than 25 million people visited the unusual tower, which at 984 feet was (until the construction of the 1,284-foot-high Empire State Building in New York City in 1930) the tallest structure in the world. Controversial and despised by many, it was nearly torn down in 1909 when its first 20-year lease expired, only to be saved when the invention of the wireless gave it a new lease on life — as a radio transmitter. Beneath the tower's north pillar is a statue by Antoine Bourdelle of Alexandre-Gustave Eiffel, its architect and engineer.

Having ceremoniously celebrated its 100th anniversary in 1989, the Eiffel

Tower continues to make its glorious presence known at the northwestern end of the Champ-de-Mars, facing the Palais de Chaillot on the opposite bank of the Seine. Be sure to view the tower from as many perspectives as possible. Walk down the middle of the Champ-de-Mars, with its tree-lined paths and children's park; from there note the graceful lines and impressive craftsmanship of Eiffel's work, even more fascinating as one climbs the stairs to the second level to take an elevator to the top. On an exceptionally clear day, it is possible to see for about 50 miles. There are three restaurants within the tower, but the *Jules Verne* (open daily for lunch and dinner; phone: 45-55-61-44) is the one that we recommend, though it requires a month or two advance reservation and is expensive.

After leaving the tower, walk across the Pont d'Iéna facing it, which leads to the Place du Trocadéro and the Palais de Chaillot (both of which can be visited at the end of this walk). After crossing the bridge, don't take the easy route straight ahead, but turn left and walk along the footpath bordering the Seine, avoiding the noise and traffic of the upper level of the Avenue du Président-Kennedy. This route offers yet another view of the Eiffel Tower, as well as a skyline of the high-rise buildings to the west in a tableau that looks something like Paris confronting Manhattan. This unlikely homage to America continues farther along the walk at the Pont de Grenelle, site of a bronze replica of Bartholdi's *Statue of Liberty* (the original was presented to the United States as a gesture of friendship). However, a better view of the lady with the torch can be enjoyed from the Seine, on one of the excursion boats (*bateaux-mouches*) that ply the river day and night.

The walk along the river ends back at Pont de Bir-Hakeim, where there is a pedestrian tunnel and another bridge across noisy Avenue du Président-Kennedy leading to Rue de l'Alboni.

Follow the signs up Rue de l'Alboni to Rue des Eaux at Square Charles-Dickens to the *Musée Du Vin* (Wine Museum; 5-7 Sq. Charles-Dickens; phone: 45-25-63-26). Located in the cellar of the former Abbey of Passy, which was built during the second half of the 14th century by St. Francis of Paule, the museum couldn't be better situated. During that time, many of the hills around Paris were found to be covered with vineyards and several, operated by local monks, produced some very good wine. Between 1650 and 1720, mineral water sources were discovered here, which explains the name Rue des Eaux (Street of Waters). Passy became a very famous thermal site and was visited by such luminaries as Benjamin Franklin and Jean-Jacques Rousseau. The abbey was destroyed after the Revolution, but during the 1960s the foundations were rediscovered by a Parisian restaurateur, who transformed the space into wine cellars in order to supply the restaurants of the Eiffel Tower. The museum, which opened in 1981, now hosts the wine brotherhood (Conseil des Echansons de France), an order dedicated to the promotion of high-quality French wines.

Within its cave-like environment, the museum displays interesting scenes depicting the history of wine — from harvesting to bottling — as well as examples of vintage pressing equipment, casks, corkscrews, and labels, that give the visitor a good overview of oenology. One can also buy wines, champagnes, and spirits at prices lower than those at many of the wine shops, or visit the tasting room to enjoy a simple lunch served with a selection of wines by the glass or bottle. (A free glass of wine is included in the admission price.) Private parties, complete with traditional wine tasting ceremonies, can also be arranged. Even for those familiar with Paris, a visit to this museum is a unique experience. Open daily from noon to 6 PM.

For an interesting detour, take a round trip from the Passy métro stop to the Pasteur métro stop (toward Nation). This is one of the city's most scenic rides, beginning in "Le Seizième" (the 16th *arrondissement*), one of Paris's richest, most elegant neighborhoods. The main part of the ride goes above-ground for several stops, crossing over the Seine and affording a great view of the Eiffel Tower. The ride along the Boulevards de Grenelle and Garibaldi at second-story level provides a refreshing perspective of Parisian life. To get to the Passy métro after leaving the *Wine Museum,* go back down Rue de l'Alboni to the first corner and turn left.

Those who decide against the métro excursion should walk up Rue de l'Alboni to Place de Costa-Rica, and make a left onto Rue Raynouard to the *Maison de Balzac* (No. 47). The plain exterior of his house belies the flamboyant excesses of its renowned inhabitant; the treasures in art and antiques he once accumulated are no longer to be found, as they were sacrificed to creditors during his colorful life. However, this unassuming house is a testament to his hard work, evidenced by the manuscripts and memorabilia on display in the museum-library (closed Mondays and holidays).

As you ramble around this well-tended neighborhood, complete with discreet doormen and private roads, remember that the Passy quarter is the city home to Paris's wealthy class. For a change of scene, walk back past the Place de Costa-Rica and up Rue Benjamin Franklin (he was the US Ambassador to France from 1776 to 1785); note the *Café Franklin* on the corner. On the left above Place du Trocadéro is the terraced Cimetière de Passy, enclosed by high walls. Among the prominent people buried here are artists Edouard Manet and Berthe Morisot, composers Debussy and Fauré, and the actor Fernandel. Proceed to the large open space of Trocadéro to fully appreciate still another view of the Eiffel Tower and the Left Bank, as well as the elegance of the stunning, white-stone Palais de Chaillot. Its dazzling twin pavilions and sweeping horizontal lines contrast nicely with the verticality of the Eiffel Tower. Housed in the palace complex are the national theater, the *Cinémathèque,* and several museums: the *Museum of French Monuments,* the *Museum of Man,* the *Maritime Museum,* and the *Cinema Museum.* The gardens are a nice place around which to stroll and unwind, and at night, the verdant area takes on a whole new look when its powerful fountains are illuminated.

Walk 4: Montparnasse

The Montparnasse quarter on the Left Bank, on the southern side of Paris, was once a bastion of nonconformity; it was chronicled by author Henri Murger in his *Scenes of Bohemian Life,* the work that inspired Puccini to write *La Bohème.*

To walk almost full circle, begin at the Montparnasse-Bienvenüe métro station at the Place du 18 Juin 1940 (named for the date on which de Gaulle made his famous speech to the nation while in exile in London). Walk southeast down Boulevard du Montparnasse, a busy avenue lined with cafés, restaurants, and cinema complexes. The cafés and cabarets date to post-Revolution days, when afternoon and late-night fancy dress balls were held here.

Montparnasse was also the artistic center of Paris at one time. At the turn of the century, artists, poets, and writers relocated here from Montmartre; they would spend hours conferring in such local cafés as *Le Dôme, La Rotonde, Le Select,* and *La Coupole.* These establishments still exist, fueled by the mystique of Hemingway and other expatriates who frequented and chronicled them. Among the artists who visited *La Coupole* were Foujita, Picasso, Chagall, Soutine, and Léger. It was a stop on Hemingway's itinerary when in Paris, and also attracted fellow scribes Samuel Beckett, James Jones, and Ezra Pound and political exiles Lenin and Trotsky. These days, few struggling artists can afford to live in this popular neighborhood, much less afford the price of a *café crème.* However, some of the old regulars who do come tend to sit on the left side of the large room under the posters of current exhibitions, reading a newspaper in a traditional bamboo frame. Oddly enough, members of the fashion, publishing, and international film communities tend to sit on the right side. Catherine Deneuve, Yves Saint Laurent, and Gérard Départieu are said to be regular visitors. Though it has changed owners and was recently remodeled, *La Coupole* (102 Bd. du Montparnasse; phone: 43-20-14-20; open daily until 2 AM) remains the largest brasserie in France — with a bar, two restaurants, a terrace, and a discotheque — seating 500 people at a time. Happily, one doesn't feel rushed here. (In some of the smaller cafés on Boulevard St.-Germain, like *Café de Flore* or *Cafe Les Deux Magots,* excessive lingering over coffee is definitely discouraged.) Traditional tea dances are still held here, and Sunday is still the time for family lunches, when reservations are essential.

Le Dôme (on the corner of Boulevard du Montparnasse and Boulevard Raspail) is a good place to stop for a *croque-monsieur* (toasted cheese sandwich) and glass of *citron pressé* (fresh lemon juice served with a carafe of tap water and sugar). When it first opened at the turn of the century, *Le Dôme* was just a drinking place, but it has evolved over the years to become a popular fixture of Montparnasse café life.

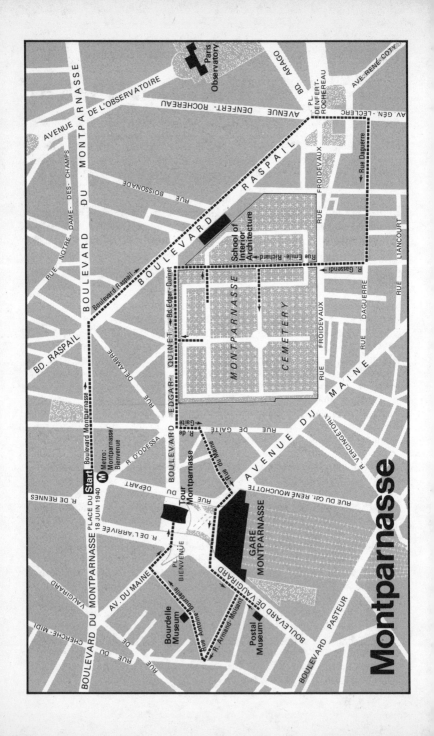

Montparnasse

Turn right on Boulevard Raspail. On the left is the famous statue of Balzac by Rodin, commissioned from the Société des Gens de Lettres in 1891, but nearly taken away from the artist when he kept missing his deadlines. It took him more than 10 attempts in over 3 years to come up with the final result, and it is a work that Rodin himself humbly called "a stirring point of departure . . . a decisive step towards open-air sculpture." Critics agree that it was a major bellwether of modern sculpture in the 20th century. Continue down the Boulevard Raspail, which may seem rather nondescript until you see a modern building on the right designed in the same daring style and in the same spirit as the *Centre Georges-Pompidou,* with red elevators on the outside. Fittingly, the building houses a school for interior architects.

Continue on to the Place Denfert-Rochereau, once a tollgate inspection point for goods arriving into the city during the 18th century. Opera buffs may recognize this area from a scene in the third act of *La Bohème.* The middle of the square is guarded by a colossal sculpture of a lion, a duplicate of one that was done on the site by Bartholdi in commemoration of Colonel Rochereau's successful defense of Belfort in the Franco-Prussian War of 1870–71. The elegant structures, with their sculptured friezes, are two of the remaining Ledoux buildings that once functioned as city gates and toll-houses. Today, men play *boules* (boccie) as calmly as if they were in the south of France instead of at a busy intersection enclosed by a few trees in the center of Paris.

At 1 Place Denfert-Rochereau is the entrance to the Catacombs, the tunnels of a former quarry where over a million skeletons were placed during the late 18th century after Les Innocents cemetery was closed. Note the *Denfert* cinema (across the road at 24 Place Denfert-Rochereau), which screens various classic art films daily. Walk down Avenue du Général Leclerc to the Rue Daguerre (named in honor of one of the founders of photography) and view a pleasant pocket of Parisian life. *Café Daguerre* (on the corner) is a good place to have a breakfast *en passant* or a good brasserie lunch. The *omelette forestière,* made with wild mushrooms and potatoes, is a good choice, or try the *salade niçoise,* with tuna and anchovies, accompanied by a glass of sauvignon blanc. Stroll along the Rue Daguerre; rich in local color, it has a lively food market, open 7 days a week. Filmmaker Agnes Varda, who lives nearby, made a documentary of daily life in the neighborhood called *Daguerrotypes.* About 5 blocks up Rue Daguerre at Rue Gassendi, turn right and cross Rue Froidevaux. The wall-enclosed street ahead, Rue Emile-Richard, divides the Montparnasse Cemetery into a large section on the left and a smaller section on the right. If you aren't interested in cemeteries, continue down Rue Emile-Richard toward Boulevard Edgar-Quinet and turn left. Otherwise enter the cemetery and stroll at leisure. Compared to the green expanse of Père-Lachaise, the first things evident here are the lack of trees and the view of the massive Tour Montparnasse, a high-rise that was derisively dismissed by Parisians as "La Tour" when it intruded on the Paris skyline more than a decade ago. From within the cemetery, the building resembles an oversize tombstone.

After entering the cemetery, turn left at Avenue du Midi, and turn right into Avenue de l'Est. Ask for a leaflet that maps out the exact positions of the graves, some of which are still not so easy to find; in Parisian cemeteries, actual street names are used.

Buried here are such notables as Simone de Beauvoir, next to Jean-Paul Sartre, interred in the understated grave they requested. The composer Saint-Saëns is buried in a family tomb topped with a lyre. Painter Chaim Soutine and writer Guy de Maupassant also have simple graves, unlike that of the poet Baudelaire, whose dramatic monument by J. de Charmoy depicts the struggle between genius and evil; many claim it is very much in the spirit of the anguished work of Michelangelo and Rodin. As with other Parisian cemeteries, it is often the uncelebrated who have more elaborate and eccentric tombs, with dramatically perched angels and sculptured figures in gentle repose.

After touring the grounds, exit right to Boulevard Edgar-Quinet, past benches that have become resting places for *clochards* (vagabonds or, less romantically, street people).

Turn left up the tree-lined boulevard to Rue de la Gaîté, once a street filled with dance halls and nightlife, now a place where many of the Paris theaters are still located. (Unfortunately, they are now easily outnumbered by a few too many X-rated video shops and arcades.) For theater lovers, there are often French-language productions of popular plays by American playwrights, sometimes featuring a well-known French actor in a leading role.

Turn right again at the Rue du Maine. Cross the busy Avenue du Maine with the Tour Montparnasse on the left, and the Montparnasse railroad station, filled with boutiques and restaurants, on the right. Continue left into the Boulevard de Vaugirard. At No. 34 is the *Musée de la Poste,* with its unusual façade of light panels. The museum's exhibition space focuses on the history of postal services.

Walk along Boulevard de Vaugirard and turn right into Rue Armand-Moisant. At the end of the street, take a very sharp right turn into the Rue Antoine-Bourdelle. Just ahead at No. 16 is the *Musée Bourdelle,* which exhibits the sculptures, paintings, and drawings of Rodin's former student. Most notable are the original plaster casts of his great sculptures and huge bronzes, as well as busts of his contemporaries, including 21 different studies of Beethoven. Continue along the Rue Antoine-Bourdelle and turn right into the Avenue du Maine, back to the Montparnasse Tower. Dominating the entire *quartier,* the 688-foot-high, 59-story office building was very controversial when it was built over a decade ago. However, for a onetime experience, visit the terrace on the top floor, and dine or drink at the bar/restaurant on the 56th floor around dusk to watch the lights of the city go on. Some people say it's worth the extra price for drinks and/or dinner because of the spectacular view, day or night. As for those who detest it, one is reminded of a remark by de Maupassant, who once said he preferred to eat his lunch in the shade of the Tour Eiffel because then he didn't have to look at it.

Walk 5: Haussmann's Master Plan

This walk begins at the rococo *Opéra,* which, when it was completed in 1875, was touted as the largest theater in the world (though with a capacity of only 2,156, it holds fewer people than the *Vienna Opera House* or *La Scala* in Milan). Designed by Charles Garnier, it covers nearly 3 acres and took 13 years to complete. At one time visitors could enter only if attending a performance; but today its magnificent interior and special exhibitions are open to the public (call first to find out days and hours; phone: 47-42-57-50, ext. 3514). The Place de l'Opéra is intersected by the Boulevard des Capucines and five other main avenues that lead to many of the city's — and the world's — most elegant shops. Just behind the *Opéra,* on Boulevard Haussmann, are Paris's two major department stores, or *grands magasins: Printemps* (No. 64) and *Galeries Lafayette* (No. 40). One can spend hours wandering from one cosmetic counter to another on the main floor before entering any one of a number of elegant galleries carrying high-fashion designs — at prices to match. Both stores are open Mondays through Saturdays from 9:30 AM to 6:30 PM.

Just outside these department stores are rows of sidewalk displays with clothing and various products for sale. Be sure and shop carefully, as these are operated by private vendors who are not affiliated with the stores.

From the Place de l'Opéra, walk southwest along the Boulevard des Capucines toward La Madeleine. At the corner of Rue Scribe is the monumental 19th-century *Grand* hotel (2 Rue Scribe), which houses the famous *Café de la Paix* (you can also enter at 12 Bd. des Capucines), where generations have come to watch the diverse parade of passersby. Just next door was the equally popular (but no longer standing) *Grand Café.* It was here, on December 28, 1895, that the first public showing of a motion picture was held. In 1990s parlance, it was a bomb; only 33 people (the house held 100), paying one franc each, attended the program of 10 short films.

Past the Rue Scribe on the right, where the Grand Boulevards come to an end, is the Church of St. Mary Magdalene, or La Madeleine. This late Roman adaptation of a Greek temple, constructed between 1764 and 1842, is surrounded by an imposing group of massive Corinthian columns. In 1806, Napoleon Bonaparte had it consecrated as a "Temple of Glory." The bronze doors are adorned with illustrations of the Ten Commandments, and inside there are many distinctive murals and sculptures. It is currently undergoing renovation, but unlike the ugly metal and wood paneling that covers the *Louvre* and Luxembourg Palace reconstructions, the renovation of the Madeleine is going on behind an amusing life-size Impressionist painting of the

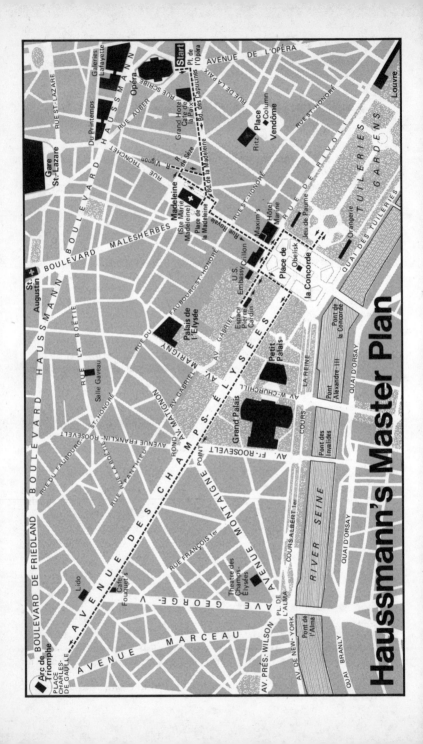

Haussmann's Master Plan

actual church front. It catches the eye of the *flâneur* (stroller) from as far as the Place de la Concorde. Some will probably even miss it when it is gone.

While other neighborhoods pay homage to haute couture, the Madeleine quarter pays homage to *haute gastronomie*. Near this temple of worship are several culinary "temples" that cater to their own following of gourmands. Just opposite the small flower market next to the Madeleine métro station — and also across the street — is *Fauchon* (26, 28, and 30 Pl. de la Madeleine; phone: 47-42-60-11), with its distinctive chocolate brown logo emblazoned on the walls and canopies of its complex of three shops. Whether you choose just to look or to partake, this is the ultimate movable feast. *Fauchon* has always been known for its presentations, which some have even called high art. One doesn't ask the price of the varieties of caviar and pâté; any exotic fruit or vegetable out of season is here — even grapes are displayed as if they were the crown jewels. The sculptured pâtés are so finely detailed that it's almost a shame to eat them. But lest you think you must dress up and bring a king's ransom with you, remember that only in Paris will you see such an eclectic clientele: At lunchtime, the bakery and pastry shop is frequented by everyone from royalty to workers who stop for a baguette or a bagatelle cake. If you are calorie-conscious, don't even approach the chocolate counter with its tempting rows of truffles and liqueur-filled bonbons.

Although discerning shoppers will find several other smaller places in the neighborhood with better prices and more patient service, *Fauchon* is still a good place to get a delicious souvenir of your visit to enjoy back home: a pound of house blend coffee, a tin of aged sardines from Brittany, or a decanter of peaches soaked in armagnac. We particularly admire Fauchon vinegar (try the tarragon) and *tchando* (lotus) tea. *Fauchon* also ships anywhere. Closed Sundays. On Mondays, only the pastry shop is open.

Just across the street is *Hédiard* (21 Pl. de la Madeleine; phone: 42-66-44-36), another gastronomic emporium on a smaller scale, with exotic spices, flavored vinegars and oils, and at least 30 varieties of tea. The wine cellar offers an extensive selection (sorry, no bargains). Closed Sundays.

Still in an eating mode, *Maison de la Truffe* (19 Pl. de la Madeleine; phone: 42-65-53-22) is the place to come from November to March for the best fresh truffles. Otherwise, there are preserved truffles from which to choose, and rich foie gras, exotic fruit, and a variety of charcuterie (closed Sundays). *Creplet-Brussol* (17 Pl. de la Madeleine; phone: 42-65-34-32) is regarded as one of the city's best cheese shops. Although the windows are filled with a lot of fancy packaged cheeses, the classic collection of aged brie and fine raw milk camembert, among others, is inside (closed Sundays and Mondays).

In the same building is *Caviar Kaspia* (phone: 42-65-33-52), a simple, straightforward store that specializes in (what else?) caviar. Choose from a selection of well-priced pressed caviar, excellent smoked salmon, and tasty fresh blinis. If you like, go upstairs to their elegant, informal restaurant and sample a few dishes along with a frosty glass of vodka (open from 9 AM to midnight daily except Sundays).

Cross back to *Fauchon* at the corner of Rue de Sèze. Enter Rue de Sèze and turn left on Rue Vignon. A few steps from the corner is *La Maison du Miel* (The House of Honey; 24 Rue Vignon, off La Madeleine; phone: 47-42-

26-70), which has been operated by the Galland family at this location since 1908. Devoted totally to honey and honey products, it produces about one-fourth of the 53 tons of honey sold here each year. There are many varieties from which to choose and sample tastings are available (closed Sundays). *Tanrade* (No. 18; phone: 47-42-26-99) is a family-run shop that specializes in the freshest candied chestnuts (marrons glacés) in the city. There are also 50 kinds of bonbons, chocolates, and special jams (confitures). Closed Sundays, Mondays, and the month of August. Just across the street is *La Ferme Saint-Hubert* (No. 21; phone: 47-42-79-20), a compact little shop that has extraordinary varieties of cheese and a friendly staff to advise you. They have one of the best selections of roquefort, dozens of goat cheeses (*chèvres*) from which to choose, and a fine assortment of reasonably priced house wines, as well as bread from the famous *Poilâne* bakery. For a unique experience, visit their adjoining lunchroom/restaurant, which offers special degustation (sampler) plates of cheese and raclette (a melted cheese dish from Switzerland served with boiled potatoes, pickled onions, and *cornichons*) in the evening. Closed Sundays and Mondays.

Continue along Rue Vignon to the end, and take a sharp left turn into Rue Tronchet, leading to the back of La Madeleine. Keep right, walking around the church until you reach the front, then turn right on Rue Royale. Walk down Rue Royale, past the chic shopping street of Rue du Faubourg-St.-Honoré on the right (see *Quintessential Paris,* DIVERSIONS), to Place de la Concorde, dominated by its famous obelisk. Considered to be one of the finest public squares in the world, with its eight massive statues designed by Gabriel, representing provincial capitals in France, and its two bronze fountains, Place de la Concorde is bounded on the left by the Tuileries Gardens, nearby the Seine and the Concorde bridge, and on the right by the Avenue des Champs-Elysées. Looking in any direction at this point will bring you face to face with one of the major monuments of Paris.

The central monument of the square is the Obelisk of Luxor. At 75 feet high and weighing more than 220 tons, it is quite similar to its London counterpart, Cleopatra's Needle. The obelisk was presented by the government of Egypt to the government of Louis-Philippe and was erected on its present site between 1834 and 1836. It had quite an ambitious journey: It was removed from the Temple of Luxor and brought to the Nile; it was then shipped 600 miles to Alexandria, where it crossed the Mediterranean and traveled up the Atlantic to Cherbourg, and was finally transported by road through Normandy to Paris.

In this same square in 1793 stood a guillotine that took the lives of some 3,000 victims of the Reign of Terror, including King Louis XVI, his queen, Marie-Antoinette, and other members of the royal family. The site was originally called Place Louis-XV, and, afterward, the Place de la Révolution. It was then renamed Place de la Concorde, but altered once again to Place Louis-XVI until 1830, when its present name was restored. The name "Concorde" was given to erase the memory of the deeds performed here.

To the right, on Rue Royale near the Place de la Concorde, is *Maxim's* (No. 3; phone: 42-65-27-94); long a legend for its Belle Epoque decor and atmosphere, it remains a formal and exclusive bastion of fine dining (see *Eating Out* in THE CITY).

At the corner of Rue Royale and Place de la Concorde are two stately mansions designed by Gabriel, with colonnades similar to those at the *Louvre*. The pavilion across the street on the left is the Hôtel de la Marine, now headquarters of the French navy. The pavilion at the right is shared by the French Automobile Club and the *Crillon* hotel (phone: 42-65-24-24), with its discreet sign and elegant gold C's on the door (see *Checking In* in THE CITY).

Walk around this part of the Tuileries, a lovely park framed at its western end by two small museums, the *Jeu de Paume* and the *Orangerie,* flanking a large pond that's usually surrounded by children and young couples; at the eastern end of the Tuileries is the *Louvre,* one of the world's greatest museums (see *Memorable Museums and Monuments* in DIVERSIONS). Cross the Place de la Concorde — carefully, and preferably not directly across the heavily trafficked square — to the park-like, tree-lined street, which is the eastern end of the Champs-Elysées, the most famous thoroughfare in Paris. It was first called the Grand Allée du Roule and, afterward, the Avenue des Tuileries. The American Embassy is on the right at 2 Avenue Gabriel. At No. 1 is *L'Espace Cardin* (phone: 42-66-11-70), a theater complex and restaurant owned by fashion designer Pierre Cardin, who is also the owner of *Maxim's.* You might want to return and see a theatrical or musical performance, or else sample the buffet at the restaurant, with its amusingly funky decor (open daily).

As you continue down the Champs-Elysées, set in a large garden off to the right is the Palais de l'Elysée. A magnificent structure that dates from 1718, it has been the residence of the French president since 1873.

Just ahead is the Rond-Point des Champs-Elysées, a large, circular, flower-filled place at the intersection of Avenues Matignon, Franklin-D.-Roosevelt, and Montaigne. The city of Paris once actually ended at this point; beyond the Arc de Triomphe, there was nothing but suburbs.

It was only after the construction of the Grand Palais and Petit Palais (they are just to the left) for the *1900 Paris International Exposition* that the Champs-Elysées became the scene of numerous street festivals. Though now considered one of the finest promenades in the world, before 1830 it was unsafe to walk here after dark. The only lights were from a few gas lamps, candles shining from small retail shops, and the red lanterns of the orange vendors' stands. These days, many of the bright lights belong to fast-food franchises, which intrude on the ambience of this high-rent neighborhood.

Once lined only by private hotels and mansions, the area grew to include banks, corporate headquarters, luxury shops, and a number of automobile dealers; during the last few decades, many large cinemas with attached shopping complexes were built on both sides of the broad street, as well as more restaurants and cafés to accommodate the growing number of visitors. *Café Fouquet's* (pronounced Foo-*kett*) is on the left (99 Champs-Elysées, at the corner of Avenue George-V; phone: 47-23-70-60). It is definitely the most famous of the cafés along the route, for decades the place for *tout* Paris to see and be seen (open daily).

Just down Avenue George-V at No. 31 is the famed hostelry of the same name (see *Checking In* in THE CITY), where many of the rich and celebrated have stayed at least once (phone: 47-23-54-00). Directly ahead is the Arc de Triomphe, and Place Charles-de-Gaulle (l'Etoile). The large, circular traffic hub from which 12 avenues radiate out into various parts of the city is the centerpiece of Baron Haussmann's inspired master plan. The famous arch — as synonymous with Paris as the Eiffel Tower — crowns the long vista of the Champs-Elysées. Conceived by Napoleon I to commemorate his victories of 1805–6 and later in memory of the Unknown Soldier, it was at the time the largest monument of its kind in the world. In front of the arch are four amazing groups of statuary symbolizing triumph, peace, resistance, and departure. A 260-step climb up to the platform at the top is rewarded by a magnificent view of the city, including the Champs-Elysées and the Bois de Boulogne. (The platform can also be reached by elevator.) A small museum under the platform contains souvenirs relating to Napoleon I, the Arc de Triomphe, and both world wars.

Walk 6: La Rive Gauche (The Left Bank)

Begin this walk on the Right Bank, at the main entrance to the Tuileries Gardens, at the east side of the Place de la Concorde. Designed by Lenôtre, the celebrated landscape gardener of Louis XIV, the main path of the gardens crosses through the center and leads straight to the *Louvre.* The Tuileries were originally commissioned in 1563 by Catherine de Medici, the queen mother, who wanted an Italianate park next to the palace (now the *Louvre*) that she shared with King Henri II. These were to be no ordinary gardens; they would include fountains, a maze, a grotto, and a menagerie. It is said that the Tuileries epitomize formal French design. Years later, sensual sculptures by Maillol were placed on the lawns, as were busts of prominent figures, like Lenôtre, and mythical figures, like Mercury, the messenger of the gods, who sits here atop his winged horse.

The Tuileries were enlarged in 1889 with more garden space created on the site of the former Tuileries palace, which was destroyed by the Communards during the Revolution. It remains the most popular promenade in Paris, most likely because of its central location. Nannies stroll with baby carriages; lovers embrace on benches; mimes entertain among groves of trees; lines of school-children wait for ice cream cones at a kiosk; and in a nearby pond, charming miniature sailboats complete this idyllic Parisian parkscape.

As you enter, on the immediate left is the *Jeu de Paume,* and on the right, the *Orangerie,* which has been undergoing renovation and should reopen by the middle of this year. Each of these elegant pavilions was built during the Second Empire and has served as an art gallery since the turn of the 20th century. Before the main works of the collection were moved to the *Musée d'Orsay,* the *Jeu de Paume* was known for its Impressionist exhibitions. The *Orangerie* holds temporary exhibitions, in addition to housing the prestigious Walter-Guillaume collection, which includes works by Picasso, Matisse, Cézanne, Modigliani, Renoir, and others. On the ground floor in two oval rooms are a series of Monet's *Nymphéas* (water lilies) paintings, done in the garden of his house at Giverny. Entering this special exhibition, illuminated with diffused light, is a most spiritual experience. Those who appreciate these works should visit the Monet collection in the *Musée Marmottan,* near the Bois de Boulogne (see *Museums* in THE CITY). The museums in the Tuileries are closed on Tuesdays.

To the left outside the Tuileries is Rue de Rivoli, with its uniformly de-signed 19th-century arcades of bookstores, cafés, hotels, and boutiques. To the far right are the quays bordering the Seine. Walk a while, look back, and enjoy the panoramic view, impressive despite the renovations currently taking

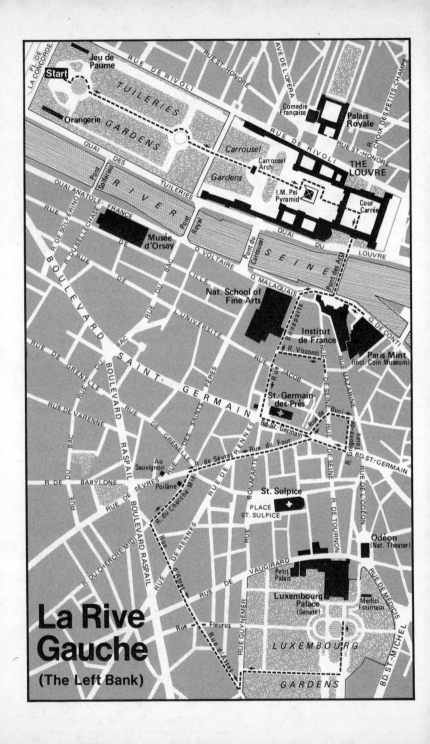

place around the *Louvre* complex (which should be complete sometime this year). The *Louvre* enjoys the distinction of being the largest museum in the world, and when the renovation is eventually completed — including an ambitious plan for a new bridge and pedestrian pathway linking *Musée d'Orsay* and the Palais Royale — that distinction will surely be unrivaled (also see *Memorable Museums and Monuments* in DIVERSIONS).

Stroll around the glass pyramid, designed by I. M. Pei, for an entirely updated perspective of the former fortress/palace. Some (like us) believe that the Egyptian-inspired design is out of place here. Continue straight ahead to the last building, the Cour Carrée (Square Court), considered to be the most impressive of the old *Louvre* buildings. Walk through the elegant courtyard and out the door to the right toward the Seine. Enjoy the impressive view across the Pont des Arts (Bridge of Arts), taking in the domed complex of the Institute of France across the river, on the Left Bank. Cross the Pont des Arts to the institute, which encompasses several prestigious academies. Designed by Levau and opened in 1688, it was a poor contrast to his more illustrious monument across the Seine (the *Louvre*). Even though the buildings were meant to complement one another, the institute was actually considered one of the prominent architect's failures.

The institute has had an interesting history as a college for scholars, and is notorious for its former exclusion of women and for the notable male candidates it has refused. Among the rejects were Descartes, Pascal, Molière, Proust, Balzac, and Zola. Today, it accepts women members; author Marguerite Yourcenar was the first to be admitted. The institute incorporates the French Academy and the schools of Fine Arts, Literature, Science, and Political Science.

To the left of this rarefied intellectual complex is the Hôtel des Monnaies (Paris Mint), a fine, unpretentious building by Antoine, who lived here until his death in 1801. The *Musée de la Monnaie,* with its wonderful collection of coins and exhibitions on the art of engraving, is on the premises (closed Mondays and holidays; phone: 40-46-55-33). Walk west along the Quai de Conti and then the Quai Malaquais to the National School of Fine Arts at the corner of Rue Bonaparte. This former monastery was founded in 1608 and closed down in 1791. It later became the *Museum of French Monuments,* displaying busts and statues from other monuments that had been destroyed. The school was created at the time of the Revolution by the union of the Painting and Sculpture Academy and the Architecture School. Although the museum was closed in 1816, it is still possible to tour the courtyard today to see some of the monuments (entrance is at 14 Rue Bonaparte).

Turn up Rue Bonaparte to see rows of exclusive and pricey antiques shops and art galleries. Turn left off Rue Bonaparte and walk 1 block over to Rue de Seine, where there are more art galleries through which to browse. Walk back to Rue Bonaparte. This narrow street dates to 1250, and today it can barely accommodate the steady flow of city traffic crossing from the Left to the Right Bank. Walk a bit farther to the Boulevard St.-Germain. On the left is the Eglise St.-Germain-des-Prés; to the right is the *Café Les Deux Magots* (No. 170), said to be the birthplace of Surrealism. Just next door is *Café de Flore* (No. 172), long the existentialist hangout where Jean-Paul Sartre and

Simone de Beauvoir held court over *café espresso*. Each is worth a visit, depending on where your nostalgic loyalties lie, and if you don't mind paying inflated prices to soak in the ambience of people watching people, which is basically what happens here. On weekend nights, this stretch of boulevard is the place to get a front-row seat to watch the lively stream of street entertainers — from mimes to fire eaters to acrobats. *Café de Flore* is closed in July; *Café Les Deux Magots* is closed in August.

Across the street at *Brasserie Lipp* (No. 151; phone: 45-48-53-91), politicians rub well-tailored elbows with the fashion and publishing crowds who work in the surrounding quarter. It is so crowded that one's only chance to sample the house specialty of *choucroute* is in the Siberia section in the upper dining room. This Alsatian combination plate of sausages, smoked meats, and sauerkraut found its way into the French capital during the middle of the 19th century, when there was a large immigration of people from the Alsace region into Paris. Many of them opened brasseries (which are beer halls distinguished by their brass dispensers). There are reports these days that even some *Lipp* regulars are saying the food here has lost much of its charm, so why not just settle for a glass of Alsatian beer and take in the atmosphere. Closed Mondays and in July.

Cross the street once again and visit the unassuming St.-Germain-des-Prés, the oldest church in Paris. Originally founded about 543 by Childebert I, it belonged to the powerful Benedictine Monastery of St. Germain. It was built on the advice of St. Germain, the Bishop of Paris, who is buried here.

With the church on the left, turn left and walk a short distance down Boulevard St.-Germain, taking a left at the first corner to Rue de Buci and Rue de Seine. This is where Paris's most expensive, and usually jam-packed, market street begins. Here (each morning until noon) are a jumble of fruit, vegetable, and *fromage* vendors alongside fish dealers, bread sellers, and meat merchants. If you don't want to grab a bite here — or would like to sit down — why not go to where many of the market vendors themselves go: *Orestia's* Greek taverna (4 Rue Grégoire-de-Tours; phone: 43-54-62-01), around the corner. Here you will squeeze into rickety chairs and sit at a long table with tourists and locals from all walks of life. Founded in 1929, this place is as busy and noisy as it is welcoming and friendly. Try the mixed appetizer plate, and if you want to please the waiter, order retsina, the unique resin-flavored wine called the "Blood of the Gods."

From Rue de Buci, walk south on Rue Grégoire-de-Tours and turn right at Boulevard St.-Germain onto Rue du Four, which leads to a busy crossroads. Continue into Rue de Sèvres, or turn left to Rue de Rennes; either way, this area has shop after shop of fashionable clothing by such famous designers as *Issey Miyake* (201 Bd. St.-Germain), *Dorothée Bis* (33 Rue de Sèvres), and *Sonia Rykiel* (6 Rue de Grenelle). Make a note to return for a bite at *Au Sauvignon* (80 Rue des Sts.-Pères, at the corner of Rue de Sèvres; phone: 45-48-49-02). Try their special sandwiches, with either the thin-sliced *jambon* (ham), a light pâté, or a mellow *chèvre* (goat cheese), served on bite-size pieces of delicious bread from *Poilâne.* Try a glass of either red or white sauvignon, bottled especially for the café. Closed Sundays, 2 weeks in January, *Easter,* and the month of August.

Those who enjoyed the bread should visit the *Poilâne* bakery shop just up the road from the café, at 8 Rue du Cherche-Midi. There will probably be lines of customers waiting to buy the trademark flour-dusted sourdough loaves. Available also by the slice, it is sold by the ounce. Their apple tarts are also worth tasting. If the place is not too hectic, visit the basement and watch the bread being mixed, kneaded, and baked in ancient wood-burning ovens. Open from 7 AM to 8 PM daily, except Sundays.

Walk past *Poilâne* and turn left at the upcoming street, Rue d'Assas, which will lead to a side entrance of the Luxembourg Gardens and the adjacent palace. Along the way, there are interesting shops, galleries, and old bookstores through which to browse. *J-C & C* (16 Rue d'Assas) is an aromatic tea shop with a good selection of tea and coffee, as well as an unusual selection of tea-flavored honey and jam.

Continuing down Rue d'Assas, briefly turn left onto Rue Fleurus, where Gertrude Stein once resided with Alice B. Toklas at No. 27. There were many spirited salons held here, with the likes of Picasso and Hemingway sparring for attention.

Continue down Rue d'Assas and enter through the gate of the Luxembourg Gardens on Rue Guynemer. These surrounding streets were originally part of the garden complex, developed after 1870. The Jardin du Luxembourg was built in 1613 on the site of an ancient Roman encampment, and a 13th-century convent of Chartreux. When the monastery was demolished in 1790, the surrounding gardens were enlarged and remodeled. There are several entrances to this park: Boulevard St.-Michel, Rue de Vaugirard near the historic *Odéon* theater, Rue Guynemer, and the Avenue de l'Observatoire.

The impressive Palais du Luxembourg at Rue de Vaugirard was originally built between 1615 and 1620 for Marie de Médici, mother of Louis XIII. It was inhabited by successive generations of the royal family until the time of Louis XVI. During the dark days of World War II, it served as German Air Force headquarters. It now houses the French Senate. Though the palace could be viewed at one time, visits have been canceled to allow for renovations.

The Petit Palais next door is now the residence of the President of the Senate, and it includes the original Hôtel de Luxembourg that Marie de Médici presented to Cardinal Richelieu as a residence.

These gardens are, after the Tuileries, one of the more favored of the Parisian promenades, particularly during the summer when many outdoor concerts are held here. Each section of the park is different, with tennis courts, pony rides, a large fountain with toy sailboats gliding by. A relief of Leda and the Swan is one of the more original examples of the statuary; located near the Médicis fountain, it is worth seeing. In addition to the ubiquitous park benches, there are hundreds of chairs that people can freely move to a spot of their choice. This is indeed a tranquil setting in which to conclude this tour of the Left Bank.

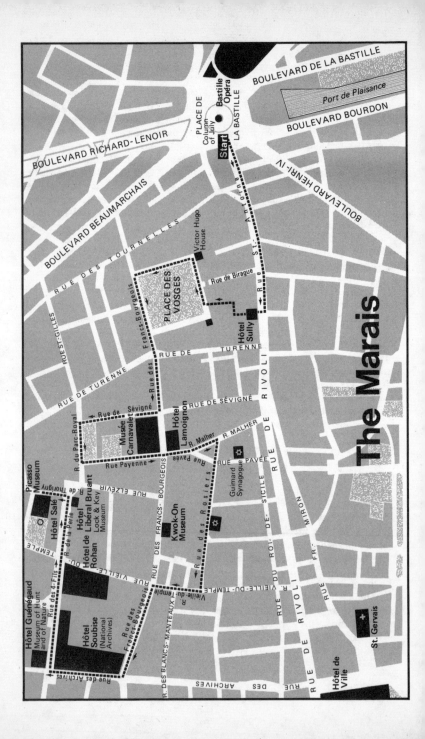

The Marais

BOULEVARD DE LA BASTILLE

Port de Plaisance

BOULEVARD BOURDON

BOULEVARD HENRI-IV

PLACE DE
Column
of July

Start

Bastille
Opéra

LA BASTILLE

BOULEVARD RICHARD-LENOIR

BOULEVARD BEAUMARCHAIS

RUE DES TOURNELLES

Victor Hugo
House

PLACE DES
VOSGES

Rue de Birague

Rue St. Antoine

RUE ST-GILLES

Rue des Francs-Bourgeois

Hôtel
Sully

RUE DE
TURENNE

RUE DE TURENNE

Rue des

Rue de   Sévigné

R. du Parc-Royal

Hôtel
Lamoignon

RUE DE SÉVIGNÉ

RUE DE RIVOLI

Musée
Carnavalet

R. Malher

R. MALHER

Rue Payenne

Rue Pavée

RUE

Guimard
Synagogue

RUE   PAVÉE

RUE DE- SICILE

Picasso
Museum

Rue de Thorigny

Hôtel Salé

Hôtel de Libéral Bruant
Lock & Key
Museum

RUE ELZÉVIR

RUE DES FRANCS- BOURGEOIS

Kwok-On
Museum

Rue des Rosiers

RUE DU ROI-DE-

FR.   MIRON

RUE   DE   RIVOLI

Hôtel
Rohan

Rue de la Perle

RUE VIEILLE-

RUE DES FRANCS-BOURGEOIS

R. Vieille-du-Temple

R. VIEILLE-DU-TEMPLE

Hôtel Guénégaud
Museum of Hunt
and of Nature

TEMPLE-DU-

Rue des 4-Fils

Hôtel
Soubise
(National
Archives)

Rue des
Francs-Bourgeois

RUE DES BLANCS-MANTEAUX

RUE
DES
ARCHIVES

St. Gervais

Rue des Archives

R. DES BLANCS-MANTEAUX

Hôtel de
Ville

Walk 7: The Marais

Begin at the Place de la Bastille, a historic intersection of several important thoroughfares connecting the 4th, 11th, and 12th *arrondissements,* where many events of the 1789 Revolution took place. Until the end of the 18th century, the formidable Bastille stood here. Originally built in 1369 by Charles V as a castle to defend Old Paris against the English, it later became the infamous, dreaded state prison. For some inmates, conditions were not as horrendous as one would imagine; it is rumored that some prisoners had the privilege of inviting guests over for multi-course banquets. But then, there are as many myths as truths associated with the Bastille.

Among the detainees was the so-called Man in the Iron Mask, imprisoned by Louis XIV (his mask was actually black velvet); rumors have it that he was the twin brother of the king. The writer Voltaire, who was locked up on two different occasions for writing inflammatory pamphlets (in 1717 and 1726), is said to have spread that rumor himself. After Paris was leveled in 1682, the Bastille remained standing; it was ordered destroyed after the Revolution on July 14, 1789, an event celebrated annually as *Bastille Day.* A thousand workmen were employed to raze the prison, and trumpets proclaimed the news at all the crossroads of the city. The contractor of the demolition sold some of the stones as souvenirs, but others were used to build the Pont de la Concorde (Concorde Bridge).

Begin at the Column of July, a handsome, 154-foot-tall pillar that was built in 1840. The column, which rests on a white marble base, bears the name of 615 combatants who struggled for liberty in July of 1830 and 1848. They are interred beneath the column.

Today, on the former site of the Bastille is the controversial new opera house designed by Carlos Ott, which opened in 1989. The 2,700-seat auditorium presents lyric and contemporary opera, and bears an uncanny likeness to a modern prison-fortress.

Cross the large intersection near the Column of July (opposite the opera complex) and walk down fashionable Rue St.-Antoine. Look to the right down the Rue de Birague. At the end of this narrow street is a good view of the façade of the King's Pavilion and the Place des Vosges, a spot of unique historical interest. But first proceed on Rue St.-Antoine to the Hôtel de Sully (No. 62), one of the most beautiful old houses in Paris. It was built in 1624 by a Monsieur Gallet, a gambler who was also the controller of finances. In 1634, Gallet lost his house in a game of cards to Count Sully, a minister of Henri IV. Enter the Hôtel de Sully's first courtyard, which is filled with sculptured wall reliefs that are allegories of the changing seasons. Take the small passageway into the garden, where you face the former *orangerie.* Continue through the narrow door on the far right to the southwestern corner of the Place des Vosges.

If this door could speak, it would recount the adventures of Madame Sully, the young wife of Count Sully, who was told by her much older husband to divide her monthly household allowance into three equal parts — "for the house, yourself, and your lovers. Just be discreet and have them use the back door."

The Place des Vosges, once known as the Place Royale (it was a courtyard of a royal palace), is at the site where Henri II accidentally met his death in a tournament in 1559. When the court was removed to the *Louvre* after that tragedy, the deserted courtyard became a horse market, and was also used as a dueling ground. In an attempt to beautify Paris in 1605, Henri IV had the Place des Vosges constructed as it is today; soon it became the fashionable address of more celebrities than any other residential area in Paris — among them were Richelieu, Madame de Sévigné, Prince de Condé, and Molière. This was the center of Parisian social life, the place where some of the sophisticated residents held *ruelles,* intimate gatherings at which the elegant and witty guests attempted to rival each other in repartee and social one-upmanship. These rituals, which preceded the popular salons of the 18th century, were parodied by Molière in his play *Précieuses Ridicules.*

The fashionable neighborhood became known as Place des Vosges after a unique incident in 1800 when Lucien Bonaparte (minister of finance and Napoleon's brother) announced that the first *département* to pay its entire taxes on time would have the honor of having a street named after it. The Department of Vosges was the first to pay its full contribution, and the name was eventually changed. (Note the irony that the Rue des Francs-Bourgeois, which traverses the northern end of the square, got its name in the 15th century for the poor people who lived there in almshouses and *didn't* have to pay any taxes.)

Enter the Place des Vosges from the Hôtel de Sully; follow the arcades to the right to the next corner, passing the hallway of the King's Pavilion. At the corner, at No. 6, is the house of Victor Hugo, now a museum. Among the objects of interest here are pictures illustrating the great writer's works by many well-known artists, as well as sketches by Hugo himself, who was quite a fine draftsman. Among the collection of inkstands and pens belonging to him and his peers — Dumas, Lamartine, and George Sand — is his chest-high writing table (he wrote standing up) and the bed on which he died. As you leave the Victor Hugo home, stroll on through the arcades of the Place des Vosges. Today they are occupied by expensive shops, a popular corner café, and one of Paris's most exclusive restaurants, *L'Ambroisie* (No. 9; phone: 42-78-51-45). This is the showcase for chef Bernard Pacaud's elegant culinary talents, and has earned three Michelin stars. It is very expensive and reservations are necessary. Closed Sundays, Monday lunch, the month of August, and holidays. Enter the park, where couples stroll, children play, and busy city life seems to be suspended, and have a drink or snack at *Ma Bourgogne* (No. 19; phone: 42-78-44-64), a popular meeting place since 1920 for tourists and locals alike. Try their specialty of sausages from Auvergne with a glass of burgundy or bordeaux wine. The waiters are friendly.

When leaving, turn left on Rue des Francs-Bourgeois and walk directly into the historic Marais quarter. The first street to the right is Rue de Sévigné, and at No. 23 is the *Musée Carnavalet,* the residence of Madame de Sévigné in the 17th century. However, the museum derives its name from the widow of François de Kernevenoy (corrupted to Carnavalet), tutor to Henri III, who bought it in 1572. It was built in 1550 by the architect Pierre Lescot, and over the years had many embellishments added by other architects, especially when it was officially designated as a museum. Its collection includes mementos of Madame de Sévigné, as well as exhibitions on the history of Paris from the era of François I to the turn-of-the century Belle Epoque. The gift shop has a wealth of items, from T-shirts to interesting objets d'art.

Leave the *Carnavalet Museum* and walk left up Rue de Sévigné to the end. Turn left into the Rue du Parc-Royal. At the Achille Square on the corner, the visitor is literally surrounded by the many elegant *hôtels* in the area. (Note that the term "hôtel" originally referred to the large and elegant city residences of the nobility, not the French equivalent of a Hilton or Holiday Inn.) Turn left again at the Rue Payenne, cross Rue des Francs-Bourgeois, and bear left to Rue Malher, with the post office on the right and the Hôtel de Lamoignon on the left. The hotel was originally built in 1585 by Robert de Beauvais, the comptroller general of the city of Paris. It was bought in 1658 by Lamoignon, the president of the French Parliament, and was the site of many dazzling soirees. Nearby, the *Kwok-On Oriental Theater Museum* (41 Rue des Francs-Bourgeois), named after its patron, and devoted to traditions in the Oriental theater, has a large collection of costumes, masks, and musical instruments, as well as changing exhibitions. Closed Saturdays, Sundays, and holidays.

During the 18th century, the Marais started to lose its fashionable cachet as the aristocracy and their social activities moved on to the area around the Concorde and Faubourg-St.-Honoré. Many of the superb palaces were divided up into apartments, or turned over to trade. The entire area became industrialized and was a center of small businesses and crafts shops well into the early part of the 20th century. After the Second World War, the trend reversed again as Parisians who had settled in the distant suburbs sought to live within the heart of the city once more. Renewal of the Marais district began after 1972, and there was no lack of people who wanted to live here — especially at such reasonable rents. In recent years, however, with the proliferation of chic shops that have spread through the quarter, it once again has a fashionable image and is no longer a low-rent district.

Walk ahead on Rue Malher and turn right into the narrow Rue des Rosiers, the heart of Paris's Jewish quarter. It was here that the Jews came at the end of the 19th century when they fled the pogroms of Eastern Europe, and still again after fleeing the Nazis in Germany. (This is also the street down which the Nazis marched as they led 75,000 Jews to concentration camps.) As a result of the French exodus from Algeria, a third wave of Jews settled in the Marais. Like New York City's Lower East Side, it is a hectic neighborhood, whose streets are always blocked with traffic. These days, the traffic is not the fashionable carriages of years gone by, but a stubborn ballet of bicycles, motorcycle couriers, and assorted French automobiles competing for the right of way. Walk through the Rue des Rosiers and its surrounding streets with its small neighborhood synagogues, kosher meat markets (with signs that say *strictement cachère*), and shops that sell Jewish artifacts, and you are in a totally different part of Paris. Walk to Rue Pavée, a tiny street off Rue des Rosiers and near Rue Malher. At 10 Rue Pavée is the synagogue built in 1913 by Hector Guimard, the famous Art Nouveau architect of the métro. The design recalls the shape of the tablets of the Ten Commandments. If you are there on a Saturday morning, the doors will be open.

Back again to Rue des Rosiers; drop in to *Le Loir dans la Théière* (The Dormouse in the Teapot; No. 3; phone: 42-72-90-61), a cozy tearoom in a loft-like space with long wooden tables and comfortable chairs. At the counter, choose from a display of delicious homemade pastries. Relax in the Alice in Wonderland ambience, then look around at their art and photo gallery. Closed Mondays. Stop at *Jo Goldenberg's* (No. 7; phone: 48-87-20-16), a traditional Jewish delicatessen with very Parisian prices, yet still a good spot to take a break; try the mushroom and barley soup. Open daily. Farther up the road on the left is *Café des Psaumes* (No. 14; phone: 48-04-74-77), which serves kosher specialties Sundays through Friday afternoons. A definite experience is a falafel on pita while wandering these narrow streets. This Middle Eastern treat of mashed chick-peas fried up and served with roasted eggplant, carrots, and a tasty yogurt sauce is healthy fuel and a bargain at around $3.50. There are several stands along the road; *Le Roi du Falafel* (Falafel King; No. 34; phone: 48-87-63-60) is one of the most popular. Closed Friday evenings and Saturdays. A bit farther, at the corner of Rue des Rosiers and Rue des Hospitalières-St.-Gervais, is *Chez Marianne* (No. 2; phone: 42-72-18-86), a restaurant and falafel stand that is one of our favorites. The tables upstairs and downstairs always seem to be full, but it's worth the wait for the tasty buffet. Otherwise, buy a falafel from their take-out window and continue walking. Closed Fridays.

Turn right onto Rue Vieille-du-Temple and notice a school with a placard that is a memorial to hundreds of Jewish children who were sent to war camps. There is a bench where you can sit a moment to reflect. Continue along Rue Vieille-du-Temple, crossing Rue des Francs-Bourgeois again.

A block to the left, at 60 Rue des Francs-Bourgeois, is the Hôtel de Soubise, a palace with an illustrious history that today houses the National Archives, containing about 220 miles of information. In 1700, the house was acquired by François de Rohan, the Prince of Soubise, thanks to the generosity of Louis XIV. Over the next few years, extensive remodeling transformed the mansion into a palace; the best painters and artisans were brought in to enhance the classical architecture into something more formal.

On the ground floor were the apartments of the Prince of Rohan-Soubise (which can be visited by groups when arranged in advance). The princess's apartment on the first floor is now a museum, with interesting historical documents, among them the wills of Louis XIV and Napoleon, the diary of Louis XVI, and the Declaration of Human Rights. There is also a model of the Bastille that was carved from one of its original stones. Outside, walk to the right past the National Archives complex around the Rue des Quatre-Fils. At the corner, at 60 Rue des Archives, is the Hôtel Guénégaud, still another mansion built by Mansart in 1650, regarded as one of the finest in the Marais. It has been remodeled twice since the 18th century, retaining its simple lines.

Turn to the left at Rue des Quatre-Fils, and visit the small formal garden. On the same property is the *Musée de la Chasse et de la Nature,* which features a collection of hunting souvenirs and an arms collection from a Monsieur Sommer, who had restored the house in later years. There is also a collection of tapestries, ceramics, and sculptures related to the hunt. Closed Tuesdays and holidays (phone: 42-72-86-43).

Walk ahead to Rue Vieille-du-Temple and turn right. At No. 87 is the Hôtel de Rohan, converted into the imperial printing house under Napoleon, and another annex to the National Archives in 1927. It was the residence at one time of Cardinal de Rohan, who was the son of the Prince of Soubise, and became home to four other members of the Rohan family, who were also cardinals. Though the courtyard is not as elaborate as the one in the Soubise mansion, the former stables are quite interesting, simply because of the splendor of the sculptured façade, which depicts the Horses of Apollo, drinking at the trough.

If this inspires thirst, walk directly across the street to *Le Clos Follainville* (72 Rue Vieille-du-Temple; phone: 42-78-21-22), a casual and rustic tea salon/restaurant/wine bar, suitable for a light lunch and a selection of wine sold by the half glass, glass, or bottle. With their more intimate ambience, the Paris wine bars are a refreshing contrast from the hectic Paris sidewalk cafés. Open Mondays through Fridays, Saturdays after 7:30 PM; closed Sundays.

Back at the corner, turn right onto Rue de la Perle. At No. 1 is the Hôtel Libéral Bruant, built in 1685 by the architect of the Invalides for his own residence. This stately mansion has been restored to its original appearance and now houses the *Musée Bricard* (Lock and Key Museum; phone: 42-77-79-62). Inside is an exhibit tracing the history of the lock from the Roman Empire, as well as a collection of locks. Closed Sundays, Mondays, holidays, and the month of August.

Walk to the left to Rue de Thorigny and the former Hôtel Salé (No. 5). This house was built in 1656–59 for a gentleman who made a fortune out of the salt tax, which is how it got its name (*salé* is French for "salty"). In the 17th century, the right to collect taxes was sold by the state to private enterprises working on a percentage basis. The 3-story house has been restored over the years, and following the death of Pablo Picasso in 1973 his heirs donated an outstanding collection of the artist's works in lieu of inheritance tax; it is now the site of the *Musée Picasso* (phone: 42-71-25-21), with more than 200 paintings, 3,000 drawings and engravings, and other objets d'art. The works are arranged in chronological order, providing a fascinating insight into Picasso's various periods. Especially interesting is his private collection of paintings of other artists, with works by Cézanne, Braque, and Rousseau. There are also films on the prodigious artist's life and work. The courtyard and the museum's garden are relaxing places to pause before or after touring the museum. Be sure to see the lovely fountain by Simounet in the formal garden. Open daily except Tuesdays, from 9:15 AM to 5:15 PM (until 10 PM Wednesdays).

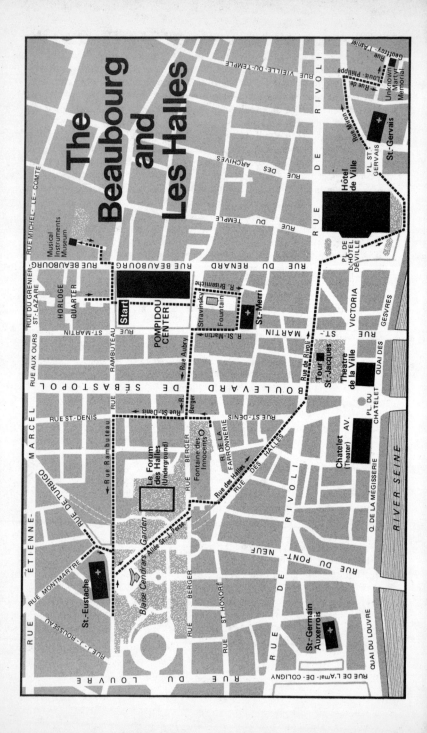

Walk 8: The Beaubourg and Les Halles

Le Centre Georges-Pompidou and the bustle of the Beaubourg, with its street entertainers, have become a center for international youth of all ages. One either loves it or detests it; there is no middle ground. The *Centre Georges-Pompidou* was built on the initiative of former President Georges Pompidou, to create a multi-purpose cultural center and regenerate life into the neighborhood following the demise of the old *Les Halles* food markets. Unfortunately, one can only imagine the once colorful hustle and bustle of Paris's colorful wholesale market, the scents and sights, and especially the bowl of onion soup one could always get on a cold morning at the height of the near-dawn shopping hours.

Before starting this walk, an interesting detour in the area is the Horloge Quarter, just north of the *Centre Georges-Pompidou,* between Rue Beaubourg and Rue St.-Martin. This is another pedestrian area with a lot of shops, and although the neighborhood is still experiencing transition, it is a dynamic melting pot with a real sense of street life. The landmark *horloge* (clock) is an unusual design of brass and steel that is electronically operated by a life-size figure, known as "a defender of time." Not far to the east, at the end of the Impasse Berthaud off Rue Beaubourg, is the *Musée de la Musique Méchanique,* whose collection includes over 100 mechanical reproducers of music dating from the late 19th century.

The *Centre Georges-Pompidou* — designed by the young team of British architect Richard Rogers and Italian architect Renzo Piano, and built between 1972 and 1977 — is a futuristic concoction of steel and glass and piping with bright colors, like a surrealistic refinery. Widely accepted, it attracts thousands of visitors each year.

What you first notice are the oversize see-through escalators, which look like giant caterpillars transporting a constant flux of people up and into the building. The piazza, which is directly in front of the main entrance, is swarming with spectators and the ubiquitous fire eaters, jugglers, musicians, and mimes. Be aware that there may be pickpockets around.

Take the time to visit the center, which in addition to housing the *National Museum of Modern Art* and the *Industrial Design Center* also boasts a public information library and an Institute for Acoustic and Musical Research. The permanent collection of contemporary art traces modern art's roots back to Fauvism and Cubism. There is something for every taste, from Picasso and Matisse to Mondrian, Rauschenberg, and Warhol. The temporary exhibitions are always quite spectacular, and the bookstore and poster shop are also worth a visit. Go up the escalator to the fifth floor and step outside for a view of Paris's distinctive rooftops. The café is a nice place to relax before moving on, or stay awhile for one of the classic films shown at the center.

Once back at the entrance, leave the building and walk to the left for a pleasant and peaceful diversion. Place Igor-Stravinsky is the site of a delightful pool-size fountain, a creation that is a collaboration between the playful artists Nikki de Saint-Phalle and Jean Tinguely. In homage to the works of the great composer of *The Firebird* and *Rite of Spring,* colorful Saint-Phalle creations, including water-spouting lips, twirling female torsos, and a dancing skeleton, all happily interact with the animated black steel sculptures of Tinguely.

Walk gingerly, taking care not to be sprayed by the fountain. Consider this fountain to be a little satire on the monumental fountains that have long graced Paris's boulevards. You are in the St.-Merri quarter of Beaubourg, the name of the old village that stood on this site in the 12th century. At the southern end of the Place Igor-Stravinsky is the Eglise St.-Merri, the name being a corruption of St. Mederic, a monk who lived in a cell until his death in 700. The church dates from 1612, when the tower was finally completed, but it was actually built in its unusual Gothic style during the reign of François I, between 1520 and 1530. If you would like to stay in a hotel in the area with bizarre furnishings, try the *St. Merri* just beyond the church (78 Rue de la Verrerie; phone: 42-78-14-15).

After circling the Stravinsky fountain, follow the crowds on the pedestrian road west to Rue Aubry, cross the Boulevard de Sébastopol into Rue Berger, and enjoy the active street life around the Fontaine des Innocents. The fountain itself is a Renaissance work by Pierre Lescot — much altered and restored — that once adorned the old *Marché des Innocents* (which preceded the *Halles* market) and also graced the Church of Innocents.

There are several cafés along this pedestrian area, which borders *Le Forum des Halles.* One of the more popular ones is *Café Costes* (Square des Innocents; phone: 45-08-54-39), a post-modern–looking place designed by French wunderkind Philippe Starck. Prices are expensive, and even more so at one of the sought-after outdoor tables. Always remember that there is a three-level price structure — for dining outdoors, sitting indoors, and standing at the bar. When you sit on a terrace on a lovely day with a good vantage point, you are literally "renting" your chair. But it is worth a visit just for the contrast in design compared to other more typical French cafés. Open daily.

After leaving the café, follow Rue St.-Denis north and turn left on Rue Rambuteau, site of the grand St.-Eustache, considered to be one of Paris's most beautiful churches after Notre-Dame. A mixture of late Gothic and Renaissance architecture constructed between 1532 and 1637, the front portion of the church, with its Ionic and Doric columns, was added in 1778. The church is known for its organ, one of the finest and largest in the city; it is here that Berlioz and Liszt composed some of their finest works. The white marble altar, with its sculptured canopy, is also remarkable. The church's collection of 16th- and 17th-century paintings, sculpture, and painted glass is definitely worth noting. Across the street, visible from the church, is the underground *Forum des Halles* complex of shops, food outlets, and movie houses. The gigantic *FNAC* store sells everything from stereos and cameras to books and records at discount prices; another diversion is a walk through the Blaise Cendrars garden, which is between the church and *Le Forum des Halles.*

Happily, some traditions still exist around *Le Forum des Halles.* In keeping with its historic identity as a market, it remains a regular stop for professional cooks and restaurateurs, as well as enthusiastic amateurs in search of the best in cooking equipment. *E. Dehillerin* (18-20 Rue Coquillière; phone: 42-36-53-13) has an overwhelming selection of cookware, from copper pans to unusual kitchen tools. There are merchandise catalogues available, and if you need copper retinned, this is the place. They do mail orders on most everything, and though the staff is said to be unfriendly, the merchandise is worth the temporary inconvenience. Open Mondays through Saturdays from 8 AM to 12:30 PM and 2 to 6 PM.

Duthilleul et Minart (13-15 Rue de Turbigo; phone: 42-33-44-36) has been selling artisans' uniforms since 1850. So if you've been dying to have a chef's hat or apron, or waiter's vest or smock, look no farther. Open only on weekdays from 9 AM to 12:30 PM and 2 to 6 PM. Closed during August.

M.O.R.A. (13 Rue Montmartre; phone: 45-08-19-24) is another cookware shop in the *Forum des Halles* area that is still frequented by professionals. They have a large assortment of baking tools, including baguette pans, special cake molds, and oversize pans for professional ovens. Check their excellent cookbook selection. Open weekdays from 8:30 AM to noon and 1:30 to 5:30 PM; 8:30 AM to noon Saturdays; closed Sundays. *La Bovida* (36 Rue Montmartre; phone: 42-36-09-99) carries an impressive selection of stainless steel, copper, porcelain, and earthenware equipment. Open Mondays through Fridays from 6:30 AM to 6 PM; 7 to 11:45 AM Saturdays; closed Saturday afternoons and Sundays.

Our favorite shop in the neighborhood is *Papeterie Moderne* (12 Rue de la Ferronnerie; phone: 42-36-21-72), which for decades has been the source of many of the city's signs. You can choose from among hundreds of typical Parisian signs or else have your own made to order: everything from the ordinary *"defense de fumer"* (no smoking) to an 18th-century saying outside a cemetery: *"De par le roi, defense à Dieu, de faire miracle en ce lieu"* (By order of the king, even God isn't allowed to work any miracles here). Open daily from 7:30 AM to noon and 1 to 7 PM; closed Sundays and two weeks in August.

For a change of scenery, walk up Rue des Halles to Rue de Rivoli. Turn left at Rue de Rivoli and continue to the Hôtel de Ville, about a 15-minute walk. On the way, notice the 16th-century Tour St.-Jacques, the former belfry of a church torn down in 1802. A statue of the scientist-philosopher Blaise Pascal is in the tower. The Place de l'Hôtel de Ville, originally known as the Place du Grève until 1830, was the scene of many important historical events. From 1310 until 1832, public executions took place here, and Dr. Guillotin's machine was first put into action on humans on April 25, 1792, before being moved to the Place de la Concorde. Foulon, one of the first victims of the Revolution, was hanged here by a mob whom he had exasperated by saying that "the hungry should eat grass."

During the late 1800s it was a meeting place for men waiting in line for jobs, specifically those in the building trade. On some mornings as many as 4,000 men were assembled, with only a few gendarmes on duty to keep the road clear. The Hôtel de Ville (1533–1628), or Town Hall (city government building), has always been considered one of the city's most splendid buildings. The design of the present building is French Renaissance, with distinctive mansard windows and sculpture-adorned columns. Statues grace the courtyard and gilded figures decorate the roof. It was rebuilt between 1878 and 1882, with alterations and enlargements very much along the lines of the original Town Hall, which was burned down during the fierce street fights in the days ending the Commune in 1871.

A memorial worth a visit is at 17 Rue Geoffroy-l'Asnier (near Rue de Rivoli a bit east of the Hôtel de Ville). A tribute to the Unknown Jewish Martyr, dedicated to Jews killed in the Holocaust, it has an impressive crypt with a torch burning on the lower level; upstairs is a museum that documents the Holocaust. Closed Saturdays, Sundays (except afternoons in July and August), May 1, and Jewish holidays.

Closer to the Hôtel de Ville is the Eglise St.-Gervais-St.-Protais, built between 1616 and 1621, the first example of the imposing classical-style façade in Paris. The interior maintains the 17th-century theme with its finely carved stalls. The organ, said to be the oldest in Paris, was built in 1601. The elm tree that stands in the square was, according to medieval custom, the place where people came to pay their taxes. Naturally, sometimes some of them didn't show up, and the cynical expression "Wait for me under the elm tree" was born. So if you find yourself exhausted by this final walk, and longing only for a comfortable place to rest, fear not. There's no one under the elm tree — except for a few squirrels.

INDEX

Index

BIRNBAUM TRAVEL GUIDES

Order by phone, toll-free: 1-800-331-3761

Name_____ Phone_____

Address_____

City_____ State_____ Zip_____

Discover the Birnbaum Difference
More Details and Discounts Than Any Other Travel Guide

Get the best advice on what to see and do and where to stay while benefiting from money-saving information from America's foremost Birnbaum Travel Guides.

Country Guides—$17.00 Each

☐ Canada   ☐ Great Britain   ☐ Portugal
☐ Caribbean   ☐ Hawaii   ☐ South America
☐ Eastern Europe   ☐ Ireland   ☐ Spain
☐ Europe   ☐ Italy   ☐ United States
☐ France   ☐ Mexico   ☐ Western Europe

New Warm Weather Destination Guides 1992—$10.00 Each

☐ Acapulco   ☐ Bermuda   ☐ Ixtapa &
☐ Bahamas   ☐ Cancun/Cozumel/Isla   Zihuatanejo
  (including Turks   Mujeres (including Playa
  & Caicos)   Del Carmen

New City Guides 1992—$10.00 Each

☐ Barcelona   ☐ London   ☐ Paris
☐ Boston   ☐ Los Angeles   ☐ Rome
☐ Chicago   ☐ Miami   ☐ San Francisco
☐ Florence   ☐ New York   ☐ Venice

Business Guides 1992—$17.00 Each

☐ Europe 1992 for the Business Traveler
☐ USA 1992 for the Business Traveler

Total for Birnbaum Travel Guides	$
For PA delivery, please include sales tax	
Add $4.00 for first Book S&H, $1.00 each additional book	
Total	$

☐ Check or Money order enclosed. Plase make payable to HarperCollins Publishers.
☐ Charge my credit card ☐ American Express ☐ Visa ☐ Mastercard

Card no._____ Exp. date_____

Signature_____

Send orders to:
HarperCollins Publishers, P.O. Box 588, Dunmore, PA 18512-0588